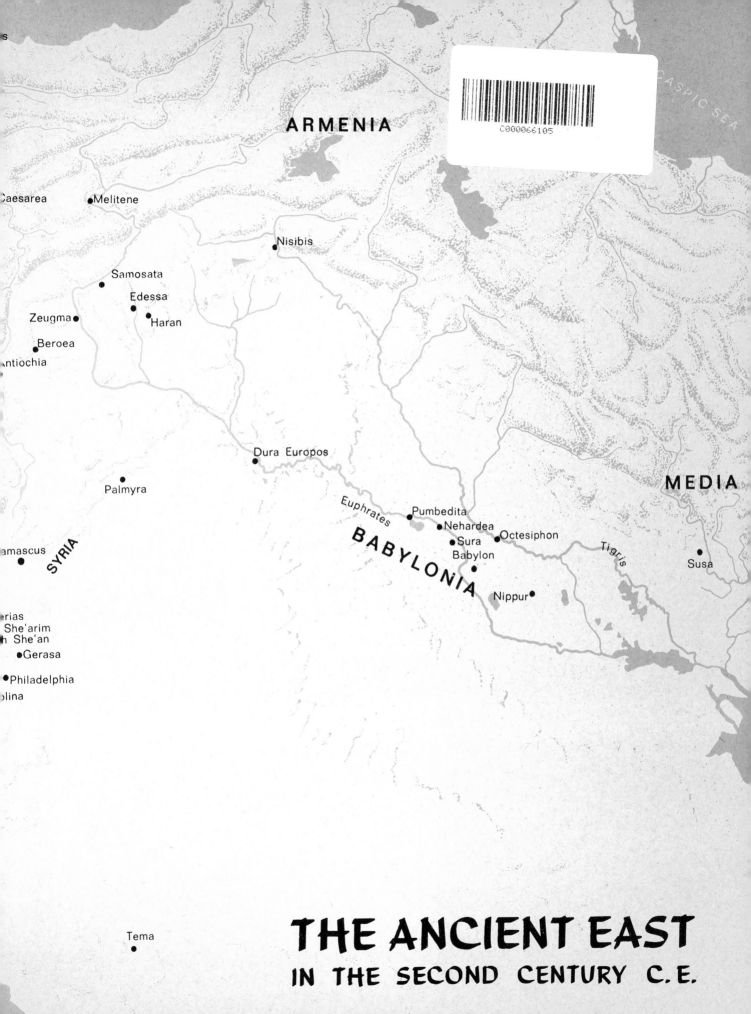

ARMENIA

CASPIC SEA

Caesarea

Melitene

Nisibis

Samosata

Edessa

Zeugma

Haran

Beroea

ntiochia

MEDIA

Dura Europos

Palmyra

Euphrates

Pumbedita

Nehardea

Octesiphon

amascus SYRIA

BABYLONIA

Sura

Tigris

Babylon

Susa

Nippur

rias

She'arim

She'an

Gerasa

Philadelphia

lina

Tema

THE ANCIENT EAST
IN THE SECOND CENTURY C.E.

BETH

RUTGERS UNIVERSITY PRESS, NEW BRUNSWICK, N.J.

SHE'ARIM

REPORT ON THE EXCAVATIONS DURING 1953–1958

Volume III: CATACOMBS 12–23

by

Nahman Avigad

on behalf of The Israel Exploration Society and
The Institute of Archaeology, Hebrew University

THE HEBREW EDITION OF BETH SHE'ARIM III
WAS PUBLISHED BY THE ISRAEL EXPLORATION SOCIETY

ISBN 0-8135-0763-4
Library of Congress Catalog Card Number: 72-2177

© 1971 Hebrew Edition by The Israel Exploration Society
© 1976 International Copyright by Massada Press Ltd., Jerusalem

PRINTED IN ISRAEL
by Peli Printing Works Ltd.

TABLE OF CONTENTS

LIST OF PLATES

LIST OF FIGURES

LIST OF BIBLIOGRAPHICAL ABBREVIATIONS

AA = *Archäologischer Anzeiger.*

ADAJ = *Annual of the Department of Antiquities of Jordan.*

AJA = *American Journal of Archaeology.*

Avi-Yonah, *QDAP* = M. Avi-Yonah, Oriental Elements in the Art of Palestine in the Roman and Byzantine Periods, *QDAP*, X, 1942; XII, 1948; XIV, 1950.

BASOR = *Bulletin of the American Schools of Oriental Research.*

BBSAJ = *Bulletin of the British School of Archaeology in Jerusalem.*

BIES = *Yediot, Bulletin of Israel Exploration Society.*

BMB = *Bulletin du Musée de Beyrouth.*

BRF = *Bulletin, Louis M. Rabinowitz Fund for the Exploration of Ancient Synagogues.*

CIJ = J.-B. Frey, *Corpus Inscriptionum Iudaicarum,* I: *Europe,* Rome 1936; II: *Asie-Afrique,* Rome 1952.

Cumont, *Symbolisme funéraire* = F. Cumont, *Recherches sur le symbolisme funéraire des Romains,* Paris 1942.

Dominus Flevit = P. B. Bagatti & J. T. Milik, *Gli scavi del "Dominus Flevit",* I, Jerusalem 1958.

EI = *Eretz-Israel,* Jerusalem 1950*ff.*

Gerasa = C. H. Kraeling et al., *Gerasa — City of the Decapolis,* New Haven 1938.

Goodenough, *Symbols* = E. R. Goodenough, *Jewish Symbols in the Greco-Roman Periods,* I–XII (*Bollingen Series,* XXXVII), *New York* 1953–1964.

Harden, *Karanis* = D. B. Harden, *Roman Glass from Karanis,* Ann Arbor 1936.

IEJ = *Israel Exploration Journal.*

JGS = *Journal of Glass Studies.*

JHS = *Journal of Hellenic Studies.*

Kohl & Watzinger, *Synagogen* = H. Kohl & C. Watzinger, *Antike Synagogen in Galilaea,* Leipzig 1916.

Macalister, *Gezer* = R. A. S. Macalister, *The Excavation of Gezer,* I–III, London 1912.

Morey, *Sarcophagi* = C. R. Morey, The Sarcophagus of Claudia Antonia Sabina and the Asiatic Sarcophagi, *Sardis,* V, 1, London 1924.

PEFQSt = *Palestine Exploration Fund Quarterly Statement.*

PEFA = *Palestine Exploration Fund Annual.*

QDAP = *Quarterly of the Department of Antiquities in Palestine.*

RB = *Revue biblique.*

Reinach, *Statuaire* = S. Reinach, *Répertoire de la statuaire grecque et romaine,* I, Paris 1906.

Robert, *Sarkophagreliefs* = C. Robert, *Die antiken Sarkophagreliefs,* Berlin 1890.

Samaria-Sebaste = I: J. W. Crowfoot, K. M. Kenyon & E. L. Sukenik, *The Buildings at Samaria,* London 1942.

II: J. W. Crowfoot, G. M. Crowfoot & K. M. Kenyon, *The Objects from Samaria,* London 1957.

Watzinger, *Denkmäler* = C. Watzinger, *Denkmäler Palästinas,* I–II, Leipzig 1933–1935.

ZDPV = *Zeitschrift des deutschen Palästinavereins.*

PREFACE

The excavations at Beth She'arim were one of the most important archaeological projects undertaken by the Israel Exploration Society. Since these excavations shed much light on an important chapter in Jewish history, they aroused great interest both in the academic and the general public. The first excavations were conducted during 1936–40 under the direction of Professor Benjamin Mazar. The report of these excavation seasons was published in volume I of *Beth She'arim*.

When, after a prolonged interruption, the Israel Exploration Society decided to resume the excavations, Professor Mazar — at that time President of the Hebrew University in Jerusalem — suggested that I undertake the direction of the excavations, and I readily accepted his offer. The excavations were carried out between 1953–58, in conjunction with the Hebrew University. The results of these excavations, which were carried out mainly in the necropolis of Beth She'arim, are the subject of the present volume. The results of the limited excavations in the city area on the summit of the hill were published in the preliminary reports.

The late Moshe Schwabe joined our party as the Greek epigrapher. Not only was he the right man in the right place, but also his rich knowledge, his intellectual stature, and his warm personality were a source of inspiration for all the staff. After the first season he suddenly became ill and had to leave the excavations; to our great regret, he never returned to Beth She'arim. The important contributions he made to the research on Beth She'arim are reflected in his numerous epigraphic studies and in the comprehensive book on the Greek inscriptions, *Beth She'arim,* volume II.

Another member of our expedition whose untimely death took place during this period was Immanuel Dunayevsky. Mr. Dunayevsky was associated with the Beth She'arim excavations right from the beginning and, though he could not work with us regularly, he visited the site frequently — even between official excavation seasons. He devoted a great deal of thought to clarifying the problems connected with the layout of Beth She'arim and spared no effort preparing the plans published here.

The archaeological staff consisted mainly of archaeology students who worked with us for various periods of time. Since then, many of them have become well-known scholars in their own right: Magen Broshi and Dr. Joseph Elgavish, who were the chief assistants, Dr. Trude Dothan, Uzza Eilam-Zebulun, Ram Gofna, Simcha Cohen-Goldstein. Dr. Joseph Naveh, Dr. Orah Negbi, Dr. Avraham Negev, Yael Namir-Olnick, Naomi Vogelman, Naomi Zirin, and others.

The photography for the expedition was begun by R. Weinstein but was pursued most of the time by A. Volk; it was completed by S. I. Schweig, who produced most of the plates appearing in this volume. I. Kolodny was the surveyor for the expedition in 1958.

Moshe Jaffe was the main work supervisor throughout the excavations. His broad experience made him indispensable in the specific work of excavating catacombs. Ze'ev Berkovitz and Yiftah Seid supervised the work at different stages. The Seid and Jaffe families, who were the first settlers at Shêkh 'Abrêq, and the Berkovitz family were most hospitable and helpful to the expedition staff. We extend our most sincere thanks to all of them.

We also wish to express our gratitude to the various people and organizations who assisted us in carrying out the excavations: to the Department of Labor of the Government of Israel for supplying the required laborers; to the American Fund for Israel Institutions for its contributions to the Excavations Fund; to the Jewish Agency of Eretz-Israel; to the Solel Boneh Company; to Mr. Matityahu Lunz who devoted much effort to raising funds; and to the National Parks Authority for developing the site and preparing it for visitors. Finally, special mention must be made of the workers, most of them newcomers from nearby immigrants' camps, who — though of limited working capacity — did their best under very difficult circumstances of acclimatization to Israel; they, too, felt a special identification with Beth She'arim when, with their own hands, they uncovered the Hebrew inscriptions on the tombs of their forefathers.

This volume, the third in the series *Beth She'arim,* was published in Hebrew in 1971, thirteen years after the excavations were completed. Various factors beyond our control delayed its publication. In the meantime we attempted to keep up to date with the new publications related to the subjects discussed here, to refer to them in the book itself, and to supplement the bibliography; for technical reasons, however, this was not always possible.

The Greek inscriptions discovered during the excavations were treated by the late Professor Schwabe. However, some of the inscriptions which were discovered after his resignation were published in brief by us in the preliminary reports. The file of Greek inscriptions was afterward handed over to Professor Baruch Lifshitz for publication in volume II of *Beth She'arim.* All the Greek inscriptions discovered in catacombs 12–20 are discussed there in full, except for four inscriptions published here for the first time (see p. 256, note 2). In this volume, therefore, the Greek inscriptions are presented in their original text and translation only, without any discussion, as part of the general description of the tombs. On the other hand, almost all the photographs and facsimiles of the inscriptions have been included here.

I wish to express my deepest thanks to all those who assisted me in this work: first and foremost, to Professor Mazar, whose suggestions and advice were of great help and who also read the chapter on the typology and chronology of the catacombs; to the late Professor Y. Kutscher who was kind enough to read the chapter on the Aramaic and Hebrew inscriptions and who made several important comments; to Dr. D. Barag who wrote the chapter on glass vessels and who assisted me in writing up the small finds; to Dr. A. Wirzburger and Dr. S. Gross of the Geological Institute of the Ministry of Development who wrote the reports included in the Appendix; to Mr. Joseph Aviram, the honorary secretary of the Israel Exploration Society who, during all the years, devotedly bore the responsibility for the organization of the excavations and who also contributed greatly to the publication of this book; to Mrs. Pennina Shagiv who ably translated the book into English; and to Massada Press Ltd. for the care and skill in printing this volume. Lastly, thanks are due to my wife Shulamith, who typed the original Hebrew manuscript, helped in arranging the indices, and was an unfailing source of encouragement and assistance throughout my work.

N. Avigad

Jerusalem, 1973

CHAPTER 1

INTRODUCTION

1 THE HISTORY OF BETH SHE'ARIM

The history of Beth She'arim has been described in detail by B. Mazar in the first volume of this series of reports on the excavations of Beth She'arim.[1] This description includes a comprehensive discussion on the name of the place, on Beth She'arim in the literary sources,[2] and on the identification of the site. For the convenience of the reader, a short general survey of the history of Beth She'arim will be presented here, based on the above-mentioned discussion and on additional archaeological finds discovered during the excavations.

Today it is undisputed that ancient Beth She'arim is to be identified with the hill known by the Arabic name Shêkh 'Abrêq. This hill juts out of the lower southern extensions of the Galilean highlands, south of the Haifa–Nazareth highway, near modern Kiryat Tiv'on, overlooking the Jezreel Valley to the southeast and the Carmel range to the west. In ancient times there was a network of settlements in the vicinity, through which the main roads passed from the seacoast to the east. However, Beth She'arim itself was not an important thoroughfare.

According to the archaeological evidence, the first settlement on the hill was established during the time of the Israelite monarchy, circa the ninth century B.C.E. Shards found during the excavations on the summit of the hill from the Iron Age II, the Persian, and the Hellenistic periods, revealed that the site was occupied continuously.[3] However, no traces of building from these periods have been discovered so far. There may have been a small settlement here whose name is not mentioned in the sources. In any case, the summit of the hill has not been sufficiently excavated as yet to provide any information about the settlement, other than the fact of its existence.

Beth She'arim is mentioned for the first time by Josephus Flavius (66 C.E.)[7] by its Greek name, Βησάρα. It is described as the center of the estates of Berenice, the daughter of Agrippas I. Beth She'arim and the surrounding Jewish villages were part of a large land tenancy held by the Herodian dynasty in the Jezreel Valley. Apparently this land tenancy formerly belonged to the Hasmoneans. The earliest building remains discovered so far in Beth She'arim are Herodian. Small ashlar stones with coarse, protruding bosses are characteristic of these few remains. The major part of our historical knowledge of Beth She'arim is derived from the Talmudic literature, in which the place is called by its original Hebrew name, Beth She'arim, or by variants influenced by the local dialect and the Aramaic accent: Beth Sharei or Beth Sharein. In its first appearance in the Talmud Beth She'arim is described as a Jewish agricultural settlement and as the place of residence of one of the important Tannaim, Rabbi Johanan ben Nuri, who lived in the first half of the second century C.E.[5]

The historical events which took place in Judah during 132–135 C.E. led to a decisive change in the history of Beth She'arim. The Bar Kochba revolt of those years resulted in the uprooting of masses of Jews from the cities and villages in Judah and their moving to Galilee, which thus became the center of national and religious life for Palestinian Jewry. The Antonine and Severine periods (second half of the second century to beginning of the third century C.E.) were a time of normal relations between the Roman government and the

Jewish population. This was a prosperous and flourishing period for the Jewish settlements in Galilee, evidenced by the numerous remains of magnificent synagogues from that time which are scattered throughout Galilee.

Beth She'arim became one of the important cities of refuge for scholars among whom the greatest was Rabbi Judah Ha-Nassî who established the seat of the Sanhedrin here.[6] On the time of Rabbi Judah's arrival in Beth She'arim, Mazar writes: "Even though we lack evidence for the date of Rabbi Judah Ha-Nassî's settling there, and the reasons that led him to establish there the seat of the Sanhedrin, we can assume that this occurred in the days of Antoninus, the Rabbi's friend; this apparently was the Emperor Marcus Aurelius Antoninus (161–180 C.E.). From the Talmud, we learn that the Rabbi received as tenancies towns and villages in various parts of the country. It is very possible that one of these was Beth She'arim (and its immediate neighborhood), which was still considered royal land in the Second Temple period. If this supposition is correct, then the problem of the ownership of Beth She'arim and its necropolis during the time of Rabbi Judah and his heir has been solved. The tenancy of Beth She'arim thus belonged to the Nassî-hood, and provided the income of the family of the president of the Sanhedrin."[7]

Rabbi Judah Ha-Nassî, head of the Sanhedrin and editor of the Mishnah, was the recognized and highly esteemed leader of the Jewish people and was also respected by the Roman authorities. During his lifetime Beth She'arim—the city of the Sanhedrin and the center of learning—developed enormously. Proof of this development are the large public buildings of outstanding quality and the tombs of remarkably rich architectural details dating from this period. At no other time did building flourish in Beth She'arim to such an extent. While it became a center of Torah and Jewish learn-

ing, Beth She'arim also absorbed Greek cultural values in language and art, as proved by the archaeological finds. It is well known that these values did not offend Rabbi. After some time Rabbi Judah Ha-Nassî moved to Sepphoris, where he lived for seventeen years. The Talmudic tradition attributes this move to Rabbi's illness, for which the healthy air of Sepphoris was beneficial. Rabbi died in Sepphoris (circa 220 C.E.) but was brought for burial to Beth She'arim, where he had prepared a burial vault in his lifetime.[8] The Talmud and the Midrash tell lengthy stories of miracles which occurred during his funeral.[9]

After the burial of Rabbi, leader of the nation and guiding spirit of his generation, the cemetery at Beth She'arim became sacred for the Jewish people. Many Jews from all over the country and from the Diaspora brought their dead for burial at Beth She'arim. Mention of this can even be found in the Jerusalem Talmud;[10] however, the main evidence comes from the archaeological finds. Many extensive catacombs were discovered, whose dimensions are in no proportion to the size or needs of Beth She'arim. On many graves inscriptions were found pertaining to the origin of the deceased: cities on the Phoenician coast, in Syria, Mesopotamia, and Southern Arabia. Probably a decisive reason for the conversion of Beth She'arim into a central necropolis for Diaspora Jewry was the fact that, after the Bar Kochba revolt, burial of Jews was prohibited in the cemetery on the Mount of Olives. Thus, Beth She'arim became the main cemetery for those who wished to be buried in the Holy Land.

The character and the economy of the city were influenced to a large extent by its becoming a burial center. This function was certainly connected with large-scale organizational activities by public institutions and with the employment of many workers —for example, quarrymen and undertakers, architects and builders, stonecutters and sculptors who prepared the stone coffins in local workshops. It was also connected with the import of marble coffins from foreign countries. It may well be assumed that the deceased were accompanied by members of their family from the Diaspora; and thus Beth She'arim became an "international" meeting place for Jews. This "internationalism" is reflected to a large extent in the epitaphs, but it may be surmised that it left its mark on the life of the city as well. In the synagogue of Beth She'arim a marble tablet was found with an inscription dedicated to a respected person from distant Palmyra. The same name appeared in an epitaph in a catacomb belonging to a Palmyrene family.[11] This instance proves that there were Jews who came to spend their last days at Beth She'arim in order to be buried there, just as it was customary in all generations for Jews to come to Jerusalem to die and be buried there.

The synagogue was apparently erected at the beginning of the third century C.E. It was built in the best decorative style of the Galilean synagogues of that period. While Beth She'arim continued to flourish, it seems that its golden era came to an end with the death of Rabbi and the transfer of the Sanhedrin to Sepphoris. A decline in the quality of the buildings is seen at the end of the third and the beginning of the fourth centuries: the graves continued to multiply, but they became simpler. The last literary information on the existence of Beth She'arim is about one of the late Amoraim (Talmudic interpreters) from the end of the third century C.E.: "Rabbi Menahem of Kefar She'arim, also called Beth She'arim."[12] At that time, therefore, the settlement was called Kefar She'arim, though it was well known that the correct original name was Beth She'arim.

The archaeological finds demonstrate that Beth She'arim existed without any particular upheavals until the middle of the fourth century C.E. when it was destroyed and burned. In one of the buildings that was exposed from the conflagration stratum

of the city a hoard of 1,200 copper coins was discovered, all minted before 350 C.E., during the time of Constantine the Great and Constantius II. This is conclusive evidence that the city was destroyed in the middle of the fourth century. Mazar is of the opinion that this destruction should be connected with the Gallus Revolt of 352 C.E., during the reign of Emperor Constantius II. In this revolt against Byzantine rule, the troops of Gallus attacked many settlements, for example, Tiberias, Sepphoris, and Lydda, and certainly Beth She'arim was attacked as well.

Beth She'arim never recovered from this destruction. Though it continued to exist in the Byzantine, period, it was a small, poor settlement whose inhabitants built their houses amid the ruins of the demolished city. The large cemetery ceased to be used. Only in very few places in the catacombs were traces found of burials which could be attributed to the second half of the fourth and the fifth centuries C.E. This fact also is evidence of the basic change which occurred in the history of Beth She'arim in the middle of the fourth century. We do not know to what extent the settlement in the Byzantine period remained Jewish or when it lost its Jewish character, since to this day no symbols or inscriptions from this period have been found in the city or in the graves. In the silt which filled a water reservoir (no. 24 figs. 1 and 2) that at one time had supplied the cemetery but was later abandoned Mazar found a cache of pottery and glass vessels and coins from the Byzantine period,[13] on several of which were Christian symbols. At present we do not know the origin of these vessels. If, indeed, they did come from the city, then it means that Christians were already living there at the end of the sixth century. In any case it is clear that at that time, approximately the end of the Byzantine period, the robbing of the Beth She'arim tombs had already begun —an occurrence which increased greatly during the Early Arab period. Eventually the courtyards of the catacombs were filled with debris, but this did not prevent adventurous people from penetrating into the caves. Inspired by the atmosphere which prevailed in this special necropolis, an Arab poetess with a sensitive soul inscribed on one of the catacomb walls a lament unique in early Arabic epigraphy.[14] The date written beside it corresponds to the month of April in the year 900 C.E. Several visitors from the time of the Crusades left Crusader-style graffiti incised on the walls. Arab shepherds used many of the caves for shelter and protection. In the Mameluke period a number of families still lived on the hill; but, ultimately, the ruins of the abandoned settlement were covered with earth, the place was deserted, and even its name was forgotten. During the Middle Ages when Jewish pilgrims wanted to pray at the grave of Rabbi Judah Ha-Nassî, they did not even know where Beth She'arim was located; thus, Jewish tradition transferred his place of burial to Sepphoris. Modern scholars tried unsuccessfully to identify the place, but it was not until present-day Jewish settlement had reached the hill of Shêkh 'Abrêq that ancient Beth She'arim was discovered. The identification was definitively confirmed during the excavations with the discovery of a Jewish epitaph bearing the name Βησάρα.[15]

2 DESCRIPTION OF THE SITE

Since the publication of the first report on the excavations of Beth She'arim, in which the topography of the site was described in detail, new data have been added to the topographical map of Beth She'arim which enables us — even if only in an experimental and fragmentary fashion — to distinguish the general outline of the plan of the city and its necropolis.[16]

The General Plan. All the places which have been excavated to this day at Beth She'arim are marked in the general topographical map (fig. 1). On the summit of the hill are the three major excavation sites within the city area: the synagogue and the public building, the gate, and the basilica. Several modern buildings are also indicated to facilitate orientation. A large part of the summit of the hill is occupied today by agricultural farms. No excavations were conducted on the southern and southeastern gentle slopes of the hill. On the western slope are catacombs 1–4, 11, and 32 (called Mughâret el-Jehennem).[17] In the lower slopes of the opposite hill to the Northwest are catacombs 5–10.[18] From here there is a river bed running to the Northeast. On its southern bank, which is the northern slope of the hill of Beth She'arim, are concentrated all the catacombs excavated since 1953. The rock of this hill and the hills nearby is composed of Eocene limestone covered with *nari,* that is to say, soft, chalky limestone which is very suitable for the quarrying of caves. There is no water source near the hill; the closest spring is 2 km away.

In figure 2, the shape of the hill of Beth She'arim stands out very clearly. The summit rises to a height of 137.80 m above sea level. This elongated summit, over which the city extends, is bottle shaped: its neck to the east and its body to the west.[19] The length of the summit is approximately 400–500 m; its maximum width, circa 200 m.

From three buildings that were discovered it is possible to determine the approximate boundaries of the built-up area of the city on three sides of the hill. The synagogue and the nearby public building are at the end of the "neck of the bottle" (square 21 in fig. 2) and are probably not far from the eastern boundary of the city. The basilica was discovered at the western edge of the summit, near the "base of the bottle" (squares 14–15, fig. 2). This means that the

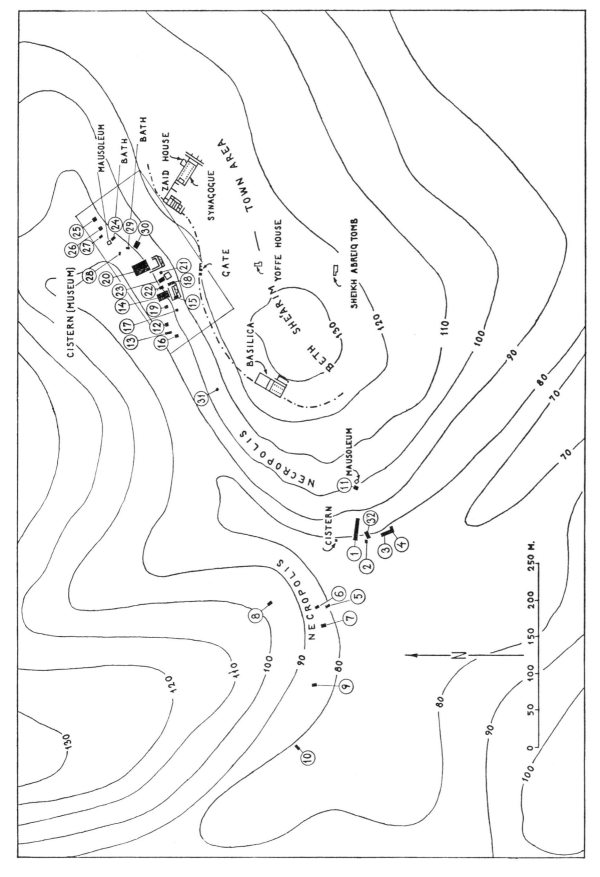

Fig. 1 General plan of the Beth She'arim excavations

large public buildings were located on the two highest points of the hill. Between these two points at contour line 119 remains of a gate were exposed (square 13:B9). If we draw a line joining these three buildings, in keeping with the topography, we shall obtain — more or less — the building line of the city to the North, and a little beyond this line to the East and to the West as well. This was not a fortification line since it became clear in the course of the work that Beth She'arim was not a walled city. Apparently, the city's defense line was formed by the compactly placed buildings at the city's borders. The entrance gates were probably placed in various parts of the city, between blocks of houses. One of them was discovered on the northern side, as mentioned above. It can clearly be seen at this gate that the gate stones were placed between two existing buildings.[20]

In seeking an answer to the question of why an entrance gate was placed precisely at this spot, our attention is inevitably drawn to a large, well-constructed water reservoir hewn at the foot of the slope, opposite the gate and at a distance of about 110 m from it (no. 28 on the plan).[21] This pool, 700–800 m3 in volume, received its water from a riverbed to the North, via a conduit whose remains were found in situ in front of the pool. Obviously, a water reservoir of such dimensions was too large to supply the needs of the cemetery only, and we must, therefore, suppose that it was also intended to supply the city which did not have a natural spring. Since the water had to be drawn up to the city by human or animal labor, the gate was placed at the point closest to the reservoir. It may be assumed that this also necessitated the paving of a road or path between the gate and the reservoir (see the plan at the end of the book). Proof of this assumption, in the opinion of Mr. Dunayevsky, is the existence of certain buildings along this course which were most likely served by the road on the slope between these two points. Thus, for

example, remains of walls were discovered on the slope parallel to the course of the surmised road. Unusual buildings were found on the sides of the road, e.g., a square structure, apparently the foundation of a memorial, and two water pools (nos. 24 and 29). In catacomb 30, of which only the courtyard has been excavated so far, the entrance faces the path and not North like the other courtyards. Finally, the explanation of the cut-off corner of the open-air assembly place above catacomb 20 (square 12:G5) probably lies in the assumption that a public road passed by. It seems that even the entrance to the assembly place was from this road.

Basically similar planning may also be discerned on the western slope of the hill, where a group of catacombs was excavated in 1936–40. Near catacomb 1 there is a reservoir called Mugharet es-Sikh (fig. 1), similar in size to the northern reservoir mentioned above. This reservoir supplied the water to the western part of the city. While the excavations were in progress, Mazar already suggested that perhaps a path descended from the city to the reservoir. Here, also, the road passes near a mausoleum, the memorial of catacomb 11 (fig. 2); and here, too, the opening of the cave faces the road. At the foot of the hill a road passed westward from the North, with several paths branching off to the catacombs. The area on the slope between the groups of catacombs uncovered on the North and West has not been excavated as yet but doubtlessly it, too, contains many catacombs.

Catacombs 12–23. Catacombs 12–23, the subject of this report, are concentrated on the northern slope of the hill, West of the road which led from reservoir 28 to the northern gate of the city. The plan at the end of the book gives a clear picture of the general arrangement of these twelve catacombs, including their courtyards and rooms. The large numerals (within the circles) indicate the catacombs; the small numerals, the height of the rock above sea level. The dotted areas represent the courtyards and the visible floors of the buildings. The burial rooms are marked by unbroken lines; however, they are below the rock surface and are therefore invisible, except for the outer graves in front of courtyards 21 and 23 (sq. 12:J3, H3). Stone construction is marked in black.

The crowded arrangement of the caves is conspicuous. The twelve courtyards extend over a length of 110 m; the caves below the surface, to a length of circa 150 m. It is obvious that the quarrymen tried to save space by hewing the courtyards as closely together as possible, without one catacomb interfering with the other. As a matter of fact, they were most successful in taking best advantage of the topographic conditions of the slope, conditions which enabled the quarrying of caves at small differences of height. Maximal exploitation of the area was thus attained. Catacombs 12, 13, and 14 were cut into the lowest level of the slope; catacombs 16, 19, and 22, into a higher level; catacombs 17, 21, and 22, into a still higher level; and catacombs 15 and 18, into the highest level excavated so far. It may be presumed that additional catacombs lie hidden further up the slope.

Catacomb 20 is a singular phenomenon. It is larger, both in area and in the number of its extensions, than the other caves and was very probably hewn while space was still plentiful and other caves did not interfere. Due to the exceptional height of one of its western rooms, the ceiling was broken into by one of the arcosolia of catacomb 23, and a breach was formed between them. Similarly, one of the arcosolia of catacomb 13 was joined with one of the kokhim of catacomb 16 above it. It was impossible to avoid junctions between the ends of the caves which were, more or less, on the same level. At many points it is possible to penetrate from one cave to the other through breaches formed by the junction of two rooms, e.g., between catacombs 12 and 13 or between catacombs 14 and 19.

The courtyards are hewn perpendicular to the slope, so that the southern wall of the courtyard is always the highest. In this wall, the entrance leads consistently into the main hall; thus the main façades of all the tombs hewn out of this slope face North. The courtyards are of various shapes. The most common is the small, square courtyard into which there is a descent of wide steps (catacombs 12, 16, 19, and 21). The elongated courtyard (catacombs 15 and 18) is the result of special conditions. The rarest courtyard, intended only for multiple-storied catacombs is the narrow, deep one of catacomb 13, into which one descends by flights of steps (compare also with the corridor of catacomb 1).

Catacombs 14, 20, and, to some extent, also 23 have spacious, elaborate courtyards, exceptional in that an open-air assembly place was erected above each of them. While the rest of the catacombs had sunken courtyards that were only partly visible to the onlooker, these three catacombs added architectural splendor to the landscape of the necropolis.

3 THE HISTORY OF THE EXCAVATIONS

The first excavations at Beth She'arim began in 1936 under the direction of Prof. B. Mazar and continued until 1940. During these four excavation campaigns catacombs 1–11 were exposed. Our expedition excavated from 1953 to 1958, four seasons in total. The first campaign, which was the fifth excavation season at Beth She'arim, began on August 11, 1953, and lasted only one month. In this campaign the expedition set itself two specific, modest aims in keeping with the limited means and time at its

Fig. 2 Topographical map of the Beth She'arim hill with the excavated sites

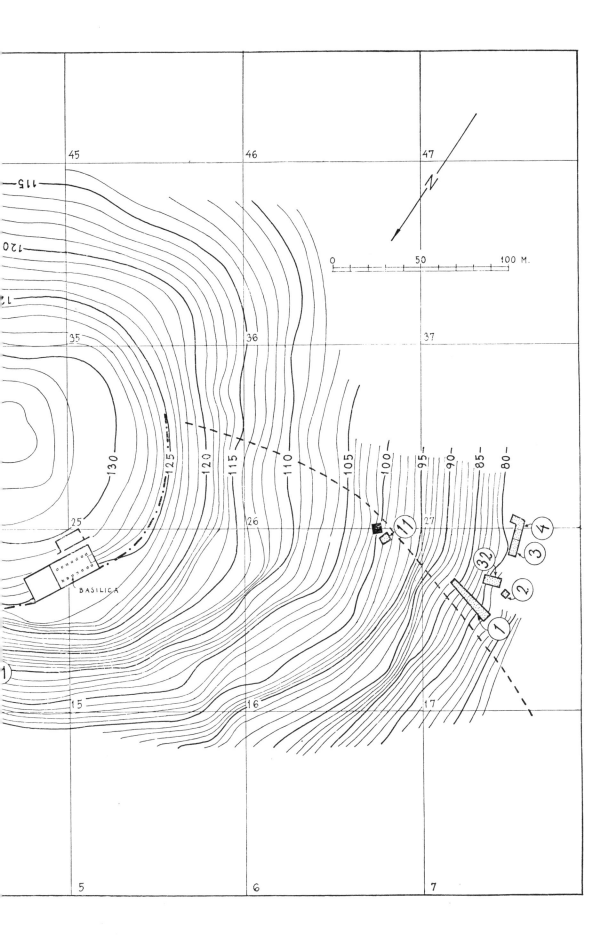

BASILICA

disposal: *(a)* to study the remains of buildings higher up on the slope which were discovered during the construction of a roadbed to the catacombs excavated in the previous seasons; *(b)* to examine this slope, which had not been investigated as yet and to search for new catacombs. Our assumption was that, since this area was close to the synagogue and public buildings, chances were good that tombs discovered here would provide new data likely to broaden our knowledge about the character of the necropolis.

As to the structural remains mentioned previously, it finally emerged that they belonged: *(a)* to an oil press erected at the northern end of the city, and *(b)* to a gate through which the city was entered from this side. On the basis of the pottery which was found it was possible to assign the various occupation phases of these structures to the fourth–sixth centuries C.E., though there is a possibility that they were built earlier.[22]

Our main efforts were directed to unearthing the catacombs, and it should be mentioned here that the finds exceeded all our expectations. We began our work at the foot of the slope, where a section of rock face was visible (sq. 13:E1). In the course of the excavations it turned out that this was none other than the courtyard of the first catacomb to be excavated (no. 12). On the fifth day of our work, after digging about 5 m deep into the slope of the hill, we came upon a breach in the vertical rock face, above the lintel of the door to hall A. Apparently this was the hole through which tomb robbers had entered long ago. During the excavation the evidence became convincing that entering the caves via holes above the lintels was a well-tested method used by grave robbers. By using this method there was no need to break through the rock. All that was necessary was to dismantle a few of the stones which generally blocked up the holes formed above the lintels when the doors were fixed in place.

Indeed, when we crawled into the cave on August 16, 1953, the scene unveiled before us was one of destruction and disarray. Stone slabs which had covered the graves were thrown onto the floor, some smashed and some piled up. While hunting for valuable articles, the grave robbers exhumed the bones from many graves and scattered them on the floor of the cave where they disintegrated to dust. A similar picture was revealed in the other catacombs as well. The most interesting discoveries in this hall were two Aramaic execration inscriptions. Through a breach in a kokh of room II we penetrated into hall B where we found many Greek epitaphs concerning deceased brought here from cities in Phoenicia and Syria.

The next day we entered catacomb 13 through a breach in arcosolium 3 in room III. During the quarrying of the catacombs many breaches were formed between the different halls so that we could easily pass from one hall to another and from one storey to another. Since we had to find our way by crawling in the dark with lighting only from pocket flashlight and kerosene lamps (which smoked and flickered constantly for lack of oxygen), it seemed that we had covered an infinite distance. The confusion which we found here was even greater than that in the previous catacomb. Many doors were opened inwards and thus dust accumulated in the rooms. Because of the large number of doors, we surmised that this catacomb had a long courtyard with many openings. Even in the poor light we could discern an abundance of Greek inscriptions painted on the walls.

This wealth of discoveries, upon which we came suddenly and surprisingly, demanded an enormous effort on our part to keep up with the work. With help from Kibbutz Alonim a power extension was drawn from the Jaffe house at the top of the hill, providing us with two electric lights. The clearing of catacomb 12 proceeded at a quickened pace: the courtyard was cleaned, the doors were opened, and two additional small halls were also discovered, C and D. We were amazed by the heavy stone door of hall A which still turned on its hinges with astonishing ease! In room VI a small cache of vessels was found, unique in this excavation season which, on the whole, was scanty in small finds.

Here I would like to devote a few words to our method of dealing with the bones found in the catacombs. Certain Jewish circles accused us of disrespectful treatment of the bones. However, these accusations were unfounded: never were bones thrown outside the cave. Our instructions were followed meticulously by the workers, among whom there were older pious men whose reverence for each bone almost verged on superstition. The practice, which was observed very strictly, was to gather all the bones found in the dust and those which remained in the looted graves (there were catacombs in which not even one bone remained in its grave) and to place them in special graves within the catacomb. These graves were then well covered with earth and stone slabs. In the few graves which were not touched by the robbers the bones were left in place and covered anew.

A large share of the burden fell upon our colleague, the late Prof. M. Schwabe, who was excited and thrilled by the rich epigraphic material discovered during this season. This was the first time he had come upon such a find as a member of an archaeological expedition. At first he deciphered the inscriptions of what he called the "Phoenician community" in hall B of catacomb 12. Then, with unbelievable energy, he set to work on the many Greek inscriptions discovered in catacomb 13. He would not pay attention to our pleading that he be satisfied in the meantime with the tracings of the inscriptions prepared for him by Mrs. Trude Dothan, and that he postpone the examination of the original inscription until the entrance to the cave from the outside was discovered. It was as though he had a premonition that he must hurry and do at once as much as possible. Every day, with great physical effort, he undertook the "crawling trip" between piles of fallen rocks, through holes and breaches, toward the inscriptions of catacomb 13. There he would spend many hours under poor conditions of light and air. With equal patience he would wait in total darkness whenever there was a breakdown in the temporary lighting arrangements. Schwabe enjoyed conversing with his colleagues. Every day he would return from his deciphering tour with news, and he liked to tell us about the problems which arose in reading the inscriptions. He often used to debate with himself aloud, and we the listeners were the fascinated participants in his great excitement when he succeeded in solving a difficult epigraphic problem.

Somewhat later we managed to locate the courtyard of catacomb 13. By the end of the season, we succeeded in exposing the entrances to the upper halls, D and E. In hall D there was a breach through which we entered a new catacomb, no. 16.

While continuing work in catacomb 12, we also searched for new catacombs. In square 12:K5 we followed up a rock face that was visible on the surface, but without success; after a week's work we abandoned the place. Only three years later did it become clear that this rock face was formed by the collapse of the ceiling in catacomb 23.

After this fruitless attempt, we began excavating a trial trench in square 13:B4–5, where a depression was noticeable on the surface. Our reasoning was that this depression might be the indication of a courtyard. And indeed, after six days' work and at a depth of 4 m, we had the good fortune to hit exactly upon the upper keystone of the right arch in the façade of catacomb 14.

When it became obvious that we would never be able to clear all the debris by hand in order to reach the newly-discovered structure, we enlisted the help of a bulldozer. Within two days a large quantity of debris was removed. It contained almost no shards. At this point we again began excavating by hand, and by the end of the season we exposed most of the façade, which was composed of three arches. On Friday, August 28, we entered the catacomb through a hole above the lintel of the main door. Here an entirely new type of catacomb of exceptionally large dimensions was revealed before our eyes. In this cave we made an exciting discovery — two epitaphs mentioning Rabbi Shim'on and Rabbi Gamaliel, which furnished us with material for daring hypotheses concerning the identification of the graves.

The sixth excavation campaign — our second season — began on August 26, 1954, and ended on October 17, 1954. Prof. Schwabe did not participate in this expedition because of the serious illness from which he never recovered. Nevertheless, during this season he followed from afar the discovery of the Greek inscriptions.

In this season also the excavations were conducted in two places: in the city area on the summit of the hill and in the necropolis. In the Seid yard, about 37 m southwest of the synagogue, we conducted a trial sounding by digging a trench 27 × 5 m. The object of this sounding was to determine the nature of the remains on the site before it was prepared for construction work. Remains of several rooms which were part of a residential building were discovered. One room had a mosaic floor. Of special interest were two cisterns found inside the building. Eventually, their use as reservoirs had been discontinued and they were used as refuse pits for broken pottery. By means of the numerous lamps and one coin found in the cisterns, it was possible to date this pottery cache to the third and the first half of the fourth centuries C.E. The buildings were razed, apparently, in the general destruction of Beth She'arim in the fourth century.[23]

We unearthed the entire courtyard of catacomb 13, including the staircase and all the stories. In addition to the nine halls known from the previous season, another three halls and their entrances were discovered. Here, for the first time, a hall was found whose graves had not been robbed, hall M. According to the Greek inscriptions on one of the graves, it belonged to a Sidonian Jew. All twelve halls were cleared of debris and were then thoroughly examined.

The focal point of this season's work was catacomb 14, the main features of which were already known from the previous season. We completed the uncovering of the façade and cleared most of the courtyard of its debris. Electric lighting was installed in the cave so that we could continue clearing and examining it. Another two inscriptions were discovered. At our request, the Public Works Department built concrete supports and erected iron posts to prevent the ceiling from collapsing.

In the courtyard we found many scattered building stones. In order to find the building from which these stones originated, we excavated on the slope above the cave. In fact, we discovered a wall with a niche in the middle and several rows of benches. To the west of these benches and adjoining them catacomb 15 was discovered, also entered through a breach above the lintel. However, this catacomb was of a different type. In hall B, which was destroyed prior to the looting of the graves, a group of glass vessels was discovered in a tomb for the first time. Hall C was just below the benches, and its excavation was postponed.

West of catacomb 15 catacomb 17 was discovered; it was full of debris which had to be removed. Several lamps and the first and only coin were found here. East of the structure with the benches, above catacomb 14, the courtyard of catacomb 18 was exposed. On the lintel above the doorway there was a Greek inscription; and in the debris of the courtyard fragments of a marble tablet were discovered bearing a long Greek epigram with a symbol of a menorah at the top. When I brought a photograph of this inscription to Prof. Schwabe who was very ill at the time, his sad eyes began to shine again. Unfortunately, the interpretation of this epigram was his last contribution to Judaeo-Greek epigraphy — a subject to which he had devoted most of his life.

This was an excavation season replete with astonishing events and exciting discoveries which aroused great interest among the general public as well.

Catacomb 14 was the center of interest since it was suggested that members of Rabbi Judah Ha-Nassî's family were buried here. This possibility fired everyone's imagination. The place bustled with visitors from all sections of the community: the president of Israel, the late Yitzhak Ben-Zvi; the prime minister, the late Moshe Sharett; the late David Ben Gurion; Mrs. Golda Meir (then minister of labor); cabinet ministers; the chairman and members of the Knesseth (the Parliament of Israel); the chairman of the Jewish Agency; the heads of the Hebrew University; teachers and students; citizens and tourists. All shared the wish to view the inscriptions of Rabbi Shim'on and Rabbi Gamaliel — vivid evidence of so important a chapter in Jewish history and a tangible reminder of two outstanding personalities among the spiritual leaders of the people.

The seventh excavation season began on July 26, 1955, and ended on October 14, 1955. This time again our work was centered mainly on the cemetery area, though some soundings were conducted on the summit in preparation for future systematic excavations in the city area. Thus we decided to examine a portion of a wall in the northwestern part of the hill and to trace its course. After we uncovered about 40 m, it became obvious that this was not a city wall as we had originally assumed, but the outer wall of a large public building — later to be known as "the basilica" — built of perfectly drafted masonry. In fact, during the excavations conducted by Prof. Mazar

in 1956, our suppositions as to the nature of the building were confirmed. Evidently there was an important center on this part of the summit, similar to that on the northern part where the remains of a synagogue and a public building were found.

In the necropolis area, we completed several bits of work left unfinished from the previous season — mainly the clearing of catacomb 18. In between excavation seasons a group of workers was usually employed to continue clearance and restoration work and to dig drainage ditches above the catacombs. This time, the northern end of the courtyard of catacomb 14 was cleared. In the process, burial hall B was discovered. Opposite it hall C was exposed, its entrance blocked with stones. This hall was only a small burial chamber. In one of its arcosolia there was a breach into catacomb 19. We located the courtyard of this catacomb and uncovered all three of its halls. Several interesting Greek inscriptions were discovered in the catacomb, and a relief of a human head was found on one of the lintels.

We set out to look for a new excavation site and finally decided upon a depression at the foot of the slope, about 40 m east of the courtyard of catacomb 14 (sq. 12:FG3). Here there was a broad artificial terrace (Pl. II, 1) composed almost entirely of chipped rocks piled up in ancient times. We conjectured that a large cave must have been quarried nearby, from which this large quantity of material originated. The crescent-shaped depression near the terrace seemed, therefore, a promising site for excavation. After digging a trial trench for five days, we discovered the first signs of a stone structure; and after four more days, on August 5, 1955, we crawled through a hole beneath the lintel of an entrance into the catacomb numbered 20.

What was revealed before us, even in the weak light of our flashlights, was so different from what we were accustomed to in Beth She'arim that we could hardly believe our eyes. Stumbling and slipping on wet blocks of rock — water had penetrated through the ceiling and caused the formation of a layer of mud on the floor of the cave — we made our way through what seemed to us like interminably long halls. Wherever we looked, we saw rows or groups of large stone sarcophagi, all broken into. Sometimes the heavy lids were flung onto the floor. Obviously, the grave robbers had reached this catacomb as well. Every now and then, someone of our group would call out in excitement: "Here are lions! Here is a Hebrew inscription!" When we reached a large rock fall at the end of the catacomb with frightening hanging rocks, we continued climbing heedless of the slippery rocks until we reached more rooms which seemed to us to be "beyond the mountains." With no mean effort and some anxiety we worked our way back to the small hole through which daylight penetrated.

That day we dismissed the workers early and held council on how to continue the work. Clearly we had a difficult long-term task ahead of us. We prepared a work schedule for the present campaign and an additional, long-range program. We hired a bulldozer to clear the debris from the front part of the courtyard. This enabled us to expose the façade of the catacomb in a relatively short time. The façade consisted of three arches, similar to the façade of catacomb 14, except that it was largely destroyed. At our request, Tahal (the Israel Water Planning Company) sent us a Swedish expert on mining and tunneling who at that time was directing the digging operations on the tunnel at Eilabun for the new trans-Israel water carrier. He suggested strengthening the loose rock by a system of rock bolts in the weak spots. This did not seem feasible to us since the rock of the cave was soft and friable. Other experts too, whose advice we sought, did not find a suitable solution.

We finally decided to rely on our foreman, Moshe Jaffe, for a solution to this problem as well. He carried out his task very well indeed, using his own methods. Though it was dangerous, he knocked down all the loose rock suspended from the ceiling until a kind of solid rock dome was formed, strong enough to hold itself. Parts of the walls and entrances which were in poor condition were dismantled and rebuilt with stones taken from the fallen rocks of the cave. These repairs, by the way, also helped to strengthen the ceiling. This work was carried out in stages during the excavations and between seasons.

Despite the unfavorable conditions, Mr. Aryeh Volk succeeded in photographing everything most successfully before clearing and cleaning operations began. This work was carried out under difficult circumstances: poor lighting, lifting of heavy loads, hauling large quantities of rock and debris over long distances and slippery ground. In addition, the manpower at our disposal was insufficient. Actually, the clearance work in this catacomb went on intermittently for several years, supervised by Moshe Jaffe. Among the small finds the lamps are particularly noteworthy, both the ones used by the undertakers and those of tomb robbers.

The rains caused a severe problem since water seeped through the rock and turned the floor of the cave into a smooth slippery mass with muddy puddles. Eventually, we found a remedy to this problem also, digging drainage ditches and removing the earth above the catacomb. While digging one of these ditches, we came across building remains. We deepened the trench and reached a beaten-earth floor. We immediately thought that this could be part of another upper structure similar to that above catacomb 14. However, we had to postpone the verification of this matter to the next season.

At the end of the ceiling of room XXI, which was full of fallen rocks from the original ceiling, we discovered a small gap through which earth penetrated. This was an indication of some connection either with the outside or with another catacomb. After careful measuring, we located the spot from the outside. It was on the very place where we had conducted an unsuccessful sounding two years ago. Now we renewed our excavation there. After exposing remains of walls and a mosaic floor, we again reached the rock face, proof that a catacomb had existed here but that its ceiling had collapsed (no. 23). We were forced to discontinue our work due to manpower shortage.

During this season we also discovered a small catacomb of the kokh type. This catacomb, no. 31 (sq. 14 on contour line 105), was exposed at the bend of the path descending to the recently discovered catacombs. When this road was widened in 1963, the tomb was entirely destroyed.

The eighth excavation season was conducted in the summer of 1956 under the direction of Prof. Mazar; therefore, its results are not included in this report. That year I was on sabbatical leave. During this excavation[24] the important fact was established that the first settlement on this site existed in the ninth and eighth centuries B.C.E., i.e., in the time of the Israelite monarchy. In this season the basilica in the southwestern part of the city was uncovered at the spot where we had exposed the long ashlar wall during the previous season. In the necropolis several catacombs were discovered. At Prof. Mazar's suggestion, two of them have been included in this report since they form an integral part of the group of catacombs which were uncovered by our expedition.

The ninth excavation season, the last in this report, was conducted in August, 1958. Because of the many discoveries made in the previous seasons and the large quantity of material which had accumulated, we decided not to excavate any new areas but rather to clarify some of the problems which arose during the previous campaigns as well as from work done between seasons.

We also decided to continue our investigation of the rich finds from catacomb 20. It appears, however, that even limited operations at Beth She'arim are likely to produce important finds.

The examination conducted above catacomb 20 in order to determine the nature of the building remains which had come to light in the previous season led to the discovery of an open square surrounded by benches, similar to that above catacomb 14, but more spacious. Near this area, to the west, a drainage channel was dug during the previous winter, and a built grave was uncovered containing a lead coffin decorated with menoroth. This was a somewhat surprising discovery for two reasons: *(a)* Until now, the only evidence of the use of lead coffins at Beth She'arim were small fragments found in various catacombs. Also, and even more important, this was the first lead coffin found in the country which could be defined with absolute certainty as Jewish because of the symbols on it. *(b)* This was the first time at Beth She'arim that a tomb was discovered outside the catacombs. Was this accidental or the beginning of a new development?

In order to investigate the matter, we conducted a systematic excavation of this area. Several additional graves were discovered, also containing lead coffins. Thus, a new type of tomb was added to Beth She'arim, which we named "outer tombs."

While searching for other tombs of this type, we came across catacomb 21 which consisted of a chamber with kokhim and other burial rooms. On one of the lintels a Greek inscription dedicated to a woman from Tyre was discovered. We also found a marble tablet with an epitaph of a freed woman slave.

Another surprise awaited us when we cleared the area in front of the entrance to catacomb 23 of the debris which had accumulated during our excavation of the "outer tombs": two deep shaft graves with brick-lined walls, of a type without parallel in this country. This brought to a close the number of catacombs and other tombs which our expedition excavated.[25]

In this campaign we devoted particular attention to catacomb 20. During the last few months, the courtyard was cleared of the debris which filled it. In the process, the entrance to the courtyard was exposed, and additional architectural fragments of the upper part of the façade were found. Moshe Jaffe later inserted them in the restored façade. The clearance operations in the catacomb itself also progressed steadily. An additional examination of the sarcophagi revealed several more Hebrew inscriptions — one of them about the man ("who made this cave") — and some new decorations. The clearance of the large rock fall continued intermittently for several years and was terminated, for the time being, at the stage indicated in the plan of the catacomb (fig. 44).[26] In order to complete the clearance of the catacomb large, complicated supports will have to be built to prevent the rock from collapsing — a project entailing much expenditure.

For the time being, this brings the account of our excavations at Beth She'arim to a close. However, this narrative cannot be concluded without mentioning an important factor which contributed greatly in all matters concerning the preservation of the remains that were discovered. I am referring to the Department of Improvement of Natural Landscape and Historical Sites,[27] attached to the prime minister's office, and to its director, Mr. Y. Yanai. Its activities at Beth She'arim justified its name fully. The landscape of Beth She'arim was improved by planting trees, shrubs, and lawns; the monuments were restored in consultation with us; electric lighting was installed in catacombs 14 and 20; and a small local museum was erected inside an ancient cave (no. 28), which had once served as a water reservoir. A convenient road for vehicles enables thousands of visitors to reach the site. Beth She'arim has become one of the most popular historical sites in the country. The charm of the place, the mystery surrounding the necropolis with its many catacombs, a tour of catacomb 20, unique in the ancient world because of its numerous sarcophagi, the historical background of the site — all these leave a lasting impression on every visitor.

NOTES

1 B. Mazar, *Beth She'arim*, vol. I, New Brunswick, N. J., and Jerusalem, 1973, pp. 7–20.

2 On this see now: S. Safrai, "Beth She'arim in Talmudic Literature," *Eretz-Israel,* V (1958), pp. 206–12 (Hebrew); also: *Sefer haYishuv,* I, p. 18 (Hebrew).

3 B. Mazar, *BIES,* XXI (1957), p. 159 (Hebrew).

4 Josephus, *Life,* 24.

5 Tosefta Terumah 7, 14, p. 38; Jerusalem Talmud, *ibid.,* 8, 46, top of a.

6 "The Sanhedrin was transferred... from Jerusalem to Jabneh and from Jabneh to Usha... and from Usha to Shefar'am and from Shefar'am to Beth She'arim and from Beth She'arim to Sepphoris, and from Sepphoris to Tiberias." Rosh Hashanah 30a-b; Genesis Rabba 97, Albeck ed., pp. 1220–21; Sanhedrin 32b: "...it went... after Rabbi to Beth She'arim."

7 *Beth She'arim,* I, p. 5.

8 "Rabbi was at Beth She'arim, but since he became ill, they brought him to Sepphoris, which was a high place with fragrant air." Ketubot 103b.

9 Jerusalem Talmud Kelaim 9, 32a-b; Ketubot 12, 35b.

10 "Thus they bear him [the deceased] from place to place, such as those who are buried in Beth She'arim." Jerusalem Talmud Mo'ed Qatan 3, 82c. Safrai suggests the following reading: אילין דקיסרין דקברין, meaning "like the people of Caesarea who bury [their dead] in Beth She'arim." *Eretz-Israel,* V, p. 211.

11 *Beth She'arim,* I, p. 18.

12 Niddah, 27a.

13 B. Mazar, *BIES,* XXI (1957), p. 163 (Hebrew).

14 A. Ben-Horin, *BIES,* XXI (1957), pp. 165–68 (Hebrew).

15 M. Schwabe and B. Lifshitz, *Beth She'arim,* II, New Brunswick, N. J., 1974, p. 45, no. 127.

16 This section was written according to data supplied by our architect, Immanuel Dunayevsky.

17 All of these, except for catacomb 11, are published in *Beth She'arim,* I.

18 These catacombs have not yet been published.

19 The exact direction of the hill's axis is from East-North-East to West-South-West but, for convenience, only the main compass points will be drawn henceforth.

20 N. Avigad, *IEJ,* IV (1954), p. 90.

21 This cistern is now used as a local museum.

22 See: N. Avigad, *IEJ,* IV (1954), p. 92.

23 N. Avigad, *IEJ,* V (1955), pp. 207–11.

24 B. Mazar, *BIES,* XXI (1957), pp. 153 *ff.* (Hebrew).

25 It is noteworthy that we began excavating an additional catacomb discovered near the path west of catacomb 16. We managed to locate a small room in a rather destroyed state, which contained several Greek inscriptions. For various reasons we were forced to stop the excavation and cover it up. The cave still awaits the excavator.

26 After writing these lines, we made additional clearing excavations. Room XXIII was entirely cleared of rock debris, and a spacious passage was discovered between this room and room XXII.

27 Now the "Parks Authority."

CHAPTER II

THE TOMBS

1 CATACOMB 12 (figs. 3–4)

This catacomb comprises four halls which branch off from the four walls of a square courtyard, 4.90 m long and 4.10 m wide. This courtyard is entered from the north through a flight of five rough steps hewn into the western half of the rock face. The steps begin on the northern side at a height of 90.95 m above sea level, and descend about 2 m. On the southern side of the courtyard, the floor level is about 4.70 m below the rock surface and about 6.60 m below the present slope (fig. 4).[1]

A square sunk courtyard, entered through a descending flight of steps and with entrances leading into a burial hall in three or all four of its walls is the plan most commonly encountered in the Beth She'arim catacombs. The main hall is usually found behind the southern wall of the courtyard, opposite the steps, since the rockface is highest on that side. This made it possible to quarry deeply into the hill and to hew out an extensive cave. This could not be done in the side walls which were not high enough. The main hall was always hewn first and was generally of superior workmanship to the other halls. The lateral halls were sometimes hewn considerably later than the main hall and were usually smaller and simpler. In the entire catacomb there are sixty-nine burial places.

Hall A

The entrance to the central hall, in the southern wall of the courtyard, is well preserved. Since it comprises all the features generally characteristic of the tomb doors in this cemetery, it is a fine example of the doorways common at Beth She'arim. One of the most fascinating experiences of every visitor is to see how this heavy door still turns with relative ease on its hinges. We

shall describe this doorway in detail here so as to avoid repeated description of similar doors in other catacombs.[2]

The Central Entrance (fig. 5). In order to fix the door in place, a wide irregular opening was first cut out of the rock and then the stones of the door frame put in their proper position. The spaces between the rock and the doorposts and lintel were filled with small stones and then covered with plaster.

This door system is composed of five elements: the threshold, two jambs, and a lintel forming the door frame; and the door slab fixed by its hinges into sockets in the lintel and the threshold. All these members are monolithic except the right doorpost which is composed of two stones. The keyhole is found in the joint between these two stones. The hard, light-colored limestone is finely dressed with a toothed chisel. The lintel and the doorposts carry a cyma recta molding on the outer edges. The lintel extends beyond the jambs, forming something like "ears" — a stylistic feature popular in the architecture of the period both in synagogues and in tombs.[3]

The door and hinges are made of one piece. The upper hinge is cylindrical and juts out about 8 cm; the lower hinge is rounded or slightly conical and is shorter. The sockets in the lintel and the threshold are adapted to the shape of the hinges. The door is decorated in the style characteristic of all the doors in Beth She'arim — in imitation of a paneled wooden door. A vertical fillet divides the door into two "wings," imitating a double door, each decorated with two panels.[4] Each half is also studded with three groups of conical knobs in imitation of round nailheads (Pl. IV, 1). There is a row of such "doornails" in the

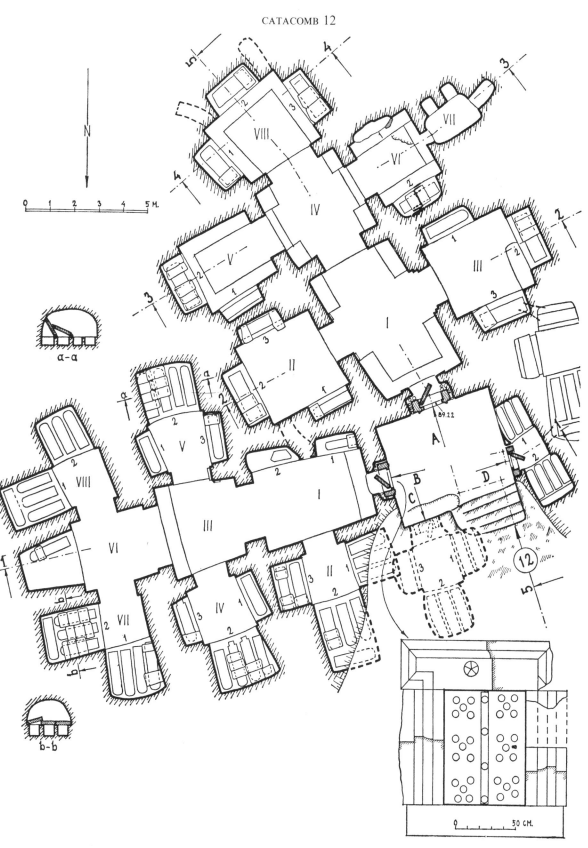

Fig. 3 Plan of catacomb 12   *The door of hall B*

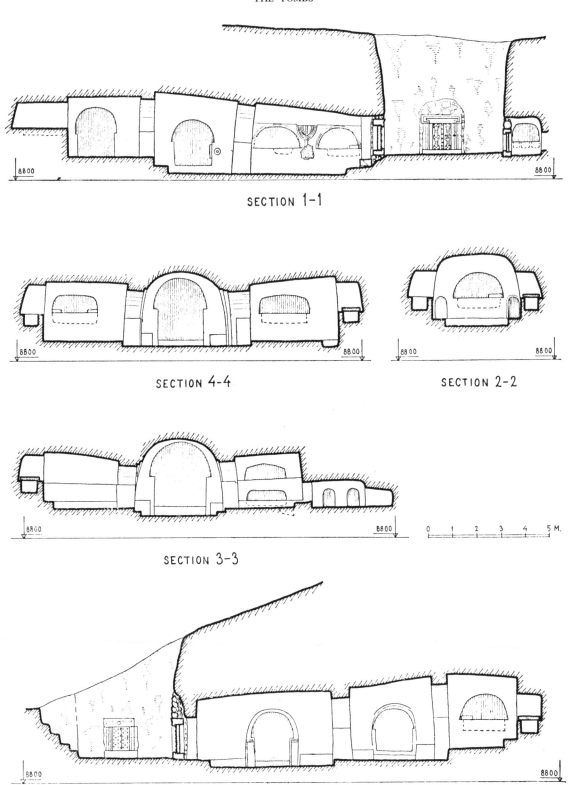

SECTION 1-1

SECTION 4-4

SECTION 2-2

SECTION 3-3

SECTION 5-5

Fig. 4 Sections of catacomb 12

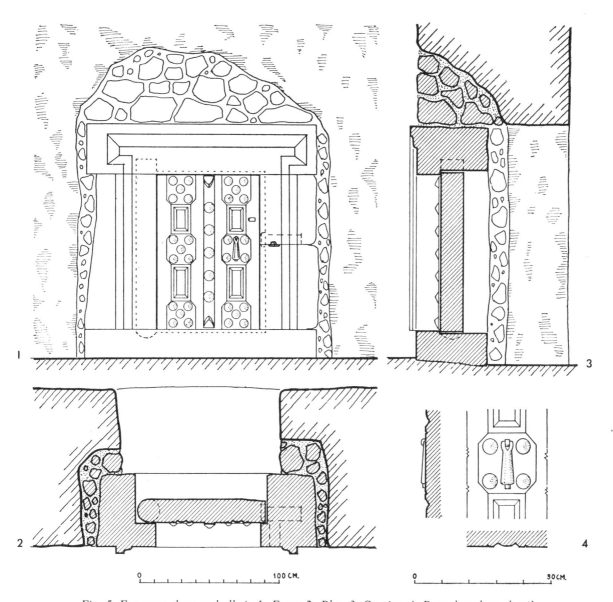

Fig. 5 Entrance door to hall A. 1. Front 2. Plan 3. Section 4. Door knocker, detail

central fillet also. In the middle of the right "wing," a suspended handle imitating a door knocker is carved. An iron loop is inserted at the upper right side in order to secure the iron ring, now missing, by which the door was pulled. The keyhole joins up with the bolt slot. The bolt itself, in the form of a stone bar, was missing, but its shape is well known from other doors (Pl. LVII, bottom). It had two or three notches where the key teeth were inserted to move the bolt into a recess in the door slab.

The internal measurements of the entrance are .75 m wide and 1.09 m high. The lintel is 1.61 m long and .35 m high. The door slab is .95 m wide, 1.13 m high, and .17 m thick. The height of the entire door frame is 1.62 m.

The Plan of the Hall. The total length of the hall is 13.60 m. The plan is strictly symmetrical except for the addition of room VII. The central hall comprises two rooms (I, IV) which do not contain any burials. From these rooms five burial

21

chambers branch out; each of the chamber walls contains one arcosolium. The hall contains a total of twenty burial places, including the small kokhim for secondary burial. The ceilings of the rooms are vaulted. The openings between the rooms are arched (see Pls. III and IV). These arches are not always perfectly rounded and seem to have been borne by projecting doorposts. The walls were dressed with a sharp-edged adz; some places, like the posts of the archways, were well smoothed in straight lines and right angles.

The arcosolia are also arched, sometimes semicircular and sometimes squat. Only one trough-shaped grave is quarried in the shelf of each arcosolium. These trough graves were covered with stone slabs sealed with mortar. A few of the slabs were found in situ; the majority, however, were scattered over the floor. The arcosolia are not all equal in size: they range between 1.80 to 2.40 m in length, .65–1.00 m in width, and .70–1.00 m in height. In a few of the arcosolia walls small, sooty recesses were found, used as receptacles for pottery lamps.

R o o m I. This room served as the main passageway to the other rooms. It is 5.70 m long, 3.60 m wide, and 2.90 m high. All along the walls there are rock benches for seating mourners. These benches are .45 m high. An archway in the left wall leads into room II. The image of an eagle, 25 cm high, is incised in fine sketchy lines on the right side of the arch (fig. 6). Since the eagle is not associated with any specific grave, it is assumed to be the handiwork of one of the visitors. This is the only animal depicted in this catacomb and, except for the sarcophagi, the only image of an eagle found in all the catacombs we excavated.

R o o m II. This room is 3.50 m long, and 3.40 m wide. One arcosolium is hewn in each of the three walls, and each arcosolium contains one trough grave. In the northern wall to the right of the arcosolium, an irregular kokh was hewn, and through it a hole was breached into room I of hall B.

Fig. 6 Graffito of eagle

On the jambs of the archway between rooms I and II two graffiti were discovered. On the southern post a short Greek inscription was incised:[5]

ΑΕΚΣΟ ΕΦ

"[May] I attain [happiness]."

In the line of the inscription around the corner of the post, a small schematic menorah is engraved (fig. 7).

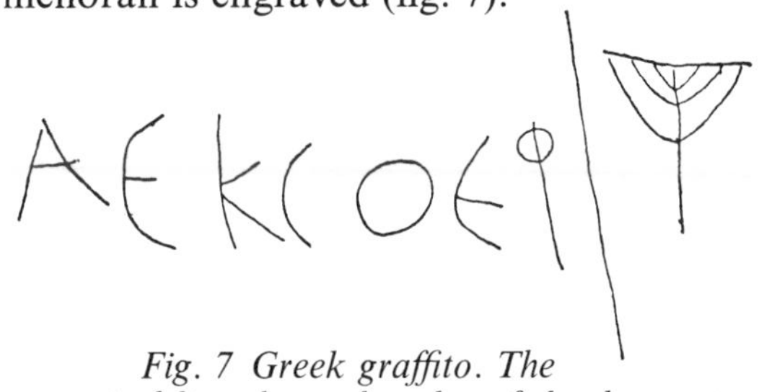

Fig. 7 Greek graffito. The vertical line shows the edge of the doorpost

On the northern jamb the first word of the previous inscription is engraved in Hebrew transliteration (no. 4):

עא]יקק[ו

A small menorah is engraved near this inscription as well (fig. 8).

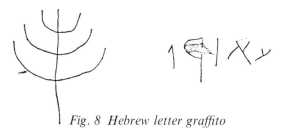

Fig. 8 Hebrew letter graffito

The late Moshe Schwabe interpreted this inscription as an expression of the belief of the deceased that he would attain light and happiness in the next world. If this interesting interpretation is correct, then we have here a rare instance of a combination of words and a symbol into a semi-pictographic sentence. It does seem strange, however, that the inscription is incised at the entrance to the room and not on the grave of the deceased since, according to this interpretation, the first person singular is used by the writer.

R o o m III. In this room (3.54 × 3.30 m; 2.35 m high) also there are three arcosolia, each having one grave. In the corner of the floor between arcosolia 2 and 3 is a sunken rectangular grave, the only one added in the floor of this hall. Arcosolium 3 is noteworthy for its two inscriptions (see Pl. III, 5). On the back wall, there is an Aramaic dipinto in red (inscription no. 1; see Pl. III, 3):

כל מן דיפתח

הדא קבורתה

על מן דבגוה

ימות בסוף ביש

"Anyone who shall open this burial
upon whomever is inside
shall die of an evil end."

This inscription will be fully discussed later in the chapter on inscriptions.

Its author was not content to address his warning to the Aramaic-speaking public only, and he repeated it in Greek as well, in a slightly altered formula (Pl. III, 4):

MHΔIC ANYΞE[I]
KATA THN OCIAN
KATA ΠΡΟCTAΓ[M]A

"Nobody shall open, in the name of the
divine and secular law."

Because of the particular importance of this inscription, we shall present Professor Schwabe's opinion in full: "...the author of the inscription demands protection in the name of both religious and secular laws. The famous imperial edict is the only known epigraphic evidence as to the existence of a law against the violation of graves, especially prohibiting the removal of the dead from their graves and the burial of other dead in their stead."[6]

In the corner of arcosolium 3 there is a breach into catacomb 13. Incidentally, it was through this very opening that we crawled into this catacomb before it was exposed from the outside.

R o o m IV. This room (3.75 × 3.50 m; 3.20 m high in average) served as a passageway for three burial chambers. Benches were hewn in its four corners. Room V lies to the West of room IV.

R o o m V. This room (3.60 × 2.85 m; 1.90 m high in average) was entered by a descent of two steps (Pl. III, 2) and contained only two arcosolia. There were benches along three walls. Almost all the cover stones of the arcosolium were found in situ. The slab farthest to the left was partly lifted and a small stone placed underneath for support. Apparently, this was one of the grave robbers' methods for lifting cover stones in order to pillage the graves. In the wall of this arcosolium there was a small recess, doubtlessly for a lamp since the rock above it was blackened with soot.

R o o m VI. The arrangement of this room (2.70 × 2.60 m; 2.10 m high) differs from that of the other rooms, a small room (VII) having been hewn in its western wall. At first there was no arcosolium in the southern wall, as was the case in the corresponding wall of room V. However, the hewing of an arcosolium was started at a later stage but not completed. Instead, an irregular arcosolium was hewn lower down, partially cutting into the bench. One of the vertical cover stones remained in situ. Above this arcosolium there is a blurred Greek inscription painted in black:[7]

ΤΟΠΟC [E]ΛΠΙΔΙΑC

"The place [of burial] of Elpidia"

In the southwestern corner an irregular depression was cut into the floor. Here a group of vessels was concealed (see fig. 9), which included five clay lamps (nos. 5, 9, 11, 11a, and 11b; see also Pl. LXX), a glass unguentarium (Pl. LXVIII, 4), a bronze cosmetics spatula (Pl. LXXIII, 15), and a necklace of mother-of-pearl beads (Pl. LXXIII, 23). For some reason these articles were hidden in this depression in the floor and covered with earth and thus escaped the notice of the tomb robbers. Since, in our excavations, this was one of the two groups of vessels found in situ, it was of great value in dating the catacomb. As will be seen later, this group should be assigned

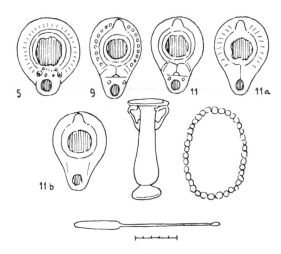

Fig. 9 The finds in room VI

approximately to the middle of the third century C.E.

R o o m V I I. This chamber contained three short kokhim, probably intended for secondary burial.

R o o m V I I I. This room (3.50 × 3.20 m; 2.90 m high) terminates the series of rooms in this catacomb. Its floor is one step higher than that of room IV (Pl. IV, 3). There are benches all along three walls. Here, too, there are three arcosolia. In the southern wall, flanking both sides of arcosolium 2, kokhim were added. Above the right kokh there is an Aramaic inscription (no. 2; Pl. IV, 4):

דקביר בהדין
שמעון בר יוחנן
ובשבועה דכל
דיפתח עליו יהי
מאית בסוף
ביש

"He who is buried here is Shim'on, the son of Yoḥanan; and on oath, whoever shall open upon him shall die of an evil end."

The text of this inscription is similar to that of the inscription in room III, except that here the name of the deceased is also mentioned. Part of a stone slab (.56 × .72 m) was also found in this room. It bore traces of the beginning of an inscription phrased like the Aramaic inscription in room III (no. 3):

כל מן דיפתח...

"Anyone who shall open..."

It is likely that this stone slab closed the opening of the kokh, though it is also possible that it was one of the stones covering a trough grave.

Judging by its overall layout, the plan of hall A should be classified with the usual plans of catacombs prevalent at Beth She'arim, i.e., a series of rooms with arcosolia. However, this catacomb differs from the others in several respects. First, mention must be made of the two central rooms which serve as a passageway to the various chambers, the spacious, handsome burial chambers, the steps rising from room to room, and the numerous benches. Secondly, there is a great contrast between the vastness of the rooms and the limited number of graves, only twenty. These distinctive features plus the fact that there are no decorations whatsoever give this catacomb an atmosphere of spaciousness and monumentality which does not prevail in other catacombs of this type. Most probably, burial in this hall was very expensive and, therefore, only wealthy persons could afford to acquire a burial chamber here.

We know nothing about the origin of those interred in hall A. As we shall see later on, hall B was acquired in its entirety by Jews from Syrian and Phoenician cities. Did the same thing occur in hall A? Judging by the Aramaic inscriptions found in hall A, we may well assume that the answer is negative since, to this day, no Aramaic inscriptions have been found at Beth She‘arim on graves of Jews from the Diaspora — certainly not pure Palestinian Aramaic. Actually, no Aramaic inscriptions were found anywhere else at Beth She‘arim, a problem which will be discussed later in the chapter on inscriptions.

Based on considerations of style the date of hall A may be attributed to the first half of the third century, as we shall attempt to prove in the chapter on the classification of the catacombs. Additional confirmation for this date may also be found in the small cache of lamps and other articles which were concealed in the floor of room VIII. Since the lamps are typical of the mid-third century (see the discussion on lamps), we may presume that hall A was hewn at a somewhat earlier date.

Hall B

The entrance leading into hall B is in the eastern wall of the courtyard. The size of the entrance is .72 × .90 m. It is constructed of hard, light-colored stones, partially smoothed. The stone dressing of the entrance is not combed, unlike that of the previous hall. The door jambs are partly broken and the door is cracked. The moldings of the jambs and the lintel do not match exactly. The door is not paneled; it is decorated with studs only. A small schematic rosette is carved on the lintel (see fig. 3, bottom).

The descent into the hall is by two steps, the lower one serving also as a bench along the entrance wall (Pl. V, 1). The plan of this hall also is symmetrical: it consists mainly of three rooms (I, III, and VI) arranged in a row, 11.50 m in total length. From each of these rooms two burial chambers with arcosolia branch off. The hall has thirty-six burial place altogether. The symmetry of the plan is broken in the southern wall of room I where two arcosolia are hewn instead of a burial chamber, the reason being that room II of hall A is situated just behind this wall. All the rooms are vaulted. The passageways between the rooms are arched and their posts rise to a height of 1.00–1.20 m above the floor.

R o o m I. This room is 4.50 m long, 3.10 m wide, and on the average 2.60 m high. It has smoothed walls, except for the entrance wall and a band all along the foot of the walls where the dressing is rough. The walls jut out a bit at their junction with the vault. In the southern wall there are two arcosolia with molded edges. In arcosolium 1 the grave is not cut out along the entire length. One of the vertical cover stones was found in situ, covered with rough plaster. On the right side of arcosolium 2 the quarrying was not completed because the stonecutter struck a kokh behind it. The cutting of the grave was also stopped soon after it was started. In order to compensate for the space thus lost, the stonecutters extended the shelf of the arcosolium toward the left so as to prepare sufficient space for a coffin or a body. Traces of mortar were noticeable along the rim of the arch — an indication that the arcosolium had been sealed with vertical stone slabs.

A menorah is carved in relief on the wall between the two arcosolia (Pl. V, 1–2). The height of the relief is 1.35 m; its width at the top is .83 m. The branches of the menorah are plain; its stem is straight, without legs, and was partly destroyed when an opening was breached during the quarrying of a kokh in room II of hall A. This menorah is the only one carved in relief in this catacomb, and is one of the few encountered in all the catacombs excavated by us. On the other hand, in the catacombs discovered in 1936–40, reliefs of menoroth are quite common, several of them similar in style to the menorah described here.[8]

On each side of arcosolium 1 there is a Greek inscription. On the right side (see Pl. V, 4) the inscription reads:[9]

ΘΑΡΣΙ
ΚΑΛΙΟΠΗ ΜΑΤΡΩΝΑ
ΟΥΔΙΣ ΑΘΑΝΑ
ΤΟΣ Η
ΑΠΟ ΒΙΒΛΟΥ

"Be of good courage, lady Kalliope from Byblos; no one is immortal."

This is a stereotype consolation formula, very common among the inscriptions of Beth She'arim.

On the left side of the arch of the arcosolium, the inscription reads:[10]

ΑΨΙΣ
ΚΑΛΙΟΠΗΣ
ΒΙΒΛΙ
ΑΣ
ΜΑΤΡΩ
ΝΗΣ

"The tomb of Kalliope from Byblos, the lady."

On the left side of the archway to room II the following inscription is incised:[11]

ΙΕΣΟΥΟΣ
ΙΑΜΟΥΡΙΤΗΣ

"Belonging to Jesus of Yaḥmur"

The city of Yaḥmur lies 30 km east of Sidon. The same inscription is found twice more on the left post of the arch.

R o o m I I. This room is 2.00 m long and 2.00 m wide. There are three arcosolia in the room. In arcosolium 1 there are three longitudinal trough graves; in arcosolium 2, one transverse and three longitudinal graves; in arcosolium 3, two graves hewn transversely. Several of the cover stones were found in situ.

R o o m I I I. The archway leading into this room was partly destroyed. The room is 3.40 m long, 3.00 m wide, and 3.00 m high. The walls are roughly finished. The intersection between the walls and the ceiling vault is sharp. On the wall to the right of the entrance to room V, a concave disc with a knob in the center is carved (Pl. V, 3). In front of the entrance to room VI, all along the wall, there is a step. Flint balls protrude from the ceiling of rooms I–III. There is a rise of one step into room IV.

R o o m I V. This room is 2.25 m long and 2.20 m wide. In each of the three walls there is one arcosolium. The arcosolia in the side walls contain one trough grave each, while the arcosolium in the wall opposite the entrance has four graves cut lengthwise. The back end of each grave is rounded, and the bottom is somewhat raised to serve as a pillow for the head of the deceased. This arrangement is common to the other graves as well. A number of graves were slightly extended in order to make place for the feet. Several cover slabs were found in situ.

This room is distinguished by its numerous Greek inscriptions which indicate that six members of a respected family from Antioch were buried here.

On the right side of the entrance is the following inscription (Pl. VI, 3):[12]

АΨIC
AIΔECIOY
ΓΕΡΟΥCΙΑΡΧΟΥ
ΑΝΤΙΟΧΕΩC

"The tomb of Aidesios, the head of the Council of Elders, from Antiochia"

On the right jamb, the inscription reads (Pl. VI, 1):[13]

EICIN EN TH A
ΨIΔI KPHΠI
ΔEC EΞ ς
ΔΙΑΦΕΡΟΥ
CAI AIΔECIΩ

"There are in the burial chamber six tombs which belong to Aidesios."

The head of the family, Aidesios, who acquired the burial chamber was interred in arcosolium 3, as proved by the name written on it: AIΔECIC (see Pl. VI, 1, back wall). In arcosolium 2 (see Pl. VI, 2), buried from right to left were: Hesychis (HCYXIC — apparently the wife of Aidesios), Magnos (MAΓNOC), and Kyrilla (KYPIΛΛA).[14] There are no inscriptions on the two remaining graves.

Room V. The arcosolia in this room (2.20 × 2.10 m) are similar to those in room IV. A noteworthy point is the manner in which the two graves to the left in arcosolium 2 are covered (see plan, section a–a). The cover slabs were lain slantwise, the first row leaning against the wall of the arcosolium, and the second row leaning against the first. The joints between the slabs were filled with chips of stone and mortar. This arrangement was necessary due to the use of oversized slabs.

Room VI. This room is 3.00 m long, 2.80 m wide, and 2.35 m high. One ascends it by two steps, through an arch with a smoothed soffit. The lower part of the walls is very roughly finished. In the eastern wall there is an arcosolium containing only one longitudinal grave. The remaining space on the shelf was not utilized.

Room VII. This room (1.75 × 1.65) has two arcosolia, each containing four graves. In arcosolium 2, most of the cover stones remained in situ. Below arcosolium 2, the following Greek inscription was found (Pl. V, 5):[15]

ΕΝΘΑΔΕ ΚΙΤΕ ΑC
ΘΗΡ ΑΝΘΟΥ
ΤΥΡΙΑ

"Here lies Esther, daughter of Anthos, from Tyre."

Room VIII. The arrangement of this room (2.00 × 1.70 m) is similar to that of room VII. It, too, contains a total of eight burial places.

It seems that hall B was hewn after hall A. This is evidenced by the fact that no chamber could be hewn in the southern wall of room I because of the burials which already existed behind it. It also seems that the door to hall B, different and of poorer workmanship than the door to hall A, was made later as well. In addition, the large number of graves in the arcosolia of hall B seems to indicate that these arcosolia are later than those in hall A. Nevertheless, this does not necessarily mean that there was a large disparity in time between the two halls.

In its general features, the plan of hall B is similar to that of hall A. Hall B is smaller and does not make so monumental an impression as hall A with its high rooms, its large archways, its arcosolia with one burial only, and its many benches. The reasons for this are twofold: (a) the impossibility of cutting out high rooms into the lateral sides of the courtyard and (b) the desire to supply the demand for cheaper graves by utilizing the arcosolia for the interment of whole families.

What singles out hall B from the rest of the burial halls at Beth She'arim is the exceptional concentration of inscriptions mentioning the places of origin of the deceased. These inscriptions prove that the deceased were brought here from cities on the Syro-Phoenician coast — Tyre, Byblos, and Antioch; and from inland Syria — Yaḥmur. It seems that all of the deceased were from the wealthy class. The most outstanding among them was Aidesios, the head of the Council of Elders in Antioch, who acquired a whole burial room for his family.

Schwabe suggested that Aidesios and his wife are the very persons mentioned in the synagogue inscriptions of Apamea in Syria, together with their grandson, the head of the synagogue in Antioch, and other members of the family. Basing his calculations on this hypothesis, Schwabe concluded that Aidesios acted as the head of the Council of Elders in the first quarter of the fourth century C.E., and that he was brought to Beth She'arim for burial in the second quarter of this century. If this is indeed correct, it would mean that Aidesios was buried in this hall considerably later than the construction of hall A. However, there is no conclusive evidence in this theory for establishing the date when the hall was hewn or when it was first used for burial. Regrettably, the finds in the hall were too scarce to be helpful in dating it. Two small blurred coins discovered in this hall date, apparently, to the fourth century. On the other hand, lamp no. 10, similar to the type of lamps found in the small cache in hall A, doubtlessly dates to the third century.

Hall C

This hall lies on the northern side of the courtyard. Its main door, in contrast to the doors of halls A and B, is made of soft stone which yellowed in the course of time. The only decoration on the door face is a vertical strip (see Pl. VI, 5). The lintel and door jambs are entirely plain. The entrance is .40 m wide and .78 m high. The hall has only one room with three arcosolia, each containing one to three graves. The room is 2.00 m long and 1.70 m wide. The workmanship in this room is very coarse.

Hall D

This hall is situated on the western side of the courtyard. This door too is made of soft stone, nicely smoothed. The entrance is .48 m wide and .64 m high. The entire hall consists of only one small square chamber (1.10 × 1.10 m), two of its walls containing an arcosolium with shallow trough graves. The hall was very roughly hewn. During the cutting of arcosolium 1 a breach was formed into the courtyard; and in the wall opposite the door a hole was breached into catacomb 13.

There is no doubt that hall D is a late addition and that it was hewn when catacomb 13, which is of a later date than catacomb 12, was already in use.

2   CATACOMB 13 (figs. 11–14)

This catacomb — 19 m west of catacom 12 — has twelve halls arranged in four stories, centered around a long, narrow courtyard. Most of the doors were found half opened so that earth penetrated into the burial halls, especially near the entrances. Only the door of hall L was closed and thus the room was free of dust. In several rooms there was a partial collapse of the ceiling or walls. Most of the slabs which covered the graves were removed by grave robbers and thrown onto the floor. Here too, most of the bones were scattered in the rooms and only a few graves were left untouched.

The Courtyard (Pl. VII–VIII)

The courtyard runs from north to south. At floor level, it is 8.50 m long and 1.10–1.40 m wide; at the top it is 10.60 m long and 1.60–2.20 m wide. On the entrance side to the north, it cuts 4.50 m deep into the rock of the slope; however, the other end on the southern side is 7.50 beneath the rock surface, and an additional 1.50 m deeper than the present surface of the slope. The lowest level of the courtyard floor is 85.30 m above sea level (see section 1–1, fig. 13).

The walls of the courtyard were not properly aligned or smoothed. There are three rock-cut flights of steps, ranging in width from .40 to .90 m. These steps are not equal in size—neither in width nor in height—and they are so roughly finished that it is difficult to climb them. It is, however, possible that their shape deteriorated owing to the softness of the rock and the frequent use to which they were put.[17] The first flight of steps descends from the North at a height of 89.90 m above sea level; the second flight continues in the same direction and rises to the southern entrances. A third flight, the shortest of the three, leads to the lowest part of the courtyard at the northern end. The halls are marked in alphabetical order according to the direction of the steps from top to bottom.

The burial halls are arranged in four floor levels: halls C–E in the top level; halls A and B in the second level; halls F–H in the third level; and halls J–M—there is no hall I—in the lowest level (see section 1–1). In the drawings of the plan, the halls are divided into two distinct groups according to their levels: halls A–E in figure 11; halls F–M in figure 12. The plans of both groups have the same x–y axis.

The Burial Halls

The halls are hewn in the customary Beth She'arim fashion, their plan consisting of a long, narrow hall divided by archways into two or more rooms. In the walls of the rooms there are arcosolia with trough graves. Generally the halls are contiguous, and breaches were frequently formed between them during quarrying.

All the entrances were found intact. The doors still turn on their hinges. They are decorated in the conventional style described above (see catacomb 12), except for two doors which are decorated differently. The workmanship is not of the best.

Since the details may be seen in the plans and sections (see figs. 11–14), we shall describe this catacomb only briefly.

Hall A

This hall has two rooms which contain eleven burial places. The entrance to the hall is in the western wall of the courtyard. This entrance is .50 m wide and .95 m high. Above the lintel there is a sort of small "window," similar to the ones found in this courtyard above two other entrances. The purpose of these "windows" is unclear since, obviously, there is no need for lighting in the tombs. We may assume, therefore, that they were blocked. The total length of the rooms is 8.70 m.

R o o m I. Three narrow steps descend into this room. It is 2.10 m high and has a sloping ceiling. In each of the two walls there are arcosolia; and in each arcosolium there is only one trough grave. Arcosolia 1 and 2 were breached all along their width into the arcosolia of adjacent hall B. Both the ceiling and the arcosolia are partially destroyed. Above arcosolium 4 there are traces of a red dipinto inscription. It is, however, illegible.

R o o m II. One descends into the room via two additional steps, through an archway. This room—better preserved than room I—has four arcosolia, each with one grave, and one arcosolium with two graves.

Hall B

In this hall there are thirteen burial places. The entrance is on the same level as that leading into hall A and is equal in size as well. Above the lintel there is a Greek inscription incised in fine lines (fig. 10):[18]

XΩHN BYPITIOC

"Cohen from Beirut"

Fig. 10 Greek inscription

At first[19] I interpreted XΩHN as the Hebrew title for "priest," in accordance with the Greek ἱερεύς ("priest") in the other inscriptions. However, Prof. Saul Lieberman pointed out to me that it is quite possible that the word "cohen" as used here does not imply a title, but a family name, i.e., a man by the name of Cohen who came from Beirut. This interpretation seems quite likely, especially when compared with the interpretation of the lintel inscription of catacomb 18 where CAKEPΔOC (Latin for "priest") appears as a family name.

In this hall there are also two rooms, totaling 6.50 m in length (Pl. X, 1). The arcosolia have squat arches.

R o o m I. This room, the larger of the two, is 2.20 m high, and two steps lead down into it. The ceiling and a small part of the walls were damaged. In the northern wall there are two arcosolia, each containing one grave. In the southern wall there are two arcosolia with two graves each.

On the western side of arcosolium 3 there is a Hebrew dipinto inscription (no. 5; see Pl. X, 2):

זה משכבו
שליודן בן לוי
לוי לעולם
בשולם
יהי
שוי שוי

משכבו
בשולם
שליודן
בן לוי

"This is the resting place of Yudan, son of Levi, forever in peace. May his resting place be set [?] in peace. Of Yudan, son of Levi."

On the wall below the arcosolium there is an additional painted inscription (no.6):

זה משכבו
שליודן בן
לוי לעו]ל[ם

"This is the resting place of Yudan, son of Levi, forever."

These inscriptions are discussed in detail in the chapter on the Hebrew inscriptions.

It is evident that both a Cohen and a Levi were interred in this hall among the other deceased. It is difficult to know why Cohen from Beirut had his name inscribed above the entrance. It is unlikely that he was the head of a family who acquired the entire hall since at least one member of a Levi family is also buried here. It seems more reasonable to assume that Cohen was the first to be buried in this room and that his name was thus carved on the lintel.

R o o m II. This very small room has three arcosolia, each with one to three graves.

Hall C

To our present knowledge, this hall has ten burial places. The ceiling collapsed, and the room was full of earth and broken rock. We did not clear this room because of the potential danger of another collapse. We penetrated into the hall, in reality a single room, through a breach from hall D. The southern wall has two arcosolia with one grave each, whereas the western wall has two arcosolia with four graves each. The northern wall was not exposed.

Hall D

This long hall, which has twenty-four burial places, is particularly rich in Greek inscriptions. Judged only by the abundance of inscriptions, this hall is the most important in the entire catacomb. Its entrance is at the northern end of the courtyard, on the highest platform (Pl. IX, 1). The door is decorated in standard fashion, but it is taller than the others. It is 1.05 m high and .75 m wide. On the lintel the following inscription is engraved:[20]

CATOPNIΛOY

"Belonging to Satornilos"

Apparently, Satornilos was one of the important heads of the family that was buried in this hall. The hall consists of two rooms of a total length of 8.80 m.
R o o m I (Pl. XI, 2). This room is 6.00 m long, 4.50–5.40 m wide, and 2.20 m high on the average. The ceiling is flat and roughly dressed; the walls are smoothed. In each wall there are three arcosolia, and in each arcosolium there are between one and five graves. Benches were hewn all along the walls. There is a breach from arcosolium 1 into hall E. Arcosolium 6 was destroyed, and a breach was formed into hall C. The arrangement of the graves in arcosolia 2–4 is unusual: The first trough grave was cut out transversely, i.e., parallel to the wall, and the graves behind it are hewn longitudinally. There was probably only one grave in each arcosolium originally and, in the course of time, the arcosolia were enlarged and graves added.

Beneath arcosolium 3 the following inscription is incised:[21]

ENΘA KITE CAPA
ΓYNH BAPIΩCH

"Here lies Sarah, the wife of Bariosē."

Above the arcosolium the same woman is mentioned alongside her virtues:[22]

ΩΔE KITE
CAPA IOYΔEA OCIA

"Here lies Sarah, the pious Jewess."

This is the only inscription at Beth She'a-rim in which the fact that the deceased was Jewish is mentioned. Apparently the purpose of this inscription was not to emphasize Sarah's Jewishness — this seems superfluous in a Jewish cemetery — but rather to praise her in idiomatic terms in use even today, for example, "a wise Jew," "a good Jew," etc. At the same time, it should be noted[23] that in two inscriptions in Rome, the women proselytes are so designated in order to emphasize their Jewishness.[24]

Above arcosolium 4 is a partly obliterated Greek inscription, its contents being: "Here lies Fabonius, son of Sabinus and the mother....."[25]

Between arcosolia 4 and 5 the following inscription is incised:[26]

ENΘA KITE
CIPIKIA

"Here lies Sirikia."

In arcosolium 5 a man and a woman are interred. The following words are written on the upper left side:[27]

ʹTOΠOC EIACONOC

"The burial place of Jason."

On the right side the following inscription appears:[28]

ΘEOΔΩ
PA
ENΘAΔE
KITE

"Theodora lies here."

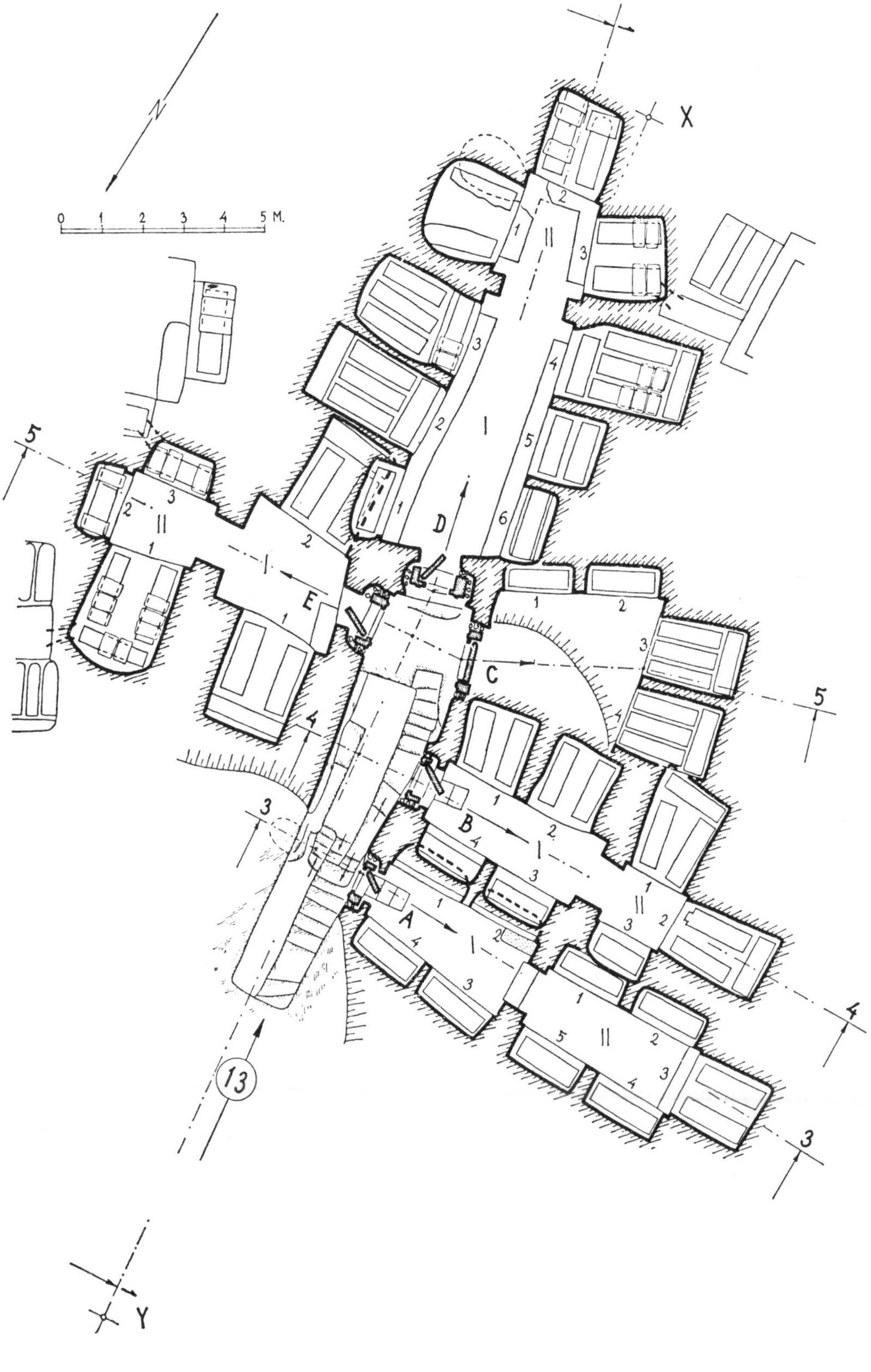

Fig. 11 Plan of catacomb 13; halls A–E

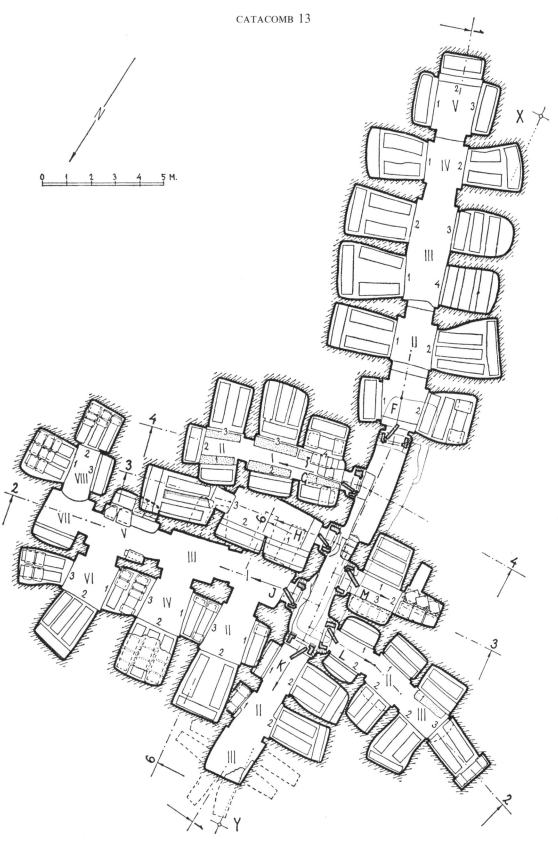

Fig. 12 Plan of catacomb 13; halls F–L

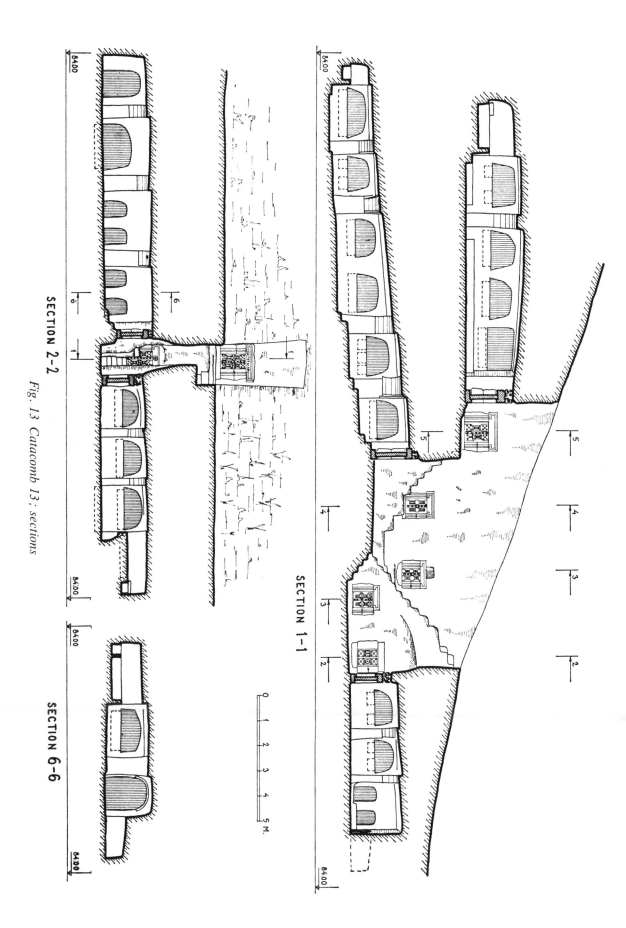

SECTION 2-2

SECTION 1-1

SECTION 6-6

Fig. 13 Catacomb 13; sections

34

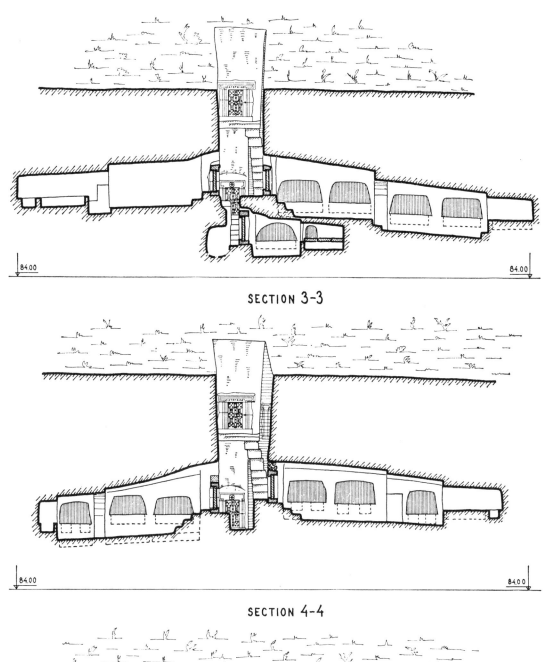

SECTION 3-3

SECTION 4-4

SECTION 5-5

0 1 2 3 4 5 M.

Fig. 14 Catacomb 13; sections

Room II. This is a small room which has benches along its three walls. Each wall has one arcosolium containing two graves. In arcosolium 1 the space available for a third grave was not utilized. In the left corner the benches were destroyed and a kokh was cut into the wall, perhaps for a bone depository. In arcosolium 3 a hole was breached into catacomb 16. The ceiling of the room is flat.

Several interesting Greek inscriptions were discovered in this room. Above arcosolium 1 there is a red dipinto inscription (Pl. XI, 1):[29]

OC EAN METAΘH TAYTHN O[C] EΠANTIΛΛAMENOC ZΩ[O]ΠOIHCE[I] TOYC NEKPOYC AYTOC KPINE[I]

"Whosoever shall change the place of this one,[30] God who resurrects the dead shall judge [him]."

This is another one of the warning inscriptions discovered at Beth She'arim whose purpose was to deter anyone from disturbing the rest of the deceased and to threaten any trespasser with punishment from God. (See above, catacomb 12, Hebrew inscription no. 1.) The late Moshe Schwabe wrote about this interesting inscription: "The formula of this inscription has no parallel — not in the inscriptions found at Beth She'arim, nor in the inscriptions found anywhere else in Eretz Yisrael. Noteworthy about this inscription is the conclusive evidence it bears that belief in the resurrection of the dead was accepted in that period by the Jews who used to bring their dead to Beth She'arim for burial."[31]

On the right soffit of arcosolium 3 there is a partially obliterated red dipinto inscription:[32]

ENΘA KITE EYCEBIC O [Λ]AM

ΠPOTATOC AP XICYNAΓΩΓO C ΩN BHPITΩ[N]

"Here lies Eusebius the most illustrious, the head of the synagogue of the people of Beirut."

This inscription may be compared to the one mentioned above concerning "Cohen from Beirut." As to Eusebius' title, see the Greek inscription discovered in catacomb 26 which refers to "Yosé, the head of the Sidonian synagogue."[33]

The last noteworthy inscription in this room was written on a cover stone that had been thrown onto the floor of the room (Pl. XI, 3):[34]

ΩΔE KEITE O OCIOC CA TOPNEIΛOC

"Here lies Satornilus the pious."

Satornilus is the very person whose name is engraved on the lintel of the entrance to the hall. Schwabe had already noted[35] that we need not assume that Satornilus owned the entire hall since, from the inscriptions, it appears that a number of families used to bury their dead here. Schwabe suggested that perhaps Satornilus was interred in arcosolium 1 and that his wife had the warning inscription written subsequently. However, this is by no means certain.

Hall E
There are ten burial places in this hall. The entrance to the hall is on the left of that to hall D, in the eastern wall of the courtyard. This doorway is one of two in which the stone bolts were found in the jambs. The hall has two rooms totaling 5.70 m in length.
Room I. The room is 2.65 m high. The floor is 1.15 m lower than the step platform outside. This room contains two arcosolia

with three graves each. Arcosolium 2 has a breach into hall D. The walls of the room were roughly plastered and are cracked in several places.

Room II. This room has three arcosolia containing five graves. In two of the arcosolia (1, 3), holes were breached into catacomb 12.

Hall F

The entrance to this hall is in the narrow southern end of the courtyard, on the third level. This is the tallest entrance in the catacomb (Pl. IX, 2). It is 1.20 m high and .65 m wide. The rock above the lintel was cut in the form of an arch. The space between the arch and the lintel was blocked with stones and then plastered. The bolt was preserved in the jamb so that it is still possible to lock the door. On the lintel a rosette was carved and the following inscription was incised on either side of it:

CABIN CIPIKIA

There are thirty-two burial places in this hall, distributed among five small rooms. This is the longest hall in catacomb 13. It is 14.20 m long and 3.30 m wide. The rooms are arranged consecutively in a single row (see Pl. XI, 5), and they have arcosolia in the walls. Both the ceiling and the floor gradually slant downward from the doorway. The hall is well preserved and the walls are smoothed. It is quite obvious that many of the graves in this hall were never used as they do not contain any bone remains and in several of them scattered stone chips from the quarrying can still be found. In addition, there are very few sealing stones. From these facts, we may conclude that the hall was hewn shortly before the destruction of Beth She'arim, and in that short period not all the graves were used.

There are several short Greek inscriptions incised on the walls of the hall.

In room I, above arcosolium 2, the following inscription appears (fig. 15):[36]

KYPA MIKKH

"The lady Mikkē"

Fig. 15 Greek inscription

In room III, above arcosolium 1 (fig. 16):[37]

ANNIANOC
ΠPOCΔOKIO[C]

Fig. 16 Greek inscription

In room III, above arcosolium 4 on the left side (Pl. XI, 6):[38]

KOYΦA IH

Lifshitz corrects the iota to gamma and is of the opinion that here we have a formula, not conventionally used by Jews, in which the deceased is blessed with rest in "the light earth."

Hall G

This hall has eighteen burial places in two rooms with a total length of 5.90 m. The entrance (Pl. XII, 1) is in the eastern wall of the courtyard at the bottom, the first to the right. The door is of the usual type, and above the lintel there is a "window." Except for one stone resting on the lintel, there is no evidence that the "window" was blocked. As noted previously (see above, description of hall A), it is difficult to understand what the function of such windows could have been in a catacomb as, normally, tombs do not have windows. It seems

37

likely, therefore, that these "windows" were blocked. Above the window Greek letters incised; however, they are scarcely legible. On the lintel of the entrance, the following inscription is incised (Pl. XII, 3):[39]

ΠΑΥΛΙΝΟΥ
ΜΥΡΕΨ[ΟΥ]

"Belonging to Paulinus,
the perfume merchant."

This trade is also mentioned in another inscription at Beth She'arim (no. 79). As we shall see shortly, Paulinus the perfume merchant acquired at least one room in this burial hall.

R o o m I. This is a long narrow room which slopes down to the east. It is 3.90 m long, 1.25 m wide, and 2.20 m high. A flight of four narrow steps descends into the room (Pl. XII, 2). The walls contain seven arcosolia with one to four graves each. In the floor of the room, along two of the walls, four rectangular graves were dug. The southernmost grave, nearest the entrance, was covered with stone slabs. In this grave, which we covered anew, a skeleton was found without any funerary deposits. On the left soffit of arcosolium 2, two words were written (Pl. XII, 9):

KYPIC KYPA

"The lady Kyris"

R o o m II. This room, smaller than the former, belonged in its entirety to the family of Paulinus. This is evidenced by the inscription incised above each of the three arcosolia (Pl. XII, 4–8):

ΠΑΥΛΙΝΟΥ

"Belonging to Paulinus"

Two graves were quarried in the floor of this room also.

Hall H

A half-blocked "window" was found above the entrance to this hall also. The hall has only one room with five burial places. In the left wall there are two arcosolia with single graves. In the right wall it was impossible to cut out an arcosolium since there was a breach into hall G. In the eastern wall there is a conventionally-styled archway; however, instead of a room, there are three trough graves behind it. Between the first two graves is a trench through which the last grave could be reached.

Hall J

This hall has thirty-two burial places. On the lintel of the entrance there is a carved rosette to the right of which a schematic branch is incised. The plan of this hall differs from that of the other halls: The central hall is long and narrow (10.60 × 1.60 m) and is divided by archways into four small rooms. Each of these rooms leads into another small room with arcosolia and graves in three of the walls. Here we have an unusual arrangement: the arcosolia between rooms II, IV, and VI are open, without dividing walls, i.e., each arcosolium which has two graves is common to two rooms. It is thus possible to look through the arcosolium from one room to the other (Pl. X, 4).

R o o m s I and III. There are two kokhim in the southern wall of each of these rooms.

R o o m II. Room II has one of the "look-through" arcosolia (3) mentioned above, with one grave belonging to this room and the other to room IV. Arcosolium 1 has a single grave and arcosolium 2 contains three graves with an empty space left for a fourth.

R o o m IV. This room has two arcosolia (1 and 3) in common with the neighboring rooms. Arcosolium 2 with its three graves has a fine, well-preserved example of a cover constructed of stone slabs and plaster.

R o o m V. An arcosolium was hewn in the southern wall of the room at floor level.

A grave was also dug in the floor in front of this arcosolium and in the northwest corner as well.

Room VI. Arcosolium 1 is open to room IV; arcosolia 2 and 3 have six graves.

Room VII. In the eastern wall of the room the place for an arcosolium was marked, but it was never hewn.

Room VIII. This is a small chamber, very roughly dressed. It contains three arcosolia with seven burial places.

The order in which halls G, H, and J were hewn can be studied from their excessive crowding and proximity. First, hall G was hewn; after that, hall H, in which no arcosolia could be cut in the southern wall; and lastly, hall J, where again no arcosolia could be cut in the wall adjacent to hall H. However, since the floor of hall J is lower than that of hall H, kokhim could be hewn into the southern wall of hall J at floor level.

Hall K

This narrow, long (6.00 m) hall contains fourteen burial places in three rooms. Its entrance is in the northern end of the lowest level of the courtyard. The door is not fashioned in the conventional style; rather the lintel and door slab are well smoothed, and the door jambs resemble pilasters with molded based and capitals (Pl. IX, 3).[40] The entrance is .52 m wide and .85 m high. The rock above the lintel is arcuated. The empty space between the rock and the lintel was blocked with stones. Rooms I–III. The walls of these rooms are well dressed. The arcosolia are 1.00 m above the floor. Below arcosolium 1 in room II is the following Greek inscription (Pl. XIII, 6):[41]

KYPIAC

ΓΥΝΗ CYMMAXOY

"Belonging to Kyria, the wife of Symmachos."

The eastern arcosolia of rooms I and II are breached into hall J, a fact which implies perhaps that hall K was hewn after hall J.

Room III. This room differs from the others in that it contains only kokhim, two in each wall (Pl. XIII, 5). While rooms with kokhim are more typical of tombs of the early type (first and second centuries C.E.), they are found occasionally in later tombs also, and often in catacombs with arcosolia.

Hall L

This hall contains sixteen burial places in three small rooms, 5.70 m long altogether. The entrance, near the one to hall K in the western wall of the courtyard, is not conventional. It is .60 m wide and .87 m high. The lintel and jambs are plain. The door slab is decorated with unusual geometric designs: above and below there are double triangles resembling an hourglass and in the center, rectangles and a circle (Pl. IX, 4).[42]

Room II. Below arcosolium 2 at floor level, another arcosolium was added. Between the two arcosolia there is a menorah formed by a series of holes bored on the wall (Pl. X, 3). The straight branches of the menorah form triangles; the base is the shape of a tripod. The "hooks" on either side of the top and the legs of the menorah are quite interesting. This is the only menorah depicted in catacomb 13. This technique of holes representing the links of the menorah is quite unusual.

Room III. A rectangular grave was dug in the floor of the room. Beneath arcosolium 3 the hewing of an additional grave was started but not completed. The ceiling of the arcosolium is shaped in the form of a pointed vault.

Hall M

This hall, the smallest in the entire catacomb, has seven burial places. It is the only hall in which there were no traces of pillage. The door was found closed but not locked, since the bolt was missing. The hall is actually one small room containing three arcosolia. It is 2.00 m long, 1.00 m wide, and 1.60 m high. Arcosolium 1 was clean and did not seem to have been used. The graves in arcosolia 2–3 were sealed with slabs of stone and covered with rough mud plaster. Among the excavators there was great excitement at the opening of these graves since they were the first and only ones found still sealed.

There are two graves in arcosolium 2. In the grave to the right which was covered with large slabs, only a handful of scattered bones were found, obviously brought here for secondary burial. The grave to the left was covered most carelessly: three stone slabs were irregularly laid down and the gaps between them filled with coarse plaster. Here, a complete body had been interred. The skeleton was in its proper position but the bones had badly disintegrated. In neither of the burials were there any funerary gifts. Incidentally, we closed both graves and covered them anew. In the left wall of the arcosolium an unusual feature was added: a short kokh, apparently intended for a bone depository.

In arcosolium 3 there was only one trough grave. It, too, was covered with stone slabs and rough plaster. We opened a hole through the cover, but here too we found only a few bones concentrated at the bottom of the grave. Naturally, we were keenly disappointed at not finding any artifacts which could be of help in dating the burials. We were consoled, however, by the three Greek inscriptions discovered on this arcosolium which gave us information about the deceased whose bones had been brought here for secondary burial. Above the arch to the right of the arcosolium, the following inscription was painted in red (Pl. XIII, 3):[43]

ΟΛΟΣ ΟΙΚΟΣ
ΑΡΙCΤΕΟΥ ΕΥΜΟΙΡΕΙ
ΑΡΙCΤΕ[Α]

"The whole room belongs to Aristeas; may your lot be happy, Aristeas."

The word οἶκος, which literally means "house," is used here in the sense of "burial room."

There is an inscription on the left upper side of the arcosolium also (Pl. XIII, 4):[44]

Η ΜΑΚΡΑ
ΑΡΙCΤΕΟΥ
CΙΔΩΝΙ
ΟΥ

"The sarcophagus (i.e., tomb) of Aristeas the Sidonian"

The word μακρά which literally means "bathtub," is sometimes used to designate "sarcophagus" also; but here the meaning is, of course, "tomb."

The third inscription was incised in large letters in the rough plaster on the cover slabs of the grave. The engraving was done by means of a stick, or perhaps even a finger dipped in red paint, while the plaster was still soft. The inscription was very difficult to decipher; but it seems likely that it should read as follows (fig. 17):[45]

ΕΥΜΟΙΡΙ ΑΡΙCΤΕ[Α ΕΝ ΕΙ]Ρ[Η]
ΝΗΙ Η ΚΥΜΙCΙC ΤΟΥ
ΟCΙΟΥ ΑΡΙCΤΕΟΥ ΤΟΥ
ΟCΙΟΥ

"May your lot be good, Aristeas. May the resting place of Aristeas the pious be in peace. Of the pious."

This is another instance of secondary burial of a Jew from the Diaspora — this time from Sidon. In this grave, as well as in the grave to the right of arcosolium 2, only a few bones were found. From this fact we may conclude that they were brought to Beth She'arim considerably later than their primary interment when very little remained of the skeleton. Also, the fact that no tomb deposits of any sort were placed

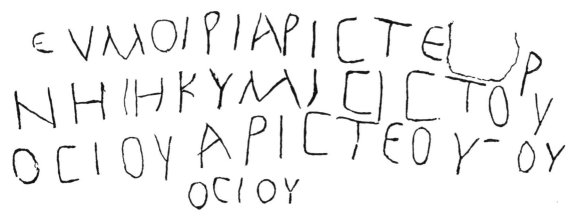

Fig. 17 Greek inscription

alongside the bones is particularly instructive when one tries to deduce the burial practices of Beth She'arim.

Miscellaneous Finds

Only a small number of artifacts were found in this extensive catacomb. Even if we assume that it was customary to place very few funerary gifts beside the deceased or even none at all as revealed by the graves found intact, it is, nevertheless, surprising that in all twelve halls, comprising so many rooms and graves, not a single clay lamp was found. Lamps are not only gifts to the deceased but objects used regularly by undertakers and visitors. Apparently the lamps were also valuable booty for the tomb robbers.

Only in the courtyard were two lamps found (Pl. LXX, 16, 19), dating from the first half of the fourth century C.E. Four complete amphoriskoi were the only vessels discovered in the halls (but not in the graves), two in hall A, one in hall J, and one in hall L. These vessels are not indigenous to Palestine and most likely have their origin in Phoenicia. In front of the entrance to hall M the bottom of a jug was found of the type of jugs illustrated in Plate LXXII, 6–7. It served as a container for ocher used in painting inscriptions.[46]

Potsherds and pieces of glass vessels were scattered in various places.

The few iron nails and iron plates that were found in the rooms and in the courtyard, as well as some pieces of lead, are evidence of burial in wooden or lead coffins and wooden ossuaries. Nevertheless, there is no doubt that the customary burial practice in this catacomb was without coffins.

A particularly noteworthy find was a marble tablet uncovered in the debris of the courtyard, near the entrance to hall C (see Pl. XI, 4). It is 18 cm wide and 37 cm high. In its upper part the conventional Jewish symbols are schematically engraved in deep lines: a menorah without a base, whose seven branches terminate on top in a horizontal bar; a shofar; an incense shovel; and a lulab. Below the symbols seven lines of a Greek inscription are incised:[47]

ΤΟΠΟC
ΜΑΡΙΝΟΥ
ΚΑΙ ΕΙΟΥ
CCΤΑC
ΓΥΝΕΚ
ΟC ΑΥ
ΤΟΥ

"The tomb of Marinos and Justa his wife"

We could not determine in which hall this couple was buried. Usually, marble tablets of this kind were placed in a special recess above one of the entrances in the courtyard to mark the tomb. For example, a tablet of this type was found in catacomb 1 above the entrance to hall G[48] and in catacomb 19 above the entrance to hall C (fig. 33). However, no such recess was found in the courtyard of catacomb 13.

Catacomb 13, characterized by its long, narrow courtyard and its halls in different levels, is unique among the catacombs we excavated. The only parallel at Beth She'arim is catacomb 1 which was uncovered in 1936 by Professor Mazar. However, this similarity is really superficial since there are considerable differences in the details of execution. Catacomb 1 is far more complex and ramified and includes many more burial places (about 380). The rooms are decorated with architectural ornaments carved in the rock, with reliefs and drawings, and are distinguished by great variety in the forms of the tombs. In catacomb 13, on the other hand, the workmanship is simpler and more conventional; and except for one menorah the catacomb contains no decorations whatsoever.

The stonecutters succeeded in fully utilizing the small courtyard and managed to convert the catacomb, which extends over an area 32 m long (from north to south) by 26 m wide (from east to west) only, into a compact arrangement of 190 graves. The economy in space and work is striking. This was clearly a public catacomb intended for people of more limited means than those who acquired tombs in catacomb 12. Who were these people and where did they come from?

Fortunately, this catacomb contained quite a number of inscriptions which shed some light on the human element. The origin of three of the deceased is known: two were from Beirut and one, from Sidon. We also know the position and occupation of two of them: one was the head of the synagogue in Beirut and the other, a perfumer. Of the twenty-six inscriptions found in this catacomb, twenty-four are in Greek and only two are in Hebrew, i.e., almost all the interred were Greek speaking. The majority had Greek or Hellenized names, and only a few had Jewish names.

While it is true that the Greek language and Greek names were widely in use among the Jews of Palestine, there is reason to believe that catacomb 13, like hall B in catacomb 12, served as a burial place for Jews from Syrian and Phoenician cities. In any case, the inscriptions are evidence that these Jews acquired a number of halls. Confirming evidence for this assumption may also be seen in the four tall amphoriskoi with ear handles that were found in this catacomb. From the fact that vessels of this type have not be discovered anywhere in Palestine and that the only parallels come from Tyre, we are inclined to think that they were brought here by the people who brought the bones from Phoenicia for burial at Beth She'arim.

The criteria for dating this catacomb are very limited. On the basis of the few artifacts found in the catacomb, it should be assigned to the first half of the fourth century C.E. Also, judging by the plan of the tombs, this catacomb seems to be late in the scale of catacomb development (see below the discussion on chronology).

3 CATACOMB 14 (figs. 18–19)

This catacomb differs completely from the thirteen preceding catacombs — in its large dimensions, in the layout of its spacious rooms, in the forms of its tombs, and in its external architecture. In general features only catacomb 20 is similar to catacomb 14.

It is composed of three main units: a courtyard, the cave, and an overlaying structure. The catacomb is circa 44 m long from north to south. This description refers to hall A; halls B and C have nothing in common with the main cave and its particulars.

The Courtyard

This spacious courtyard (16.70 × 9.30 m) is hewn into the slope of the hill with a North–South direction at its long axis. Flat, wide steps hewn in the rock led originally into the courtyard from the South, but they were apparently destroyed during clearance work by the bulldozer. There are three halls hewn behind the walls of the courtyard. The main hall, actually the major feature of the catacomb, lies on the southern side. In the two remaining walls on both sides of the entrance to the courtyard, there are two small halls, hall B to the East and hall C to the West. In the eastern wall, about 4.50 m from the façade, a breach was cut into catacomb 22. This breach, situated about 1.20 m above the courtyard floor, was blocked with several courses of stone (Pl. XXI, 4).[49] The problems concerning this breach will be dealt with later. Near the façade of hall A on the southern side, the altitude of the courtyard floor is 92.01 m above sea level; however, the floor slopes gradually to the north, and at the north-western corner the altitude is 91.50 m. In this corner the beginning of a ditch hewn in the rock, apparently for the drainage of the courtyard, was found.

Hall A

The Façade (fig. 20; Pl. XIV)

The rock wall of the façade of this hall rises to a height of 8 m. Two entrances are cut into this wall: the larger in the center, the smaller to the left. In front of the rock wall three arches are built, supported by engaged pillars. This arcaded façade is constructed of ashlar masonry. The total length of the façade is 8.95 m. All four pillars, which were preserved intact, are laid in seven to nine courses of ashlars with a total height of 2.84 m. The width of the outer pillars is .50 m, whereas the width of the inner pillars is .82 m. The distances between the pillars are unequal: 1.94 m in the left arch, 2.60 m in the central arch, and 1.70 m in the right arch. Only in the right arch were all thirteen voussoirs preserved (Pl. XVII, 1). They have a cyma reversa molding between a wide band and a narrow fillet. The voussoirs are .43 m high and .72 m thick. The internal height of the arch above the floor is 3.70 m; the external height is 4.14. One voussoir only was preserved in the central arch. From the width of this arch we may deduce that it was taller than the right arch. Three voussoirs were preserved in the left (eastern) arch.

The pillars are faced with very thin pilasters, 2 cm thick. These pilasters have molded capitals and bases (Pl. XVII, 2–3). The profile of the capitals consists of an ovolo, cavetto, and abacus. The two central capitals have lateral extensions carved in the same profile (fig. 20, top; Pl. XVII, 2). These extensions were made in order to enlarge the width of the capitals and thus adapt them to the arches above. The bases of the pilasters are of the Attic type consisting of a plinth, torus, scotia, and torus. The profile, slightly more upright than usual, is neatly carved and of good workmanship. The bases are molded in the same manner as the capitals (fig. 20, below). Their lateral extensions, however, seem superfluous since they do not carry pilasters.

It is uncertain to what height the façade continued above the arches, since only a few stones above the right arch were preserved. In our reconstruction (fig. 19, sections 1–1 and 3–3) eight additional courses were added, ending in a simple horizontal cornice. On both sides of the façade, the rock walls were faced with eight courses of ashlar masonry (Pl. XVII, 3). The courses are not equal in length. Their denticulated ends give the impression that the stone-masons intended to continue the building of the wall. However, this impression is misleading since the stones are sunk into the rock face and no room is left for extending the courses. Apparently the purpose of this seemingly incomplete construction was to impart a suitable architectural finish to both sides of the arched façade.[50]

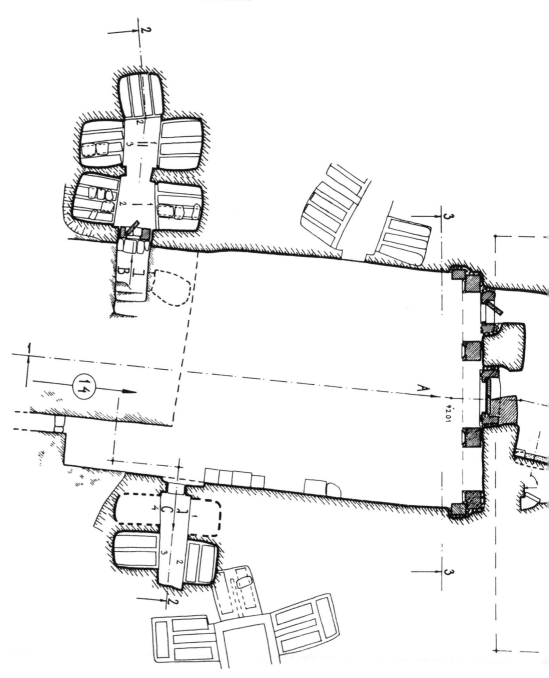

Fig. 18 Plan of catacomb 14

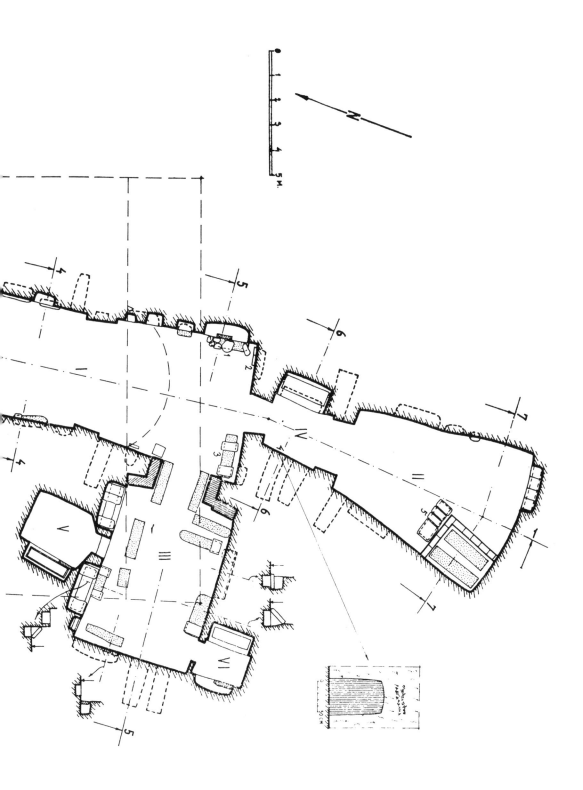

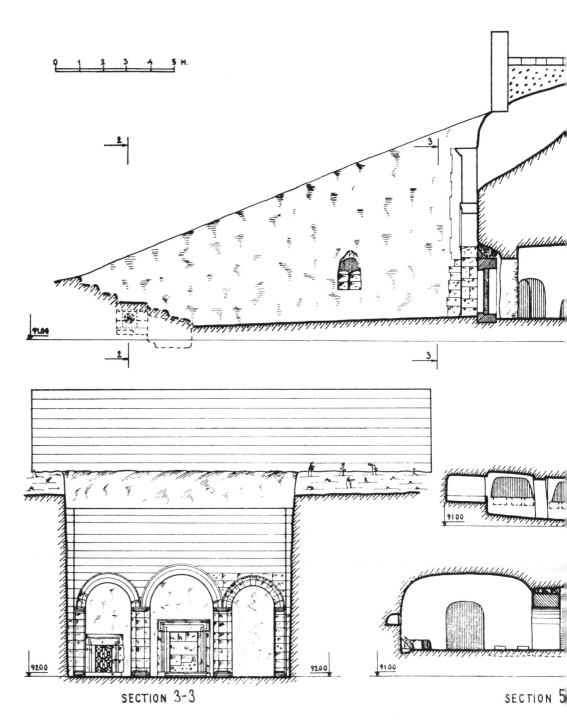

Fig. 19 Catacomb 14; sections

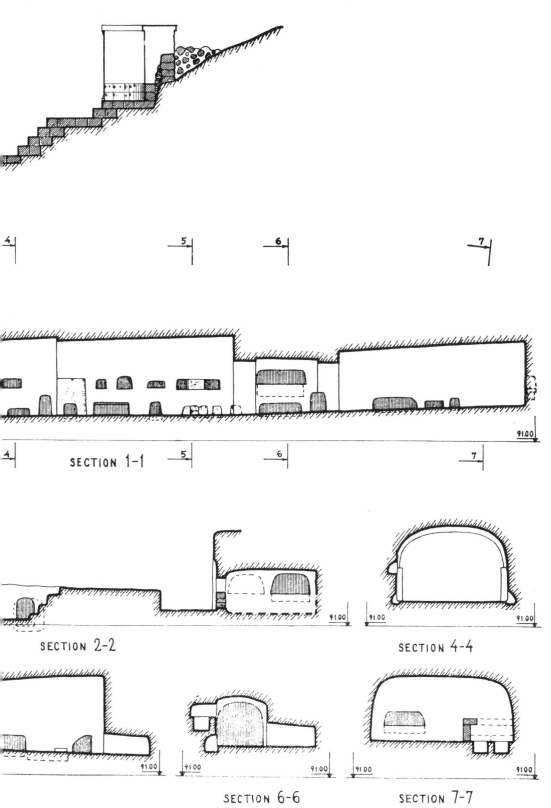

SECTION 1-1

SECTION 2-2

SECTION 4-4

SECTION 6-6

SECTION 7-7

The Entrances. The main gate to the catacomb is in the central arch. The term "gate" is used in this case because of the large size and the impressive architecture of the entrance (Pl. XVIII, 1). We have here one of the two gates with double doors that were found in the Beth She'arim excavations and the only one of its kind in the country that was preserved intact. Its members are made of hard, light-colored limestone, finely comb dressed and of excellent workmanship. The entrance is 1.20 m wide and 1.70 m high; the length of the lintel is 2.24 m, its height, .49 m. The total height of the gate frame, including the threshold, is 2.40 m. The threshold is monolithic and has drafted margins and a raised boss. In contrast to the other doors, the right jamb of this door is also monolithic and does not contain the usual keyhole. The lintel and jambs have a continuous profile of ovolo, fillets, and plain astragal which create the familiar "ear-like" effect on either side of the door jambs.

The two door slabs open inward. The hinge mechanism is unusual. The upper hinges are similar in shape to those in the rest of the doors: they are made of stone, in one piece with the door slab, and are cylindrical in shape. On the other hand, the two lower hinges are made of square bronze plates $9 \times 9 \times .6$ cm in size, with a hemispherical projection 7 cm in diameter beneath each of them. Above the plates there are four protruding elongated "teeth," arranged diagonally. These teeth were sunk into the door slab and fixed into place with lead and cement. These hemispherical hinges turned inside the round sockets of the threshold (see fig. 21). The lines of friction are readily discerned on the hinges. The hard stone sockets did not suffer particularly from the friction with the bronze hinges despite the heavy load of the door. The reason for this may lie in the fact that this door was not used frequently, the side door serving instead.

The installation of bronze hinges in the doors is a significant improvement over the conventional stone ones. To the best of our knowledge, no bronze hinges similar to those found at Beth She'arim have been discovered anywhere else in the country.[51] Rather, it was customary to mount a "shoe" or "cap" of bronze onto the stone or wooden hinges. Traces of such construction, already known in earlier periods, were found on fragments of a magnificent Roman stone door discovered in Jaffa.[52] Another method was to cover the socket of the threshold with a bronze plate within which the stone hinge turned. This, apparently, was the hinging method used for the door in the tomb of Queen Helena in Jerusalem.[53] As we shall see later, the double door in catacomb 20 was hinged in the exact opposite manner to that in catacomb 14, i.e., the bronze hinge protruded from the threshold, and the socket was in the door slab. The most efficient construction technique is that in which both the hinge and the socket are made of bronze as, for example, in the heavy marble door of a tomb in Macedonia.[54]

The two doors are decorated in the conventional Beth She'arim style of panels and studs. The vertical fillet on the right door wing is real and the second wing closes directly upon it. Also present is the customary door knocker in the middle of the left wing; there is, however, no iron ring for pulling the door. In neither door wing is there a place for mounting a lock, nor is there a recess for a bolt. Also, there is no keyhole in the door jamb. Obviously, this double door could not be locked from the outside. Thus, it must have been locked from the inside, probably with a horizontal bar which was inserted in two recesses in the jambs. This being the case, the only exit from the cave was through the small door. It seems likely that the small door served for daily use, whereas the double door was opened for special occasions, e.g., during burial ceremonies.

This arrangement was probably adopted

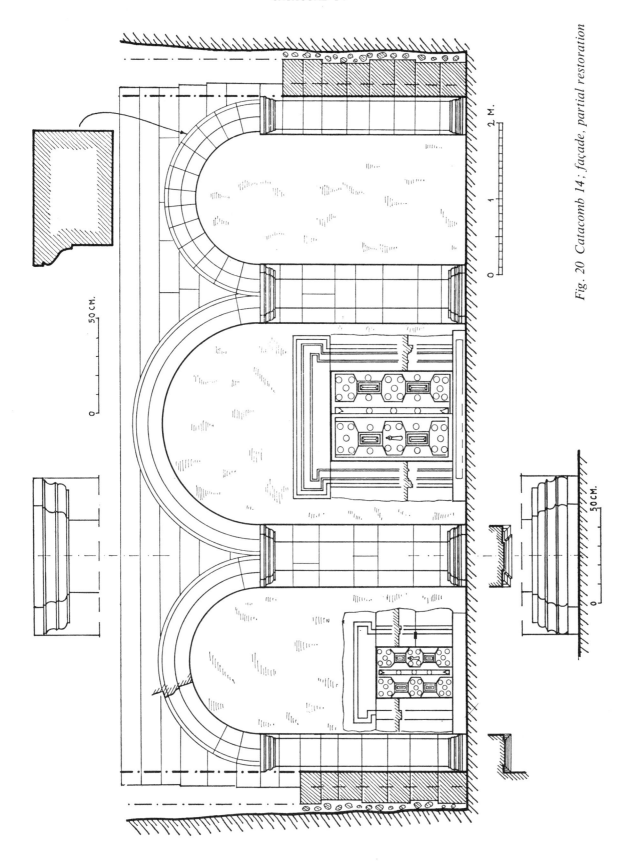

Fig. 20 Catacomb 14; façade, partial restoration

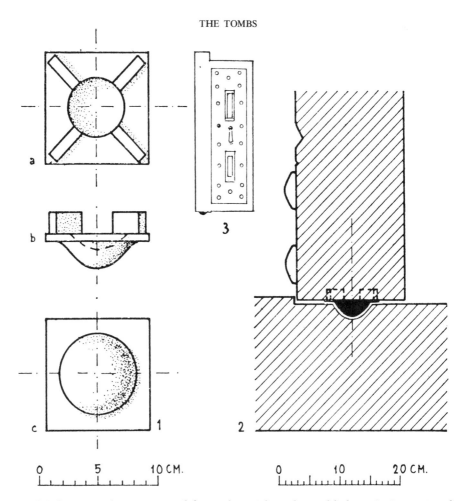

Fig. 21 1. Bronze hinges, viewed from above, the side, and below. 2. Operational system of door, hinges, and socket. 3. Door panel with bronze hinge at the bottom

for two reasons: *(a)* The locking system normally used for single doors was not suitable for double doors because it was impossible to install a bolt in the center between the two door wings. *(b)* The door wings, each weighing about 450 kg, were extremely heavy and could only be moved with great effort. Therefore, the hinges which were cut in one piece with the door were in constant danger of breaking from being turned too frequently. Indeed, the door ultimately suffered a hard fate: at first, the upper hinge of the right wing broke, putting this door out of use. At this point the inside of this wing was blocked with stones (Pl. XVIII, 3) and only the left wing remained in use. This blocking was very massive and was possibly necessary

because the rock above the door was weak and had to be supported. Later on, the lower hinge of the second door also cracked and broke at its joint with the bronze hinge.[55] Since the door could no longer be repaired, it was entirely blocked from the outside with dressed stones (Pl. XVIII, 2), and only the side door remained in use. It is astonishing that the second door wing was not blocked from the inside as well so as not to conceal the impressive doorway from the outside. The reason apparently is that the date of this final blocking was quite late, at a time when the floor of the court-yard was already covered with a layer of debris. Proof of this lies in the fact that the blocking stones were not laid directly on the threshold but on a layer of debris, of the same type as that found in the courtyard. While dismantling the blocking, we found the base of a long flat clay lamp of the "Beth She'arim type" between the blocking and the door (Pl. LXX, 19). This led us to the conclusion that the door was blocked before the middle of the fourth century.

The door in the left arch is of the usual type found at Beth She'arim. It, too, is made of hard limestone but not so light colored as the double door and without the combed dressing. The size of the opening is 1.06 × .68 m. The lintel is 1.52 m long and .46 m high. The total height of the door frame, including the threshold, is 1.62 m. The lintel and right jamb are molded with a small cavetto; the profile on the left jamb, however, was left unfinished. As customary at Beth She'arim, the door slab was decorated with a central fillet, panels, and studs. It, too has a knocker and an iron holder for the door ring. The keyhole is placed, as usual, between the two parts of the right door jamb. The bolt housing was partly faced with lead, apparently to facilitate the sliding of the bolt. It is quite likely that other bolt housings were similarly faced, and that one of the main reasons why the tomb robbers dismantled most of the bolts from the doors was to obtain the lead.

On the door frame a name was incised in Greek, apparently the handiwork of a visitor (fig. 22):

ΑΛΥΠΙC

Fig. 22 Greek inscription

The closest parallel to this arcaded façade is that of catacomb 20 (see below). Single arches may be found in front of entrances in several other tombs in Beth She'arim. However, none of these arches has any

functional value, their purpose being to impart a monumental effect to the catacomb.

There is no close parallel in this country to the triple-arched façade of the Beth She'arim type. The triple gate in the southern wall of the Temple Mound in Jerusalem has three separate arched entrances, with plain pillars and arches.[56] The triple-arched gateway is mainly typical of the Roman triumphal arches. It is characterized by a high central arch flanked by two lower side arches.[57] Incidentally, gates of this type were also found at Gerasa in Transjordan.[58] In Palestine the closest parallel is the triple-arched structure known as *Ecce Homo* (first/second century C.E.) in Jerusalem.[59] However, there are basic differences between the entrances of these gates and the arches at Beth She'arim. In the Roman triumphal arches the side entrances are much lower than the central arch, and each arch rests on its own capitals. At Beth She'arim, however, the arches rest on joint capitals. The slight discrepancy in the height of the arches is due to the difference in the width of the spans.

In summation, we may conclude that the Beth She'arim archways are not an imitation of a triple gateway but an architectural pattern derived from the multi-arched arcade so characteristic of Roman architecture. There are two kinds of arcades: in the first type, the arches rest on pillars; in the second, the arches are supported by columns. In the Theater of Marcellus,[60] in the Colosseum at Rome (first century C.E.),[61] and in other structures, the columns are integrally engaged to the façade of the columned arcade. These engaged columns, bearing a horizontal frieze, are strictly ornamental. At Beth She'arim we find a new combination of these elements: the pillars and engaged columns (pilasters in this case) are integrated, and these new units support the arches. The columned arcade is of a different character and the result of a later development.[62] Nevertheless, the fine arcade which appears as the ornamental motif on a first century ossuary from Jerusalem is evidence that structures of this type were in existence in Jerusalem during the Herodian period.[63]

In this connection, one should note the schematic carving of an arcade with three arches on columns in one of the burial rooms of catacomb 1, dated to the third century C.E.[64] Some scholars interpret this carving as a symbol of Herod's Temple. However, it seems more likely that the artist who carved the relief had in mind the arched façades of catacombs 14 and 20. Similarly, it is reasonable to assume that the arcade motif which surrounds the large glass plate found in catacomb 15 is also derived from the existing structures at Beth She'arim (see below).

As for the architectural features of the triple-arched façade of catacomb 14, they have close parallels at Beth She'arim itself. The capitals and bases of the pillars are identical in form with those in the arch at the entrance to catacomb 11 and with those of the mausoleum whose remains were found above this catacomb.[65] Another example is the façade of catacomb 6, noted for its excellent workmanship of these very same architectural features.[66] Mazar assigns these structures to the first half of the third century C.E., or to the end of Period II at Beth She'arim. Moreover, there is a close parallel in the capitals and bases found among the remains of the Beth She'arim synagogue. In addition, cornice stones were found, very similar in their cyma reversa profile to the voussoirs of catacomb 14.[67] The synagogue is dated to the middle of the third century, i.e., the beginning of Period III in Beth She'arim.

Similar stones, in which the cyma reversa is the main ornament while the strip below is of secondary importance, can also be found in other Galilean synagogues.[68] A most interesting parallel to the profile of one of the Beth She'arim arches is to be found in the northern gate and in the triumphal arch at Gerasa (first half of the second century C.E.),[69] except that at Gerasa there are two or three fasciae instead of the one at Beth She'arim.

It seems, therefore, that strictly from architectural considerations the triple-arched façade should be dated to the first half of the third century C.E., perhaps even to the beginning of that century.

The Catacomb

One enters through the side door into a Γ-shaped vestibule which leads into the hall; however, the main entrance into this hall was originally from the central gate. The catacomb was severely damaged by the collapse of parts of the walls and ceilings and by the fall of blocks of rock at the farther end of the central hall and the rooms branching off from it. Evidently, the rock from which this catacomb was hewn was not solid and cracked easily. That the danger of collapse had already worried the inhabitants of ancient Beth She'arim[70] is proved by the massive arch that was constructed in the passageway to room III in order to prevent the ceiling from falling. By the end of our work, we were forced to strengthen the passageway to room II with concrete and to support the ceiling of room I with iron posts.

The plan of this catacomb (see fig. 18) in no way resembles the stereotype plan of the other catacombs at Beth She'arim. It is characterized by large rooms with few burial places, usually small niches intended for bone depositories. A major difference is the absence of the traditional arcosolia containing several trough graves, even though some tombs with a single trough grave were found. The cover stones of these graves were smeared with a black substance mixed with soot.

This catacomb also was completely robbed. Many cover stones were thrown off, and only scanty traces of bones were left in the graves. Almost no artifacts were found either inside or outside the graves. The little that was found is described below.

Room I. (Pl. XIX, 1). This is a large hall, 14.00 m long, 4.60 m wide, and 3.00 m high. It is divided in the middle by an arch almost as wide as the room itself. The ceiling is in the form of a squat vault. Two rows of niches are hewn in the eastern wall (fig. 19, section 1–1). One row is at floor level and contains two regular kokhim and seven niches (one of them in the jamb of the arch), which are .46–1.30 m long. In the second niche from the left fifteen iron nails were found — evidence that a wooden ossuary was once deposited here. The second row was located about 1 m above the floor and consisted of five niches, the shortest, .46 m long and the longest, 1.83 m. This last niche at the end of the wall (no. 1 on the plan) was .38 m high and was sealed with three stones. On the middle stone, found in situ (Pl. XIX, 2), the name of the deceased was written (no. 8; Pl. XXII, 3):

רבי

שמעון

"Rabbi Shim'on"

Within the niche only scanty remains of bones and a few pieces of glass were found. In the floor directly below the niche a grave was dug and carelessly covered with coarse stones. The form of the grave and its location give the impression that the deceased had requested to be buried at the foot of Rabbi Shim'on's grave. On the southern wall of this corner a niche, 1.20 m long, was hewn at floor level. Above the niche, which was covered with several upright stones, this inscription was written (no. 11; Pl. XXII, 5):

אנינא

הקטן

"Anina the Little"

After our excavation, the rock collapsed at this spot and the inscription was destroyed (Pl. XIX, 12). In the floor of the opposite corner, there is a sunken rectangular grave (no. 3 in the plan) with a small niche hewn

in the wall above it. Among the debris in this corner, a stone was found bearing the following bilingual inscription (no.10; Pl. XXII, 6):

זו שלרבי

אניאנא

PABBI ANIANOY
TOY NANOY

"This is Rabbi Aniana's (tomb)"
"Of Rabbi Anianos, the Little"

Since the Greek word νάνος means "dwarf" or "small," it seems reasonable to ascribe this inscription to the grave of "Aniana the Little," and to assume that the two names are identical (for details, see the chapter on the inscriptions).

In the western wall of room I there are five niches and one kokh, all at floor level. A few of the niches in this room are slightly lower than the floor, and all of them are sealed with upright stone slabs leaning against the wall. Several of these uprights were found in situ. Approximately in the middle of the western wall, there is an enigmatic inscription in seven lines (Pl. XXII, 2). This certainly is not an epitaph since it was not found near a grave. Thus, it seems likely that it is the work of a visitor to this catacomb. Several of the characters are somewhat similar to the Paḥlevi (Persian) script, whereas others resemble the square Hebrew letters. Since the publication of this strange inscription, we have not as yet succeeded in deciphering it nor have we received any suggestions from readers.[71] Beside this inscription there is a similar shorter one incised on the wall.

Room IV. This is actually a small passageway between room I and room II. Two long niches were hewn in its left wall. The first niche is slightly sunken into the floor; the second is hewn above it and contains a trough grave. In this room a kokh was also found, partially cutting into the posts of the archway. This is not to be interpreted as due to lack of space but rather as somebody's desire to be buried near the niches. In the right wall there are two additional kokhim, 1.80 m long. Above the opening of the first kokh (no. 4 in the plan) the following bilingual inscription was found (no. 9; Pl. XXII, 4):

זו שלרבי גמליאל

PABI ΓΑΜΑΛΙΗΛ

"This (is the tomb) of Rabbi Gamaliel Rabbi Gamaliel"

R o o m II. The entrance to this room is through the above passageway (room IV) which has an archway at the end. Room II is trapezoidal in shape: 3.20–6.00 m wide and 7.60 m long. Only a few graves are cut into the walls: in the eastern wall, at floor level, three niches; in the southern wall, an arcosolium containing a trough grave; in the western wall, a niche and a kokh. However, this room also contains a feature which has no parallel in all the tombs of Beth She'arim: in the southwest corner there is a built structure enclosing a double grave (Pl. XXI, 1). These two rectangular graves are hewn side by side in the floor. The double grave, originally sealed with heavy stone slabs (Pl. XXI, 2), was fenced off and surrounded by a structure of smooth ashlar masonry. This structure consisted of two walls at right angles, having one course .70 m high, above which were sealing stones .30 m thick. These sealing stones were smoothly plastered. Three of them remained in situ, resting on the northern wall. How the horizontal slabs were supported above the empty space of the structure is still unclear. It may be that they rested on upright supporting stones. The area of this structure is 2.40 × 1.10 m; its height, 1.00 m.

The tomb robbers who plundered the catacomb dismantled the cover of the structure, as evidenced by the plastered slabs and the sealing stones of the two graves which were thrown in a heap. The bones were scattered. Only one thigh bone was

found in the left grave; it belonged to an individual of above-medium height. In the right grave small fragments of lead were found, remains of a lead coffin which was broken and robbed. In this grave a grooved cylindrical bone handle was also found (Pl. LXXIII, 24). On the basis of this single small artifact on the one hand, and the large thigh bone on the other, we may assume that the double grave belonged to a man and his wife. The plastered stones were scrupulously examined for traces of an inscription which might shed light on the identity of the deceased who were buried in this particular grave, but unfortunately none were found.

Near the northern wall of this structure an additional grave was hewn in the floor and also covered with stones (no. 5 in the plan). Here too, the desire to be buried close to the built tomb is obvious. This grave was left untouched by the robbers. Bones and three plain bronze rings were found in it (Pl. LXXIII, 18–20).

Rooms I, IV, and II are located consecutively from North to South. Their total length is 25.60 m.

R o o m III. This is a large room, 6.70 m long, 4.70 m wide, and 2.95 m high, which branches off from the southwestern end of room I. Between the two rooms there is an ashlar-built archway, 1.97 m wide and 1.70 m high. The width of the supporting posts is 1.20 m. The face of the arch in room I was built of a single row of stones (Pl. XX, 1), while in room III large stones were added on both sides of the built arch in order to strengthen the wall. In this face of the arch black mortar was used; it contrasts sharply with the white stone and creates a misleadingly modern impression (Pl. XX, 2). This massive archway was intended to support the ceiling.

In the southern wall of the room a trough niche was hewn at floor level. In the western wall, at floor level, there are two kokhim and a long niche which was sealed with two upright stones. In the northern wall, on both sides of the entrances leading into room V, there are two arcosolia, each with one grave still partially covered with a few sealing stones. Near the left corner a very small niche was cut out.

This room has one remarkable feature: nine graves which were sunk at random into the floor — in the archway, near the walls, and in the middle of the room. The commonly accepted opinion is that graves were hewn in the floor of the catacomb when there was no more space in the walls, and that such graves were cheaper and less respectable. However, this feature might also be interpreted as the wish of the deceased to be buried near a particular grave. It seems unreasonable to explain the numerous graves of this type in so spacious a catacomb as due to lack of space in the walls. We may, therefore, assume that, for some reason the deceased wished to be buried in this specific room. The graves were completely empty. On the western wall an inscription of four letters was incised but so far it has not been interpreted satisfactorily (no. 12; Pl. XXII, 1):

אב
על

Two small rooms branch off from room III: room V to the North and room VI to the South.

R o o m V. Here we have an exclusive burial room in which only one body was interred. This room, 3.00 × 2.10 m, was closed by a heavy boulder which had been moved from its original position. In the left wall of the room a long niche was hewn, the only one in this room. On the low shelf a complete clay coffin was found, empty and without a lid (Pl. XXI, 3). From previous fragmentary finds discovered in various places during the excavations, we knew that clay coffins were used at Beth She'arim; but this was the only time we found a complete coffin of this type in situ (see below for a discussion of the clay coffins).

R o o m V I. This room also served as an exclusive burial chamber — this time for two people. The size of the room is 1.30 × 2.00 m. There are two burial places: in one wall, a long niche similar to that in room V, except that it was empty; in the opposite wall, a trough niche.

Hall B

The entrance into this hall is in the eastern wall of the courtyard, about 13 m from the façade. At this point, the rock wall was too low for hewing a catacomb. A rectangular shaft had to be cut, therefore, in front of the entrance from which the opening into the catacomb was hewn. This shaft is 1.27 m deep, approximately 3.00 m long, 1.30 m wide, and it has a descent of four steps. In the southern side of the shaft, at floor level, there is a rounded pit about .50 m deep and 2.00 m long, which served most likely as a receptacle for rainwater. A row of stones was built in front of the entrance.

The frame of the entrance is built of smooth stones. The entrance itself is smaller than usual (.55 × .70 m). The door slab is made of soft stone and decorated in low relief with a large geometric six-leaf rosette, drawn with a compass (Pl. XVII, 4). Only in catacomb 15 was a similar decoration found — a door with two rosettes of this type. It is worth mentioning that in the right door jamb the keyhole was blocked with a stone as if to lock the catacomb permanently. However, at the time of the excavations we did not find the door actually locked, and the bolt was missing.

In the hall itself, there are two small rooms totaling 4.35 m in length. The hall is 1.50 m wide and circa 1.60 m high. The two rooms are separated by an archway. In the first room, there are two arcosolia with four graves; in the second room, three arcosolia with four graves. The ceilings of the arcosolia are squat. The rooms were almost entirely filled with earth, and no artifacts were discovered. Only the merest traces of bones remained.

Hall C

The entrance into this hall is in the western wall of the courtyard about 10.50 m from the main façade, almost opposite hall B. This tall, narrow entrance (.75 × 1.20 m) was blocked with dressed stones and did not have a frame or door.

The burial room is long and narrow: 3.70 × 1.20 m. While cutting out one of the arcosolia, the stonecutters encountered another catacomb (no. 19). The room contains four arcosolia, two on each side. The two front arcosolia collapsed entirely, together with part of the ceiling.

It seems that here, too, these two small halls (B and C) are somewhat later than hall A.

The Upper Structure Fig. 23; Pls. XV; XVI, 1
Above catacomb 14 remains were discovered of a structure built on the principle of a rectangular enclosure with stepped benches and a paved square (fig. 23). When the boundaries of the structure were laid out, catacomb 15 was apparently already in existence and had to be taken into account. The structure was, therefore, planned so that the courtyard of catacomb 15 would be within its limits but surrounded by walls of its own. This inconvenience could have been avoided simply by locating the whole structure somewhat to the east; however, the fact remains that the first solution was deliberately chosen, out of considerations still obscure to us. As a result, the approach to catacomb 15 was through the open square of the upper structure.

We shall first describe the remains that were found and later present our suggestions for the reconstruction of this structure. The most important remnant is the massive southern wall, of which three courses were preserved. The lowest course served as a projecting socle upon which the two courses of the wall proper were laid. The total height of the courses is 60 cm; the top of the wall is at an altitude of 105.16 m above sea level (Pl. XV). In the center of the wall, there is an apsidal niche paved with large stones. This apse is almost semicircular in shape. It is 5.60 m long and 1.75 m wide. Its floor level is at an altitude of 104.56 m, i.e., 12.55 m above the floor of the courtyard of catacomb 14. The face of the wall, including that of the apse, is built of one row of dressed stone, whereas the core is of rubble. An irregular rock scarp backs the wall. On this rock scarp there is a wall approximately .60 m thick. It is made of three–four courses of large undressed stones, laid without mortar. This wall is parallel to the apse wall, only it extends somewhat further to the East. It seems that this was a supporting wall for an earthen terrace. When this wall was discovered, some of the courses were already on the verge of collapsing due to earth pressure. In the reconstruction drawing (fig. 23), this supporting wall is part of the apse wall since it seems reasonable to assume that such was the case originally. Its function was to carry the weight of the sloping ground in order to decrease the pressure on the apse wall.

On both sides of the apse the wall is decorated with thin pilasters which have tall, concave bases (Pl. XV, 2). At the end of the wall, 5.20 m East of the apse, an additional pilaster was found. The wall to the West of the apse was preserved up to the courtyard of catacomb 15. There are good reasons for presuming that this wall extended westward above the entrance to catacomb 15 to the second corner of the courtyard, and that it terminated in a pilaster similar to that at the eastern end. This would make the total length of the wall 17.00 m.

The western wall of the structure is constructed partly of one row of stones (at an altitude of 102.75 m), and partly of two rows (102.18 m) as shown in figure 23. It continues beyond the western rock wall of the courtyard of catacomb 15 and extends about 9.50 m until it reaches the corner (altitude 101.30 m). Of this corner, which

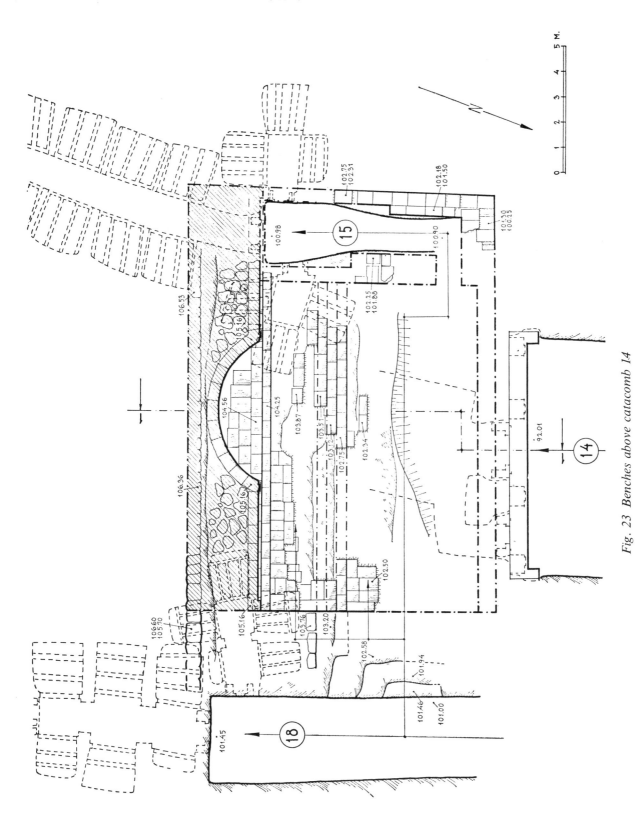

Fig. 23 Benches above catacomb 14

rested on a low rock step, four courses were preserved (Pl. XV, 1). From here the wall originally continued to the East. In our estimation, this wall rested on a rock step (which subsequently collapsed) and extended above the entrances to catacomb 14 below, at a distance of circa 1.30 m South of the arcaded façade (see section 1–1 in fig. 19). It may be taken for granted that this wall terminated in line with the eastern end of the apse wall. On the eastern side, no remains whatsoever were discovered of an enclosing wall parallel to the western wall. Instead there is an irregular, stepped rock exposure at this spot. In the drawing of the reconstruction (fig. 23) this side of the upper structure was left open, without a wall, since Mr. Dunayevsky conjectured that there was an approach from the courtyard of catacomb 18, through the stepped rock, to the benches. However, there is no certainty that this indeed was the original layout. If this were only a fence wall, the stones could have easily disappeared, just as it was only accidental that a few stones remained of the western wall of this structure. If these stones also had disappeared, we would have known nothing about the existence of a wall at this spot.

The western wall separated the bench courtyard from the courtyard of catacomb 15. Only a small section of this wall was preserved, a course of stones in two rows, 1.20 m thick (altitude 120.25 m). It seems certain that the entrance into the courtyard of catacomb 15 was at the northern end of the wall since this was the only possible place of access. However, it is impossible to prove this conjecture since the rock collapsed at this point.

Thus, the walls formed a rectangle, 16.60 m long from East–West and 12.60 m wide from North–South. The internal area, excluding the courtyard of catacomb 15 in the western part, was 13.00 m long from East–West by circa 8.80 m wide from North–South. This area is crossed by rows of benches, running from East to West,

built on steps hewn in the rock especially for this purpose (fig. 19, section 1–1). The first bench was at an approximate distance of 5.40 m from the northern wall. Between the wall and the bench there is a platform paved with stones, of which a few were preserved on the eastern side (altitude 102.50 m) and a few in the center (102.34 m). This platform is 10.33 m above the floor level of the underlying courtyard (catacomb 14). Altogether, there were five benches; fairly large portions of these were preserved intact, especially in the center. The height of each bench ranges from 36 to 39 cm. To the West the last stones of the benches sank due to the collapse of the small cave underneath. The fourth bench (1.30 m wide, 103.87 m altitude), of which many stones remained in situ, actually served as a sidewalk. The fifth and highest bench (104.25 m) adjoins the apse wall. The apse itself, which had additional seating places, was 2.22 m higher than the floor level of the platform.

Reconstruction and Function of the Upper Structure

In attempting to reconstruct this remarkable structure and to comprehend its function, we must first point out that a similar structure surrounded by benches on three sides was discovered above catacomb 20. This implies that the stepped rises found in the structure above catacomb 14 are also benches and not ordinary steps. Since the roofing of so large a structure would have necessitated columns of which no traces were found, we must deduce that here we have a kind of open-air theater or assembly hall in which the people sat facing the courtyard of the catacomb with their backs to the apse wall.

How the apse wall ended at the top cannot be established with certainty. The truncated pilasters seem to indicate that they were originally higher and terminated in capitals. In the axonometric drawing (fig. 24), Mr. Dunayevsky reconstructed the wall to a conjectured height of circa 3 m,

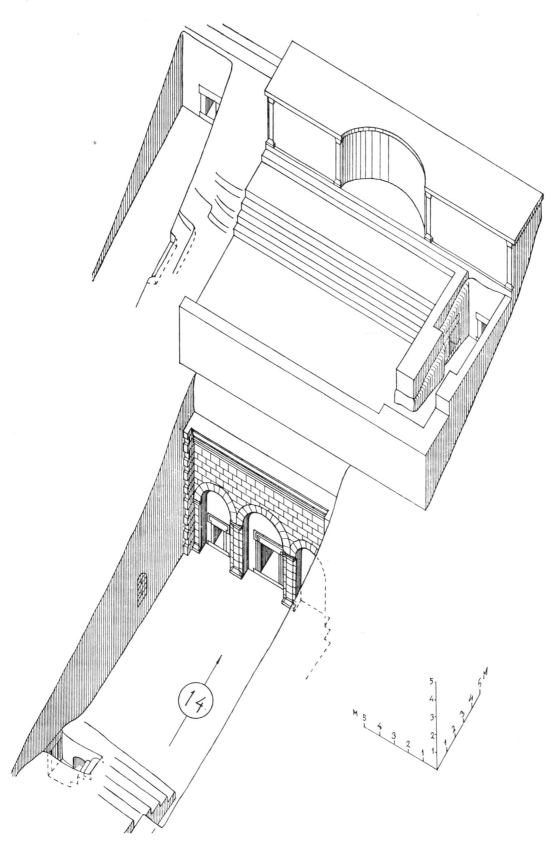

Fig. 24 Courtyard and benches of catacomb 14; reconstruction

with the apse open to the sky, without roofing. It cannot be ascertained whether the apse had a semidome. It should be noted, however, that in order to build a semidome, the workers would have had to raise the height of the wall to such an extent that the resulting size would have been totally out of proportion.

Apparently, the thick wall was built not only for architectural decoration, to add beauty and prominence to the spot, but also for functional reasons: *(a)* to serve as a supporting wall for the earth terrace behind it; this is also one of the reasons for the unusual thickness of the wall; *(b)* to enclose the apse. Similar architectural elements are also found in the structure above catacomb 20 (see below). Both apses face South toward Jerusalem, as does that of the synagogue of Beth She'arim at the summit of the hill. Although the orientation of the wall is largely determined by topographical conditions, still an apse did not need to have been inserted if it did not fulfil some particular function.

It is reasonable to presume that this upper structure served for memorial day gatherings which were intended for study, sermons, and prayer. Among the prayers there were probably some which had to be recited facing Jerusalem. It seems to us, therefore, that the apse was used by the prayer leader and was designed to indicate the direction of Jerusalem. This would mean that the benches were oriented in the opposite direction. However, it was quite acceptable to sit in a synagogue with one's back to the wall facing Jerusalem and to turn around at the required moments. Even though there were generally no apses of this type in the walls of the Galilean synagogues of this period, there are examples of apses raised above the synagogue floor in Eshtemoa, dated to the period of the early synagogues.[72]

The apses of Beth She'arim should not be confused with those of the later synagogues where they served to house the Ark of the Law, even though the Beth She'arim apses may be viewed as a kind of prototype for this later development. Semicircular apses and exedrae providing seats for respected persons, officials, and the like were common in public buildings in the Roman period.[73]

The western and northern walls of the structure were not high and apparently served only as a kind of fence. The northern wall functioned both as a supporting wall for the platform fill and as a parapet on the courtyard side, for the safety of the assembled people. Of this parapet only the western corner has remained. The rest, together with the rock upon which it was built, collapsed into the courtyard and dragged with it a large portion of the platform. During the excavation, many of the stones and much rock material were found in the courtyard below.

From the above description it may be deduced that the structure above catacomb 14 — including the upper wall and the benches — was indeed also designed to adorn the catacomb but was mainly intended to serve a functional purpose. It is very doubtful whether this monumental structure was an integral part of catacomb 15 even though its walls surround the courtyard of this catacomb. Catacomb 15 is so small and insignificant that the addition of so large a structure to it seems entirely unreasonable. This supposition is also unacceptable from the point of view of the overall plan in which catacomb 15 appears as a marginal component.

On the other hand, it does seem reasonable that the upper structure was intentionally designed for catacomb 14: it is located directly above it and is exactly parallel to the arcaded façade below. While the apsidal niche in the upper wall is not accurately aligned with the central arch below, this slight discrepancy is not actually felt. The observer of the whole complex of architectural units would hardly notice the assymetry. Thus, we may assume that this monumental upper structure is directly connected with the large catacomb immediately below it. This suggestion was made in the preliminary report on catacomb 14. If we had any doubts about the issue then, they were completely dismissed by the discovery of a similar structure above catacomb 20. It became evident that in the necropolis of Beth She'arim it was customary to erect open-air structures of this type above large and prominent catacombs.

Several facts justify the contention that the upper structure is later in date than the façade. The northern wall of the structure, i.e., the parapet facing the courtyard, is not built directly over the façade below and is not an integral part of it as is the case in catacomb 20. It is a separate construction upon whose completion the rock between the parapet and the façade was left exposed (see fig. 19, sections 1–1 and 3–3). This feature seems to indicate that the upper structure as a whole — just like the parapet — is not the product of an early plan but rather the result of two distinct construction phases, i.e., it was not constructed contemporaneously with the façade. If this contention is correct, it would provide a reasonable explanation for the inclusion of catacomb 15 within the bounds of the upper structure even though typologically catacomb 15 seems to be later than catacomb 14 (see below the chapter on the chronology of the catacombs).

In those days it was common custom to place a tombstone or memorial monument above the graves. These monuments took various forms, ranging from simple stelae to elaborate buildings. The custom is mentioned by the Sages and has been confirmed by archaeological finds both in Palestine and the neighboring countries.[74] Even prior to our excavations a monument was found in Beth She'arim above one of the catacombs: In the excavations of 1936–40 remains of a mausoleum were discovered above catacomb 11.[75] The mausoleum had four façades. One of them, which was entirely blind, contained a large niche. This was an elaborately decorated architectural monument which served to mark the tomb and commemorate the deceased. We may well suppose that this was exactly the type of monument against which our Sages often spoke.[76] However, the monument with which we are concerned here is of an entirely different nature. This is not an ornamental monument but a fairly simple structure whose purpose was mainly functional: a gathering place on mourning and memorial days for prayer, study, and sermons. What we have here is a monument suitable for the commemoration of pious men. It seems that a structure of this type is recorded in the scriptures,[77] as evidenced by the Midrash to II Chronicles, 32:33: "And Hezekiah slept with his fathers, and they buried him in the ascent of the sepulchres of the sons of David; and all Judah and the inhabitants of Jerusalem did him honour at his death. Rabbi Yehuda Berabi Simon said: And they built a house of assembly above the grave of Hezekiah, and when the people used to go there, they used to say to him 'teach us.' "[78]

The house of assembly was a well-known institution among the Jews and provided a gathering place for study and teaching the Torah. Apparently, in the time of the Sages assembly places were built above the graves of outstanding persons. Indeed, the same passage in II Chronicles (as quoted above) is explained in another source: " 'And they did him honour at his death' means that they paid respect by holding a meeting on his grave."[79] In his will to the Sages of Israel Rabbi Judah Ha-Nassî says: "Hold a meeting after thirty days." [80] While his own grave is not specifically mentioned here, it is clearly implied.

Exactly how a "meeting was held on a grave" is clarified in Rashi's writings: "In Teshuvoth Hage'onim ('Answers of the Sages'), I found various customs of the Amoraim ('teachers'); for example, 'On the anniversaries of the deaths of distinguished men, scholars from the surrounding localities as well as the general public assembled round the respective graves for study and discussion of matters of law.' "[81]

It appears to us that an assembly of this sort was particularly appropriate to the people who were interred in catacomb 14, and whose identity we shall try to determine presently. Actually the upper structure is very suitable for a large gathering, as is the structure above catacomb 20 (see below).

Identity of the Individuals Interred in Catacomb 14

At this point, it seems appropriate to attempt an identification of the individuals whose names are mentioned in the inscriptions found in the catacomb. The problem is undoubtedly difficult; however, this does not exempt us from attempting to answer the question that has been asked over and over again since the discovery of the catacomb. In the preliminary publication, the hypothesis was proposed that this catacomb is none other than the burial vault of Rabbi Judah Ha-Nassî's family.[82] We had hoped that in the course of the excavations additional facts would be discovered which would shed new light on the problem; however, our hopes were not realized. Of the new information that was relevant to our problem, none was decisive. Therefore, the best course would seem to present a full discussion of the most likely solutions and their limitations.

The question of the identification of the catacomb and the deceased buried there will be examined from four points of view: architectural, chronological, epigraphic, and literary. As has already been shown, this catacomb is distinguished by several characteristics: large rooms, a magnificent arcaded façade, and an open-air assembly place above it. All these features prove that those interred here were not only people of wealth but also of status, highly respected and admired by the community, and that it was customary to hold gatherings above

their graves. The same could be said of catacomb 20 (see below) except for one important difference: Catacomb 20 is a large public burial place including, among others, many rabbinical families, whereas catacomb 14 is a perfect example of a family burial vault. Only in a family burial vault would it have been possible to allot so much space to so few individuals and to waste the costly space of the walls of the large hall on a trivial number of small niches for bone depositories. In addition, we must remember that here, in contrast to catacomb 20, the hall was not utilized to the utmost by the introduction of sarcophagi. This fact alone proves that in catacomb 14 no effort was made to exploit the space to the maximum or to apportion the graves in a rational or aesthetic manner. Catacomb 14 contains very few graves with primary interments; most of the burial places were intended for secondary burial. Another fact is of particular interest: while the internal spaciousness of the catacomb and the external magnificence are evidence of the wealth of the interred and of their respected position, the graves themselves are exceedingly simple and modest and were rather carelessly constructed.

To what family did this catacomb belong? In general terms, we must assume that this family was large, wealthy, and very esteemed. If we want to specify a family, even by way of conjecture only, we must rely on the literary and epigraphic sources as well. From these it emerges that the only family described in the literary sources to have been buried at Beth She'arim is that of Rabbi Judah Ha-Nassî. The epigraphic material discovered in the catacomb gives evidence about two of the interred: Rabbi Shim'on and Rabbi Gamaliel. These are the very names of Rabbi Judah's two sons, both of them great sages and leaders of the nation. It seems also that the inscribing of personal names only, without the patronymic, is indicative that these people were so well known that their first names alone were sufficient for identification. In the other catacombs there is not a single individual among those bearing the title "Rabbi" whose patronymic is not also mentioned in the inscription. Therefore, on the basis of all the information outlined above, it seems justified to conjecture that these two deceased are none other than the two sons of Rabbi Judah Ha-Nassî. The next question naturally is: If these, indeed, are the burial places of Rabbi Judah's sons, why are their graves so plain? Perhaps the answer is that respect and honor were conferred upon the deceased by the size and external architectural splendor of the catacomb and not by the kokh and niche-like bone depository which, intrinsically, are always simple.

On the other hand, there is one grave in the catacomb which is made unusually conspicuous by its unique though modest construction — that is the built tomb in the corner of room II. We have already noted that this is the most important grave in the entire catacomb, and that in all probability it belonged to especially esteemed persons, possibly to the head of the family and his wife. To our regret, no trace of an inscription whatsoever was found on the grave and, therefore, the identity of the interred could not be definitively determined. However, if we accept the hypothesis that Rabbi Shim'on and Rabbi Gamaliel buried here are indeed members of Rabbi Judah's family, then it seems quite plausible that Rabbi himself and his wife were buried in the double grave in the corner of the room, and that an ashlar-masonry construction was erected there in order to distinguish it from the other graves.

Here we reach another link in the chain of evidence for identifying those interred in this catacomb: the inscriptions of "Anina the Little" and "Rabbi Aniana," who, as explained previously, are one and the same person. Without going again into the meaning of the word "the Little," we must point out that the bearer of this name was a Rabbi

too. In addition, it is important to note that his name, too, is written without a patronymic, like the names of the other deceased in this catacomb. This means that he, too, was well known in the community and that it was not necessary to append his second name. It seems to us that the name "Anina" (Ḥanina in Hebrew) is particularly germane to our problem. According to the Talmud (Ketuboth 103, 72) before his death Rabbi Judah delegated the various duties of the leadership of the Sanhedrin thus: "Shim'on, my son, the Sage; Gamaliel, my son, the President; Ḥanina bar Ḥama, the Chairman." Can it be mere coincidence that three people called Shim'on, Gamaliel, and Anina (= Ḥanina) were buried in one catacomb at Beth She'arim? Does it not seem more likely that this was not accidental at all, and that the logical conclusion must be that the people interred here are the very ones mentioned in the sources? Even if we do not know whether Ḥanina bar Ḥama belonged to Rabbi's family, it is not unreasonable to suppose that in so large a catacomb sages and scholars close to Rabbi Judah were buried here, as well as immediate members of the family. This conclusion is also confirmed by folk tradition (see below).

Now one may ask: What was the point of writing the names of all those interred and not the name of Rabbi Judah himself, i.e., how can we explain the absence of an epitaph on the most important grave in the catacomb? We shall venture a reply, but of course it can only be a conjecture.

It is well known that the purpose of the grave inscriptions at Beth She'arim was mainly to mark the burial places of the deceased in order to assist visitors in finding the graves of parents and relatives. This would explain the brevity of the formulas of the inscriptions and the sloppiness of the writing, evidently the product of the inexperienced hand of members of the family or of the caretakers. Also, the inscriptions were written considerably later than the burial when visitors coming to pray at the graves of the Sages might no longer be able to identify the graves. Since the kokhim and niches are all so similar, their identity could easily be mistaken unless they were named. However, the tomb at the end of the cave, built of large stones, conspicuous in its unconventional form, and famous for its importance, did not need to be marked since there was no chance of its being forgotten.

Only after the destruction of Beth She'arim, when interment there ceased and the entrances to the caves and, ultimately, the whole city were covered with earth, was the burial place of Rabbi Judah Ha-Nassî lost from memory. In fact, even the location of Beth She'arim itself was forgotten until it was rediscovered in recent times by archaeological excavations. However, Rabbi Judah's grave was so vividly preserved in folk memory that pilgrims in the Middle Ages and the masses at all times wanted to pay homage at his grave. To satisfy this need ancient folk tradition transferred his grave to Sepphoris, the city where Rabbi Judah spent his last years and died but not where he was buried. In those times it was quite customary for tradition to transfer the site of important graves from place to place.[83] The first to mention Sepphoris as the burial place of Rabbi Judah Ha-Nassî was Benjamin of Tudela; after him came Petaḥyah from Regensburg, Rabbi Jacob Shaliaḥ, Rabbi Yeḥiel of Paris, an anonymous student of the Ramban, Rabbi Issac Ibn-Alpra, the Traveler from Candia, and others.[84] The first to cast doubt on the authenticity of this folk tradition was R. Eshtori Ha-Parḥi (1322 C.E.). This scholar with his keen critical faculty wrote about Sepphoris: "And thus today, his grave [i.e., Rabbi Judah Ha-Nassî's] is *alleged* to be in the cave, which has a slab of stone at its entrance for a door. Northeast of Sepphoris, at a half-hour distance, there is another cave *attributed* to Rabbi Gamaliel, and at the side of this cave another one

attributed to his brother, Rabbi Shim'on. These must be the sons of Rabbi Judah."[85] In the words *alleged* and *attributed,* R. Eshtori Ha-Parḥi wanted to imply that he had misgivings about these "allegations" and "attributions" because they contradicted the Talmudic evidence which held that Rabbi Judah was buried at Beth She'arim.

Of all the sources which contend that Rabbi Judah's grave is located in Sepphoris, two are of particular importance:

1. In the book *Yiḥus ha-Zadikim* ("The Genealogy of the Pious") by R. Gershom of Scarmilla, printed in Mantua in 1561 C.E.,[86] the following description appears: "Zifra (in the Luncz edition "Zippori") — the place where our holy Rabbi and his sons R. Gamaliel and R. Shim'on are buried; in front of them, at the sides of the cave, are ten Geonim, and opposite the opening is the grave of Rabbi; and the door to the cave is of one solid stone." Rabbi Gershom did not compose this list of graves but only edited a traditional list[87] — to which he added various prayers to be repeated at the graveside when visiting it.

2. Similar to the description in the *Yiḥus ha-Zadikim* is the account given by R. Moshe Yerushalmi (1769) who also had before him a traditional grave list. This is what he writes about Sepphoris: "On the slope of the hill, to the west, in a beautiful cave-like chamber, our holy Rabbi and his two sons, R. Gamaliel and R. Shim'on, and ten students are buried in kokhim. And the monument in the cave opposite the entrance is the monument of our holy Rabbi; and the entrance to the cave is hewn in one stone."[88]

From these passages we learn that there was a widespread tradition not only as to the location of Rabbi Judah Ha-Nassî's grave, but as to its form as well. When tradition transferred the site of the grave from Beth She'arim to Sepphoris, it also carried along the traditional shape of the grave, even though this no longer suited the conditions of the new location. This inconsistency is further demonstrated by the fact that in the time of R. Eshtori Ha-Parḥi the graves of Rabbi Judah and his sons were shown to be in three separate caves in Sepphoris, whereas in the days of R. Isaac Ibn Alpra the graves of R. Shim'on and R. Gamaliel were shown to be below the cave of R. Judah Ha-Nassî.

Certain aspects of these descriptions of R. Gershom of Scarmilla and R. Moshe Yerushalmi are especially instructive. If we exchange the name *Beth She'arim* for *Sepphoris,* we obtain a description of extraordinary similarity to the archaeological findings at Beth She'arim. Catacomb 14 is indeed a cave hewn "in the side of the hill," and naturally creates the impression that it is "below the village." Even more important, the cave is to the west of the center of the city, where the synagogue was found. In the cave we discovered a tomb built of large stones ("the monument"), placed opposite the entrance ("the monument of our holy Rabbi"?). Also we found the graves of R. Shim'on and R. Gamaliel and, on both sides of the cave, the graves of other learned sages, one of whose names is known to us: Anina the Little or Rabbi Aniana. Of special interest is the folk tradition which claims that others, aside from Rabbi Judah and his sons, were buried in the cave. The description of the entrance to the cave as being "hewn out of one stone" is insufficient for specific identification since this is a feature common to many graves in the country.

For our discussion, the important question is, of course, whether ·we can prove that catacomb 14 was already in existence during the last years of Rabbi Judah's lifetime (Rabbi's death is estimated to have occurred circa 220 C.E.). In order to solve this problem we must view it from several standpoints, both architectural and paleographic. The typological comparisons of the architectural style and the arcaded façade demonstrate that this façade may well date to the beginning of the third century. The plan of the catacomb seems to suggest approximately the same date, i.e., earlier than the conventional plans which became regular practice at Beth She'arim with the enlargement of the necropolis after the death of Rabbi Judah (see the chapter on the typology of catacombs). The paleographic aspect of the inscriptions is also likely to confirm the thesis that the catacomb was already in existence at the beginning of the third century (see the chapter on the inscriptions). To our regret, the catacomb yielded a very meager amount of small artifacts, none of which could serve as a chronological criterion. This factor, therefore, could not be used as an additional confirmation for our hypothesis.

We may, therefore, conclude that the archaeological and epigraphic finds in catacomb 14, in conjunction with the facts mentioned in the Talmudic sources, justify the hypothesis — with reservations — that here, indeed, we have uncovered the long-lost burial vault of Rabbi Judah Ha-Nassî's family. It appears to us that the descriptions of R. Judah's grave in the folk tradition may increase the degree of credibility of this hypothesis from "with reservations" to "very likely." Nevertheless, the hypothesis remains unproven, even though it may seem well founded. Definitive scientific proof of this supposition could only be provided by epigraphic evidence in the form of an epitaph on Rabbi Judah's grave. This was not found; nor does it seem likely that it will ever be found. In view of the fact that Jews apparently seldom wrote inscriptions on the graves of great and outstanding persons, it is very doubtful indeed that an inscription had ever existed on Rabbi Judah's grave.

4 CATACOMB 15 (fig. 25)

We have already described the courtyard of the catacomb which is located at the western end of the upper structure of catacomb 14 — a courtyard surrounded by masonry walls upon lower rock walls within the precincts of the upper structure. It is 8.20 m long, 1.30 m wide at its northern end, and 2.40 m wide at its southern end. Its altitude is 100.98 m. The long rock walls were not hewn in a straight line. Therefore, in order to align the inside of the courtyard properly, the stone walls erected on the rock walls are of uneven thickness. This fact proves that, when the courtyard was hewn, the original plan did not include masonry walls — otherwise the rock walls would have been straight. To the North, the courtyard was blocked by a thick wall; thus, the entrance was apparently from the East, through the platform of the upper structure. The form of the entrance cannot be determined since the rock collapsed at this spot and the stones are missing. During the excavations, numerous stones that had fallen from the walls were found in the courtyard. There is no reason for assuming that this narrow courtyard was roofed.

Three entrances lead from the courtyard into three burial halls. The frames of the entrances and the doors were made of soft stone; thus, the weathering of the lintels and door jambs was severe.

Hall A

This hall, located on the southern side of the courtyard, is the major feature of the catacomb as might well be expected. Its entrance is 1.40 m high and .60 m wide. On the jambs there are still traces of broad bands of molding which apparently surrounded the lintel; however, their details are completely erased. The decorations on the door are quite different from those on the other doors.[89] Here there is a relief of two rosettes with six petals drawn by compass (Pl. XXIII, 1). In the horizontal panel between the two rosettes, which has the form of a spool, the remnant of a mounted iron ring was found imbedded in lead. Above the top rosette several Greek characters were written.

From the standpoint of layout, hall A has no parallel among the burial halls at Beth She'arim. Actually, it is a narrow, long corridor (.89–1.30 m wide and 10.70 m long) whose two long walls slant outward gradually toward the top. The average width of the floor is 1.00 m and that of the ceiling, 1.40 m. In each wall, at an average height of 1.63 m, four arcosolia are hewn (Pl. XXIII, 2). It is not clear why the arcosolia were cut so high that a ladder had to be used during burial ceremonies. The average size of the arcosolia is 2.00×2.00 m, and the height is .90 m. Each arcosolium has three spacious trough graves that were sealed with stones. While most of these sealing stones were removed and thrown into the hall, a sufficient number remained in situ allowing us to see how the trough graves and arcosolia were sealed. There is a total of twenty-four graves in the hall.

In the last arcosolium on the left-hand side (no. 5) most of the cover stones of the trough graves were found in situ, coated with coarse plaster. In arcosolium 6 the trough graves were covered with large tiles ($.40 \times .52$ m), several of which were still whole. A few of them were also found in arcosolium 2. This was the first time we found tiles in situ, though we had seen scattered fragments in other catacombs. The openings of arcosolia 5 and 6 were blocked with stones which were also covered with plaster. These two closures were partially dislodged by tomb robbers (see fig. 25, section 3–3).

A Greek inscription, semicircular in shape, was written on the plaster covering the blocking of arcosolium 5 (Pl. XXIV, 1). Only half of the inscription remained; the other half was lost due to the destruction of

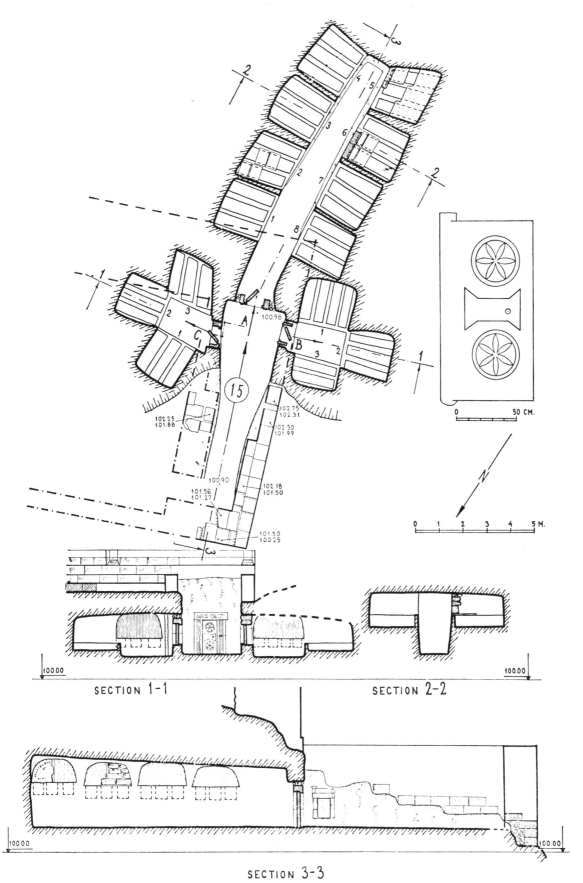

SECTION 1-1

SECTION 2-2

SECTION 3-3

Fig. 25 Catacomb 15

the closure. The inscription was painted in red on the soft plaster. It runs:[90]

ΩΔΕ ΚΙΝΤΕ Η ΜΑΚΑΡΙΑ

"Here lie the blessed..."

Beneath this inscription, the following word is inscribed in small letters: ΑϹΤΗΡ (= Esther). This is apparently the name of another woman buried here, in addition to the woman mentioned in the main inscription. Quite probably the name of the third person interred in this arcosolium was written on the right-hand side of the semicircle. In the center of the closure and on one of the fallen stones there were some traces of thin lines of paint; however, it is hard to decide whether these are traces of ornamentation or of an inscription. Some bear a slight resemblance to Hebrew characters (e.g., alef, samekh); even so, the evidence is still inconclusive.

Near the entrance, underneath arcosolium 8, a Greek inscription was written in large letters, but they are so blurred that it is almost impossible to decipher them. Opposite this inscription, below arcosolium 1, the following Greek inscription is incised (fig. 26):[91]

ΛΑΖΑΡ
ΒΑΡΙΟϹΛΙ[Μ?]

"Lazar bar Yosē (?)"

Fig. 26 Greek inscription

This Lazar,[92] whose surname is still uncertain, was apparently the head of the family buried in the tomb since it seems that his name was written on the entrance door also.

Below arcosolium 2, a number of interlacing circles were inscribed by compass. Under arcosolium 4 a menorah, 8 cm high, was incised in fine lines.

Hall B

The entrance to this hall is in the western wall of the courtyard. It is a small entrance (.55 × .80 m) made of soft, plain stones. The left jamb disintegrated altogether. A remnant of an iron ring is still fastened to the plain door. The entire hall is actually a small room, 1.30 × 2.00 m in size. It contains three arcosolia, one in each wall, with a total of nine graves. The ceiling of the room collapsed completely. As far as could be ascertained from the remains, the quality of the hewing was not of the best. The trough graves in the arcosolia are shallower than usual. In arcosolium 1 a group of glass vessels was found. Amazingly enough, several of these vessels were not damaged despite the fall of the ceiling (see below). Clearly, the ceiling collapsed in antiquity, before the graves were robbed. In all our excavations here this was the only instance that vessels were found in situ within a grave. The group of vessels found in situ in catacomb 12, room VI, was not in a grave but in a concealed hollow in the floor of the room.

Hall C

This hall is hewn in the eastern wall of the courtyard and is very similar to hall B. Its entrance, too, is small and plain; it, too, is no more than a small room with three arcosolia; here, as well, the ceiling collapsed entirely. The room was hewn under the upper structure of catacomb 14. The collapse of the thin ceiling caused the stone benches to sink, proof that the ceiling caved in when the benches were no longer in use, for otherwise the damage would have been repaired. In this room which had to be excavated from above no artifacts were found.

We tried to establish whether the benches were built when it was known that a cave existed below or whether, on the contrary, the cave was hewn when the upper structure already existed above it, i.e., when the danger of the ceiling collapsing could have been foreseen. From the existing structural data this question could not be settled. However, since the glass vessels in hall B are to be dated no earlier than the fourth century and since the upper structure is dated earlier (for reasons given above), it is our opinion that the two small halls were added to catacomb 15 when the upper structure was already in existence.

Small Finds

In hall A no artifacts were discovered. In hall B, as described above, a group of glass vessels was found which contained the following items (fig. 27):
1. A tall jug, preserved intact
2. The neck of a bottle
3. The neck of a bottle
4. The lower part of a double perfume bottle
5. A bottle
6. A lamp in the form of a goblet
7. The body of a bottle
8. A large decorated plate

In addition, several broken glass bracelets

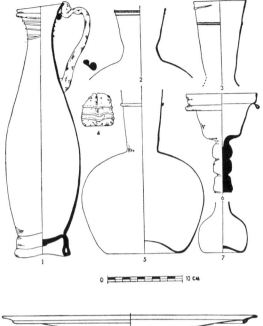

Fig. 27 Glassware from hall B

were found (Pl. LXXIII, 22). The glass vessels date to the first half of the fourth century C.E., i.e., to the end of the period in which the catacombs were still in active use. Presumably, hall A was hewn earlier, perhaps in the third century C.E. For a full discussion of the finds, the reader is referred to the chapter on glass vessels.

5 CATACOMB 16 (fig. 28)

This is the westernmost catacomb of the group we examined. It consists of two halls with a total of twenty-four burial places. The courtyard was located just a few meters southwest of the courtyard of catacomb 13. Its length is 4.80 m from North to South; its width, 3.50 m. This courtyard differs from the others in the group in that it was surrounded by a stone fence at the top of the rock walls. Only a few stones of this fence were preserved in situ. Almost the entire courtyard is occupied by broad descending steps which end near the entrances

to the burial halls. The entrance to the courtyard was from the North (altitude 95.00 m). Of the eight steps leading to the narrow courtyard (altitude 92.53 m) the top two are built of stone, whereas the rest are cut into the rock. Near the rock walls two shallow pits were hewn, evidently as receptacles for rainwater.

Hall A

Hall A is situated in the southern part of the catacomb. The door frame is constructed of soft, plain stones. The door slab has

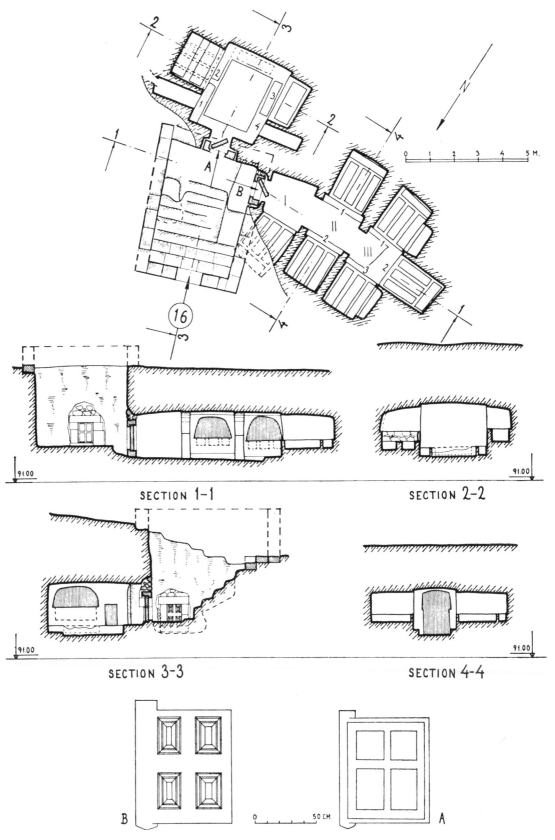

SECTION 1-1

SECTION 2-2

SECTION 3-3

SECTION 4-4

Fig. 28 Catacomb 16

four plain panels creating a design of two intersecting bands (Pl. XXIV, 2). This pattern is rare in the other catacombs. The hall consists of one room only, 2.80 × 3.40 m and 2.00 m high. Benches run along all four walls. A kokh and an arcosolium were cut into each of the two long walls.

At the end of kokh 1 in the eastern wall, a hole was breached into one of the graves of catacomb 13. Above the opening of the kokh the following bilingual inscription is written:[93]

ΙΩCHΦ ΦΑΙΝHCΙΟC שלום

"Joseph of Phaene, peace!"

The city of Phaene is located in the district of Trachona, East of Tyre and South of Damascus. The addition of the Hebrew word *shalom* is quite common among the Greco-Jewish burial inscriptions; in this catacomb, however, it appears in one other inscription only.

Arcosolium 2, located near kokh 1, contains two trough graves hewn transversely. Above them four additional graves were built out of stone, only two of which remained. Below the arcosolium a long Greek inscription of six lines was painted; however, it has not been satisfactorily deciphered as yet.[94]

In arcosolium 3, situated in the opposite wall, one grave was cut. It contained some iron nails and flat plates indicating that a wooden coffin had been placed there. Above

kokh 4, the following Greek inscription was found:[95]

ΕΙΟΥΔΑC ΙΕΡΕΩC

"Judah the priest"

The word *priest* is also mentioned in the long inscription. Perhaps this means that a family of priests from the Syrian Diaspora was buried here.

The room was small, but apparently more graves were needed. For some reason, however, the southern wall was not utilized. Instead, graves were added to arcosolium 2, as mentioned above. In addition, four graves were hewn in the benches along the walls.

The plan of the hall seems relatively early. The only find useful for dating is lamp no. 6 from the third century C.E. This, in fact, seems to be a reasonable date for the hall. The fragment of a Herodian lamp (no. 1), which was also found in this hall, was most probably deposited there with the debris.

Hall B
The western side of this hall was full of debris up to the ceiling. No artifacts whatsoever were discovered here. The entrance stones are plain. The door is decorated with panels as usual but without studs. The hall consists of three small rooms arranged consecutively, totaling 6 m in length. Each wall, except the southern wall of room I, has one arcosolium containing 3–4 graves. The dressing of the rock is quite coarse.

6   CATACOMB 17 (fig. 29)

This catacomb has two halls containing 28 burial places. Its courtyard is located about 20 m West of the arcaded façade of catacomb 14. It is small (2.40 × 3.30 m) and exceptionally deep: The floor level of the courtyard is at an altitude of 96.80 m; the rock level at the southern end is 100.40 m, to which 2 m of earth should be added. One enters the courtyard from the North

through three steps but has to jump another 1.20 m. A small pit was cut out under the steps for collecting rainwater. The courtyard contains three doorways (Pl. XXIV, 3).

Hall A
This hall is entered through the southern doorway of the courtyard which is exceptional for several reasons. One has to

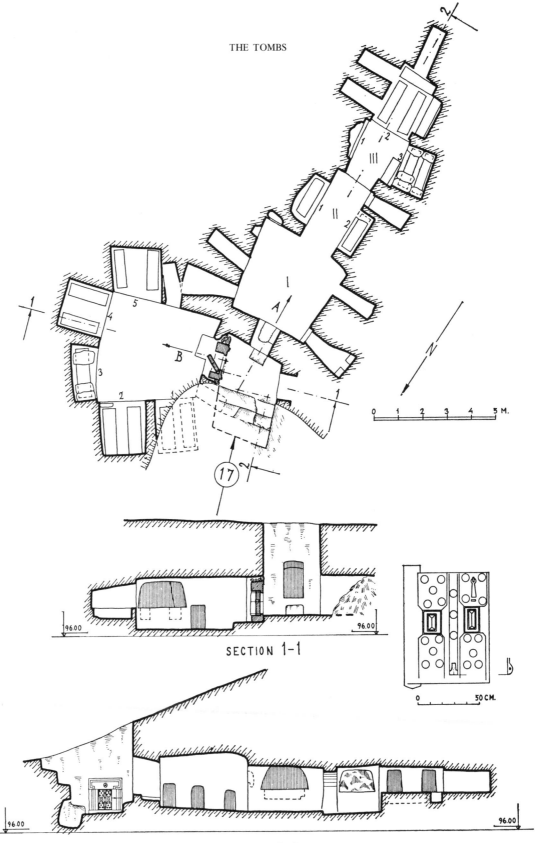

SECTION 1-1

SECTION 2-2

Fig. 29 Catacomb 17

ascend a high step because the threshold is .70 m above the courtyard floor. The entrance is .80 m wide and 1.45 m high. Its form indicates that a stone door could not have been installed. It is difficult to conceive how the doorway was closed when the catacomb was in use, unless it is assumed that a wooden door had been installed.

The hall consists of three rooms arranged in a row. Their total length is 9.00 m.

R o o m I. This room was full of debris which penetrated through the doorless opening. It is larger than the other rooms (3.50 × 3.50 m; 2.20 m high) and different in shape as well. It contains only kokhim, two on the right side and two on the left. In the left wall the hewing of a third kokh was begun but not completed, apparently because of the numerous veins of flint in the rock. In the southeast corner of the room there is a small niche for a bone depository.

R o o m II. This room is in fact a narrow passageway between rooms I and III. It contains two arcosolia, each with a kokh for a single burial.

R o o m III. This room is 2.00 × 2.00 m in area. In the western wall there is an arcosolium containing two graves; in the eastern wall the hewing of an arcosolium was left unfinished. In the arcosolium on the southern side there were originally two longitudinal graves and one transverse. However, burial places were added by cutting out a trough grave to the right, two kokhim to the left, and a kokh to the South. The stonecutting in this hall is particularly coarse.

It seems that this room, a typical kokh room, was hewn first, perhaps even before hinged doors were introduced to the tomb entrances of Beth She'arim (begining of the second century). The opening may originally have been small, as customary in early kokh caves, but was subsequently enlarged in the third century, when the cave itself was expanded.

In the western side of the courtyard also there is a doorless entrance, similar to the opening of hall A. Apparently the cutting of this entrance was interrupted almost immediately by collapse of the rock.

Hall B

This hall was hewn after hall A. The entrance has a door of the conventional Beth She'arim type, complete with decorations. In the center of the door there are two small panels only; the rest of the door is decorated with groups of five studs. The "knocker" was placed in the upper right-hand corner, a rather unusual position (fig. 29, right). The vertical fillet is different in that it has a perforated projection at its base. The lintel is decorated with a five-petaled rosette, in high relief, neatly executed.[96] The molding on the lintel and the jambs is not well matched; even the door jambs differ one from the other.

This hall consists of a single spacious room. The average area is 4.20 × 4.50 m; the height, 2.00 m. The walls are admirably smoothed. The broad arcosolia have curved sides but flat ceilings. In the northern wall there are two arcosolia, each containing two graves. In the eastern wall there are also two arcosolia. In the southern wall there is only one arcosolium; but there is also a curved kokh, imperfectly cut, since it adjoined a kokh in hall A. The entrance wall also contains a kokh. In arcosolium 2 one of the stone slabs that sealed the opening has been preserved.

Above arcosolium 1, to the left, the following Greek inscription appears (Pl. XXIV, 5):[97]

Ε[Ν]ΘΑ ΚΙΤΑΙ ΔΙΟΔΩΡΑ [Μ]ΗΤΗΡ
ΕΠΙΤΥΧΙΟΥ

"Here rests Diodora, mother of Epitychios."

The rock on which the inscription was painted is gradually disintegrating, just like a large part of the ceiling which has already crumbled and collapsed.

Small Finds

Many lamps were discovered in this catacomb — eight whole and several broken ones. Most of them were found in the debris of room I; quite likely some of them were deposited with the debris through the doorless opening. In hall B, whose door was closed, not a single lamp was found. Still, it is important to point out that there are not generally many lamps scattered about outside to make it likely that a big group would have penetrated through the opening of the cave together with debris. In any case, we did not encounter this phenomenon in the other catacombs.

The types of lamps found were: nos. 2, 12, 15, 23, 25, 26, 29, and 32 (Pls. LXX–LXXI). The first two lamps date to the third century c.e., and the rest, to the fourth century. Only the last (no. 32) cannot be dated with certainty. Lamp no. 23 is especially worthy of attention since it has the Christian monogram ☧ incised on its handle. However, in our opinion, no particular conclusion should be drawn from the appearance of such a Christian lamp at Beth She'arim; it is just accidental (see the discussion on lamps).

The remaining finds include a few fragments of glass; a piece of lead (indicating the use of a lead coffin which was robbed); and several iron nails (remains from a wooden coffin).

In the debris of room I a bronze coin from the city of Acre was found (Pl. XXIV, 4). Dr. Jacob Meshorer describes it thus:

"A bronze coin of Eleagabalus from the mint in Accho (217–222 c.e.).

Obverse: The head of Eleagabalus decorated with a wreath; facing right; a circumferential inscription:
IMP C M AVR ANTONIN...

Reverse: Tyche sitting on a rock; facing right; holds sheaves in her right hand.
Below – the river god (Na'aman River)
To the left and to the right, the inscription:
COL onia
PTOL emais
Weight: 9.55 gr
Diameter: 20.5 mm

No coin similar to this has been published so far in numismatic literature. The design on the reverse side is very common among the Acre coins. It also appears on the coins of Trajan, Hadrian, Marcus Aurelius, Lucius Verus, Commodus, and Julia Domna. Later, this design no longer appears on the Acre coins. Nevertheless, this coin indicates that this pattern was in use at least up to the year 222 c.e."

This was the only identifiable coin discovered in all the catacombs we excavated. It might be evidence of the fact that this burial room was in use at the beginning of the third century c.e. — although it is not definitive dating evidence because it was discovered near an open door. For typological reasons, we assumed, as mentioned previously, that the room was hewn in the second century, and that additional rooms as well as hall B were added in the third century.

7 CATACOMB 18 (fig. 30)

This catacomb is located East of the open structure above catacomb 14. It consists of two halls which contain thirty-eight burial places. The courtyard is long and narrow (11.00 × 3.30 m), with a North–South orientation. At the entrance the altitude is 101.45 m, i.e., this is the highest-situated courtyard among all the catacombs. It is not a closed courtyard but a kind of dromos. The entrance is on the northern side where the rock slope reaches the floor level at an altitude of 101.00 m. At the southern side,

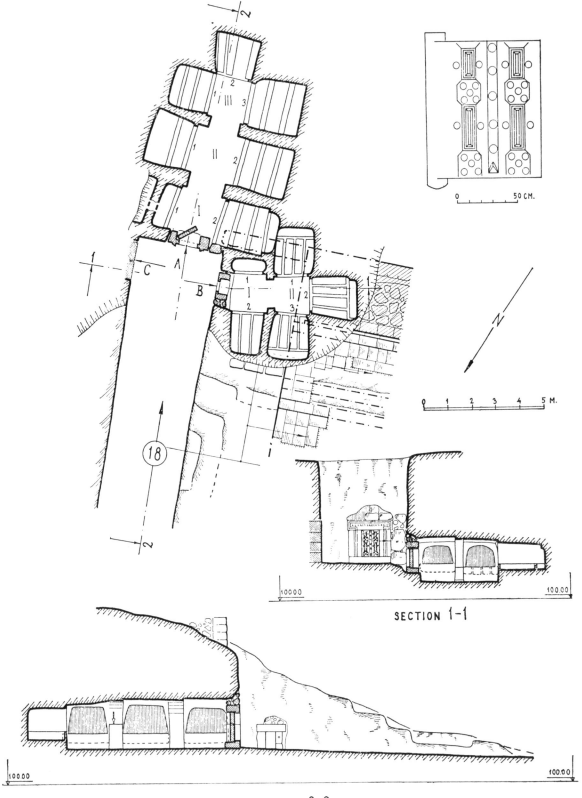

SECTION 1-1

SECTION 2-2

Fig. 30 Catacomb 18

on the other hand, the rock of the slope is at an altitude of 105.70 m. A rocky area, 3.20 m wide, separates the western wall of the catacomb from the eastern side of the upper structure. In this area, very rough steps were hewn which gave access from the courtyard to the upper structure (see fig. 23). However, from this fact alone, the conclusion that the courtyard is earlier than the upper structure cannot be reached, because the steps are so crude that it is unreasonable to assume that they were part of the original plan of the upper structure. A more acceptable assumption would be that, in this rocky area, there were other approaches whose traces disappeared in the course of time. It seems more probable that the orientation of the courtyard was determined by that of the neighboring structure rather than the contrary.

In the debris which filled the courtyard many dressed stones were found, which had apparently fallen from the walls above the courtyard. However, this is by no means certain since the area was not thoroughly excavated, and a superficial examination did not yield any results.

At one time there were three halls in this catacomb; however, the eastern hall had to be abandoned, apparently, due to the collapse of the rock. The entrance to it was then blocked with four courses of dressed stone. It might even be that the entrance was blocked before it was completed since there was no evidence of a door frame. The rock to the right of the entrance to hall A also collapsed, and the breach thus formed was blocked with stones as well.

Hall A

This hall is located on the southern side of the courtyard. The doorway to it (.70 × 1.05 m) is of outstanding workmanship (Pl. XXV, 1): The hard, bright stone is dressed to perfection, and the corners of the jambs are beveled to prevent their being damaged. A cyma molding, executed with great precision, surrounds the door frame. The lintel is 1.85 m long, its "ears" extending more than usual. The door is decorated with four panels (two long and two short) and studs. A vertical fillet gives the effect of a two-winged door. There is no carved door knocker.

We found the door closed; but when we opened it, it turned on its hinges with astonishing ease. Quite unintentionally, one of the workers pushed the door, causing it to close with such force that a crack was formed along its entire width. Since then we did not open it again for fear of enlarging the crack and breaking the door.

There were two Greek inscriptions on the lintel. One of them, incised on the lower broad surface of the lintel, reads thus:[98]

ΚΥΡΙΕ ΜΝΗCΘΗΘΙ ΤΟΥ ΔΟΥΛΟΥ COΥ CΑΚΕΡΔΩΤΟC

"Lord, remember Thy servant Sacerdos."

Sacerdos, which means "priest" in Latin, is used here as a personal name.

The second inscription is written on the narrow upper strip of the lintel. The letters are smaller and less distinct than those in the first inscription:[99]

ΚΥΡΙΕ ΜΝΗCΘΗΘΙ ΤΗC ΔΟΥΛΗC COΥ [ΠΡ]ΕΙΜΟCΑC

"Lord, remember Thy maidservant Primosa."

This inscription most likely refers to Sacerdos's wife. The formulation of these two inscriptions is common among Christian inscriptions but appears here for the first time in a Jewish cemetery.

Hall A consists of three rooms containing nineteen burial places. The total length of the rooms is 6.40 m.

R o o m I. This room has two arcosolia. Arcosolium 1 contains one grave. In its back wall there is a breach into a room which belonged to the eastern hall, the one that collapsed (see above). Arcosolium 2 has three transverse trough graves, and a fourth grave was added in the back wall. Room II. This room contains two arcosolia, each having three graves. In the posts of the archway to room III, two lulabim are carved. The lulab on the right is in high relief and is 55 cm tall (Pl. XXV, 2). However, the one on the left is carved in low relief and is 46 cm tall (Pl. XXV, 3). The handle is straight with a triangular-like basket of myrtle and a long thin branch. The carving of the first lulab was planned ahead since it was executed contemporaneously with the hewing of the arch. The second lulab, however, was added in imitation of the first after the completion of the arch. Till now, the use of a lulab as a separate motif has not been found at Beth She'arim; generally, it appears together with other religious motifs. On the whole, there were very few carvings in relief on the walls of the catacombs which we excavated. Room III. This is a small room 1.60 × 1.60 m in size. It contains three arcosolia with three graves. Several stone slabs which were used to seal the trough graves were found in the room. The hewing was roughly done, but the walls were smoothed. Cracks in the rock were filled with mortar.

Hall B

The entrance to this hall is small (.42 × .75 m)

and is made of soft, plain stone. The door slab was broken and not found in place. The hall consists of two rooms, altogether 3.20 m in length. In room I there are two arcosolia: arcosolium 1 has a single grave; arcosolium 2 has three graves. In room II there are three arcosolia containing five graves each.

In the debris of the courtyard, 16 fragments of a white marble tablet were discovered. The tablet was 88 cm long, 67 cm wide, and 3 cm thick (Pl. XXVI). At the top of the tablet the conventional Jewish symbols were carved: in the center, a menorah; to the right, a lulab and ethrog; and to the left, a shofar and incense shovel. The branches and stem of the menorah are carved in broad bands. The menorah is tripodal and terminates on top in a horizontal strip. The lulab is thin and has a triangular myrtle basket to which the ethrog is attached. The shape of the openings at both ends of the shofar lends it a naturalistic appearance. The incense shovel is open in front and has a long handle terminating in a ring. It also has dots, reminiscent of shovels depicted sometimes in mosaics.

The most important feature of the marble tablet is the incised Greco-Jewish epigram it bears. The inscription consists of ten lines. The reading and translation according to Schwabe and Lifshitz are as follows:[100]

ΕΥΛΟΓΙΑ ΤΗ ΟCΙΑ

ΚΑΡΤΕΡΙΗC ΤΟΔΕ CΗΜΑ ΛΙΨΑΝΟΝ ΦΕΡΕΙ ΦΘΙΤΟΝ

ΑΦΘΙΤΟΝ ΗΕ ΛΑΜΠΡΑΝ CΩΖΟΝ ΜΝΙΑΝ ΓΕΝΑΙΗC

ΘΗΚΑΤΟ ΔΕ ΜΙΝ ΕΝΘΑΔΕ ΖΗΝΟΒΙΑ

4 ΜΗΤΕΡΟC ΕΗC ΤΙΟΥCΑ [ΕΦ]ΗΜΟCΥΝΑC

ΤΟΥΤΟ CΟΙ ΜΑΚΑΡΤΑΤΗ ΚΑΡΠΟC CΟC ΕΔΙΜΑΤΟ

ΗΝ ΤΕΚΕC ΕΞ' ΑΓΑΝΩΝ ΕΥCΕΒΙΗΝ ΛΑΓΟΝΩΝ

ΡΕΖΕΙ ΓΑΡ ΚΛΥΤΑ ΕΡΓΑ ΕΝΙ ΦΘΙΜΕΝΟΙC ΑΙΕΙ

8 ΟΦΡΑ ΔΗ ΑΜΦΩ ΚΑΙ ΜΕΤΑ ΤΕΡΜΑ ΒΙΟΥ

ΝΕΟΝ ΗΔ' ΑCΚΥΛΕΥΤΟΝ ΑΥΘΙC ΕΧΟΙΤΕ ΠΛΟΥΤΟΝ

Eulogy to a Pious Woman   of noble Karteria
This tomb contains the dwindling remains   Preserving forever her illustrious memory.

Zenobia brought her here for burial,
fulfilling thus her mother's behest.
For you, most blessed of women, your
offspring
Whom you bore from your gentle womb,
your pious daughter,
For she always does actions
praiseworthy in the eyes of mortals
Erected this monument so that even
after the end of life's term
You may both enjoy again new
indestructible riches.

This inscription is exceptional in Beth She'arim. The description of the grave as happiness after death is not a Jewish conception at all. In the opinion of Schwabe and Lifshitz, this inscription furnishes "additional evidence to the historical fact that a considerable segment of the Jewish population in Palestine and the neighboring countries were greatly influenced by Greek civilization." While this statement is a correct generalization, it is questionable whether it directly reflects the degree of Hellenization of Palestinian Jews. Even Schwabe and

Lifshitz conjecture that both women mentioned in the epigram, Karteria and Zenobia, came from the Diaspora.

Where is the site of the tomb mentioned in the inscription? From the location of the fragments, scattered in the debris in front of the door and near the left wall on a limited area of about 2 sq m, it may be deduced that the tablet fell unbroken into the courtyard where it was shattered. As already mentioned, many dressed stones were found in this courtyard, apparently from walls surrounding it on top or from some other structure erected there. It is quite possible that the tablet is in some way associated with these dressed stones. Also, from the contents of the inscriptions on the lintel of the main entrance to catacomb 18, it appears that the epigram does not apply to this tomb but to another one, perhaps a mausoleum built above it.

On basis of the monumental style of the letters, Shwabe and Lifshitz date the inscription to circa the third century C.E. No artifacts were found in the cave itself which could be useful for dating.

8 CATACOMB 19 (fig. 31)

This catacomb is located between catacombs 12 and 14. Its plan is typical of catacombs of this class: a square sunk courtyard, steps, and three entrances into halls. Usually, at least one of the side entrances and halls is inferior to the main hall in size, quality of execution, and appearance. Here, however, the workmanship in all three halls is of equal quality.

The courtyard is rectangular, 3.00×4.75 m. The approach starts at an altitude of 95.41 m and descends through six steps to the floor of the courtyard (Pl. XXVII, 1). The first four steps are hewn across the whole width of the courtyard, but the last two are narrower and irregular. They extend along the eastern wall and terminate at an altitude of 93.08 m. There is a stone wall

across the width of the courtyard, about 1.70 m from the façade. This wall is 1.25 m high, but at the point where the steps descend near the eastern wall it is much lower. The façade wall is 3.70 m high. Above it there is a layer of earth 1.50 m thick.

Above all three entrances there are large breaches whose blockings were removed by tomb robbers.

Hall A

The entrance (.60 × 1.00 m) to this hall is in the southern wall of the courtyard. Both the door frame and the door slab are fashioned in the customary Beth She'arim manner. On the lintel a head was carved in high relief; however, it was badly mutilated so that its exact form can no longer be

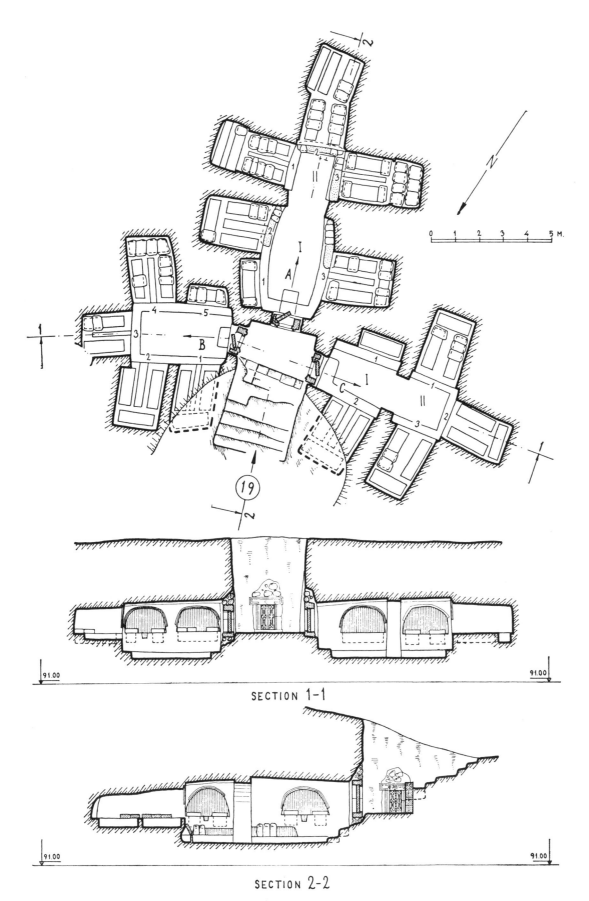

SECTION 1-1

SECTION 2-2

Fig. 31 Catacomb 19

discerned. It seems to represent an animal rather than a human head (Pl. XXVIII, 1).

The hall consists of two rooms with six arcosolia. The rooms total 6.80 m in length. Many cover stones were found, some in situ. The arcosolia have a characteristic border molded in a double recess.

Room I. This room is 4 m long, 2.00–2.85 m wide, and 2.30 m high. Its floor is 1.80 m below the level of the courtyard. Benches surround the room on three sides.

In arcosolium 1 in the eastern wall there is a single trough grave. Below the arcosolium a series of concentric circles were incised (Pl. XXVIII, 2). To the left of arcosolium 1, on the wall to the right of the entrance, two similar series of circles were carved. There is no explanation why somebody would bring a compass to the grave, and the meaning of these is obscure. Incidentally, identical circles were found in other catacombs as well.[101]

On the wall between arcosolia 1 and 2 there is a very schematic relief of a menorah, mainly a stem on a low base. It is 26 cm high. The relief widens toward the top and has seven incised indentations to represent the seven branches of a menorah (Pl. XXVIII, 4).[102]

In arcosolium 2 there are four graves: three longitudinal and one transverse. A channel between the first two graves gives access to the grave in the back. Similar channels were found in the rest of the arcosolia in this catacomb and sometimes in other catacombs as well. A Greek inscription was painted in red very distinctly on the back wall of the arcosolium (Pl. XXVIII, 3):[103]

ΕΝΘΑΔΕ

ΚΙΤΕ ϹΕΜ

..ΟΥϹ Η ΚΑΙ ϹΙ

ΡΙΚΙϹ Η ΚΙΡ

Α ΗΜΩΝ

"Here lies Sem..ous, also called Siricis, our mistress."

Lifshitz has completed the broken name to Cεμνοῦς. However, the photograph of the inscription shows that the rounded traces of the missing letter could not be part of the letter *nu*.

Arcosolium 3 is similar to the previous one. To the left, a fragmentary incised Greek inscription bears the name ΥΠΕΡΕΧΙϹ.[104] Two graves were cut into the long benches and were covered with stone slabs which leaned obliquely against the wall.

Room II. This is a small room, also surrounded by benches. It is entirely occupied by three arcosolia in its walls. At first there were only two longitudinal graves in each arcosolium but later all the arcosolia were extended by the addition of two or three graves so that the present length is 4 m. Due to the need for more burial places, graves were also hewn in the benches. The white building stones and dark brown plaster might easily be mistaken for modern masonry.

Hall B

The entrance to this hall, in the eastern wall, is constructed in the usual fashion except that it has a well-carved relief of a rosette with six petals on its lintel (Pl. XXIX, 1), similar to those discovered in catacombs 13 and 17.

The hall consists of one room only; its floor is circa 1.00 m below the level of the courtyard. The room is spacious — 2.35 m wide, 4.00 m long, and 2.25 m high — and neatly finished. There are benches surrounding three walls.

In the northern wall there are two arcosolia with three graves; in the eastern wall, a single arcosolium with two graves; in the southern wall, two arcosolia, one with three graves and the other with a single grave. All the arcosolia except the last have cut channels between the two front graves (Pl. XXIX, 2).

Beneath arcosolium 2 in the northern wall the following inscription is incised (Pl. XXIX, 3):

ΙΟΥCΤΟC
ΖΩΝ ΙΠΗΝ
ΕΥCΕ (ΠΡΩΤΗC) ΠΑ
ΝΩΜΟΥ

"Justos commanded in his lifetime,
on the first of Panemos."

The reading and interpretation are by
Prof. Lifshitz.[105] In his opinion, Justos
ordered, in the month of Πάνεμος, the grave
to be hewn. If this interpretation is indeed
correct, then this is the only date mentioned
in the Beth She'arim inscriptions. However,
only the month is designated, not the year.

There is an inscription below arcosolium
3 also, in the eastern wall (fig. 32):[106]

CΑΒΕΡΙC ΥΙΟC CΑΒ
ΙΝΟΥ ΑΡΧΙΒΑΦΘΟΥ

"Saberis, son of Sabinos the clothdyer"

Below arcosolium 4 there is a very clear
Greek inscription painted in red (Pl. XXIX,
3):[107]

BENNIAMIN
ΥΙΟC ΙΟΥΛΙΟΥ ΟΘΟΝΙ
ΑΚΟΥ ΥΙΟΥ ΜΑΚΡΟΒΙΟΥ
ΚΡΑΤΙCΤΟΥ

"Benjamin, son of Julios, the cloth
merchant, son of the excellent Makrobios."

Here we have the tomb of a family whose
members dealt in textiles: one was a dyer,
and the other a merchant. These are new
trades among those mentioned in the Beth

She'arim inscriptions so far. A textile
merchant is also cited in one of the tomb
inscriptions from Jaffa.[108]

Hall C
The entrance to this hall, on the western
side of the courtyard, is in conventional
Beth She'arim style, similar to the two
previously described entrances. On the
lintel a human head, apparently of a woman, was carved in high relief. The face is
frontal and has curly hair hung behind the
ears, like the Egyptian Hathor headdress
(Pl. XXVII, 2). The face resembles the
masks that frequently decorated Roman
sarcophagi.[109] This is the first time that a
human face was found depicted on a Beth
She'arim or on any Jewish tomb in this
country. It is obvious that the carving was
made before the lintel was fixed in place, a
fact of particular importance in the question
of the use of figurative art in the decoration
of Jewish graves (see below).

On the left side of the carved head there
is a seven-branched menorah on a square
base, incised very crudely. To the right of
the head there is a Greek inscription.[110]

CΩΚΡΑΤΟΥC

"Of Socrates"

The name and the menorah were incised
by an unskilled hand after the lintel was
fixed in place. It seems that the craftsman
found it necessary to add a menorah beside
the human head and the name Socrates, so
un-Jewish in their appearance, in order to
lend a Jewish character to the grave. It is

Fig. 32 Greek inscription

noteworthy that not a single menorah was found on any other lintel at Beth She'arim.[111]

Catacomb 19 has several outstanding features. It contained important epigraphic material, instructive not only about the origin of one of the deceased (and perhaps even of all of them) but also about the occupations of some of the deceased. The number of Biblical names used among Greek-speaking Jews was also larger. The reliefs of the heads on the lintels are exceptional for entrances to Jewish tombs and are, therefore, evidence that even a family with deep Jewish consciousness did not consider this portrayal offensive.

The name of Socrates was not the only one perpetuated on the entrance to the tomb: the name of another deceased was also preserved. In a recess in the rock wall, about 83 cm above the left end of the lintel (fig. 33), a marble tablet was affixed, 19.50 cm wide, 30 cm long, and 2 cm thick.[112] A bilingual inscription consisting of four lines in Greek and one line in Hebrew was engraved on the tablet. At the end of the sec-

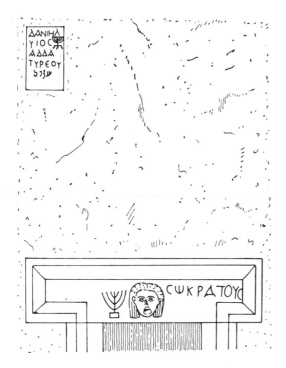

Fig. 33 Lintel with marble plaque above

ond line a seven-branched menorah was carved, having a horizontal strip on top and three stepped legs for a base (Pl. XXIX, 5). The height of the menorah is 4.50 cm, and the height of the Greek letters, 2–3 cm. The inscription runs thus:

ΔΑΝΙΗΛ

ΥΙΟC

ΑΔΔΑ

ΤΥΡΕΟΥ

שלום

"Daniel, son of 'Iddo from Tyre; peace."

This is the first time that the two Biblical names *Daniel* (translated in the Septuagint as Δανιηλ, in contrast to Δανιηλος in other sources) and *'Iddo* (Septuagint: Αδδω) are mentioned in the Beth She'arim inscriptions. Evidently this Tyrian family had very strong Jewish sentiments. Not only did the father and son have Biblical names—an unusual phenomenon among Phoenician Jews (see above, the inscriptions in catacombs 12 and 13)—but they also added a Hebrew blessing and a carving of the menorah to the Greek inscription. It seems very likely that Benjamin, Socrates, and the others interred in catacomb 19 were also brought from Daniel's country of origin. Individuals from Tyre were buried in catacombs 12, 21, and 26 also.

As to the word שלום at the end of the inscription, it is common for a Greco-Jewish epitaph to end with the blessing *shalom* in Hebrew (compare with the tomb inscriptions in Jaffa and in the Jewish catacombs of Rome).

Apparently the scribe was familiar with the Greek letters but not with the Hebrew. Note particularly the *shin* which reveals a very inexperienced hand. The tablet was probably made in Tyre and brought to Beth She'arim together with the deceased. The menorah is incised in the usual schematic manner, but it is difficult to understand why it was squeezed in between the lines of the inscription when there was ample space for it below.

This hall consists of two rooms totaling 5.50 m in length. Benches were hewn along the walls. In room I there are two arcosolia: arcosolium 1 contains one grave, and arco-solium 2 has three graves. In room II there are three arcosolia, each with three graves. The right jamb of the archway between the two rooms contains a cut recess for a tablet, but the tablet itself was not found. Recesses of this kind are generally found in court-yards but not in burial rooms.

9 CATACOMB 20

This is the largest catacomb discovered so far at Beth She'arim. In its general layout it is similar to catacomb 14. It has three major units: a courtyard, a cave, and an upper structure with benches. It extends 75 m from North to South and about the same distance from West to East. During the cut-ting of this ramified catacomb, the stone-cutters did not encounter other graves, which means that the area was still devoid of tombs. Another explanation might lie in the fact that the catacomb penetrated deeply into the slope of the hill.

One of the main problems for the builders of this catacomb was to find a dumping ground for the debris from the quarrying of this huge cave. At first, the rubble was de-posited in front of the catacomb to the North, thus creating a broad artificial ter-race which protruded into the valley (Pl. II, 1). Later on, the stonecutters wanted to heap some of the debris to the West of the catacomb; they, therefore, bounded an area of 6.00 × 16.00 m with supporting walls. When this area was also filled, it was enlarged and fenced in by a long wall (about 2.20 m high) extending from North to South on the slope of the hill at a distance of 10–12 m from the courtyard (Pl. IX, 2). Thus, a wide terrace was formed west of the courtyard, which later served for the dig-ging of individual tombs, as will be shown below (see fig. 35).

The Courtyard

This is a spacious courtyard, hewn in the slope of the hill from north to South. The three walls on the East, South, and West were faced with dressed stones; the entrance wall to the North was built entirely of stone. The internal size of the courtyard is 16.20 m from North to South and 11.72 m from East to West. The floor slopes gradually from south to north, from an altitude of 94.54 m to 94.33 m.

In the debris which filled the courtyard many dressed stones were discovered, both decorated and plain, which must have be-longed originally to the courtyard walls, the façade, and the upper structure. Two of the building stones were exceptionally large. One was 1.10 × .58 × .50 m and the other, 1.28 × .50 × .27 m. Almost no pottery was found among the debris, except for a few unimportant shards which slipped down the slope. A more important find was a stone basin, apparently used for washing hands. It is .93 m high (fig. 48, left). A frag-ment of a marble tablet incised with part of a Greek inscription also penetrated into the courtyard from the outside. A man from Sidon is mentioned in this inscription (Pl. L, 4).

The Northern Wall (fig. 34; Pl. XXX, 2). The entrance to the courtyard is located in the center of the wall. The wall, built on the rock, is 5.10 m long and 2.40 m thick; three courses of it were preserved to a total height of 1.16 m. The lowest course which forms a socle is .34 m high and protrudes 15 cm from the face of the wall. Only at the east-ern end of the wall was one stone preserved from the fourth course. Much effort was

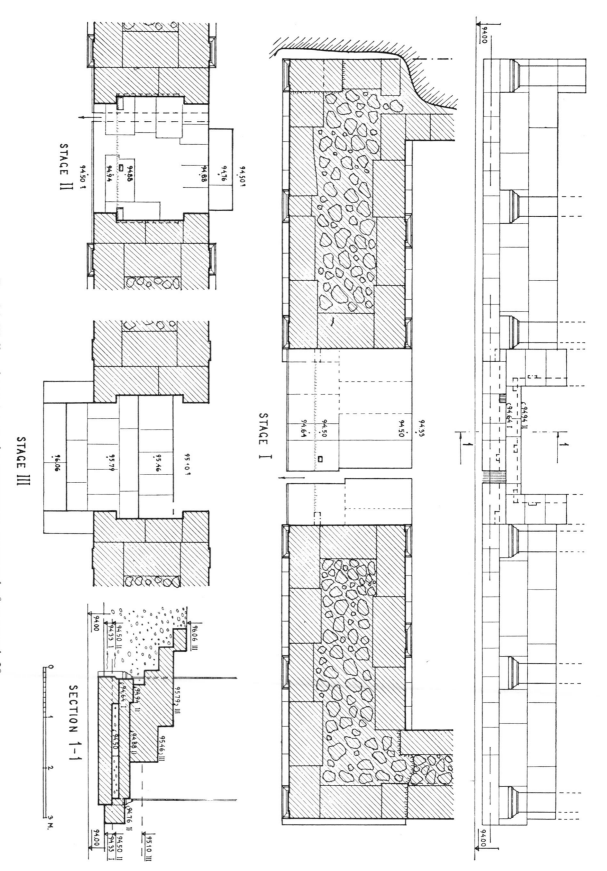

Fig. 34 Wall and opening at the entrance to courtyard of catacomb 20

84

invested in this wall, and the result is indeed remarkable. The stones were perfectly dressed and cut rectangular on all four sides. The wall had a rubble fill. Both faces of the wall are decorated with flat pilasters. On the side of the courtyard there are two pilasters on either side of the entrance; on the exterior, three pilasters on either side. The bases of the pilasters are molded with a plinth, torus, and cyma reversa (fig. 34, top). It is of interest to note that the first two exterior bases were not visible in ancient times. The corner stones were laid in a trench hewn in the rock which concealed the bases; only after we removed the rock did they come into view. It is interesting that at the time this was not considered aesthetically offensive.

In the course of time, many changes were introduced to the entrance. Three phases of construction may be discerned:

P h a s e I (fig. 34, center). The entrance was 3.50 m wide and 2.40 m thick, i.e., as thick as the wall. The threshold was built of large square stones. A drain through the threshold conducted the rainwater out of the courtyard. At this point the courtyard was level with the path in front of it: 94.33 m above sea level. The altitude of the entrance threshold is 94.64 m.

It would be natural to presume that so wide an entrance did not have a door at all; however, a recess for a bolt was found in one of the threshold stones. This leads us to surmise that a light, wooden door was installed, which did not close the opening to its full height. We did not uncover the recesses at the sides because we did not want to dismantle the construction of Phase II.

P h a s e II (fig. 34, bottom, left). Radical changes in the form of the entrance took place during this phase. The entrance was narrowed to 2.15 m by placing jamb stones on either side. New slabs of stone were laid on the threshold, thus raising the altitude to 94.94 m. In front of the entrance, on the courtyard side, a step was built. A narrow

drainage channel was cut along the left jamb, beneath the threshold stones, to replace the original trench for draining the courtyard. The threshold had two sockets and a bolt recess. There was also a proper two-winged door, most likely made of wood. These two wings, when opened, fitted into two recesses in the jambs. Long strips were cut into these recesses, apparently matching the horizontal boards which bound the door wings on the inside.

P h a s e III (fig. 34, bottom, center). Apparently the previous alteration lasted for a considerable time, during which debris from the cave accumulated on the path in front of the courtyard. The level of the path rose to approximately 96.06 m, and even the level of the courtyard floor increased to 95.10 m. In order to facilitate the descent into the courtyard, three massive steps of dressed stone were built. The first step was laid outside the opening, with two elongated vertical stones on either side as a kind of banister. The two remaining steps were built within the opening (see the sections of the three steps in fig. 34, bottom, right). At this stage, the entrance no longer had a door. How the courtyard drainage problem was solved is not clear. It is also difficult to understand the reasoning behind these alterations; instead of putting so much work into the construction of the steps which only impeded the transfer of the heavy stone coffins, the debris in front of the opening could have been cleared away and thus the previous threshold would have been accessible once more. A possible explanation might be that, at this stage, stone sarcophagi were no longer used.

The Western Wall. Sections of three to eight courses were preserved from the western wall of the courtyard. Near the façade the height of the courses is the same as the height of the nearby pillar. The lower courses are constructed in a single row along a rock scarp. The upper courses, on the other hand, are built out of two rows of dressed stones with a rubble fill between them. The wall is 1.70 m thick. The outer row lies on the rock scarp which is 4.00 m high at the southern end and less than a meter high to the North. In the southern part of the wall only the inner row had remained; however, at the northern end the wall was preserved to its full thickness. Some of the remaining stones of the wall rose to a height of 2.58 m above the floor of the courtyard.

The Eastern Wall. Only the inner row of stones of the eastern wall remained. Near the façade six courses of stones were preserved; but at the northern end only two courses remained. The other courses visible today are reconstructed. At the southern end of the wall an entrance was discovered, its stone members scattered in the courtyard. The door is decorated with the usual panels. The lintel was restored to its original place. The entrance leads to a room called "hall B" in the plan (fig. 43, bottom), 4.20 × 7.00 m in size. In the northern wall of the room there are five loculi. This room, which was filled with debris and whose ceiling was partly destroyed, contained nothing of particular interest. North of this room there was another small incomplete room, 2.00 × 2.50 m in size, which was entered through a small doorless opening. Its plain lintel was reinstalled. It most likely served as a small storeroom.

The Façade (fig. 36; Pl. XXXI). The façade of this catacomb is in the southern wall of the courtyard and faces North. It is similar to that of catacomb 14 except that it has three instead of two entrances hewn into the rock wall. It also has an arcade of three stone arches. At the time of discovery the façade was badly damaged (Pl. XXXI, 1), apparently due to the collapse of the rock. The central part suffered most severely as a large breach occurred in the entrance of the catacomb. Of the entrance stones, only the threshold and two parts of the door posts were preserved. The right-hand door remained intact whereas the left-hand door was found broken in the courtyard debris.

(The restored door was taken from catacomb 23.)

The two outer pillars of the arcade, each consisting of six courses, were entirely preserved. However, only two to four of the lower courses of the inner pillars were preserved. None of the voussoirs remained in situ. Seventeen of them were found in the debris in front of the façade. Some were still attached one to the other, as they had fallen when the arches collapsed. This must have taken place considerably after the catacomb ceased to be used for burial when the courtyard was already full of debris. This is especially evidenced by the voussoirs of the lateral arches which were found about 1.60 m above the floor of the courtyard. At this same level, shards from the Arabic period and Turkish pipes were also found. When we restored the façade (Pl. XXXI, 2), we decided to rebuild the right arch entirely with original stones and to add four voussoirs to the left arch. The rest was reconstructed with new stones.

The arched façade is built of ashlars of the *meleke* type. It consists of three arches borne on four pillars. The total length of the façade is 11.80 m. The width of the outer pillars is .90 m, the width of the inner pillars is .87 m; the width of the central arch is 2.96 m, and the width of the side arches is 2.65 m. The pillars are 2.18 m tall and .25 m thick. On the right side the total height of the restored arch is 4.50 m. The central arch was slightly higher than the side arches, in keeping with its greater width.

The pillars had flat pilasters 2 cm thick. The bases and the capitals of the pilasters are similar to those in catacomb 14. The profile of the bases includes a plinth, a torus, and a cyma reversa, exactly like the bases of the pilasters in the entrance wall. This type of base is not as common as the Attic base; however, it is very widespread in Roman architecture. In Palestine it is sometimes found in buildings of the Roman period.[113] The capitals are molded like those of the façade of catacomb 14; that is

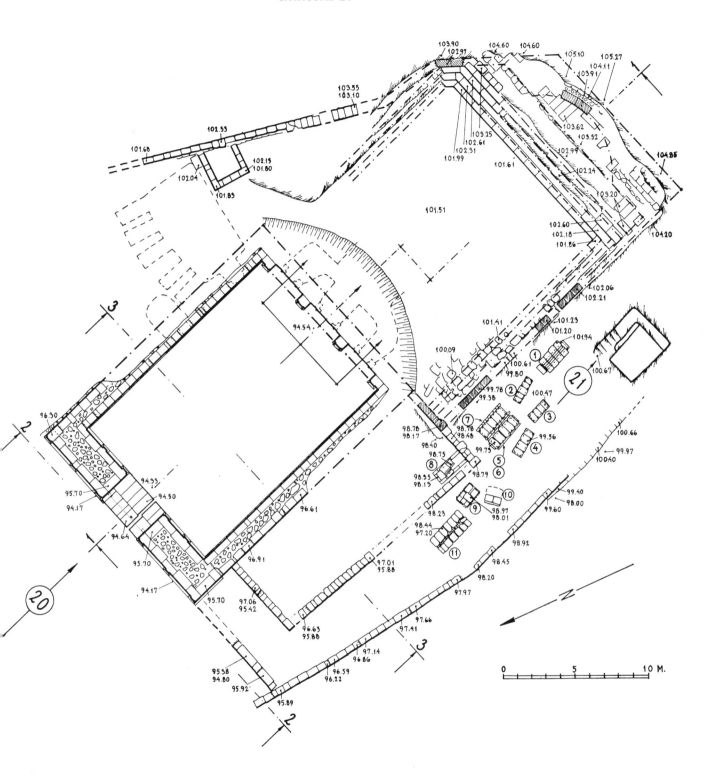

Fig. 35 Courtyard of catacomb 20, the benches above the catacomb, and the outer tombs 1–11

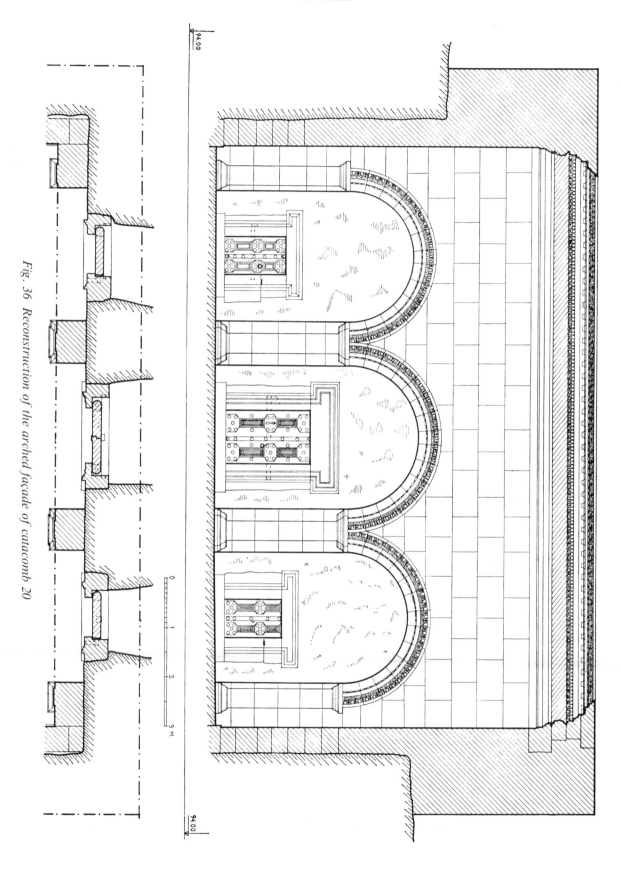

Fig. 36 Reconstruction of the arched façade of catacomb 20

to say, they have an ovolo, cavetto, and abacus. In contrast to the façade of catacomb 14, the voussoirs here are decorated with two broad fasciae separated by a bead and reel pattern; a bow-like pattern; and an ovolo decorated with egg and dart pattern (Pl. XXXII, 2).[114]

The façade wall was a number of courses higher than the arches. The estimated height of 8 m (see the restoration of the façade in fig. 36) is based on the level of the floor of the upper structure which is behind the façade, plus the estimated height of the parapet (see section 1–1, fig. 44). The upper part of the façade ended, apparently, in a richly-decorated entablature. In Plate XXXII, 1, there is a photograph of part of the entablature which was pieced together from fragments strewn in the debris of the courtyard.[115] From bottom to top the entablature is composed of an architrave (fig. 37, no. 12), a frieze (no. 11), and a cornice (nos. 9 and 10). Several stones of each part were recovered, except for no. 10 of which only two small fragments were found. The architrave, .48 m high, consists of two bands separated by a plain astragal and a cyma reversa. The convex frieze is torus shaped and fluted obliquely into a rope pattern. It is .35 m high. The cornice consists of two stones: the lower one (no. 10) has an egg and dart pattern, dentils, and cavetto. In the lower part of the upper cornice (no.9) there are square modillions separated by various geometric patterns, mainly groups of four circles. The upper part has a cyma recta decorated with schematic palmettes carved in relief. Below the cyma there is a bead and reel pattern.

Apparently this entablature was not limited to the façade alone but extended to the other walls of the courtyard as well. This assumption is based on a frieze stone with rope pattern which had an internal corner (see fig. 37, no. 17) and also on the fact that other stones were found which, because of discrepancies in details, could not have belonged to the façade. Thus, for

example, cornice stones were discovered which terminated in a cavetto instead of a cyma recta (no. 16); plain torus stones (no. 14) without the rope pattern — one of them (no. 18) a horizontal corner stone whose function is unknown; and architrave stones without an astragal separating the two bands (no. 15). Some of these stones may possibly have originated in the façade of the entrance wall.

Even though Mr. Dunayevsky's suggested restoration of the courtyard wall in figure 51 is based only on existing remnants of the lower part of the wall, it is most likely quite close to the original. The pilasters were found in situ; the arches would obviously be required since so large an opening (Phase I) could not possibly have been spanned by a horizontal lintel. Nevertheless, it is possible that the cornices were simpler. The continuation of the cornice on the western wall corresponds to the existing socle.

We have already dealt with the significance of the arched façade in the discussion on catacomb 14. Here, too, the function of the arcade was to decorate the tomb and to lend it a monumental appearance. The architecture, however, is more ornate than in catacomb 14. The closest parallel to the entablature at the top of the wall was found at Beth She'arim itself, in the mausoleum above catacomb 11. This mausoleum, discovered by Prof. Mazar, is attributed to the third century C.E., on the basis both of its architectural style and of a sarcophagus decorated with a depiction of Leda and the Swan which was found there.[116] The mausoleum also has a frieze in rope pattern, a rather rare feature. The workmanship of the carved moldings on the façade of catacomb 20 is inferior to that of the mausoleum. The explanation might perhaps lie in the fact that it was built of soft stone. In the early Galilean synagogues of the third century C.E. the combination of architrave, convex frieze, and cornice is very frequent — both above the entrances and above the

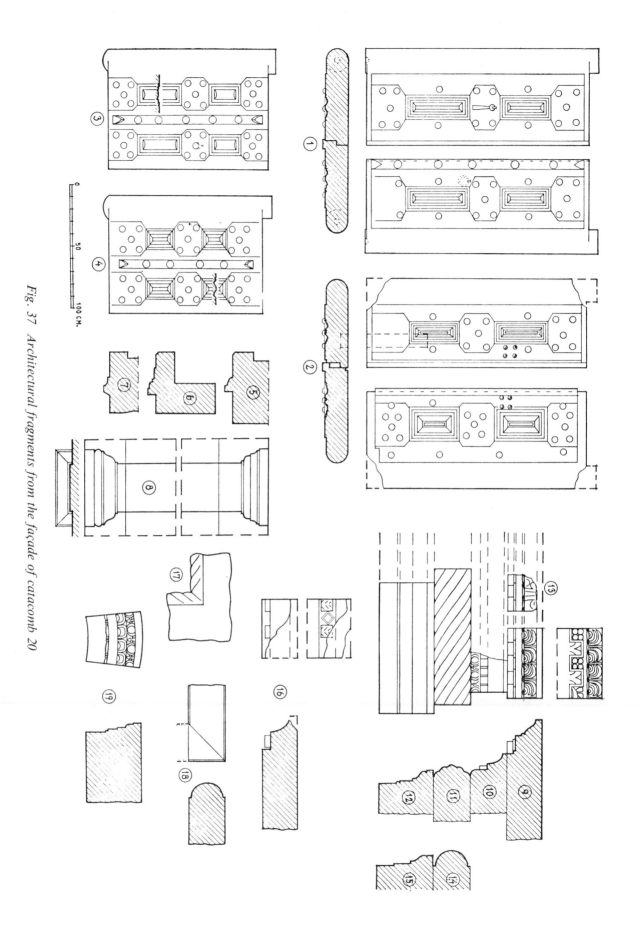

Fig. 37 Architectural fragments from the façade of catacomb 20

90

internal colonnades of the building.[117] The frieze above one of the entrances of the synagogue at Bar'am is also decorated in rope pattern.[118] In all these instances both the architrave and the frieze are made of monolithic stones, whereas in catacomb 20 each part is separate, as in the cornice.

The most characteristic feature of the entablature is the convex frieze which replaces the straight classical frieze. This type was apparently developed in the second century C.E. in Asia Minor and Syria and became an important element in monumental buildings.[119] Western Roman architecture adopted this frieze at a later period. Interesting parallels may be found in Roman temples in Syria where this entablature decorates the tops of walls,[120] or in the triumphal arch in Gerasa[121]—all from the second century C.E. It seems, therefore, reasonable to date the façade of catacomb 20 to the end of the second century or the beginning of the third. This subject will be discussed again later. Meanwhile, it should be pointed out that the classical tradition is still very prominent in the profile of the architrave with a cyma reversa and two fasciae, similar to the second century buildings in Gerasa. On the other hand, the baroque form found in the synagogues of the third century is already a deviation from this tradition.[122] The Entrances. Each arch contains an entrance which leads into the catacomb.

The central arch and the main doorway which led directly into the main hall were entirely destroyed; only the threshold and the lower parts of the two jambs remained in situ. In the courtyard, in front of the façade, four broken door slabs were found, two of them lying directly in front of the main entrance (Pl. XXXI, 1). We thus have two double doors, both fitting the main entrance. The lintel was not found at all. The entrance was made of very hard stone. The jambs of the central entrance were molded with two fasciae, an ovolo, and a fillet (see fig. 37, no. 6). The width of the entrance is 1.10 m and its estimated height is 1.75 m.

All the hinges of one of the double doors were broken (see fig. 37, no. 2). This is additional proof that heavy doors of this type could not withstand the strain of frequent use and it was, therefore, necessary to have a small door for daily use. This arrangement may be compared to the doors of catacomb 14. The height of the door slabs is 1.85 m and their total width, 1.50 m. They are decorated with the usual panels and studs. These two door slabs are not identical, nor do they close tightly, as if they had originally been intended for two separate doors. At the top of the two wings there are four holes arranged in a square; apparently, instead of the usual door ring, a different system was used here for pulling the door closed — perhaps a square metal plate held in place by four nails from which the door ring was suspended. On the inner lower part of the left door wing, there is a groove corresponding to a recess in the threshold. Evidently, there was a vertical bolt in addition to the horizontal one which closed the two doors from the inside.

After this door went out of use because the hinges broke, a new double door was installed (see fig. 37, no. 1). This door also is now broken; however, all its parts were found. The customary door decorations were used, but there is an additional carved door knocker on the left wing. Each of the door wings had rings, in contrast to the double door of catacomb 14 where there were no rings. The two wings were well matched and closed neatly. They were locked from the inside by a horizontal bar which was held in place by two recesses in the jambs. In the middle of the threshold there was also a bolt recess, evidently for an additional vertical bar to reinforce the shutting of the door.

The upper door hinges are cylindrical as usual; however, instead of the lower ones, there are hemispherical depressions 6 cm in diameter. In the threshold of the door there are flat square depressions, 20×20 cm, 1.5 cm deep, instead of the regular sockets.

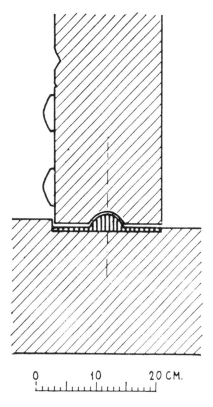

Fig. 38 Central door; reconstruction of the
hinge socket

The eastern entrance, .78 × 1.30 m, leads into a small corridor which turns sharply into the central hall. The door jambs and the lintel are surrounded by a cyma molding (fig. 37, no. 5). The door wing, of the usual pattern, was broken (fig. 37, no. 3). The door was locked with the customary bolt and key. However, the two recesses on the inside of the door jamb are evidence of another horizontal bar lock, similar to that in the double door, a rare feature in single doors. When this door was closed from the inside, the exit was via the second side entrance to the West.

The western entrance also leads to a corridor and makes a sharp turn into the main hall. This door, decorated in the usual fashion, was not damaged (Pl. XXXIII, 1). It had two locking systems as well. One was a regular lock operated by a key through a hole in the door jamb; the second was a bolt (missing at present) which moved in a vertical groove on the inner side of the door slab and was operated from the outside through an elongated slit in the middle of

Apparently, each of these recesses contained a bronze plate with a hemispherical protrusion on top. These bronze plates have disappeared; in figure 38 there is a suggested restoration of this apparatus. This system is the exact opposite of the one in the entrance of catacomb 14, where the bronze hemispherical hinge is joined to the door and turns in a socket in the threshold.

The system of hinges in catacomb 20 was also used in the double door found dismantled in the vicinity of catacombs 5–8.[123] In one wing of this door which was found intact and is now kept at the Hebrew University, there is a socket where residues of the green patina from the bronze hinges are still apparent. A similar installation was found in a heavy marble door of a Macedonian tomb.[124] Here, however, the system was improved — both the protruding hinge in the threshold and the socket in the door were bronze plated.

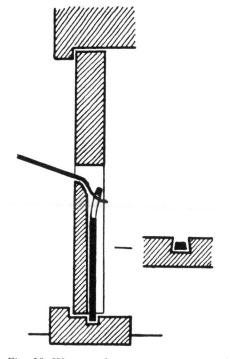

Fig. 39 Western door; reconstruction of
vertical bolt apparatus

the door (fig. 39). The key was evidently a long bar, bent at the end (see the suggested installation in fig. 39). A key of this type and its operation are described in Greek drawings (fig. 40). Great care was given to securing the catacomb against robbery and pillage to the extent that double locking systems were installed in each of the three doorways.

A section of plaster preserved near the western entrance is evidence that the rock between the entrances and the arches was plastered. The lower layer of plaster was rough and had herring-bone incisions in order to strengthen the bond with the top layer of plaster. Near the pillars of the arch a small section of red plaster was found. Another feature is worth noting: a course of stone was uncovered in front of the entrance, laid on a thin layer of earth. It is .47 m wide and .33 m high. Since this course is higher than the threshold of the entrance, it means that it was built after the door had gone out of use.

The Catacomb

In the narrative of the pillage which befell the necropolis of Beth She'arim, the plunder of catacomb 20 is a chapter in its own right. While the robbers left almost nothing behind except destruction and damage in

Fig. 40 Greek drawing showing operation of bolt with use of key

the other catacombs — and we have no way of dating these hit-and-run robberies — in this catacomb they found numerous sarcophagi whose "treatment" required considerable time. Indeed, there is evidence that their stay in the catacomb was quite prolonged. Both in the central hall in other rooms there is an accumulation of stamped earth 20–50 cm thick. In this debris there are clear traces of human occupation: soot; organic materials, like pieces of wood and cloth; shards, including shards from cooking pots; bones of animals and fowl; and above all, close to 120 clay lamps dating later than the main burial period of the catacomb. By means of these lamps, it can be established that the catacomb was first breached at the end of the Byzantine period and was finally robbed in the Arab period (see the discussion on lamps).

The catacomb was occupied from time to time even after the robbery. The large breach in the main entrance was repaired with big stones and heavy coffin lids (see photograph 1 in Pl. XXXI which shows two lids still standing in the entrance). However, even in the Mameluke period (thirteenth–fifteenth centuries C.E.) and subsequently, the catacomb still served as a shelter, e.g., for Arab shepherds. The entrance was through the left opening which was partly blocked by a coffin placed inside. This late date is evidenced by Arabic shards found inside and outside the catacomb.

After the catacomb was completely covered with debris, there was a tremendous collapse of the rock at the southern end of the cave. The *terminus post quem* of this collapse can be determined by the fact that there were no traces of human intrusion above the soft, light-colored rock debris covering the pillaged sarcophagi. The extent of this collapse is indicated in the plan of the catacomb, published in the preliminary report.[125] Since then, we have been able to clear a few rooms of debris. In addition, there were other smaller rock falls in a few places in the catacomb.

The Plan of the Catacomb (figs. 43 and 44). This catacomb was planned on the principle of a long central hall, partitioned into rooms from which wings branch off on both sides. These wings are in no way symmetrical either in size or in form, nor are they the result of unified planning and implementation. Apparently after the quarrying of the central hall, a wing was added from time to time according to need and feasibility. These wings vary in size: the first to the left is long (about 47 m) and has several rooms; the other wings contain two or three rooms or sometimes a single room only. The passage between the rooms is through archways hewn into the rock. In the central hall and in the long eastern wing ashlar archways were also built (similar to the arch in catacomb 14), in order to protect the rock ceiling from potential collapse. None of these archways has been totally preserved; in general, only the lower stones of the jambs have remained. However, these built archways did not collapse as a result of a rock fall since, with one or two exceptions, no collapse of the ceiling can be detected at these places. It seems more reasonable, therefore, to assume that they were dismantled by the tomb robbers for their ashlar stones. In fact, in the catacomb itself very few of these stones were found.

Meticulous symmetry and planning are to be found only in the entrances: the central entrance, the two side entrances and the two corridors leading into the central hall are all executed according to a plan which, it seems, has no exact parallel elsewhere. It is true that catacomb 14 was planned according to the same scheme; however, this plan was not fully implemented. It is possible to explain this unusual plan as due to the system of closing and opening the doors which demanded at least two entrances. However, it seems more likely that the façade, with its three elaborate entrances, was planned for architectural symmetry and impressiveness.[126] In this connection, the similarity with the triple entrances of the synagogues of that period should be pointed out. An earlier parallel of three entrances leading into a burial chamber may be found in a burial cave of the first century C.E. in the Valley of Ben Hinnom in Jerusalem.[127]

An important factor which influenced the planning of the catacomb and its size was the use of sarcophagi. On the one hand, this necessitated ample floor space; on the other hand, it limited the possibility of hewing graves in the walls of the rooms. It is obvious that the two methods of burial — in quarried graves and coffins — were used at one and the same time, and that the various rooms were planned in accordance with these needs. Some of the rooms were intended only for sarcophagi, for example, the row of rooms extending from room X South to room XXIV. In these rooms no graves whatsoever were hewn into the walls though there are some special recesses for sarcophagi. Most of the rooms, however, did have cut graves in addition to sarcophagi.

The hewn graves are of four types:

1. Arcosolia with one trough grave only. The arcosolia were rarely enlarged by the addition of one or two trough graves parallel to the first. It is noteworthy that the arcosolium with several trough graves, which is so common in most of the catacombs, is entirely absent from catacomb 20.

2. Niches for bone deposits. A trough grave in such a niche was covered with horizontal stone slabs; when there was a shelf in the niche, it was enclosed with vertical slabs.

3. Kokhim. Only a few single kokhim were found.

4. Rectangular graves sunk into the floor of the room. Of these too, only few were found.

In catacomb 20 a total of about 200 graves of various types was hewn.

The chronological relationship between burial in hewn graves and burial in coffins is problematic. In most cases it is clear that the accepted procedure of hewing graves into the walls preceded the placement of coffins in front of them. On the other hand, there are some arcosolia or niches which were not hewn in the usual manner or at a uniform height. This gives the impression that the location of the niches was sometimes determined by the prior placement of the coffins near the wall.

The sarcophagi are indicated in the plan of the catacomb (fig. 43) according to their position at the time of discovery — sometimes singly, sometimes in groups. They were generally left in place, and only a few were transferred to different locations. As to the arrangement of the coffins — apparently changes were made from time to time while the catacomb was still in use. Expediency dictated that sometimes they be crowded into the rooms and even into the entrances, where they barred the passage into the rooms (e.g., rooms VII, XI, and XVI). A few coffins were evidently moved by the occupants of the catacomb or tomb robbers who, after pillaging the catacomb, systematically broke the marble sarcophagi. Mere fragments remain of the marble sarcophagi; they will be discussed later.

The tomb robbers were very thorough indeed. All the arcosolia, niches, and kokhim — even those hidden behind the coffins — were breached and completely emptied of their contents. The same applies to the sarcophagi. Of 125 coffins only one remained unbreached (no. 81). In order to search for valuables, the tomb robbers used to remove the bones through the breaches and scatter them on the floor. In the course of time, these bones were covered with moist dust and rock fall; thus, nothing whatsoever remained of them. Bits of bone dust are the only evidence of the bodies that were once interred in the coffins.

The Eastern Entrance Corridor. The visitor entering this corridor will have to bend his head. If he looks carefully straight ahead of him, he will notice a Greek inscription incised on the wall in very thin lines. The inscription runs (fig. 41):[128]

ΘΑΡCΙΤΕ
ΠΑΤΕΡΕC ΟCΙΟΙ
ΟΥΔΙC ΑΘΑΝΑΤΟC

"May you be comforted holy Fathers, no one is immortal."

Fig. 41 Greek inscription

Looking at the ceiling to the left, one can discern still another graffito (fig. 42):[129]

ΕΥΤΥΧΩC
ΤΗ ΥΜΩΝ
ΑΝΑCΤΑCΙ

"Good luck in your resurrection"

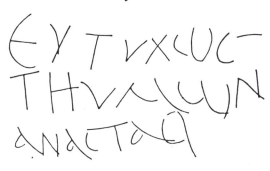

Fig. 42 Greek inscription

This inscription provides clear evidence that belief in the resurrection of the dead was widespread among Jews.[130] Apparently the two inscriptions were incised by visitors to the catacombs, perhaps well after the burial had taken place. The fact that the inscriptions were incised at the entrance of the catacomb and not near the graves leads us to believe that these words of consolation and blessing were not addressed to any particular persons whose graves were being visited, but rather to all the deceased who

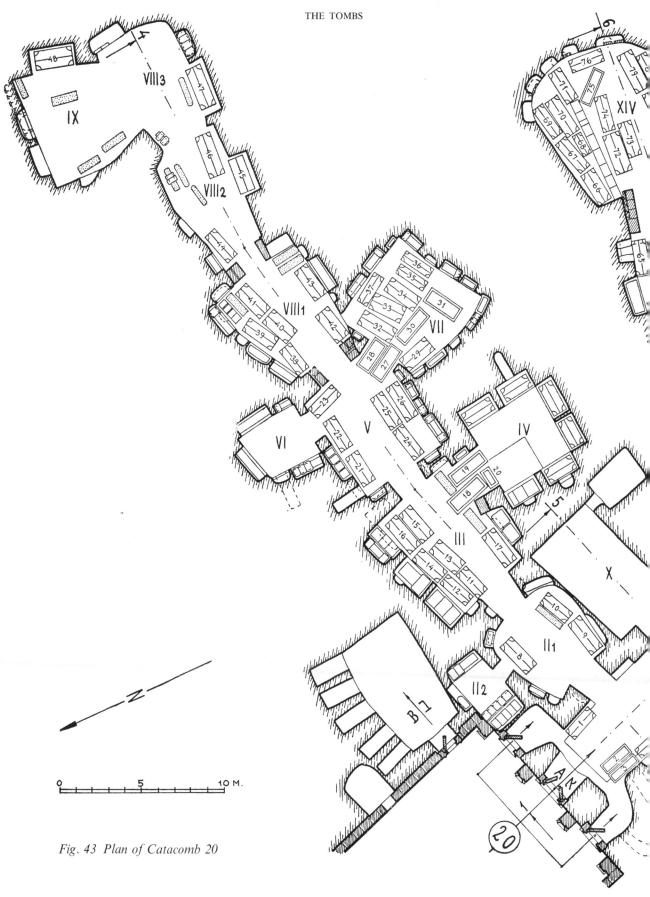

Fig. 43 Plan of Catacomb 20

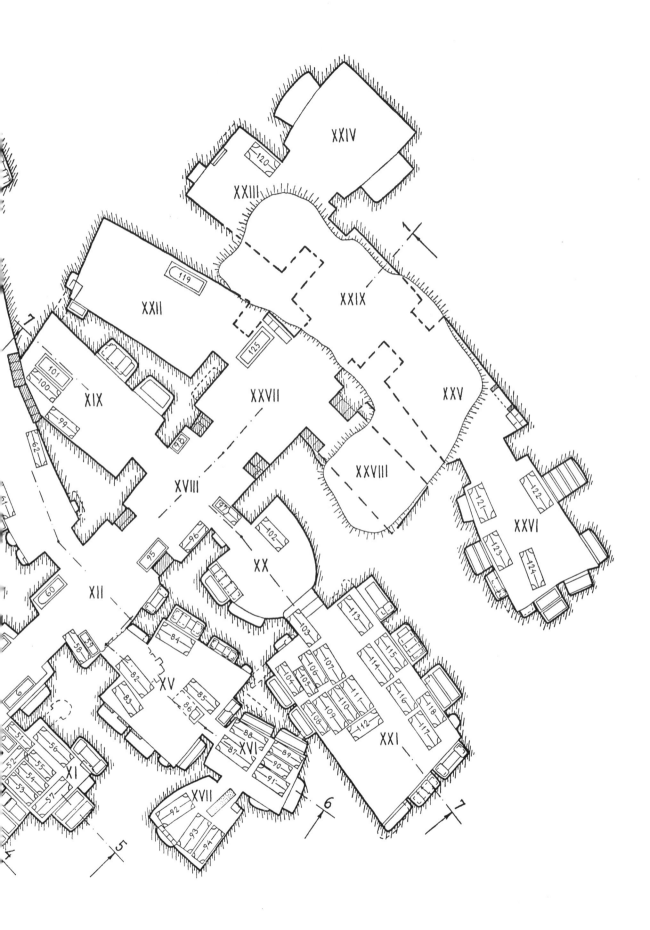

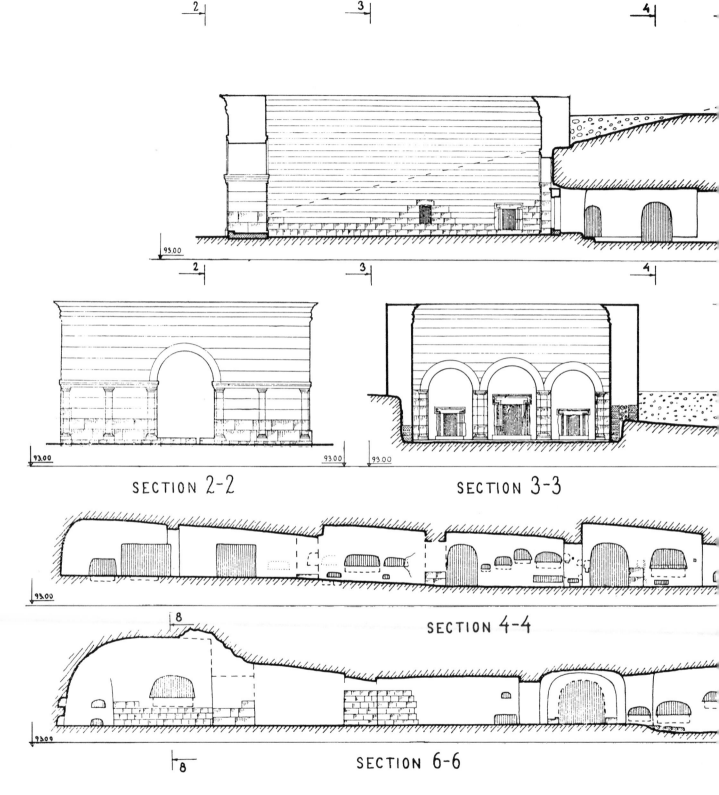

Fig. 44 Catacomb 20; sections

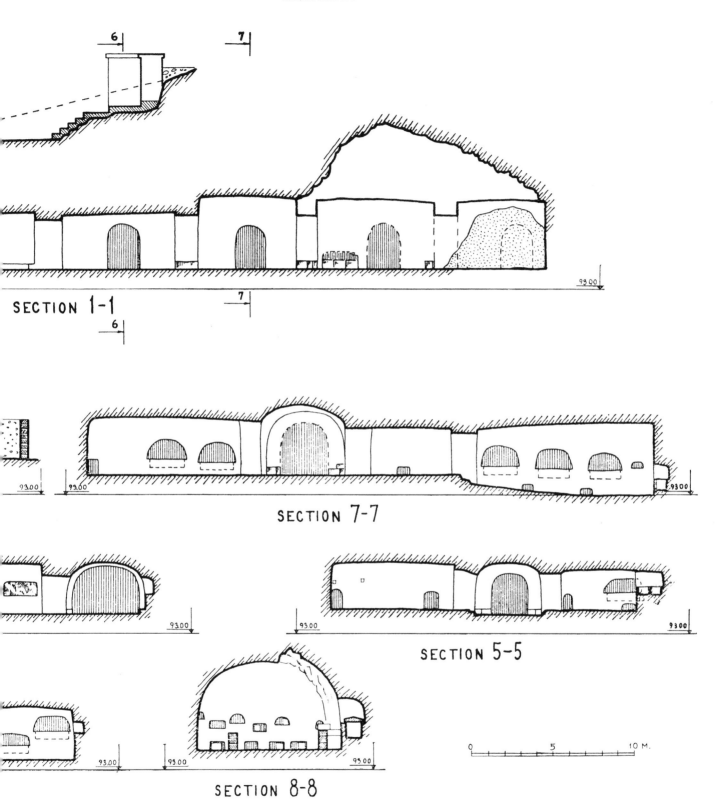

SECTION 1-1

SECTION 7-7

SECTION 5-5

SECTION 8-8

were buried in this catacomb, out of esteem and affection.[131]

On the left wall of the corridor a single Greek word was incised (fig. 45):

ΩΕΩΝΙΤΩΝ

Fig. 45 Greek inscription

We have no reasonable interpretation for this word.[132] It was doubtlessly written by a visitor, like the rest of the inscriptions in this corridor.

The Western Entrance Corridor. This corridor is the exact duplicate of the eastern one, except that its corner is rounded instead of angular. On the right-hand side there is a kokh—a puzzling feature since there is no reason to expect that someone would be buried so close to the entrance when there was ample space in the catacomb itself. On the front wall one word is incised in Hebrew (no. 13):

אחיה

"Her brother"

Apparently this is the anonymous signature of a visitor mourning for his sister.

Room I. This is the first in a row of rooms constituting the central hall — 44.50 m long and 4.00–5.00 m wide. The room itself is 13.80 m long and 2.85 m high. The ceiling is vaulted and benches are hewn all along the walls. These central rooms were not generally used for burial; however, in the western wall of this room there are two kokhim, two arcosolia, and the beginning of a niche. Sarcophagi nos. 1–7 were found in this room; they are plain and unadorned and were not found in their original position. Sarcophagi nos. 1–3 rest partly on a bench and partly on the earth. In the center of the eastern wall, an inscription is incised in fine letters (no. 14):

שלום ע...

"Peace u[pon]"

This inscription is not associated with any particular grave. To the right of it a cross was carved (perhaps by one of the first intruders at the end of the Byzantine period). On the entrance wall to the west of the door there is a short Arabic inscription which has not been deciphered as yet, probably the work of one of the occupants (pillagers?) from the Arab period.

At the beginning of room I a wing branches off to the East. In the center of the wing there is a row of rooms totaling 47.00 m in length.

Room II$_1$. The first room in this row, room II$_1$, is slightly rounded in plan and has a vaulted ceiling. It is 5.50 × 5.50 m in size. In the left jamb of the arched entranceway a niche was cut out at floor level. In the northern wall there are four small niches. In this wall there is also an entrance into room II$_2$. On the wall to the left of the entrance there was a four-line Hebrew inscription. However, it is now illegible because the red paint in which it was written was destroyed by humidity.

In the southern wall there is an incomplete arcosolium. To the right of the archway to room III there is another arcosolium above which there is a Hebrew inscription (no. 16):

רבי יהושוע בירבי הלל בן
אטיון מש...
בשלום

"Rabbi Joshua, son of Rabbi Hillel, son of Ation may his resting place be in peace."

Judging by the shallowness of the grave, we may assume that only the bones of Rabbi Yehoshua were deposited here and not his body. The three sarcophagi in this room are all plain and crude. In the floor near sarcophagus no. 10 there is a pit grave.

Room II$_2$. This is a small room, 2.40 ×3.00 m in size. In the side walls there are arcosolia containing trough graves covered with stone slabs. In the wall opposite the entrance there are two niches: one near the ceiling and one at floor level. From the second niche a breach was made into the room with the kokhim, whose actual entrance is from the courtyard. Below the western arcosolium there is a pit grave covered with stone slabs. It is noteworthy that the sealing stones of the graves in the floor were generally not found in situ.

Room III. In the jambs of the entrance which leads into this room there are two small burial niches, one flat and one arched; there are also two small recesses for clay lamps. Recesses of this type were found sporadically in many arcosolia in this catacomb and were not always recorded in the description of the cave. The room is 5.00 × 7.40 m in size. It has a squat vault ceiling, 3.40 m high. In the center of the ceiling a loop was carved, analogous to the suspension loops commonly found carved in the rock. An eternal light was perhaps suspended here.

To the left of the entrance there is a small niche. In the northern wall there are three arcosolia with fine arches. The trough graves were covered with large dressed sealing stones, 32 cm thick, which were joined with mortar. Most of them were found in situ. In the right arcosolium, behind the first grave, a second trough grave was hewn. Beneath the arcosolium in the eastern wall there is a niche. To the left of the entrance, near the ceiling, there is another long niche. To the right of the entrance two small niches were cut out, one of them at floor level. In the southern wall there is an arcosolium beneath which there is a very low niche. To the right of the entrance into room IV, the rock was strengthened by two stones; very likely there were more originally.

The sarcophagi found in this room also are plain. They are arranged along the northern wall in two rows and completely block the approach to the graves in the wall. The covers of several of the coffins have broad flat acroteria. The cover of sarcophagus no. 15 was slightly moved aside by the tomb robbers. The overhanging part of it protected the inscription on the front of the coffin from damage by water which penetrated through the ceiling (Pl. XXXIV, 1). The inscription (no. 17) runs thus:

אלו ארונות הפנימית והחיצונית

שלרבי אניאנה וש...

הקדושים בניו ש...

"These sarcophagi, the inner and the outer, belong to Rabbi Aniana and to...the holy ones, the sons of..."

The second coffin mentioned in this inscription is no. 16, which stands behind sarcophagus no. 15. This inscription is particularly interesting since the title "the holy ones" is very rare (see the discussion on the inscriptions). On sarcophagus no. 17 the following name (no. 18) is incised:

קירילא

"Kyrilla"

Incised lines are visible on the lid of this sarcophagus, perhaps of letters which are illegible. Two pit graves were cut into the floor of this room.

Room IV. The entrance into this room is blocked by the lower parts of three broken sarcophagi, one of them a child's In the left jamb of the entrance, there is a small niche for a bone depository. The room is nearly square (4.40 × 4.20 m) and has six fine arcosolia, two in each wall. All the trough graves in these arcosolia are covered with coffin lids (Pl. XXXIV, 2), except for the first arcosolium to the right of the entrance which is covered with the usual stone slabs. These coffin lids are thinner than usual. In the two arcosolia to the right, there are small niches for bone depositories. One of the arcosolia in the back wall contains a kokh. In the floor near the entrance a square recess was hewn, 40 cm deep. Its function is not clear.

R o o m V. Recesses for lamps were cut into both jambs of the entrance. In the right jamb, about 25 cm above the floor, there is a small niche. Approximately 1.10 m above it, a little to the right, a name is inscribed in fine lines:[133]

ΑΓΡΙΠΠΑC

"Agrippas"

It is doubtful whether there is any connection between the name and the niche; more likely the name was inscribed by a visitor. In the western wall, on both sides of the entrance, two small niches were cut out, one above the other. In the middle of the northern wall there is an arcosolium covered with the customary stone slabs. To the left of this, about 1.00 m above the floor, there is a kokh. At floor level there were two niches whose sealing stones were still in situ. In the southern wall there is one niche and three arcosolia of various sizes. In the right corner there is a long niche covered with several vertical slabs.

Of the six sarcophagi found in this room (Pl. XXXIV, 3), sarcophagus no. 25 is particularly noteworthy. It is decorated with garlands; on its lid is the longest Hebrew inscription found at Beth She'arim (Pl. XXXIX). The inscription (no. 15) runs thus:

כן (=כאן) הן מנחות אטיו בתו שלרבי

גמליאל בן נחמיה שמתה

בתולה בת עשרין ושתים

שנה ואטיון בתו שלרבי

יהודה בנו שלרבי גמליאל

שמתה בת תשע

שנים

וששה חודשים עמידת[ן]...

"Here they lie, Atio, the daughter of Rabbi Gamaliel, son of Neḥemiah, who

died a virgin at the age of twenty-two years, and Ation, the daughter of Rabbi Judah, the son of Rabbi Gamaliel, who died at the age of nine years and six months. May their resurrection [be with the worthy]."

Since the girl and her aunt were laid in one coffin, it may be assumed that only the bones were deposited. We moved the lid bearing the inscription to room I near the entrance in order to protect it from dampness.

R o o m VI. This room, which branches off to the north, was entirely empty. Three of its walls contain arcosolia and niches. One kokh was also discovered here.

R o o m VII. This room is outstanding for its numerous niches hewn at various levels, some of them near the floor. All of them have a small trough grave for a bone depository. In the right wall there are five niches; in the left wall, five; in the wall opposite the entrance, four. To the left of the entrance a small niche was found covered with a stone slab. When it was opened, only bone dust was discovered. In the left corner of the room a large breach was made into room VIII.

The majority of the twelve sarcophagi discovered in this room are plain and primitive. One of them is decorated with a tabula ansata and garlands similar to coffin no. 54. One of them bears three discs. On sarcophagus no. 27, standing right in the entrance, there are remnants of a long Hebrew inscription, now illegible due to the fading of the paint. On the other side of the sarcophagus, in the center, there is a protruding band on which a schematic branch is incised. These two coffins block the entrance to the room. On the left jamb there is a short, partially blurred, Hebrew inscription (no. 19): קירה

ש...

שלום

"Kyra sh ... peace"

Room VIII₁. This room is 5.40 × 6.60 m in size. The archway to the room was built of stones, but only a few remained in the jambs. The unusual arrangement of the niches and arcosolia in the northern wall is interesting: on the left side, the arcosolia were hewn above the sarcophagi; whereas on the right side, where there are no sarcophagi, the niches were cut out at various levels, some of them near the floor. In the right-hand corner of the floor there are two pit graves, one of them covered with stone slabs. On both sides of the entrance to room VIII₂ there are two niches. Originally there was a built archway here of which only one foundation stone was preserved in the right jamb and two courses of large stones in the left jamb. In the middle of the southern wall there is one arcosolium, flanked by small niches. In the left-hand corner of the room there are two pit burials. Of the six sarcophagi found in this room, no. 43 is outstanding. It is decorated with rosettes and circular incised designs. The rest of the sarcophagi are plain (Pl. XXXV, 1).

Apparently, at a certain stage in the history of the catacomb this room was the last in the wing. In the rooms quarried subsequently certain changes in the character of the previous plan can be discerned. The rock is intermingled with flint, the hewing is rougher, and a sort of improvisation is noticeable in the planning of the graves — if, indeed, there was any planning at all. Now a new element may be observed: a special recess in the wall for the placement of a sarcophagus.

Room VIII₂. This room contains several interesting sarcophagi. We called one of them (no. 44) "the hunt sarcophagus" because there is a scene of a lion chasing a gazelle to the right of the rosette in the center of the coffin front. Sarcophagus no. 46 is "the gate sarcophagus" due to the architectural motif carved on the front. The lid of this coffin was found on the floor and later returned to its former position. It is lavishly carved with bands of floral and geometrical designs. On the wall, to the right of sarcophagus no. 45, an arcosolium was marked out but not hewn.

In the floor, in front of the "gate sarcophagus," there are four pit graves arranged at random. On one of these graves several cover stones were found. One of them bore the following Greek inscription (fig. 46):[134]

ΔΟΜΝΙΚΑ Η ΜΙΚΡΑ

"Domnika the little"

Fig. 46 Greek inscription

In this grave the remains of the bones of an infant were found. Similar remains were also found in the small pit grave at the entrance to room VIII₃.

The last decorated sarcophagus in this wing of the cave was placed in a special recess in the wall. This is the "lion sarcophagus" (no. 47). On it two lions are depicted standing on either side of a vase. The heavy lid, slightly longer than the coffin, had been thrown onto the floor (Pl. XXIV, 4), and later we put it back in place. In the floor, in front of the sarcophagus, there is a pit grave. In this instance as well, one senses the wish of the deceased to be interred near a particular sarcophagus.

Room IX. This room is 6.70 m wide. It was completely empty except for one sarcophagus in a recess in the eastern wall. Because many fragments of marble were found here, it may well be assumed that this

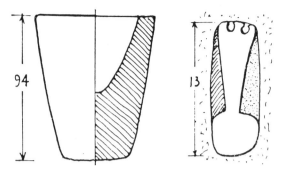

Fig. 47 Right: Carving in cave rock.
Left: Stone vessel found in courtyard

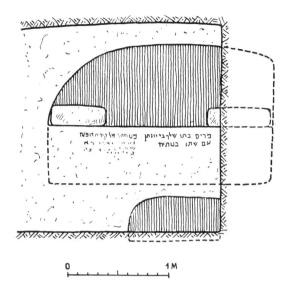

Fig. 48 Arcosolium in the corner of room XI

room originally contained more sarcophagi which were broken and removed. In the northern wall there is one arcosolium at a high level, another arcosolium and two niches at the usual height, and one arcosolium at floor level (in the northeast corner of the room). Four pit graves were cut at random into the floor.

This is the end of the eastern wing of catacomb 20. It is most impressive for its great length and for the numerous sarcophagi placed against the walls of almost the entire length of the hall.

R o o m X. This room is entered from room I in the central hall. It is 4.20 × 7.20 m in size. Apparently, it was intended for sarcophagi only since no graves at all were hewn. At the time of discovery it was entirely empty; however, various other remains proved that it was used as living quarters, perhaps by the people who pillaged the sarcophagi. Among the artifacts found were early Arabic shards, a knife, scissors, and a number of small articles. In the wall there are several recesses for clay lamps and suspension loops. In the southern wall two recesses were hewn. In one of them there was a small stone coffin and two lids of small sarcophagi.

The "eagle sarcophagus" (no. 56) is at present displayed in this room. It was transferred from room XI so that visitors might view it from all sides. In the rock of the left jamb of the entrance, above standing height, there is a strange bas-relief which is difficult

to interpret: a bottle-like object with a long neck (fig. 47). There are no means of determining when it was carved.

R o o m XI (Pl. XXXV, 2). This is the first and smallest ramification to the West. The room is 4.50 × 4.30 m in size. In the northern wall there is a deep arcosolium with an unusual feature for this catacomb: three trough graves, hewn one behind the other. To the right of this there is a small niche. In the western wall there is an arcosolium with two trough graves; and to the left of it, a niche. On the left side of the southern wall there is a kokh; and on the right side, an arcosolium below which there is a short narrow niche at floor level. The arcosolium is 1.03 m above the floor. The western end of the trough grave continues into the wall. It is 2.28 m long and .55 m deep. It is still covered with two slabs, one on either side. On the face of the grave, near the rim of the arcosolium, there are two red dipinto inscriptions, one beside the other (fig. 48). The inscription (no. 20) to the left is badly faded and only the first line is legible:

מנוחתה של קירא דומנה

"The resting place of the lady Domna"

The inscription to the right (no. 21) reads (Pl. XXXVIII, 1):

מרים בתו שלרבי יונתן
עם שתי בנותיה

"Miriam, the daughter of Rabbi Jonathan with her two daughters"

Here, then, we have additional proof of secondary burial. (For discussion about the inscriptions and associated problems, see the chapter on inscriptions.)

This small room was crammed with eight coffins, two of which blocked the entrance. Since it was not customary to place sarcophagi in this manner at the time of burial, some of them must have been brought here from other rooms. There are several interesting sarcophagi in this group. The most noteworthy is the "eagle sarcophagus" (no. 56), decorated on all sides with reliefs of eagles, lions, and bulls' heads.[135] Sarcophagus no. 57 is plain but of exceptional length: 2.65 m. It is the longest of all the coffins found, and it is 1.70 m high. The rest of the sarcophagi are identical, both in form and in ornamentation; all have a tabula ansata and plain garlands, analogous to sarcophagus no. 54 (Pl. LI, 1). In addition, the coffins are made of very hard stone and are meticulously finished. Among the finds in this room the most noteworthy is the sculpted marble hand of an Amazon (Pl. LIII, 1). Also of interest is an Arabic lamp found inside sarcophagus no. 56. Evidently this lamp slipped out of the robber's hand while he was trying to light up the interior of the sarcophagus through a small breach after he had removed all its contents.

Room XII. This room is entered through an archway, the only complete one in the central hall, entirely hewn in the rock. Of the three sarcophagi found in this room, the most noteworthy is no. 60 even though it is partially broken. It is decorated with three plain garlands and overlying discs, similar to the sarcophagus found in catacomb 23 (Pl. LIX, 3). The inside of the coffin is rounded at the head end. The bottom is slightly raised to provide a "pillow" for the head of the deceased. "Pillows" of this type were found in many sarcophagi. Near the sarcophagus numerous fragments of marble were found.

The second largest wing in catacomb 20 branches out to the east of room XII. It is 28.00 m long. In contrast to the other wings which are more or less straight, this one turns obliquely South. It has two main sections: room XIV, used as a storeroom for sarcophagi; and room XIII, which is long and narrow, actually just a passageway into room XIV.

Room XIII. This room is 19.00 m long and 4.00 m wide. It contains very few graves. At the time of discovery it contained only five coffins, all of them plain; however, there most probably were many more sarcophagi here originally. Coffin no. 65 is placed on a built foundation. At various levels in the left wall there are two arcosolia and several niches, some of which are partially closed with stone slabs. In the right hand wall, near the entrance, there are two small niches, one above the other. Approximately in the middle of the room, where this wall makes a slight turn to the right, there are indications of an arch hewn the whole width of the room. The right jamb was destroyed during the hewing of room XIX, when a large breach was formed in the wall. The breach was blocked with a wall 2.00 m high, made of seven courses of dressed stones. This wall is 4.20 m long. Apparently the protruding section replaced the archway jamb that had been destroyed (Pl. XXXVI, 2).

The passageway into room XIV consists of a very massive arch built in ashlar masonry. The three lower courses of the two jambs are preserved (Pl. XXXVII, 1). The jambs are 2.40–2.68 m wide; the total height of the three courses is 1.35 m. Their upper stones with the oblique surface are the springing courses which give rise to the arch. On the wall above the jamb the mortar lines of the missing masonry are still visible. In the debris at this spot there were many building stones but no voussoirs. Even though the rock above the arch collapsed, this could not have destroyed so massive an arch. On the contrary, it is more reasonable to assume that the rock collapsed precisely because the arch was dismantled. It, therefore, seems certain that these arch stones, too, were removed by robbers. The numerous fragments of marble found here prove that room XIII also originally contained marble sarcophagi.

Room XIV (Pl. XXXVII). This room is exceptional in several respects. It is unusually large: approximately 7.60 × 8.60 m in size. The eastern wall is rounded. The vaulted ceiling is irregular: along the length of the ceiling there is a crack that was formed, apparently, during the quarrying of the catacomb; this affected the shape of the ceiling. The curve of the vault to the left of the fissure is normal, and here the vault is 5.00 m high; however, to the right of the fissure the vault is steeper. The eastern rounded wall merges with the ceiling vault to form a dome. This is the highest room in the catacomb; the crack in the ceiling and additional rock falls added still more to its height (fig. 44, section 8–8).

In the southern wall of the room there is one arcosolium which contained a trough grave covered with stone slabs in the form of a gable. In the eastern wall there are small niches for bone deposits, some of which are still partially closed with vertical stone slabs. The niches vary in height and are either arched or flat. Five are at floor level; above them there are six additional ones, irregularly distributed (fig. 44, section 6–6 and 8–8). Another outstanding feature is the construction of two partitions of dressed stone all along the length of the room. The left partition has three courses which reach a total height of .94 m; the right partition has three courses totaling 1.02 m in height and also one stone of a

fourth course. It is not certain whether the partitions were originally higher; in any case, there were no evidential traces of mortar on the walls at the anticipated point of junction with the partition. On the other hand, it is possible that some of the dressed stones found in the debris originated from these partitions. It is obvious that they were built after the sarcophagi were placed in the room. Six sarcophagi were grouped along the northern wall; the partition was built up to sarcophagus no. 71 which was not moved from its place. Behind the right partition there was only one sarcophagus (no. 81). It is difficult to understand the purpose of these partitions since the wish to separate the coffins hardly seems to justify the investment of so much work.

In this room there were sixteen sarcophagi, all of them plain and unornamented except for one. On sarcophagus no. 71 there are carvings of a tabula ansata and plain garlands (similar to sarcophagus no. 54). One of the sarcophagi, on the left side of the partition, was placed on a built platform. Among the eight coffins standing in the center of the room a few were broken. Sarcophagus no. 72 is remarkable for its height: 1.78 m, including the lid. Coffin no. 73 was placed on two stones.

As mentioned previously, one sarcophagus (no. 81) was found behind the right partition. It was concealed in the corner and rendered invisible by the built wall. This is the only sarcophagus in the entire catacomb that was not breached — overlooked, apparently, even by the sharp eyes of the tomb robbers. It is plain and the cover is not sealed with mortar. We lifted the cover slightly (not without tense anticipation); however, the sight was rather disappointing. In the middle of the bottom there was only a small quantity of bones, with no fragments of a skull or funerary gifts. Nevertheless, we were able to make two deductions from these findings: first, it was additional evidence that funerary gifts were not interred with the bones (see above, the

description of the tomb of Aristeas in catacomb 13); second, sarcophagi were used for
bone depositories as well as body burials.
This conclusion was also reached on the
basis of several inscriptions on various
sarcophagi.

It is important to note that, even in this
crowded room, numerous marble fragments were found, several of them carved.
Many fragments of tiles — generally used
for covering clay coffins — were also discovered. It is quite possible that these
marble sarcophagi originally stood in room
XIII; after they were broken, some of the
fragments were thrown into room XIV. The
robbers left here shards of the early Arab
period.

Room XV. The left jamb of the entrance
contained an unusually wide niche which
caused the rock to weaken and, ultimately,
to collapse. In the threshold of the entrance
there was a sort of stone ramp which
sloped into the room. The purpose of this
ramp was undoubtedly to facilitate the
transfer of sarcophagi into the rooms where
the floor was lower than that of room XII.
In the left wall of this room there are two
arcosolia and a small niche, at different
levels. In the right wall there are two long
niches which were sealed with vertical slabs.
In one of them five of the six slabs were
still in situ. We were, thus, provided with
an excellent example of the method by
which niches of this type were closed (fig.
49). Near the corner of this wall there is a
low niche and above it a very small niche,

too small to have served even as a bone
depository.

In the wall opposite the entrance two
arcosolia were hewn: one to the right of the
entrance leading into room XVI, and one
to the left. The trough grave in the latter
arcosolium is covered with the broken lid
of a sarcophagus. On the back of the
arcosolium a disc was carved, a modest,
solitary decorative relief on the wall of this
catacomb. In this room there were five
sarcophagi; one of them, the "mask sarcophagus" (no. 84), is particularly interesting. It was placed in front of an arcosolium
on a built platform. It has carvings of
columns, garlands, and rosettes; and on the
narrow side, the face of a bearded man.
This sarcophagus occupies an important
place in the iconography of Beth She'arim.
Room XVI. The entrance into this room
is high and narrow. It was found badly
crumbled but was restored. The rock of
the entire room is also in poor condition.
The entrance to the room was almost completely blocked by sarcophagus no. 87;
subsequent to its introduction, burial doubtlessly ceased in rooms XVI and XVII. It is
important to note that the last two sarcophagi deposited in this room (that is to
say, those closest to the entrance) were
placed on a 30–40 cm thick layer of earth,
which must have been brought here intentionally. This can only be explained by
the desire to have the sarcophagus in con-
tact with earth.

Sarcophagus no. 89 is the most important
in this room. It stands on a rock pedestal
which was evidently planned when the
room was quarried. The arcosolium behind
the sarcophagus was hewn higher up, proving that, when the arcosolium was fashioned, the sarcophagus intended for the pedestal was already taken into consideration.
on the left side there is a second arcosolium,
lower than the first (see section 6–6 in fig.
44). Sarcophagus no. 89 is very simple.
There is a Hebrew inscription (no. 28) on
its lid:

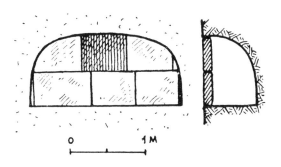

Fig. 49 Niche closed by stone ashlars

O   1 M

זו ארונו שלרבי הליל בנו שלרבי לווי שעשה
את המערה הזו

"This is the coffin of Rabbi Hillel, the son of Rabbi Levi who made this cave."

This inscription is most interesting since, for the first time, the name of a man associated with the construction of the catacomb is mentioned. It is not clear if the inscription refers to the whole catacomb or this particular room (see the chapter on the inscriptions).

Above the left arcosolium in the southern wall there are very faint traces of a red dipinto Greek inscription. It is, however, illegible. Sarcophagus no. 87 is ornamented with geometrical designs.

Room XVII. The entrance leading into this room crumbled almost entirely — as did most of the ceiling. Of the three sarcophagi in this room, no. 92 is the most worthy of attention; it is the tallest sarcophagus in the catacomb, 1.82 m including the massive lid, itself .77 m high. The sarcophagus weighs approximately eight tons. It has a very small cavity for a body burial. It is decorated with discs.

In this room there is only one shallow niche. It was cut out in the northern wall at floor level and was closed by three courses of stone totaling .95 m in height. These courses lean against the edges of the sarcophagi in front of them, i.e., the grave was cut after the placement of the sarcophagi. Evidently, somebody tried to bury these bones in an inconspicuous place.

In the floor between the sarcophagi and the entrance there is a long rectangular depression, 15 cm deep. It is too shallow to have been used for burial; however, it might possibly have been surrounded by stones. At any rate, many building stones of unknown function were found scattered on either side of the entrance, among them a nicely-dressed cornerstone molded with a cyma reversa (here doubtlessly in secondary use).

Room XVIII. This room is entered via an archway from room XII in the central hall. The arch was built of stone; however, only two of the stones were preserved, one on either side. Three sarcophagi were found in this room. Sarcophagus no. 96, decorated with a tabula ansata and garlands, is at present at the Hebrew University in Jerusalem. Sarcophagus no. 97 was restored to its original place. When discovered, this broken sarcophagus was standing near the jamb of the entrance to room XX, its decorated front facing the entrance. It was named the "acanthus sarcophagus B" and is outstanding for its fine carving. The arches leading to rooms XIX and XX had nearly disintegrated and were restored after the excavations.

Room XIX. This room faces east. As it is at right angles to the central hall, a breach was formed during quarrying into room XIII which stands obliquely to the central hall. As previously mentioned, this breach was blocked with stones. The room is spacious: 9.00×4.50 m and 3.30 m high. It is well finished and has a fine vault. In the southern wall there are two arcosolia; at the end of the wall there is a kokh. Three sarcophagi were found here of which no. 101, the "acanthus sarcophagus A," is the most noteworthy. It is broken and some parts are missing. The designs of the garlands and acanthus leaves are remarkable for their excellent workmanship. The decorated side faced sarcophagus no. 100. At present, sarcophagus no. 101 stands near the eastern wall. One of the workmen engaged in hewing the room, evidently wanting to display his talents, chiseled a human figure into the right wall of the room (Pl. XXXVI, 3).

To the West an additional wing branches off. It is 17.40 m long and consists of rooms XX and XXI.

Room XX. The semicircular form of this room is most unusual. It suffered severely from the crumbling of the walls and ceiling. The left wall was reinforced recently by a stone construction. Near the floor there was originally at least one small niche; in the right wall there are two niches. In the floor there is a pit grave covered with stones.

Room XXI. A huge rock fall covered all the sarcophagi and filled the room nearly to the height of the original ceiling. When the ceiling collapsed at the western end, a breach was opened into catacomb 23 which is at a higher level. In the northern wall there were two arcosolia that had crumbled; we, therefore, blocked them up with stones. We also had to restore the entrance to the room because of the danger of potential collapse. In the southern wall there are three well-cut arcosolia, a small niche to the right of them, and two tiny niches at floor level. In the entrance wall also, on either side of the opening there were niches.

The room is entered by a descent of two steps. The floor slopes downward. The length of the room is 11.20 m, the width 6.80 m, and the original height 4.20 m. The sixteen sarcophagi in this large room were arranged in rows. Five of them are particularly interesting because of their decorations and Hebrew inscriptions.

Sarcophagus no. 103, called the "gable sarcophagus," stands at the entrance. It has the following inscription (no. 25):

האָרון הזה...
בתו שלרבי יהושוע...
זכר
צדיקים לברכה

"This sarcophagus...the daughter of Rabbi Joshua. [May] the memory of the righteous be blessed."

The next inscription (no. 23) appears on the cover of sarcophagus no. 115. It reads:

זו ארונו שלרבי יושוע...

"This is the sarcophagus of Rabbi Joshua..."

On the front of sarcophagus no. 114, the following inscription is written (no. 22):

זוא ארונו שלשלושת בניו שלרבי יודן
בנו שלרבי ..שה

"This is the sarcophagus of the three sons of Rabbi Judan, the son of Rabbi [Mia]shah."

On the broken lid of sarcophagus no. 116,[136] the following inscription is incised (no. 24):

זו ארו[נ]ה שלקירה מגה
אשתו שלרבי יהושוע
בן לווי שלום

"This is the coffin of the lady Mega, the wife of Rabbi Joshua, son of Levi. Peace."

Sarcophagus no. 117, named the "shell sarcophagus," is exceptional for its rich decorations on the front and on the two narrow sides. The ornamental motifs include both floral and animal designs, as well as architectural and geometrical elements. On the front, the following inscription was written (no. 26):

זה ארונו ש....גמליאל בנו
שלרבי אליעזר.... בן שבע
עשרה שנה זכר צדיק
לברכה

"This is the sarcophagus of....Gamaliel the son of Rabbi Eliezer...seventeen years of age. [May] the memory of a righteous man be blessed."

Since the excavations, this inscription has faded and today it is no longer visible.

Three of the inscriptions mentioned above apparently referred to one family: Joshua, the father; Mega, his wife; and their daughter, whose name was not preserved (see the chapter on inscriptions).

The largest rock fall occurred in the southern part of the catacomb. Here such enormous quantities of rock collapsed that they piled up to a height of approximately 7 m and filled several rooms. The collapse extended to the end of room XVIII (Pl. XXXIV, 5) and entirely covered rooms XIX–XXVII and most of rooms XXII, XXIII, and XXV. We have already referred to the difficulties and dangers involved in removing such rock falls. Even today rooms XXV, XXVIII, and XXIX have not been entirely cleared.

Room XXVII. This is one of the passage rooms of the central hall. Between this room and room XVIII there was originally a built archway, of which only two courses of stone from the jamb pillars were preserved. A convex frieze stone was used in the construction of the western pillar, similar to those found in the courtyard. Apparently this was an extra stone.

In order to continue clearing the rooms and to avoid further collapse of the rock, it was necessary not only to build a new arch but also to strengthen and restore the adjacent walls. The length of the cleared room was 6.70 m and its width, 5.00 m. In the preserved part to the left of the opening in the eastern wall, a niche was hewn at floor level and was sealed with perpendicular stone slabs. We had to fill the niche in order to prevent further collapse of the wall. In front of the destroyed entranceway which led to room XXII, we discovered sarcophagus no. 25, called the "Nikae sarcophagus." It is decorated with a relief of two flying Nikae holding a wreath in their hands. Obviously, the sarcophagus was not found in its original place.

South of the sarcophagus there is a built course of stones, .42 m high, leaning against the rock wall behind it, at the side of the entrance to room XXIX. At present there is only a pile of fallen rock boulders at this spot. The jambs of the entrance are preserved to a height of about 1.00 m.

Room XXVIII. The entrance to this room also was constructed of stone. Of the jambs, two courses remained totaling .75 m in height. At the beginning of the southern wall there are traces of a burial niche, above which there are decorative red lines. The room has still not been cleared of the collapsed rock which reaches the ceiling. There are indications that the walls of the room were faced with stone.

Room XXIX. This is the last room of the central hall which begins, as previously mentioned, near the main entrance. It is still completely full of rock fall. Only the top of the back wall is visible; however, it is sufficient in order to prove that the central hall continues no further. Neverthless, we do not know whether there was a low opening or hewn graves in this wall.

Room XXII. This room was almost entirely empty. It is 9.10 m long and 5.30 m wide. It has only one sarcophagus (no. 119), decorated with rosettes and plain garlands. There were probably marble sarcophagi in this room since there are no hewn graves except for two small niches. In the northeastern corner of the floor there is a breach into a kokh of the neighboring room.

Room XXIII. (Pl. XXXVI, 1). Today this room is reached through a wide opening that had been cut, for obscure reasons, into the thick wall that separates this room from room XXII.[137]

In the northern wall of the room there are two niches, one of them at floor level. The walls of this room are smoothly dressed. This room has two unusual features: the first is a projecting cornice all along the walls beneath the vault, decorated with a zigzag pattern painted in red. The second is the relief of a large menorah in the eastern wall. This menorah is 1.90 m high and 1.25 m wide and juts out 12–36 cm from the wall. The branches of the menorah are plain; but they were partially disfigured with a sharp instrument. The shaft of the menorah was broken. The base, indistinct in shape, is attached to the floor. In our excavations this was the second carved menorah found on a wall (see above, catacomb 12). In the previous excavations, however, numerous reliefs of this kind were found in the catacombs. In this room there was only one sarcophagus (no. 120), decorated with discs.

R o o m XXIV. This room, the southernmost in the catacomb, is entered through a very wide opening. The room is 6.00 ×6.00 m in size. In the walls there are two empty recesses for sarcophagi. We may assume that at one time there were marble sarcophagi here since the room was found entirely empty.

After climbing over tall heaps of fallen rock, we finally reached the last wing to the West, which is 16.00 m long. It consists of two rooms.

R o o m XXV. Most of this room was full of rock fall. The only parts visible were the entrance leading to room XXVI and the upper part of the southwestern corner. Attached to the southern rock wall were a few courses of ashlars, 1.20 m thick. In this thick wall an arched niche, 1.26 m wide, was built (see fig. 50). The courses of stone at the sides and above the arch are missing. On the rock wall behind the niche and to the left of the arch there is a simple projecting cornice, similar to the one on the walls in room XXIII. In this corner also we were unable to clear entirely the debris and, therefore, we could not determine the purpose of the niche.

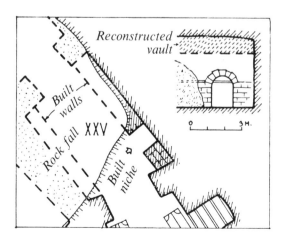

Fig. 50 Revised plan of room XXV.
Upper right corner; View of built niche

From the remaining masonry and from the traces of mortar visible on the western rock wall, it was evident that even in antiquity an impending collapse was feared. Therefore, as a preventive measure, the two long walls were faced with massive walls of stone, above which a barrel vault was built to strengthen the rock ceiling. Later on this vault, like all the built arches in this catacomb, was dismantled by the tomb robbers. As a result, the ceiling caved in; this, in turn, very probably led to a series of rock falls in the neighboring rooms where the rock was not solid.

R o o m XXVI. This room, the last in the row, has also not been entirely cleared of piles of rock (Pl. XXXIV, 6); however, at least its plan is evident. It is 7.80 m long and 4.40–5.50 m wide. The archway is completely preserved. In the southern wall there is a deep arcosolium containing four trough graves, one behind the other, and another arcosolium with one trough grave. In the northern wall there are five arcosolia and niches, varying in form and height from floor level. It is noteworthy that the arcosolia behind the two sarcophagi are hewn above them. In the western wall there are two arcosolia and three niches at different levels.

There are three sarcophagi in this room. No. 122 is named "the menorah sarcophagus" because it is decorated with a relief of a menorah on one of its narrow sides. On the other narrow side there are carved dolphins bearing a wreath. No. 124 is called the "column sarcophagus." Sarcophagus no. 123 is noteworthy because of the acroteria decorated with discs on the narrow ends of the lid. This motif does not appear on any of the other lids. All the debris surrounding the sarcophagi has not been cleared as yet.

The Upper Structure (figs. 35, 51; Pl. XXX, 1)

Above catacomb 20 remains were discovered of an open-air structure, similar to the

111

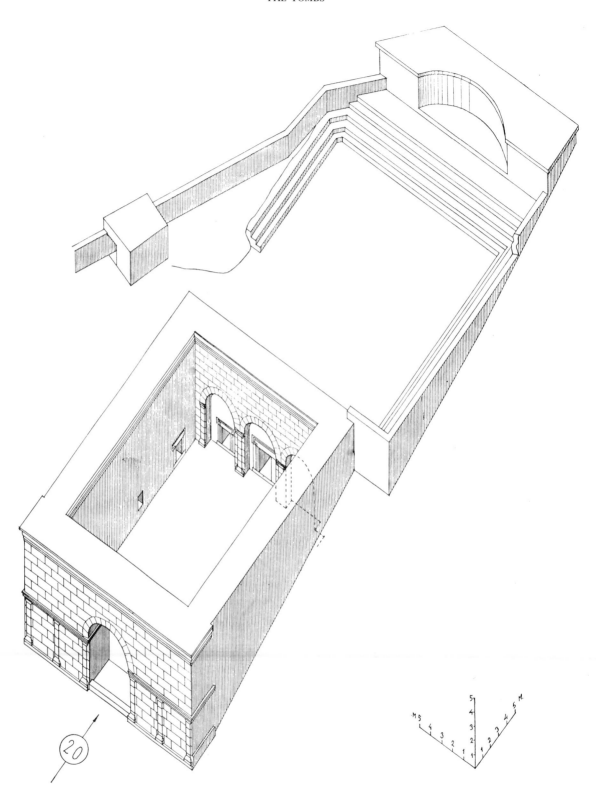

Fig. 51 Catacomb 20; restoration by I. Dunayevsky

type found above catacomb 14. To the North, it bordered on the courtyard; and to the South it terminated in a thick wall which contained an apsidal niche. The floor of the square enclosed by the benches was plastered with white *ḥawar* ("marl"), and is 101.51 m above sea level, i.e., 7.14 m above the courtyard floor. The building covers an area of 18 m from East to West, by 23.50 m from North to South. Only a few stones of the walls have remained. To the West a row of dressed stones of the first course was found in situ, laid on stepped rock. The thickness of the wall is made of one stone .50 m wide.

In the southern wall containing the apse only two stones of the first course of the apse proper remained (altitude 103.91 m), in addition to a few stones of the socle which constituted the apse floor. On the basis of these stones and the rock which rises irregularly behind them, it is possible to estimate the thickness of the wall, circa 3.50 m. The building is bounded on the East by the rising rock; however, no remains were found which would prove that the wall continued along the entire length. On the opposite side there is a diagonal wall running South to North which continues outside the boundaries of the building. This wall is 15 m long, and adjoining it are the remains of a small room, 2.50 × 2.50 m in size. This wall does not belong to the building since the course is laid on the natural slope (103.54 m on the South and 101.68 m on the North). Therefore, it may be assumed that this was a fence alongside a road which passed hereby. It seems that to the North the bench square was fenced by a parapet formed by the upper courses of the arched façade below. Several courses of the northwest corner of the building are preserved (98.78 m); they are built of ashlar masonry.

In contrast to the few stones remaining from the walls, a considerable number of stones from the benches was preserved. These stones, together with the tiers cut in the rock on which the complete benches rested formerly, give us a clear idea of the form of the bench construction. In order to create a broad flat area, the rock was leveled. Only in the northwest corner was it necessary to raise the natural level by constructing a platform of large stones. This platform very likely extended along the whole northern side; however, the rock collapsed here and everything fell down into the courtyard. To the South, along the entire width of the building, there are five benches. The fifth bench is at a height of 1.64 m above the floor and forms a sidewalk 1.50 m wide along the wall of the apse, similar to that in the open-air structure of catacomb 14. The apsidal niche is paved with large stones and is 2.01 m higher than the main floor. Its restored length is circa 8.00 m; its width, circa 2.00 m. At the western end of the wall containing the apse a few filling stones remained.

Along the western wall there are three benches of which only the lower parts hewn in the rock were preserved. The same is true of the eastern wall, where even less remained. In the southeast corner, the benches did not join at right angles, but diagonally. It is, therefore, likely that the wall was diagonal as well and that the corner of the wall containing the apse was cut diagonally. It is difficult to understand this strange arrangement except by assuming that some factor prevented right-angled construction. The road which supposedly passed through at this point was certainly not the reason, since it was not a main road. Therefore, there probably was some building — or catacomb — on the other side of the road which had to be taken into consideration during construction. Perhaps this is also the reason that the upper structure is not on the same axis as the courtyard below but is shifted slightly to the West. Nevertheless, it is worth recalling that there is also a similar phenomenon in catacomb 14, as yet unexplained. In both places the apsidal niche faces South toward Jerusalem. Because of the scanty remains, we do not know if the niche had any architectural decorations.

The upper structure of catacomb 20 was much larger and more spacious than that of catacomb 14. It extends over an internal area of 328 sq m (in comparison to the 117 sq m of catacomb 14, excluding the western part). The total length of the benches is 183 m (in comparison to the 65 m of catacomb 14), which provides a seating capacity of approximately 450 persons.

In our discussion of the structure above catacomb 14 we dealt with its function and significance. The same conclusions are applicable to the structure above catacomb 20. It also served as an assembly place for memorial days or, in the words of our fore-fathers, להושיב בו ישיבה על הקבר ("to call a meeting over the grave"). The seating of the congregation in a U-formation in the open air, on a high place overlooking the valley and the right architectural surround-ings doubtlessly made an indelible impres-sion on the participants.

Summary

The general arrangement of catacomb 20 is evidence of a broad, imaginative architec-tural conception (see the reconstruction of I. Dunayevsky, fig. 51). Viewed from the outside, the two components — i.e., the courtyard and the upper structure — are most impressive, the former in its size and monumental architecture, and the latter in its spaciousness and magnificent location. The third component, the catacomb which is not visible from the outside, is construct-ed on the same monumental scale, both in size and in its numerous ramifications. Completing the picture are the 125 large, heavy sarcophagi found in the catacomb and the many marble coffins placed there originally but subsequently broken and robbed.

The uniqueness of catacomb 20 will be discussed later in the chapter on the clas-sification and chronology of the catacombs. The finds of catacomb 20 will also be dis-

cussed further in detail. In addition, we shall deal with the various problems arising from these finds, for example: the figurative art of the Jews and the exclusive use of the Hebrew language in the inscriptions of this catacomb.

Just as the necropolis of Beth She'arim is a singular phenomenon in Palestinian ar-chaeology, so is catacomb 20 unique within the necropolis itself. This was a large project of immense proportions and demanded initiative, organization, vision, and re-sources. Extensive burials in sarcophagi is extraordinary, not only at Beth She'arim and in the whole of Palestine, but also in the entire ancient world, where hardly another single catacomb can boast so large a num-ber of sarcophagi. Generally, a mausoleum or catacomb contained only a small group of coffins.[138] It is difficult to explain what motivated the people of Beth She'arim to adopt this practice and to place so many coffins in one large catacomb. Apparently only catacomb 20 was intended for burial in sarcophagi. Since this manner of burial was very expensive, its introduction into the other catacombs as well was not feasible. In any case, till now, three isolated coffins only have been found outside this cata-comb. It is impossible to predict, of course, what remains still concealed in the extensive areas of the necropolis which have not as yet been excavated.

About 200 burial places of all types were found hewn in the rock of catacomb 20: arcosolia with trough burials, small niches, kokhim, and graves sunk in the floor. An especially outstanding feature is that while there are numerous niches for secondary burial — i.e., for the collecting of bones — there are only a few kokhim intended for burial of bodies. The trough graves in the arcosolia were generally intended for prima-ry burials but, at least in one case, the in-scription above the trough grave proves that the bones of three individuals were placed here. In other catacombs as well, trough graves were sometimes found which were used for the burial of bones brought from the Diaspora. It is very likely that the custom was to bring only the bones of the deceased, not their bodies.

By their very nature, the coffins were intended for bodies. However, the finds in coffin no. 81 and the contents of several inscriptions on the coffins are evidence that sarcophagi were also used for the burial of bones collected from other graves. It became clear, therefore, that in catacomb 20, the rock-cut graves and coffins included, there were more secondary burials than could have been assumed earlier. We do not know whether, or to what extent, catacomb 20 also served for the burial of Jews from the Diaspora. The epigraphic material will probably furnish valuable information on this subject. The abundance of Hebrew inscriptions on the one hand, and the almost total absence of Greek inscriptions in this catacomb on the other, are in conspicuous contrast to the wealth of Greek and paucity of Hebrew inscriptions in the other catacombs. This feature, together with the fact that almost all the inscriptions belong to rabbinical families, tend to support the assumption that this catacomb served as a burial vault for rabbis and their families, both local and countrywide, among whom the tradition of the Hebrew language was still strong. We may safely assume that the individuals buried in coffins — both of local limestone and of imported marble — belonged to the respected and wealthy class, since the preparation of an ornamented coffin or its transfer from the Diaspora certainly must have been very costly. Doubtless catacomb 20 must have been an ex-

clusive burial vault since it is the only one among all the catacombs excavated in Beth She'arim to this date in which extensive use was made of stone and marble coffins.

The author is inclined to think that the magnificent marble sarcophagi, decorated with Greek mythological scenes, belonged mainly to people from the Diaspora; however, there is no tangible evidence for this assumption. Up to now, we have not found in the Hebrew inscriptions of Beth She'arim any indications of the provenance of Diaspora Jewry, who customarily wrote in Greek. Perhaps there were indeed Greek inscriptions on several marble coffins, but this is difficult to determine since only small fragments of these coffins have been preserved. The use of coffins decorated with pagan motifs alongside the rabbis' graves strongly emphasizes the tolerance which the rabbis of that generation showed toward figurative art among Jews. This point will be discussed more fully later.

We did not find decisive evidence for the approximate date of the initial use of catacomb 20. Therefore, we must rely on typological considerations. Judging by the architectural features, the style of the marble coffins, the paleography of the inscriptions, the various artifacts, and the historical data, it can be estimated that the initial use of catacomb 20 may be dated to the time of Rabbi Judah Ha-Nassî, i.e., the end of the second century C.E. The catacomb served as a burial place until the destruction of Beth She'arim, in the middle of the fourth century. It was first broken into at the end of the Byzantine period and finally robbed in the Arab period.

10   CATACOMB 21 (fig. 52)

The courtyard of this catacomb is about 17.00 m to the West of the upper structure of catacomb 20 and South of the area where the outer graves were found. The courtyard is sunk about 2–3 m into the rock and is

3.60 × 3.40 m in size. A flight of irregularly hewn steps descends along the eastern side. The steps are .90 m wide. The courtyard is at an altitude of 98.64 m above sea level. There are four burial halls in this catacomb,

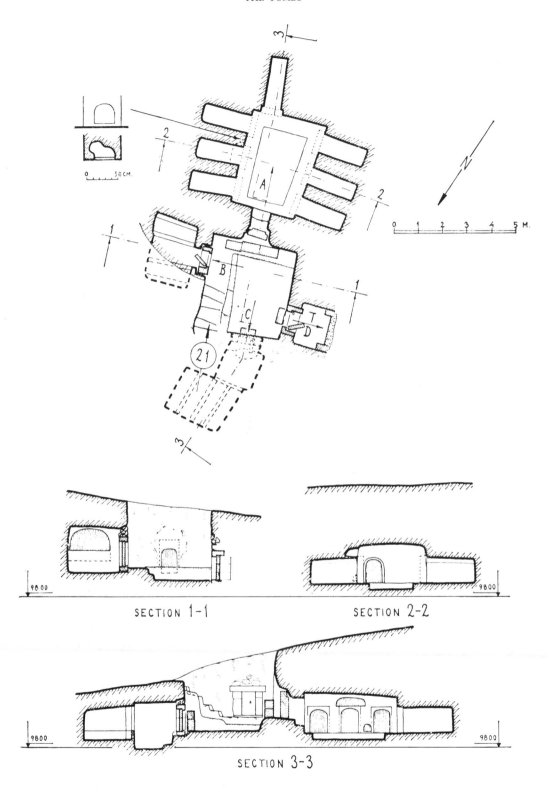

Fig. 52 Catacomb 21

one on each side of the courtyard, as shown on fig. 52.

Hall A

The entrance to this hall is at the southern end of the courtyard. Here a bench was hewn all along the wall. Five large stones in two courses were placed on this bench in order to block the approach to the entrance (Pl. LIX, 1a). The size of the opening is .69 × .55 m. A sealing stone, 1.05 × .80 m in size, closed the entrance. On the inner side of the slab there is a thin projection, rounded on top, conforming to the design of the opening (Pl. LIX, 1b). Since the tomb robbers left the door half open, a great deal of dust collected in the catacomb. The benches hewn around the room create the effect of a pit in the center of the floor. In each of the long walls there are three kokhim; in the southern wall, only one. The openings of the kokhim are arched and have rectangular frames. They were sealed by heavy stone slabs which were found scattered in the room. These slabs are 1.10 × .90 × .32 m in size. In the eastern wall, between the second and third kokhim, a tiny niche was discovered. It was so tightly sealed with a stone tablet that it was difficult to detect (Pl. LVIII, 1–2). Inside, the niche is irregular and could only have contained a few bones (see fig. 52, above to the left). Above the central kokh in this wall, an elongated niche for a bone depository was hewn at a later date in the use of the catacomb. No artifacts were discovered in this hall.

Hall B

The entrance to this hall is from the East. The entrance is constructed of flat plain stones. The room is small and contains two arcosolia, each with one trough grave.

Hall C

This hall is entered from the North. The entrance, .51 × .93 m in size, was blocked with two stones (Pl. LIX, 1d). The stones of the entrance are plain. The room is small,

1.50 × 1.60 m. In the back wall there is one arcosolium with four graves. The dressing is coarse. The stones blocking the entrance indicate that the hall had not been broken into; however, nothing was found inside.

Hall D

This hall is entered from the West. The entrance is .65 m wide and .89 m high. It was closed by a perpendicular slab in front of which another stone was lodged (Pl. LIX, 1c). The entrance frame is built of basalt stones, a most uncommon feature here. The right jamb consists of two stones. However, the left jamb is made of three stones, which is also most unusual at Beth She'arim. The lintel is plain as are the jambs. The door slab was found lying inside near the entrance.

The plan of the hall could not be determined because it had been almost completely destroyed in antiquity by a rock fall. Judging by the rock, there was space for only one room, about 1.60 m wide. Remnants of shelves of arcosolia were preserved on both sides. The wall opposite the entrance was blocked with building stones.

The door slab is made of basalt, excellently wrought. It is .92 m high, .79 m wide, and .15 m thick. It is carefully dressed and undecorated, except for a peripheral sunken band. The lower hinge is complete and there is evidence that it was sheathed in metal. The upper hinge is missing (fig. 53).

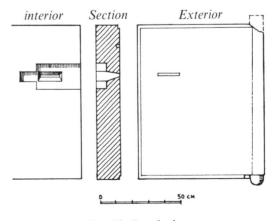

Fig. 53 Basalt door

This door slab is unique in Beth She'arim. The most conspicuous divergence is the locking mechanism: it is located on the left side and the door, therefore, opens to the right, in contrast to the rest of the doors which open to the left. In the upper part of the door slab there is a small hole in which the pulling ring was fastened. The keyhole is not in the jamb, as is customary, but in the door slab. The key was inserted through a narrow horizontal slit and moved the bolt into a recess in the left jamb. The bolt was held by a lock which was mounted into a recess behind the door. The lock itself is missing; however, we know that it was made of metal because of the rust stains in the recess and the traces of concrete which held the lock in place. The design of the lock may be studied from an identical lock found in a tomb at Sur Bahr, between Jerusalem and Bethlehem. This lock and door are the same in every detail as the door under discussion.[139] A lock mounted on a door was also preserved in a Roman grave discovered in Samaria.[140]

There is no doubt that this door was imported to Beth She'arim. This conclusion is derived not from the fact that the door was made of basalt (in other catacombs, not mentioned here, several basalt doors were discovered, ornamented in the customary designs), but from the locking mechanism which is radically different from the system conventionally employed at Beth She'arim. There are several indications that the entrance to this room underwent a number of changes. For example, in the limestone threshold there are two hinge sockets, one to the right and one to the left. This would indicate that the usual socket was indented to the left at first and that the one to the right was added later, when the basalt door with the right-hand hinges was mounted.

Together with the basalt door came, apparently, the rest of the basalt stones which were put to secondary use in the door frame. On close examination, it appeared that the present lintel once served as a threshold since it also contains two hinge sockets — a round one for the present door and a square one. The sunken square in the threshold was designed for a metal hinge plate (see the threshold in catacomb 20, fig. 38). The left jamb is not monolithic, as is customary, but is composed of three stones. It has two bolt recesses: one appropriate for the present locking mechanism and the other, slightly below the first, with no apparent function.

We know the name of the owner of the tomb from the Greek inscription incised on the lintel (fig. 54):[141]

ΤΟΠΟC ΘΕΟΔΟCΙΑC ΤΗC
ΚΑΙ CΑΡΑC ΤΥΡΙΑC

"[Burial] place of Theodosia, also called Sarah, from Tyre."

Fig. 54 Greek inscription

Here, then, is another instance of an individual from the Tyrian Diaspora. Tyrian provenance is referred to in a number of inscriptions from Beth She'arim. The woman has both a Greek and a Jewish name, an accepted practice among Diaspora Jews.

Another inscription was discovered in the upper debris of the courtyard. It attests to the widespread Hellenization of the Jews in the Diaspora. The inscription is incised on a marble tablet .37 m long and .25 m wide. Evidently, the tablet rolled down the slope and did not originally belong to catacomb 21. The inscription was incised in monumental letters (Pl. LIX, 2):[142]

ΜΝΗΜΑ ΚΑΛΛΙΟΠΗC
ΜΙΖΟΤΕΡΑC ΚΑΙ ΑΠΕΛΕΥΘΕΡΑC
ΤΟΥ ΤΗC ΛΑΜΠΡΑC
ΜΝΗΜΗC ΠΡΟΚΟΠΙΟΥ

"A memorial [tomb] of Kalliope the elder,
the freedwoman of Procopios
of glorious memory."

This inscription is very interesting epigraphic evidence of the practice of slavery among Jews in that period (the third and fourth centuries C.E.), a fact known from other historical sources as well. Perhaps Procopios had another younger slave by the name of Kalliope and therefore the expression "the elder" is used. The titles referring to her former slavery accompanied Kalliope to her grave and were even noted on her tombstone, a fact which proved that she took pride in them. At any rate, the memory of her former master is referred to affectionately. Upon receiving her freedom, Kalliope was evidently awarded a more prestigious status, otherwise she would not have been brought to Beth She'arim for burial. Even though the provenance of these individuals is not mentioned in the inscription, we may nevertheless assume on the basis of the unusual names that they were not local residents. Kalliope was probably brought from the Diaspora, perhaps from Phoenicia — like Kalliope from Byblos whose remains were interred in catacomb 12 (see p. 26).

11   CATACOMB 22 (fig. 55)

This catacomb is located to the East, near catacomb 14. It consists of a courtyard and one burial hall which was made in an unconventional manner. The courtyard is rectangular: 4.00 × 5.60 m in size. The hewing of the right-hand corner at the entrance side was not completed. The courtyard was sunk about 4.50 m into the rock. The entrance is at an altitude of 97.26 m, down a flight of narrow steps not parallel to the courtyard line. These steps lead directly to a step at an altitude of 95.26 m. At this point the cut rock turns left along the eastern wall of the courtyard. Here the steps reach the floor of the courtyard (altitude 94.00 m). The rock façade rises to a height of 4.65 m above the floor. Above the façade there is a layer of earth about 1.50 m thick. The single entrance, unusual at Beth She'arim where more than one entrance is the rule, is located in the southern wall of the courtyard. However, the design of the entrance is quite conventional, a rectangular frame of molded stones and an ornamented door, in the accepted style and of excellent workmanship. The entrance is .75 × 1.25 m in size.

The Hall

The inner threshold of the entrance is semicircular in shape, another unusual feature. The room is spacious: 4.30 m wide, 5.30 m long, and 4.15 m high. The floor is 1.10 m below that of the courtyard; the ceiling is vaulted. In the rock along the entrance wall there is a wide bench, upon which two pillars are attached to either side of the entrance. The height of the pillars is 2.00 m high. The base of each pillar is like a truncated pyramid, .50 m high, .90 m wide at the bottom, and .55 m wide at the top. The shaft of the attached pillars juts out .30 m from the wall; it is .35 m wide on the average. It culminates in a capital consisting of three projecting bands which widen toward the top, somewhat similar to an Egyptian Djed column.[143] The right capital is partly destroyed. The entire upper section of the entrance wall collapsed.

At first only six burial places were hewn symmetrically in this spacious room: two kokhim and one arcosolium in each of the long walls, one opposite the other. In the eastern wall the kokhim are about .60 m above floor level and in the western wall,

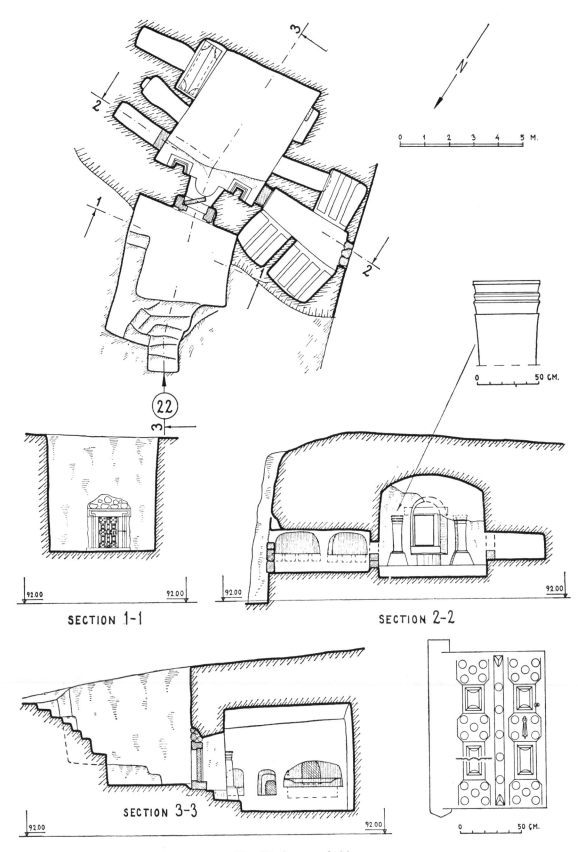

N

0 1 2 3 4 5 M.

0 50 CM.

SECTION 1-1

SECTION 2-2

SECTION 3-3

92.00

92.00

92.00

92.00

92.00

92.00

22

0 50 CM.

Fig. 55 Catacomb 22

about .35 m. Their openings are beautifully hewn. The longer kokh is 2.40 m; the shorter was lengthened a little by the opening of a small niche at its edge. The openings of the two kokhim on either side of the entrance were partially blocked with ashlar stones. It is quite possible that at one time they were entirely sealed in this manner.

Apparently, the arcosolium in the western wall was designed especially as a depository for the bones that were placed on the shelf. It is short (1.40 m) and narrow and was originally sealed with stone slabs, of which one remained in situ. On the other hand, the arcosolium in the eastern wall is exceptionally large: 2.40 × 1.00 m. In the shelf a trough grave was hewn and was covered by a gabled sarcophagus lid with acroteria. When it became necessary to add another burial place to the arcosolium, a large kokh, 2.40 m long, was hewn in the back wall.

At a certain stage it became essential to enlarge the catacomb and to add burial places. However, instead of additional graves being cut into the vacant southern wall, a new burial room was created by enlarging the first kokh on the western side. It contains ten graves, almost twice as many as the main room. This additional room was long and narrow: 1.30 × 3.50 m. In the northern wall there are two arcosolia, one with three graves and one with four. During the hewing of the first arcosolium, an opening was breached into the corner of the courtyard. In the southern wall of the room there is only one arcosolium with three graves. The loculus behind the wall prevented the hewing of an additional arcosolium.

In the western wall of the added room a breach was opened into the courtyard of catacomb 14 (see the discussion on this catacomb). The breach is 1.20 m above the floor of the courtyard. We found it mostly blocked with three courses of stone. The lower part of the breach was dressed, but the upper part was left rough (see photograph 4 in Pl. XXI). After the excavations, the rock collapsed and now the room is open along its entire width.

The breach between catacomb 22 and the courtyard of catacomb 14 raises a chronological problem: was the added room breached during the hewing of the courtyard of catacomb 14, i.e., is the courtyard later than the room; or was the breach formed during the hewing of the additional room when the courtyard was already in existence? Technically speaking, there are arguments pro and con. The dressed part of the breach could be taken as an indication that the kokh opening was cut through at this point; on the other hand, it could also be viewed as the straightening of the rock, in preparation for laying the courses of stone for blocking the breach. We may recall that a breach was also cut into the courtyard of catacomb 22, much larger than can be seen on the plan. Judging by the typology of the catacombs (see the chapter on chronology of the catacombs), the plan of catacomb 14 is earlier than that of the additional room of catacomb 22. On the other hand, the main room of catacomb 22 is typologically slightly earlier than catacomb 14 — approximately the end of the second century C.E. or the beginning of the third century.

We now come to the problem of the two attached pillars on either side of the entrance to the main room, unique in all of Beth She'arim. The few carved columns found in burial rooms up to now are an integral part of the rock architecture, supposedly fulfilling the function of supporting arches, lintels, or the like.[144] In the present case, however, the pillars are not functional because their capitals do not support anything. What then is the purpose of these pillars? What is their significance? We can only make a tentative suggestion on the basis of certain parallels.

It seems quite possible that similarities of the capitals to the Egyptian Djed pillar—

whose symbolic significance is associated with the cult of Osiris — is not accidental.[145] Comparisons may also be made with the columns placed, at various periods, on either side of the entrances to temples in Syria, Phoenicia, and Palestine. The function of these columns was not architectural, but cultic; however, opinion is divided as to their exact significance. This custom was also practiced in the Canaanite temples[146] and in Solomon's temple in Jerusalem (Jachin and Boaz). There are also indications that various buildings in Phoenicia carried this tradition up to the first centuries of the present era. Similar columns on both sides of entrances were found in cultic clay models from the Iron Age, both in Palestine and in Cyprus.[147] Furthermore, even the house-shaped pottery ossuaries from the Chalcolithic period (the end of the fourth millennium B.C.E.), found in Azor,[148] have a pair of free-standing columns on either side of the entrance. This example from the realm of sepulchral art is particularly important for our discussion, despite the large gap in time. While a fully satisfactory explanation cannot be given for the pillars in this burial room of Beth She'arim, there is a possibility that it reflects a long-continued tradition of symbolic columns.

12   CATACOMB 23 (fig. 56)

This is one of the three catacombs at Beth She'arim with remains of a superimposed structure. Like catacombs 14 and 20, it is a complex of three units: a courtyard, a cave, and an upper structure; however, this catacomb is much smaller in size.

The long axis of the courtyard has a North–South orientation. It is 8.52 m long and 4.60 m wide. The walls were first cut into the rock and then faced with ashlar masonry, .45 m thick. One to five courses of this stonework were sporadically preserved. The entrance to the courtyard was on the northern side. In the western wall there is a small entrance leading into a burial room which collapsed and was covered with debris. The façade of the southern wall was originally decorated with a built arch; however, only four to five of the lower courses of the arch posts remained in situ. The archway is 2.50 m wide. The reconstruction suggested in section 1–1 of fig. 56 implies that the built walls also rose to a proportional height and were terminated by a cornice. Courtyards faced with stone and façades with a decorative arch are characteristic of several catacombs in Beth She'arim. This architectural style is indicative of important and rich tombs.

The entrance was found destroyed. Its stones were dismantled, except for the threshold which still remained in place (altitude 97.81 m). Here the rock had collapsed, carrying part of the ceiling of the burial room in its fall. The lintel and the door slab were found in the debris of the courtyard. They are quite conventional: the molded lintel, 1.90 m long, has two horizontal ear-like extensions. The door slab is decorated with panels, studs, and a door knocker. It is slightly larger than usual: 1.40 m high and .98 m wide. The diagram in section 1–1 shows the restored lintel and door in situ.

Since this entrance was unusually wide for a single door, sarcophagi could easily be taken through. On either side of the inner face of the entrance there are two pilasters attached to the walls, somewhat similar to the attached pillars in catacomb 22 but simpler in design. Only their lower sections were preserved. In front of the entrance, along the width of the room, a shelf was hewn serving both as a step and a bench.

The room is rectangular: 8.25 m long, 4.50 m wide, and 3.30 m high. The ceiling is vaulted. This is the only room in the catacomb. Apparently, it was intended at first

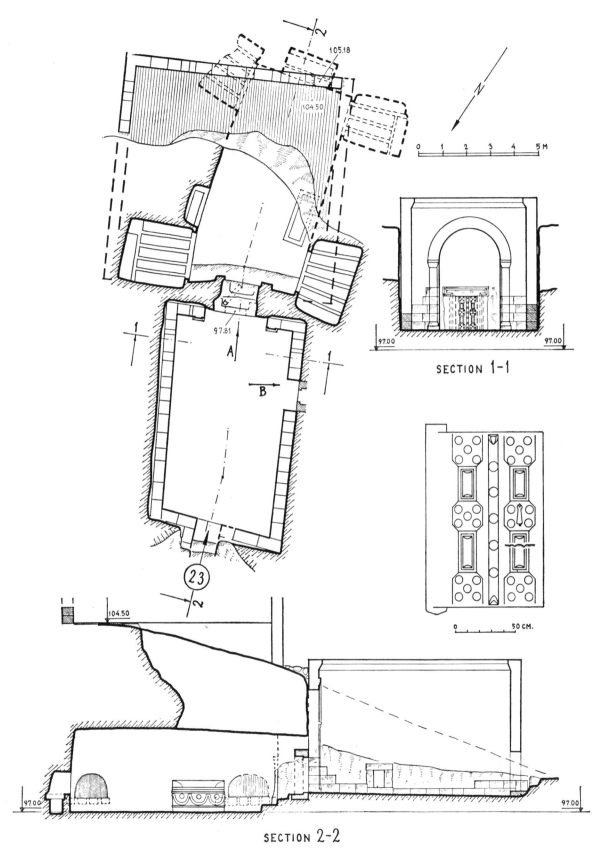

SECTION 1-1

SECTION 2-2

Fig. 56 Catacomb 23

only for burial in sarcophagi. Indeed, one sarcophagus was found in situ (Pl. LIX, 3). Only at a later stage, when additional burial places became imperative, were arcosolia hewn into the walls. Near each corner of the room there is an arcosolium with four to six trough graves. The southern and eastern walls each have an arcosolium with one grave. The arcosolium in the southeastern corner was partially destroyed by the enormous rock fall in catacomb 20; thus a breach was also formed into room XXI of catacomb 20.

The Upper Structure

Above this catacomb remains were discovered of a square structure with a plain mosaic floor. Also preserved were two courses of the southern wall (9.30 m long),

part of the eastern wall, and the southern portion of the mosaic floor, 6.60 m higher than the courtyard floor (104.50 m altitude). The northern part of the structure was destroyed by the collapse of the underlying rock; however, there is reason to assume that it was approximately 9.00 m in width.

The simple mosaic and the thin walls lead us to conjecture that the structure was not very high and that it was not roofed. By analogy with the structures above catacomb 23, we may infer that this upper structure and the catacomb below it formed an integral functional whole, and that it likewise served as a place of assembly.

On the basis of its initial plan, this catacomb is dated to the beginning of the third century C.E. (see also chapter on chronology).

13 CATACOMB 31[149] (fig. 57)

This catacomb was discovered about 120 m West of the oil press, situated on the summit of the hill, at a turn in the path descending to catacombs 12–23 (fig. 2, square

14, altitude 105 m). It was destroyed during the construction of a road.

The catacomb consisted of two rooms. The first room (3.30 × 2.00 m in size) had a sunken floor; thus benches were formed on all four sides. In the eastern wall there were three kokhim. In the western wall a kokh was begun but not completed. The floor of the second room (2.20 × 2.00 m) was also sunk in the center. This room contained five kokhim.

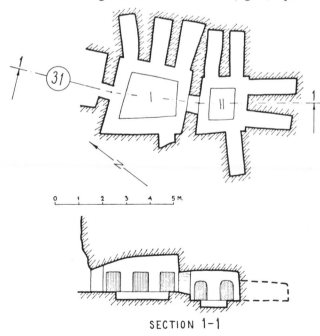

Fig. 57 Catacomb 31

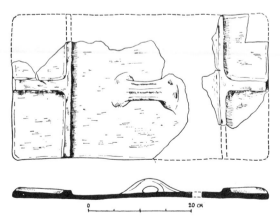

Fig. 58 Fragments of clay lid

The entrance to the catacomb was small (.50 m high). It was closed by a heavy sealing stone with a projecting boss in the center, part of which was found lying in front of the entrance. Since the catacomb was robbed in antiquity, it was found full of earth. No artifacts were discovered except for fragments of a flat pottery cover with a horizontal handle in the center (fig. 58). Apparently this cover served as a lid for a clay ossuary. However, nothing similar was discovered in any of the other tombs.

From a typological point of view, this tomb could be attributed to the Herodian period. Of the previously examined tombs, the most akin is hall A of catacomb 21. A similar catacomb was discovered in the previous excavations at Beth She'arim;[150] however, for its general arrangement, catacomb 31 is the most complete and perfect example of family tombs at Beth She'arim, attributable to the first century C.E.

14 OUTER TOMBS

By the term "outer tombs" we refer to graves found outside the catacombs; on the slope of the hill, and not in subterranean chambers as was the general practice at Beth She'arim. Graves of this type were found in two places: above catacomb 20 and in front of catacomb 23. The graves in these two locations differ in type and may be divided into two main classes: *(a)* built graves; *(b)* shaft tombs.

Built Graves[151] (figs. 35 and 59; Pl. LXI) On the slope above catacomb 20, West of the upper structure and courtyard and North of the courtyard of catacomb 21, a group of eleven graves was discovered, all with an approximate North–South orientation. No standard method was used in the construction of these graves. Some of them were hewn into the rock as a rectangular pit; some of them were cut into the fill of the artificial terrace; still others were built in cist form of stone slabs. The covers were also constructed in various ways: a single row of flat stones; two rows of sloping stones leaning against each other in gable fashion; or a rectangular structure of several courses of stone. The types of burial also vary: either in lead coffins or without coffins at all, directly in the open graves. Five lead coffins were discovered in situ, full of earth and without a single artifact. The bones disintegrated, leaving only tiny particles.

The same was true of the coffin-less burials.

After interment the burial structures were purposely covered with earth; otherwise the tombs would surely have been robbed. This is also the reason why lead coffins were discovered in situ.

G r a v e n o. 1 (fig. 59). This grave is the southernmost in the group. It is hewn into the rock in the form of a rectangular pit. It is $2.00 \times .50$ m in area and approximately .60 m deep. Lead coffin no. 1 was found in this grave. The tomb cover was built of two rows of sloping stones, like a gabled roof. The edges of the stones at the ridge of the gable were cut obliquely. The empty triangles at the two ends of the gable were sealed with stones: at the southern side by a vertical stone and at the northern, by two superimposed stones. The total length of the structure is 2.53 m. The northern half of the roof was covered with additional stones lodged at random, evidently as an extra means of preventing tomb robbery.

G r a v e n o. 2. This grave is also a rectangular pit hewn in the rock, $1.80 \times .40$ m. It was covered by five horizontal slabs of stone totaling 1.85 m in length.

G r a v e n o. 3. All that remains of this grave are four horizontal cover stones, left in situ. They doubtlessly covered a grave that was dug into the earth; however, the form of the grave is no longer discernible. The bones crumbled completely.

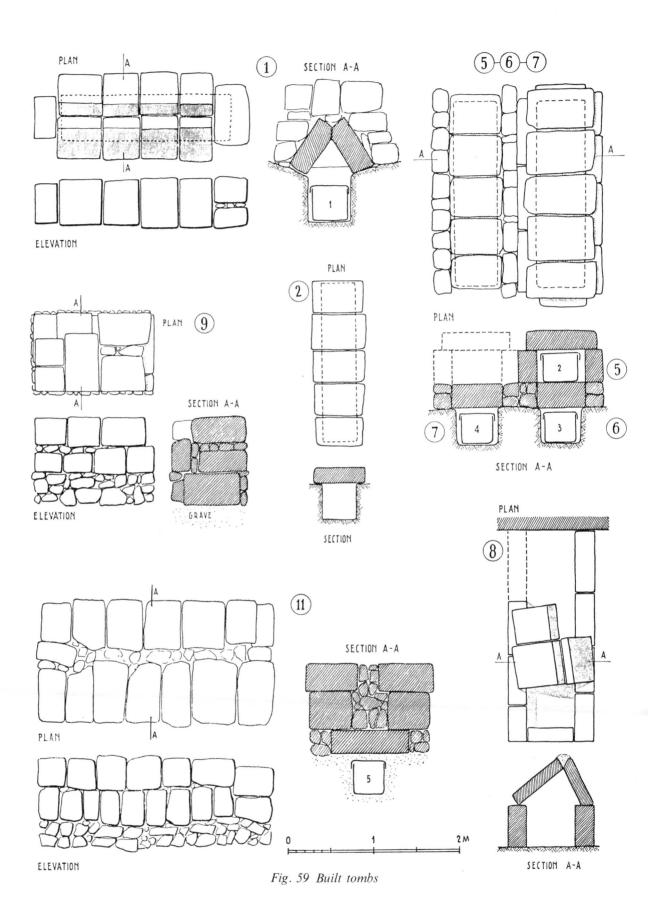

Fig. 59 Built tombs

126

Grave no. 4. Four cover stones were found in situ. Like grave no. 3, this grave was dug into the earth.

Graves nos. 5–7. This was a composite structure consisting of two stories designated for four graves, of which only three were found. The two lower rectangular graves were hewn in the rock; each contained a lead coffin: the western grave (no. 6), coffin no. 3; and the eastern grave (no. 7), coffin no. 4. Both graves were covered with horizontal stones. Above grave no. 6 a cist was built of vertical stones (no. 5), .40 m high. After coffin no. 2 was placed inside, the cist was covered with stone slabs. The intention evidently was to build a similar cist above grave no. 7; however, the plan was apparently not executed. There is no reason to assume that there was formerly a grave which was dismantled by tomb robbers as these would have surely noticed grave no. 5 as well.

The intricate construction of this tomb is evidence of a single plan and of the simultaneous interment of the three coffins.

Grave no. 8. This grave is located in the southwestern corner of the walls on the first terrace, West of the courtyard of catacomb 20. It is a rectangular cist of stone slabs, leaning against the southern side of the terrace wall. It is 2.22 × 1.00 m in size. The grave was covered with a gabled roof of stone slabs of which one pair of slanting stones and an additional single stone were preserved. Obviously, a lead coffin could not have been interred here because the gable stones would not have remained in situ had the coffin been removed.

Grave no. 9. This structure consists of three stone courses, 1.40 m long, .86 m wide, and 1.00 m high. The stones were built on the grave which had been dug into the earth, and it is possible to distinguish between the friable earth of the grave and the undisturbed earth below. It is noteworthy that the structure was too short for an adult body. Therefore, this was either the grave of a child or a bone depository.

Grave no. 10. Only two sloping stones were preserved on this grave; nevertheless, they are evidence of a gabled roof. The grave itself was dug into the earth; however, its form was indiscernible.

Grave no. 11. This grave is the northernmost of this group of outer tombs. The solid structure above the grave was preserved intact. It is 2.80 m long, 1.35 m wide, and 1.00 m high. It consists of three courses of stone. The two upper courses are built in two longitudinal rows, and the bottom course is built of one row of six smoothly dressed slabs, the longest of which is 1.22 m. This massive course, 2.50 m long, covered lead coffin no. 5 which was concealed in the ground. Apparently the builders of this grave made more serious efforts to prevent tomb robbers from opening it than was the case at the other graves.

Since graves covered with stone slabs (horizontal or diagonal) are common in Palestine, they need not be dealt with in detail here. This, however, is not the case for the other forms: the two-storey tombs, half hewn and half built, and the structures above the graves. If we suppose that it was the Beth She‘arim undertakers who built these graves, then they surely used accepted local methods. However, we have no means of knowing the common burial practice in graves outside the catacombs at Beth She‘arim, since all the tombs discovered up to now are within catacombs. We are familiar though with the types of graves elsewhere in the country; nevertheless, we have found no parallels to the Beth She‘arim types.[152]

We may, therefore, conclude that these lead coffins were brought here from Phoenicia (as will presently be shown), and were interred by the people who brought the coffins according to their particular methods of burial. The system of hewing tombs into the rock and building over them additional flagstone graves, especially many-storied graves, was extensively practiced in Sidon in that period.[153]

Shaft Tombs (fig. 60)

In front of the courtyard of catacomb 23, there is a rectangular area, 3.80 × 4.80 m (see general plan, 3J, in fig. 131) sunken into the rock of the slope, .40 m deep to the North and 1.65 m deep to the South (fig. 60, 1–2). At the northern edge of this area, five stones were found in situ, apparently the remains of a low wall. On the inner side of this surface, adjoining the western wall, there was a row of four stones whose function is difficult to determine. Two shaft graves (I–II) were hewn in the floor of this sunken area, one beside the other. The distance between them is 1.30 m. Their approximate orientation is North–South. Each grave is covered with one large stone slab. Shaft I (fig. 60, 2–5). The southern end of the stone slab covering this shaft was broken, probably when the grave was robbed. The slab was 2.15 m long, 1.03 m wide, and .28 m thick. It was placed in a recess surrounding the shaft. The hewn shaft is 1.63 m deep, 2.00 m long, and .80 m wide (fig. 60, 3). The long walls are faced with brick almost to their entire height, whereas the short walls only to a height of .35 m. The inner width of the shaft is .54 m. The burnt bricks are of the thin Roman type. They are 14–19 cm long, 13 cm wide, and 2.5 cm thick. They were bonded with a white lime mortar. 1.5 cm thick. The floor of the shaft consisted of three layers totaling 10 cm in depth. The upper layer was made of three clay slabs (fig. 60, 4), 50 × 50 × 3 cm in size. These slabs were placed on a layer of sand, 5 cm thick. Below this sand layer, there were three rows of pottery slabs: a row of square slabs in the center, 31 × 31 × 2 cm in size; and two rows of narrower slabs along the side, 31 × 13 cm in size (fig. 60, 5). The shaft was full of earth and contained no artifacts except for a fragment of a bone (probably an arm or leg).

Shaft II (fig. 60, 6–7). The stone slab covering this shaft was almost completely preserved. It is 1.97 m long, .91 m wide, and .26 m thick. For some reason, the tomb robbers did not break the slab except for a small piece at the southern edge; instead, they made laborious efforts to enter the grave by hewing a breach into the rock near the broken edge of the slab. The shaft is 1.86 m long, .72 m wide, and 1.80 m deep. The walls of this shaft also were faced with burnt bricks. Three of the walls were brick faced almost to the entire height; but on the southern side the brick wall was built only in a special recess in the lower part of the shaft. The inner measurements of the shaft are 1.60 m long and .54 m wide. The floor was constructed out of two layers of bricks.

About .68 m above the floor there are special ledges in the long brick walls, which possibly served to hold pottery cover tiles. In this connection it is important to note that numerous fragments of bricks and small pieces of pottery tiles were found, some of which probably served to cover the burial. However, we could not determine whether this covering was made of large pottery slabs placed horizontally, in gabled form or even vaulted. Similarly, there was no evidence as to the method of burial.

While it is true that deep shaft tombs, hewn into the rock, have been found in various places in Palestine, none had been found with brick facing and pottery tile flooring to date. This facing has no structural function whatsoever since the rock here is solid and compact and therefore no reinforcement is necessary. Thus, it seems certain that here we have an example of tomb owners attempting to continue the tradition of built graves, a tradition brought from another country where it was customary to construct graves out of bricks or to line pit graves with bricks.

It is known that the country where brick graves of this type were built is Mesopotamia, though the same system was also practiced in Egypt. Interesting parallels may be found in the Assyrian graves of the first millennium B.C.E.[154] These rectangular graves are constructed of bricks and paved with tiles, exactly duplicating shaft I (fig.

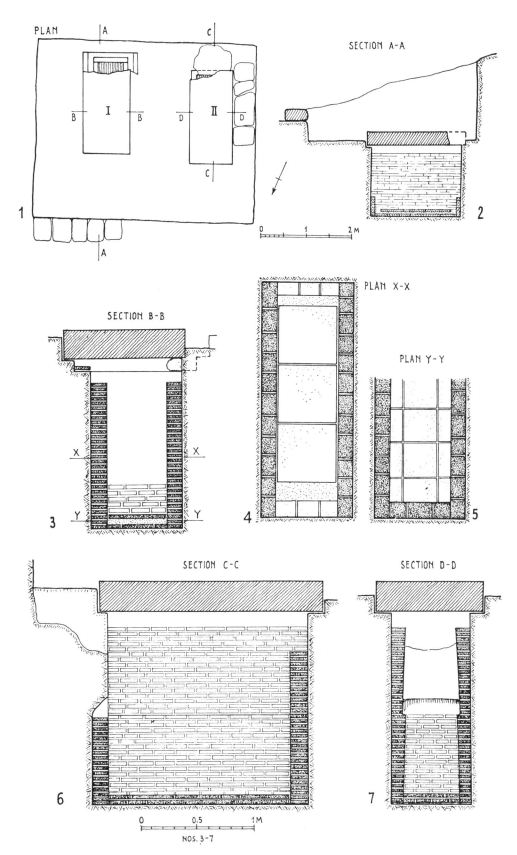

PLAN

SECTION A-A

SECTION B-B

PLAN X-X

PLAN Y-Y

SECTION C-C

SECTION D-D

NOS. 3-7

Fig. 60 Shaft tombs

60, 5). The larger graves are built of burnt brick, paved with square bricks, and roofed with a vault.[155] While these tombs are considerably earlier than those at Beth She'arim, they nevertheless reflect the long-practiced Mesopotamian tradition of building graves out of bricks.

It may be assumed, therefore, that Jews from Mesopotamia[156] were buried in these two shaft graves, and that their relatives attempted to inter them in the manner prevalent in their country of origin: in tombs lined with bricks. The excellence of the workmanship and construction of these graves — including the intricate paved flooring — is indeed remarkable. It should be noticed that in shaft I, for some reason, the narrow brick walls were not built to the full height of the shaft but only sufficiently high to accommodate the body or the bones of the deceased. In shaft II the rock in the upper part of the southern wall was unlined whereas the lower part of the wall, where the body was interred, was faced with brick. This would seem to indicate a wish to make a distinct separation between the deceased and the cold rock and, in accordance with tradition, to ensconce him in warmth. Thus, this hybrid form of tomb came into being. There is no reason to assume that coffins were used in these burials since tomb robbers would not have been able to remove them through the small breaches without breaking them, and no evidential fragments of coffins were found.

These shaft graves prove that the burial practices at Beth She'arim were more numerous and varied than previously inferred. In addition to the local customs, burial practices prevalent in the neighboring countries were also found — as evidenced by the outer graves. It is quite possible that these graves are not the only ones of this type in Beth She'arim and that similar ones, and perhaps even additional forms, will still be discovered in later excavations.

NOTES

1 In all sections only the rock surface is indicated; the soil stratum above it was not marked.

2 Cf. also the appendix on the openings and doors: *Beth She'arim*, I, p. 221.

3 On synagogue lintels see: Goodenough, III, nos. 510, 511, 543. For the lintels of tombs from the Second Temple period see *Ibid.*, nos. 23, 24, 39. Cf. also: *Beth She'arim*, I, Pls. V, 4; VI; XXXVI, 4.

4 Doors decorated in this manner were common in many countries in the Roman period, including Palestine. See several examples in Goodenough, III, nos. 44–48.

5 *Beth She'arim*, II, no. 133.

6 *Ibid.*, no. 134 and note 12.

7 *Ibid.*, no. 135.

8 Cf. the menorah illustrated in *Beth She'arim*, I, Pl. XVIII, 3. Incidentally, there the menorah has three legs.

9 *Beth She'arim*, II, no. 136.

10 *Ibid.*, no. 137.

11 *Ibid.*, nos. 138–140.

12 *Ibid.*, no. 141.

13 *Ibid.*, no. 142.

14 *Ibid.*, nos. 143–146.

15 *Ibid.*, no. 147. We translate the word κιτε as "lies," according to the text of Hebrew inscription no. 14 in catacomb 20: "Here they lie...."

17 The upper row of steps has now been replaced by concrete steps.

18 *Beth She'arim*, II, no. 148.

19 *IEJ*, V (1955), p. 217.

20 *Beth She'arim*, II, no. 150.

21 *Ibid.*, no. 161.

22 *Ibid.*, no. 158.

23 *Ibid.*

24 *CIJ*, II, 21, 202.

25 *Beth She'arim*, II, no. 156.

26 *Ibid.*, no. 155.

27 *Ibid.*, no. 154. Contrary to what was stated here, the name Jason has been meanwhile discovered in an Aramaic tomb inscription in Jerusalem. See: N. Avigad, "Aramaic Inscriptions in the Tomb of Jason," *IEJ*, XVII (1967), pp. 101 *ff.*

28 *Beth She'arim*, II, no. 153.

29 *Ibid.*, no. 162.

30 Namely, of the deceased who was buried here.

31 *BIES*, XVIII (1954), pp. 40–41 (Hebrew).

32 *Beth She'arim*, II, no. 164.

33 B. Mazar, *BIES*, XXI (1957), p. 162 (Hebrew).

34 *Beth She'arim*, II, no. 163.

35 *BIES*, XVIII, p. 42 (Hebrew).

36 *Beth She'arim*, II, no. 165.

37 *Ibid.*, no. 166.

38 *Ibid.*, no. 167.

39 *Ibid.*, no. 168.

40 It is certainly accidental that in catacomb 1 a similar door was also found precisely at the end of the corridor. See *Beth She'arim*, I, Pl. V, 3.

41 *Beth She'arim*, II, no. 170.

42 For similar doors see: *Beth She'arim*, I, Pls. XXIV, 2–3; XXXVI, 1.

43 *Beth She'arim*, II, no. 171.

44 *Ibid.*, no. 172.

45 *Ibid.*, no. 173.

46 Cf. also: *Beth She'arim*, I, p. 211.

47 *Beth She'arim*, II, no. 149.

48 *Beth She'arim*, I, Pl. VI.

49 This blocking was not indicated in the plan of the courtyard, but it can be seen in Section 1–1 in fig. 19 and in the plan of catacomb 22.

50 Cf. *Beth She'arim*, I, p. 186, the entrance arch to hall C of catacomb 4. The built wall terminates on both sides in a denticulated form and does not continue further.

51 A bronze hinge from Thassos in Greece is in the custody of the British Museum in London. It was made in the form of a cube (32 × 46 × 53 mm) with a hemispherical projection, like the hinge from Beth She'arim. I wish to thank the director of the Greek and Roman Department of the Museum for assisting me in locating comparative material for our hinges.

52 Y. Pinkerfeld, "Two Fragments of a Marble Door Slab in Jaffa," *'Atiqot*, I (1957), pp. 78–82, fig. 2 (Hebrew).

53 M. Cohen, *The Tombs of the Kings*, Tel Aviv, 1947, p. 70 (Hebrew). The author reports that he saw such remains. In note 68 he quotes Mariti from the year 1684 who found, under the bottom door hinge, a piece of bronze upon which the hinge swiveled. Thickness of piece: 1.25 cm; width: 11.25 cms.

54 A. Baumeister, *Denkmäler des klassischen Altertums*, München-Leipzig, 1888, III, p. 1806, fig. 1894. Cf. the pairs of bronze hinges from Italy that are at present in custody of the British Museum (W.T. 984; BM 1918/1–1/87–88). They consist of a hollow cylinder which enclosed a wooden hinge and a square bronze plate which serves as a door socket.

55 Were it not for the crack which revealed the bronze hinge, we would not have known of its existence.

56 C. Warren, *Excavations at Jerusalem*, London, 1884, Plans etc., Pl. XXV.

57 D.S. Robertson, *A Handbook of Greek and Roman Architecture*, Cambridge, 1943, Pl. XXIa; and cf. Pl. XXIb. This gate, with two arches, is closer in conception to the arched façades of Beth She'arim.

58 *Gerasa*, Plans IV, XIX.

59 L.H. Vincent & F.M. Abel, *Jérusalem*, II: *Jérusalem nouvelle*, Paris, 1914, fig. 6; Watzinger, *Denkmäler*, II, p. 57, fig. 4.

60 B. Fletcher, *A History of Architecture*, London, 1938, p. 186A.

61 Robertson, *Handbook*, Pl. XVIb; F. Noack, *Die Baukunst des Altertums*, Pl. 138.

62 On the arcade in architecture and as an ornamental subject see: M. Avi-Yonah, *QDAP*, X, pp. 142 *ff.*

63 Goodenough, III, no. 211; R.D. Barnett, "Reminiscences of Herod's Temple," *Christian News from Israel*,

XII (1961), no. 3, pp. 14–20. Barnett attempts to derive the form of the portico surrounding Herod's Temple from the colonnaded decoration of the ossuary.

64 *Beth She'arim*, I, Pl. VII, 5; p. 53. See there also the discussion on the arcade motif and its distribution.

65 B. Mazar, *BIES*, IX (1941), Pl. IV (Hebrew); Goodenough, III, no. 89.

66 This has not yet been published.

67 This has not yet been published.

68 Kohl & Watzinger, *Synagogen*, figs. 211, 260.

69 *Gerasa*, Plans V, 4; XX;, 4, 6.

70 Mazar (*Beth She'arim*, I, p. 142, n. 1) has already indicated the Talmudic source which refers to the cave-in that occurred in the catacomb belonging to the Patriarchal family: "When one of the Patriarchs died (the burial) cave collapsed, and lives were endangered. R. Jose came and delivered a funeral oration for him (the deceased) 'Happy is the man who leaves the world in peace.'" (Jer. Talmud, Abodah Zarah 3, 1, 42c).

71 We sent the photograph of the inscription to Prof. W. B. Henning in London. In his opinion the script is not Paḥlevi. Nevertheless, there are certain resemblances to this script.

72 L. A. Mayer and A. Reifenberg, "The Synagogue at Eshtemoa," *BIES*, IX (1942), the plan on p. 40; Goodenough, III, no. 605. See now: N. Avigad, "The Form of the Ancient Galilean Synagogues," *All the Land of Naphtali*, Jerusalem, 1968, p. 91 (Hebrew).

73 Cf. the Roman basilica building at Samaria: G. A. Reisner, C. S. Fisher, & D. G. Lyon, *Harvard Excavations at Samaria*, II, Cambridge, 1924, Plan 12.

74 See: N. Avigad, *Ancient Monuments in the Kidron Valley*, Jerusalem, 1954, pp. 66 ff. (Hebrew).

75 B. Mazar, *BIES*, IX (1941), Pl. IV (Hebrew).

76 "Burial monuments are not to be made for the righteous, their words will serve as a remembrance for them." (Jer. Talmud, Shekalim, 2, 47a).

77 I must thank Prof. S. Lieberman for pointing this out to me. I also wish to thank Dr. Y. Brandt for assisting me in presenting the sources.

78 Lamentations Rabba, Prolegomenon 25.

79 Baba Qama 16, bottom b.

80 Ketubot 103, top b.

81 Yebamot 122, top a.

82 *IEJ*, IV (1954), pp. 103–104; *IEJ*, V (1955), p. 236.

83 In my comments on the tradition about R. Judah Ha-Nassî's tomb, I am indebted to the erudition of the late Avraham Ya'ari.

84 A. Ya'ari, *Massa'oth Eretz Yisrael* Tel Aviv, 1946, pp. 44, 51, 84, 93, 109, 112 (Hebrew).

85 *Kaftor vaFeraḥ*, ed. A. M. Luntz, Jerusalem, 1897, p. 301 (Hebrew).

86 Ed. A. M. Luntz, 1897, p. 77.

87 There is reason to suppose that the origins of such lists lie in the early literature when it was customary to record the burial places of the sages. In the course of time changes were made in the lists, such as the relocation of a traditional burial site from one place to another. On the existence of such literature we learn, among others, from the book *The Lives of the Prophets*, preserved in its Greek form (the original was certainly written in Hebrew); it contains information concerning the prophets' birthplace, death, and place of burial. This book is thought to have been written in the Talmudic period because the Sages already dealt with these questions. See: S. Klein on the book *Vitae Prophetarum, Sefer Klausner*, 1933, p. 184 ff. I must thank Prof. Mazar for drawing my attention to this article.

88 Ya'ari (above, n. 84), p. 439.

89 Except for the small door in hall B of catacomb 14 in which there is one rosette.

90 *Beth She'arim*, II, no. 176.

91 *Ibid.*, no. 177.

92 The transliteration לעזר is also found in a bilingual inscription in Jaffa. See: *Sefer HaYishuv*, I, p. 81, no. 10.

93 *Beth She'arim*, II, no. 178.

94 *Ibid.*, nos. 179–180. The inscription was broken into two parts. B. Lifshitz published the two parts as two separate inscriptions (nos. 179 and 180). Apparently he relied on incomplete notes and did not examine the original. On. Pl. LXXIV there is a photograph of the inscription *in situ*.

95 *Ibid.*, no. 181.

96 Similar rosettes are engraved on the lintel of hall F in catacomb 13 and on the lintel of hall B in catacomb 19 (See Pl. XXIX, 1).

97 *Beth She'arim*, II, no. 182.

98 *Beth She'arim*, II, no. 184b.

99 *Ibid.*, no. 184a.

100 *Ibid.*, no. 183; *Eretz-Israel*, IV (1956), p. 104 (Hebrew).

101 *Beth She'arim*, II, Pl. XIV, 2.

102 This is a proven method for engraving menoroth in schematic form. Cf. *Beth She'arim*, I, Pl. XXXIII, 5, and other menoroth that are not yet published.

103 *Beth She'arim*, II, no, 191.

104 *Ibid.*, no. 192.

105 *Ibid.*, no. 190.

106 *Ibid.*, no. 188.

107 *Ibid.*, no. 189.

108 *Sefer Ha Yishuv*, p. 84, no. 35 (Hebrew).

109 Very similar faces defined as masks appear on a Roman sarcophagus in custody in Baltimore. See: K. Lehman Hartleben, *Dionysiac Sarcophagi in Baltimore*, Baltimore, 1962, fig. 26.

110 *Beth She'arim*, II, no. 185.

111 The second menorah on the lintel of a Jewish tomb was found at Kfar Tamra in Western Galilee. See: N. Avigad, "Relics of Ancient Jewish Art in Galilee," *Eretz-Israel*, VII (1964), p. 21; Pl. 1 (Hebrew).

112 The tablet was discovered in situ a short time after the excavations. This is the only time that we found a memorial tablet in its original position. As may be recalled, two similar tablets were found, but not in situ. On the other hand, a marble tablet had been found in situ in the corridor of catacomb 1, above the entrance (see: *Beth She'arim*, I, Pl. VI).

113 This profile is also encountered on the column bases of Absalom's Monument in Jerusalem (first century A.D.). See: N. Avigad, *Ancient Monuments in the Kidron Valley*, Jerusalem, 1954, fig. 56; *ibid.*, on p. 111 additional parallels from Roman architecture are also presented.

114 See the enlarged photograph in *IEJ*, VII (1957), Pl. 17c.

115 After the publication of the photograph in Pl. XXXI, 2, the top of the right end of the façade was reconstructed.

116 *BIES*, IX (1941), Pl. IV (Hebrew).

117 Kohl & Watzinger, *Synagogen*, figs. 183, 185; Pl. IV.

118 *Ibid.*, p. 95.

119 For a discussion on this see: *Ibid.*, p. 152.

120 D. Krencker & W. Zschietzschmann, *Römische Tempel in Syrien*, Berlin–Leipzig, 1938, Pls. 91, 93.

121 *Gerasa*, Plans IV; V, 1.

122 Kohl & Watzinger, *Synagogen*, figs. 47, 183.

123 *'Atiqot*, I (1957), Pl. VII, 4.

124 A. Baumeister, *Denkmäler des klassischen Altertums*, III, Munich–Leipzig, 1888, p. 1806, fig. 1894.

125 *IEJ*, VII (1957), p. 81.

126 Cf. the large gate of the Second Temple which, *Middoth*, IV, 3, says consisted of two small doors, one in the North the other in the South. The southern one was blocked and no one could enter it. However, through the northern opening, one entered into a cell and from there into the sanctuary in order to open the doors of the gate.

127 N. Avigad, "Façades of the Jerusalem Necropolis," *IEJ*, I (1950/1), p. 105, fig. 9. The accuracy of this reconstruction is doubtful.

128 *Beth She'arim*, II, no. 193.

129 *Ibid.*, no. 194.

130 Cf. M. Schwabe, *Studies in Memory of Asher Gulak and Samuel Klein*, Jerusalem, 1942, pp. 187–200 (Hebrew); see also: *Beth She'arim*, II, pp. 223–224.

131 My interpretations of these two inscriptions which were published in the first report (see now: *IEJ*, VII (1957), pp. 246*f.*) were criticized by B. Lifshitz. See: B. Lifshitz, *ZDPV*, LXXVIII (1962), pp. 73–75. Lifshitz claims that: (*a*) The words πατέρες ὅσιοι should be translated "righteous parents." (*b*) The writers of the inscriptions were not "visitors" but the relatives who were present at the time of burial. The words of consolation were intended for the parents who were buried in one of the nearby tombs. (*c*) In the first publications I did not note that the word ἀνάστασις in the second inscription is a translation of the word "resurrection" found in the Hebrew inscription on sarcophagus no. 25. As to these objections, I would like to make the following remarks: (*a–b*) The basic meaning of πατέρες is "fathers" and, even though it also means "parents," there is no particular reason for applying this meaning here. Lifshitz himself thinks that the inscription was inscribed on the day of the burial; however, is it likely that both parents of its author died on the same day? The language of the second inscription is also of a general nature and is not directed toward a specific person, even though the basic cause for writing an inscription was the fact that the writer's relatives were buried in this catacomb. It is obvious that in using the word "visitors," I meant the relatives who visited their patriarchal graves. Until the present day no bilingual inscription with an exact translation of the word ὅσιος — which is usually interpreted as "holy" — has been found. This Greek term is very common in the Beth She'arim inscriptions, and it is generally agreed that its usual translation is "righteous" or "pious," etc., according to S. Lieberman, *Greek in Jewish Palestine*, New York, 1942, p. 71. It is not my intention at all to question this; however, in this case, my translation "holy" was influenced by the Hebrew inscription on sarcophagus no. 15 (room III, next to corridor) in which the two rabbis buried there are called הקדושים ("the holy ones"). It is possible to understand the feelings of a person who came to prostrate himself upon the patriarchal graves; it is even possible that he came especially to this particular grave, visited the rest of the catacomb, saw the inscription on the "holy ones" and was so impressed that before leaving he engraved an inscription on the corridor walls. It was quite natural to translate the word הקדושים into ὅσιοι. Lifshitz himself believes (*ZDPV*, bottom of p. 72) that the deceased referred to in the inscription were buried in the vicinity of the entrance, for it is there that the word is written. On p. 75 Lifshitz writes: "Die Inschriften auf den Sarkophagen und die Graffiti sind wahrscheinlich von denselben Leuten abgebracht worden, denn sie drücken dieselben Gedanken aus und enthalten dieselbe Formel." If such is the case, then the same hand that inscribed ὅσιοι in the corridor also wrote "holy" on the sarcophagus. (*c*) In the two previously mentioned cases my translation is "resurrection."

132 B. Lifshitz (*Beth She'arim*, II, no. 197) reads Μεωνιτον and interprets it as "a name indicating provenance from Ma'on (Μαών) in Judea." According to him the inscription indicates that in this particular place, the deceased are from Ma'on and that it was they who built the burial chamber (see: *ZDPV*, p. 70). My opinion is that there are no grounds for this reading and interpretation. Furthermore, the inscription is not even located inside a burial chamber.

133 *Beth She'arim*, II, no. 195.

134 *Ibid.*, no. 198.

135 This sarcophagus now stands in room X.

136 This sarcophagus now stands near the northern wall of the room.

137 This opening was discovered after the plan of the cave in fig. 43 was drawn.

138 See, for example, the comparatively rich finds in Samaria-Sebaste. Nine sarcophagi were found in a Roman mausoleum and ten in tomb 220.

139 The door and lock are preserved at the Louvre in Paris. See: R. Dussaud, *Les monuments palestiniens et judaiques*, Paris, 1912, pp. 58–59. For photographs and discussion of the operation of the lock and the reconstruction of the key see: *idem*, "La serrure de Sour-Bahr d'après les recherches de M. Ch. Fremont," *Syria*, VI (1925), pp. 188–193.

140 *Samaria-Sebaste*, I, p. 86, fig. 43.

141 *Beth She'arim*, II, no. 199.

142 *Ibid.*, no. 200.

143 Cf. the very similar Djed column: G. Jequier, *Les éléments de l'architecture (Manuel d'archéologie égyptienne)*, Paris 1924, p. 158, fig. 86.

144 See: *Beth She'arim*, I, Pls. X, XVII, XXVII, and XXVIII.

145 Cf. Albright's discussion on "cressets" or "incense stands" illustrated on the sides of the entrances to the Phoenician tombs discovered at Marissa and the association with the Egyptian Djed columns and the pillars of Jachin and Boaz in the Temple of Solomon. W. F. Albright, "Two Cressets from Marissa and the Pillars of Jachin and Boaz," *BASOR*, 85 (1942), pp. 18–27, figs. 1–10; *idem*, *Archaeology and the Religion of Israel*, Baltimore, 1946, pp. 144–148.

146 Cf. the Canaanite temple at Hazor, Area H.

147 For the discussion on this subject and a selected bibliography see: S. Yeivin, "Jachin and Boaz," *Eretz-Israel*, V (1958), pp. 102–103 (Hebrew).

148 J. Parrot, "Une tombe à ossuaires du IVe millénaire à Azor, près de Tel-Aviv," *'Atiqot*, III (1961), Pl. III, 1–2.

149 At the time of discovery this tomb was given the serial no. 21 and is thus recorded in the preliminary report: *IEJ*, VII (1957), p. 255, n. 71. However, for technical reasons, its number was changed afterwards to 31.

150 *Beth She'arim*, I, p. 25, fig. 6.

151 This designation is not appropriate to all the tombs of this group because, generally, only the structures that are above the tombs are built of stone and not the tombs themselves; however, the term was chosen for the sake of convenience.

152 After these lines were written, a Nabatean cemetery was discovered at Kurnub (Mamshit) in the Negev from the first century C.E. with square and rectangular stone structures above the graves. See: A. Negev, The Nabatean Necropolis of Mampsis (Kurnub), *IEJ*, XXI (1971), pp. 110–129, Pls. 12–25.

153 M. Mendrac & L. Albanese, "A travers les nécropoles gréco-romaines de Sidon," *BMB*, II (1938), pp. 74, 93; Renan, *Mission de Phénicie*, Paris, 1864, Pl. XLII, 8.

154 Arndt Haller, *Die Gräber und Grüfte von Assur*, Berlin, 1954, p. 35, fig. 26; pp. 143*f.*, 169*f.*

155 *Ibid.*, p. 149.

156 On the burial at Beth She'arim of a Jewish woman from Babylonia see: *Beth She'arim*, II, no. 101.

CHAPTER III

THE FINDS

1 THE STONE SARCOPHAGI

The sarcophagi discovered at Beth She'arim were remarkable in their profusion and decoration, some being even unique specimens among finds of this type in the country. Stone sarcophagi began to appear in Palestine in the Herodian period (first century C.E.) in tombs of wealthy Jewish families, for example the tomb of Herod's family and the tomb of Queen Helena in Jerusalem.[1] Recently, new sarcophagi were discovered in Jewish graves on the Mount of Olives[2] and on Mount Scopus.[3] All are decorated with floral designs only.

During the second and third centuries C.E. sarcophagi were increasingly used in the Mediterranean countries and also became very common in Palestine. The locally-produced stone sarcophagi are essentially imitations of the imported marble ones which were frequently decorated with garlands. Sarcophagi of this type were found in various places in the country, both singly and in small groups, but only in a few cases were they of any particular interest.[4]

In catacomb 20 of Beth She'arim, however, a total of 125 sarcophagi were found. Apart from the breaches made by the tomb robbers, most of the sarcophagi were preserved intact. Only a few did not have covers; a very small number were fragmented; and in only a few were parts missing. All the sarcophagi are made of limestone — either *nari* (from the surrounding neighborhood) or *meleke* and *mizzi ḥilu* (rocks from the more distant vicinity) — cf. the appendix.

The sarcophagi range from 2.10 to 2.60 m in length, .80 to 1.00 m in width, and .80 to 1.06 m in height (without the cover); the covers range from .50 to .60 m in height. The longest sarcophagus is 2.65 m (no. 51), and the tallest sarcophagus, including the cover, is 1.82 m (no. 92).

Generally the walls were approximately .20 m thick. Frequently a raised "pillow" for the head was carved at one end of the bottom of the sarcophagus (fig. 61). Since the covers were always solid, they were tremendously heavy: an average of 4–5 tons. Doubtlessly, an enormous amount of work was involved in conveying these sarcophagi to the catacomb.

Sometimes the sarcophagi were hermetically closed: the joint between the lid and the coffin was plastered on the outside, at times so expertly that it is hardly noticeable. The great difficulty in moving these lids from their place is evidenced by the fact that even the tomb robbers generally did not try to budge them. There were two ways of fracturing coffins depending on the tools used: occasionally, if the lid was not sealed with plaster, it was removed with an iron rod; the usual method, however, was to hammer the most vulnerable part of the coffin (near the edge) or of the lid (at the corner).

Normally the coffins were placed on the floor; however, on special occasions they were deposited on a built platform. This practice would seem to indicate particular respect for the deceased and, indirectly, was also a preventive measure against moving the sarcophagus.

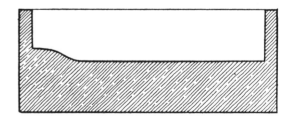

Fig. 61 Section of sarcophagus

Almost all the sarcophagi have the same kind of cover: a gabled roof with acroteria at the corners. During the Roman period, this form of lid was most commonly used in the Levant; its origin evidently lies in the desire to imitate the design of a house. Sometimes the rounded shape of the acroteria degenerated, and they became flat and broad.

Approximately 90 sarcophagi are undecorated. They are generally inferior in workmanship to the decorated sarcophagi, which form a third only of the whole collection. The decorations are usually carved in relief, in geometrical and architectural designs, or animal and floral patterns. The workmanship is often poor or mediocre, both technically and artistically. Only two sarcophagi (no. 97 and no. 101) are of almost as high a standard as the marble sarcophagi. Only a few sarcophagi (for example nos. 52, 54–56, and others) have excellent combed dressing.

The decorated stone sarcophagi may be classified into four main groups, according to decoration and to quality of workmanship:

1. Coffins decorated with geometric designs. This is the traditional pattern found on ossuaries. The workmanship rates from average to poor. They are made of various kinds of stone.

2. Sarcophagi decorated with motifs derived from coffins of the Roman period, or with designs common in decorative synagogue art. The carving is primitive. The sarcophagi are made of different kinds of stone.

3. The two "acanthus" sarcophagi, distinguished from the rest of the coffins by their superb carving. Both were manufactured of hard *nari*.

4. Sarcophagi with a tabula ansata, similar to sarcophagus no. 54 (see Pl. LI, 1). They are uniform in size, decoration, and excellence of finish. All of them were manufactured out of *mekele* stone. Similar sarcophagi were discovered in other places in Palestine and in neighboring countries.

We have no conclusive data for determining the origin of the stone sarcophagi, i.e., whether or not they originated in Beth She'arim. The truth of the matter is that this question is not particularly important unless one doubts whether they were manufactured in a Jewish workshop (this problem arises in connection with the carved figures and will be discussed later). In our opinion these doubts are unfounded.

The type of the stone is not an infallible criterion for specifying the location of the workshops where the sarcophagi were manufactured. Various types of stone were utilized, both from the nearby and the distant surroundings of Beth She'arim. It is quite possible that the sarcophagi of group 4 were made in a workshop outside Beth She'arim since they are homogeneous in form and type of stone. The two sarcophagi of group 3 might be attributed to artisans outside Beth She'arim because of their superior workmanship; however, this is by no means certain since they were both made of local *nari* stone. Many different types of stone were used for the undecorated sarcophagi of groups 1 and 2, therefore, other factors aside from the type of stone have to be considered in determining their origin.

It seems reasonable to assume that the Beth She'arim "tomb industry," which developed on a broad scale and employed many hewers, stone pointers, and artisans, would also include the workshops necessary for the manufacture of stone coffins for clients who could not afford imported marble sarcophagi. As a matter of fact, the poor quality of carving on most of the sarcophagi is of a similar standard to that found on walls in other catacombs at Beth She'arim. The chief products of the workshop (or workshops) of Beth She'arim are the sarcophagi of groups 1 and 2. They have been named "the sarcophagi of Beth She'arim," precisely because they have many properties in commom.

Before the discovery of catacomb 20 we

did not know whether the Jews of Palestine used coffins in the early centuries after the destruction of the Second Temple. The few sarcophagi from this period discovered sporadically in Palestine were generally considered as pagan since there was no evidence for designating them as Jewish. At that time, the findings on the subject were summarized by Goodenough in volume I of his book.[5] He stated there that the use of sarcophagi among the Jews of Palestine was restricted to the first century C.E., the same period when ossuaries were used, and that later on it was not Palestinian Jewish practice to inter in sarcophagi. This conclusion seemed rather arbitrary inasmuch as Jews in the Diaspora made use of sarcophagi carved with Jewish symbols alongside pagan decorations. The sarcophagus carved with Leda and the Swan, at that time the only marble sarcophagus discovered at Beth She'arim, provided Goodenough with an example of the exception which proves the rule. From this he inferred that sarcophagal art was non-existent in Palestine — an art that would have demonstrated the strong influence of Greek culture on the Jews so clearly evidenced already by other finds of the same period. The discovery of the sarcophagi in Beth She'arim enabled Goodenough to introduce corrections in his succeeding volumes.

The "daughters" sarcophagus (Pl. XXXIX)
This sarcophagus, no. 25, was discovered in room V. It is 2.27 m long, .85 m wide, and .86 m high; the cover is .56 m high.

The cover was slightly moved by tomb robbers. After the excavation it was transferred from room V to room I near the entrance of the catacomb, in order to protect the engraved inscription from humidity.

In the center of the front — the long side — of the sarcophagus, a rectangle with two intersecting diagonals is incised. The rectangle is .54 × .83 m. On either side of it

there are two wreaths. The right-hand wreath is incised in diagonal, pope-like lines, in sunk relief. The ribbon dangling from the wreath is stylized in a geometric design somewhat similar to a monogram of the letters A and Y. The wreath to the left was not completed and is only indicated by external engraved lines in the shape of the Greek letter *omega*. All the incised lines were painted red.

The acroteria on the cover are really just extensions of the gabled roof. On the long side of the cover, including the entire sloping area and the underlying margin, there is a Hebrew inscription (no. 14), incised and painted in red. According to the inscription two daughters of a rabbinical family were interred in this sarcophagus.

On the right narrow side of the sarcophagus, a concave disc was carved, .43 m in diameter, with a button jutting out of the center (fig. 62). The left narrow side is undecorated and only roughly dressed.

The wreath motif is very common in

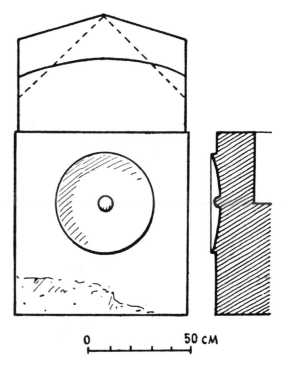

Fig. 62 The "daughters" sarcophagus

Jewish sepulchral art at the end of the Second Temple period; it is also encountered frequently in the lintels and friezes of the ancient synagogues.[6]

The "lions" sarcophagus (Pl. XL, 1)

This sarcophagus, no. 47, was discovered in room VIII₃. It is 2.48 m long, 1.00 m wide, and .95 × .53 m high.

The lid was removed by tomb robbers; at the time of discovery it was found leaning against the front of the sarcophagus. The lid is much longer than the coffin itself — 2.70 m. The sarcophagus is made of fine white stone.

The long side — the front — of the sarcophagus is decorated with a bas-relief of a lion and a lioness standing opposite each other, with what seems like an incomplete vase between them. The carving is very rough and the artistic standard quite primitive. The lions' mouths are half open, their tongues extending between two rows of sharp teeth; the large eyes are frontal. The hair of the mane is designated very schematically by straight lines and covers a large part of the body; the lioness also has a mane. The lion is differentiated only by his male organ, by the crop of short hairs around his head, and by his size — he is slightly larger than his mate. His pose, on sloping ground, gives him a dash of realism. The lions' tails lie on their backs. In the depiction of the ears the artist revealed his observational powers: one of the ears is turned toward the viewer.

The form of the lions, the proportions between the different parts of the body, and the means by which the anatomical features are emphasized, all exude both primitiveness and naivete. Nevertheless, the composition is not lacking in a certain charm of its own and is bound to arouse the interest of modern art devotees. At any rate, the artist did succeed in creating the impression he intended of the fierce power and terrifying wildness of these beasts. He also heightened this visual impression by using

another device: all the lines designating eyes, teeth, hair, and toes were painted red and were thus strongly accentuated on the white background.

A rope-like band decorates the rim of the sarcophagus. A carved column, about three quarters round, is found at either edge of the long side. The bases of the columns are plain, and their shafts are twisted. However, the capitals are blurred, and only traces of spirals are evident. The grooves, both in the rope-like band and in the columns, are painted red. On the other long side of the sarcophagus there are no decorations whatever.

The motif of two animals facing each other with a central object between them was prevalent in ancient art. Examples may be seen in the deer, sphinx, and griffins on either side of the "Sacred Tree" and the lions flanking a column in the gate of Mycenae. This theme underwent many variations; however, because of its heraldic appearance, it became so common that at times it is difficult to reconstruct its original symbolic meaning. In many cases, it even appears that the purpose of this motif is purely decorative.[7] In the Roman period, the version of two lions standing in heraldic fashion beside a vase became very widespread. Thus, for example, it appears on several sarcophagi from Greece and Rome — always on the back wall of the sarcophagus, while the front is occupied by mythological themes.[8]

It is likely that the artist from Beth She'arim saw this motif on one of the marble sarcophagi in the catacomb and copied it for its explicitly decorative character. At the same time, he might have borrowed it from the repertoire of decorations from local Jewish art, for example, the lintels on the synagogues in Umm el 'Amed,[9] in Capernaum,[10] and in Khirbet Samaka[11] on the Carmel, and also on the entrance of a tomb in Kh. Samaka (here a lion and an ox are depicted on either side of the vase).[12] Later on, the same heraldic motif also appears in Christian art.[13] The particular style in which the lions' tails were raised may also be found in the relief of a lion in the synagogue at Nabratein.[14] While the motif of two lions on either side of a vase is common in synagogal decorations, it seems to us that the origin of this motif lies in sepulchral decorative art, as evidenced by the aforementioned sarcophagi.

The "hunt" sarcophagus (fig. 63; Pl. XL, 2) This sarcophagus, no. 44, was discovered in room VIII$_2$. It is 2.20 m long, .88 m wide, and $1.07 + .50$ m high.

This sarcophagus is cut out of white stone. Some damage was done to the corners and the lid. In the center of the long side, there is a carved sunken relief of a geometrical rosette with six petals made with the compass. The diameter of the rosette is .39 m. To the right of this rosette a hunting scene was incised in sunken relief. It portrays an animal, probably a lion, chasing a horned animal, apparently a gazelle, whose head is turned backward. The lion is disproportionately larger than its

frightened prey. The lion's body is clumsy and maneless; the feet of the gazelle are far too short.

On either side of the façade, there is a small column carved in three-quarter round relief. The small column to the right is mostly destroyed. These colonnettes stand on bases; their capitals consist of a group of tendrils. The rim of the sarcophagus has a slightly concave band. On the upper part of the right narrow side, there is a relief of a plain tabula ansata, .35 m long and .22 m high.

This sarcophagus is remarkable for its hunting scene. This picture is a far cry from the stereotyped and conventional style which characterized the animals on the other sarcophagi. It was rendered by a deft hand. The artist succeeded in portraying a lively scene full of movement with rapid, simple strokes. The location of the hunting scene (at one side of the rosette which was intended to be the central decoration) and the depiction of these animals (suspended in the air, without any framework or ground line) are incompatible with the

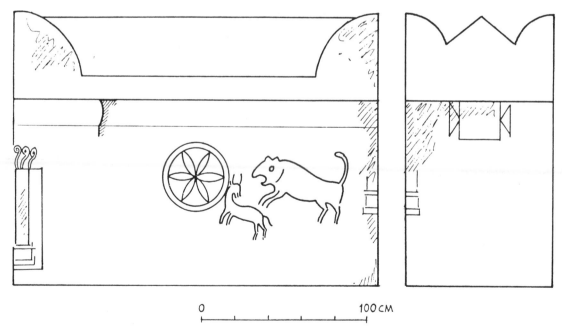

0   100 CM

Fig. 63 The "hunt" sarcophagus

customary artistic conception of these sarcophagi. These factors lead us to conjecture that this scene is a later addition, possibly introduced at the request of the customer.

If this hypothesis is correct, then it seems likely that here we have an example not of a conventional design, but of a depiction with symbolic significance, e.g., death striking his victim.

The motif of a lion chasing a gazelle or preying on his victim and similar hunting scenes are very common in the art of the ancient East (e.g., in ivory carvings and others).[15] A few of these motifs also appear on tombs from the Hellenistic-Roman period. For example, hunting scenes in which the lion pounces on his prey are quite frequently found on a particular type of Roman fluted sarcophagi.[16] A relief very similar to that of Beth She'arim also occurs in Nabatean art.[17] In the course of time, the motif became more abstract and finally evolved into the depiction of a lion laying his paw on the head of a bull (see the discussion on the next sarcophagus).

The "eagle" sarcophagus (Pl. XLI; XLII, 1–2)

This sarcophagus, no. 56, was discovered in room XI.[18] It is 2.60 m long, .88 m wide, and 1.05 + .50 m high.

The lid was placed on the rim of the coffin without mortar. Inside the sarcophagus, a lamp from the Early Arab period was found (type 51). It certainly must have belonged to a tomb robber; probably it fell out of his hand through the narrow hole while he was examining the interior of the coffin in its light to see if any valuables remained.

The sarcophagus is made of hard stone; the front is comb dressed. It has more decorations than other sarcophagi: each side has carved reliefs, both on the coffin itself and on the lid. The top and the bottom of the coffin have a cyma-reversa type molding. The reliefs of the animals are low

and protrude about 2 cm. On each of the long sides of the coffin there are identical reliefs of two lions standing opposite each other in heraldic fashion with the head of a bull between them. They are half crouched and have three (!) feet extending forward (Pl. XLI). The style of carving is different from that of the lions of the previous sarcophagus; however, it is not any less primitive. The heads are disproportionately large for the small degenerate bodies, especially in one of the pairs. The large uplifted tails were also unduly stressed, as though these two members expressed the threatening power of beasts of prey. The gaping mouths of the lions, the rows of sharp teeth, and the extended tongues (seemingly hanging from the lower jaw) all display the artist's extraordinary lack of talent. The lions' manes are designated by crescent-like incisions, very awkward on one pair and slightly better on the other. The threatening faces of the lions seem carved schematically; in a few strokes the artist was able to render all the anatomical details and even the bovine expression.

The decorations on the long sides of the gabled lid are not identical.[19] On one side, there is a carved relief of two garlands of long stylized leaves, one beside the other. Above each of the garlands, an eagle is carved in heraldic style; he is depicted with his head turning to the right and his wings slightly spread. His feathers are very schematically rendered. On the other side of the cover, above the garland, bulls' heads were carved in the style described previously.

On the narrow end of the sarcophagus (on the right side according to the original position of the sarcophagus near the wall), a garland was carved; above it there is an eagle resembling those on the front of the lid. On this side of the lid, a bull's head was carved (Pl. XLII, 1). On the other narrow end of the sarcophagus (Pl. XLII, 2) two bulls' heads were carved, one on the cover and the other on the wall of the sarcophagus, above a garland.

Altogether, the carvings on this sarcophagus include four lions, seven bulls' heads, three eagles, and six garlands.

This sarcophagus exemplifies some of the most characteristic motifs of funerary art from the Roman period in general, and from Jewish Palestinian art in particular. In the discussion of the previous sarcophagus, we dealt with the motif of two lions standing face to face. In this sarcophagus, the vase between them was substituted by a bull's head. The posture of the lions lends this relief a stronger impression of heraldic style than noted in the former sarcophagus. It seems reasonable to assume that the artist, here too, copied this motif from another source; however, we did not encounter an exact parallel, except for sarcophagus no. 117 in the same catacomb. From a conceptual point of view, the closest resemblances are the reliefs found on a lintel of the synagogue in Umm el 'Amed in Galilee,[20] and on a lintel from the vicinity of Tiberias,[21] also attributed to a synagogue. On both these lintels two lions are depicted, each with his front paw on a bull's head. Portrayals of single lions laying their paws on the head of an animal also appear on the murals of the synagogue in Dura-Europos.[22] Apparently this motif really evolved from the theme of two griffins placing their front paw on a human head — a motif which symbolizes a king subjugating his enemy.[23] The motif of a lion subduing a bull is one of the most prevalent in ancient oriental art; with certain modifications, it is even current in later art. It is quite possible that the lion laying his paw on the head of a bull is actually a schematization of the same motif. Since this theme was popular in the tombs of the Hellenistic and subsequent periods, a deep symbolic significance is generally attributed to it, according to which the lion represents death claiming its victim.[24] Thus, it seems reasonable to

interpret the motif of two lions with a bull's head between them as a further abstraction of the same subject.

In the "eagle" sarcophagus the bull's head also appears as an independent motif; it is frequently found on altars and sarcophagi of the Roman period as well. The bucrania have garlands suspended from their horns.[25] As the main ornamentation, it appears above garlands on the "bull" sarcophagus (see below). In Palestine bucrania appear in pairs also, both on lintels[26] and on tomb doors.[27]

The eagle, usually bearing garlands, occurs quite frequently on sarcophagi from the Roman period.[28] In a marble sarcophagus discovered at Tel Barak near Caesarea,[29] the eagle appears above the garland, like the one at Beth She'arim. It also appears above a garland on the murals of the Hellenistic tomb in Marissa.[30] The figure of the eagle is widespread in the ornamentation of Galilean synagogues as well.[31] At Beth She'arim the eagle motif appears at the top of the arch of the mausoleum,[32] and in a graffito in catacomb 12. Sometimes this motif seems to assume different symbolic connotations (e.g., the eagle on the pagan tombs was assigned the task of soaring to the heavens with the soul of the deceased);[33] however, on our sarcophagus, the eagle is purely a decorative pattern.

The garland is the most common decorative pattern on sarcophagi from the Roman period, especially in Asia Minor, Syria, Palestine, and North Africa. At Beth She'arim it consists of clumps of stylized leaves, like wreaths in the synagogue reliefs of the same period.

The "bull" sarcophagus (Pl. XLII, 3)
The photograph of this sarcophagus (no. 127) is presented in Plate XLII, 3; however, the sarcophagus was not found during the present excavations, nor have we seen it. At one time it stood outside the catacomb on the slope of the hill, at a spot which now adjoins the eastern wall of the courtyard of

catacomb 20. It is referred to by many authors;[34] and during the excavations of 1936–40 it was still there. It was taken subsequently to a nearby settlement, Giv'ot Zeid.

There is no doubt that this sarcophagus belongs to the assemblage of sarcophagi from catacomb 20. It was most likely taken outside during the pillage of the catacomb, when the catacomb entrance was still open, and left on the slope of the hill.

The rim of the sarcophagus has a cyma reversa profile. The base is not visible in the photograph. On the front there is a carved relief of three garlands consisting of long stylized leaves. Above each garland a bull's head is carved. The narrow side, visible in the photograph, is also decorated with a garland and a bull's head. The details of the flat face are not clearly discernible. The eyes and brows were indicated with incised lines. From the photograph, it would seem that the bulls on the front of the sarcophagus are extending their tongues. The first head on the front seems more like a ram than a bull.

If this sarcophagus is compared to the "eagle" sarcophagus (no. 56), many similarities in detail are revealed, e.g., the rim of the sarcophagus, the long leaves, and even the style of the bull's heads. All these features are evidence that the two sarcophagi were manufactured in the same workshop.

The "shell" sarcophagus (Pl. XLIII)

This sarcophagus (no. 117) was discovered in room XXI. It is 2.33 m long, .92 m wide, and 1.00+ .47 m high. The lid was mortared to the sarcophagus. Tomb robbers made a hole in the back of the sarcophagus.

The façade. The decorations on the front of the sarcophagus blend to form a wide ornamental frieze which covers about two thirds of the upper area. The central motifs are two aediculae composed of two colonnettes supporting a shell. These aediculae resemble decorated niches in Roman architecture which imitate the form of a shrine. The aediculae are placed asymmetrically on an elongated rectangular panel which protrudes slightly from the front of the sarcophagus. In the right aedicula is the figure of a lion, and in the left, a bird with long legs and flapping wings.

Beside the right aedicula there is a carving of a schematic wreath surrounding a geometric rosette. Near the left aedicula a wreath was also roughed out, as evidenced by the fine delineation marks. The artist completed the underlying ribbon, but for some reason he did not continue with the carving of the wreath itself. In the space between the two wreaths, there was a red dipinto Hebrew inscription (no. 25) which is barely discernible today. According to this inscription, the sarcophagus belonged to "(Rabbi) Gamaliel ben Eliezer." Between the two shells of the aediculae there is a strip decorated with a heraldic motif of two lions and bull's head. To the left of the lions two birds are pecking grapes. Below the left bird a small fish is carved. Beside them a pattern of interlacing circles was carved. Under this band there is a reel and bead pattern which also extends above the shells of the two aediculae.

A cornice-like molding runs above the aforementioned strip and extends down on both sides. In the frieze below the main panel two rows of interlacing circles were carved, forming an attractive embroidery-like pattern. On both sides a band of stylized schematic vine scrolls was carved; these are independent patterns which are rather incongruous with the ornamentation as a whole. The right scroll is composed of scallops, alternately containing a cluster and a leaf. The vine to the left consists of a row of superimposed arc-like patterns, each filled with grapes. This is an unusual stylization of a vine. Traces of red paint were preserved on the decoration.

The right narrow side. This side is replete with various decorations. A broad band is carved on three sides. On the left band there is a sunken relief of a stylized vine rising from a vase and turning right before terminating. The right band remained plain, thus disturbing the balance of the ornamentation. The main field of decoration in the upper part of this side is enclosed by two bands, one vertical and one horizontal, consisting of a row of ovolos which are made from interlacing circles. The main motif in this jumble of forms is that of a lion and a lioness (looking more like calves), standing face to face in heraldic fashion. Between the two lions there is a figure of a small animal, apparently a gazelle, looking back. The gazelle replaced the bull's head on the front of this sarcophagus and on the front of the "eagle" sarcophagus. Above the lions, to the right, five fish in various sizes and facing different directions are depicted. In the upper left corner, three birds are crammed into a tangle of branches; in the opposite corner, two birds are sparring on a branch. All the figures are carved in low relief, in exceedingly primitive style. In this confusion of motifs, there is no discernible plan except for the apparent need of filling the area to the maximum *(horror vacuis)*.

Below the decorative frame the stone was trimmed so that a flat rectangle was formed with two diagonal ridges at the sides. This particular form has a parallel in the narrow side of the "gable" sarcophagus (no. 103). This is only one of several resemblances between the two sarcophagi, as will be described later.

The left narrow side. This side has a relief of a framed square tablet (34 cm) which contains two superimposed pairs of birds standing one opposite the other. The lower birds have a projection on their heads, perhaps representing the crest of a hoopoe. The lid. On the edge of the cover there is a carved row of bead and reel. The acroteria, of which the right-hand one is broken, are incised with vertical volutes. In the center of the lid, there is a projecting shell carved in flat relief and surrounded by

a bead pattern. A similar shell also appears on the other side of the cover.

The "shell" sarcophagus is remarkable for its lavish embellishment. Evidently the artist did not attempt to imitate a conventional sarcophagus but made use of the motifs familiar to him from contemporary Jewish art. He thus created an original decorative composition, entirely different from the ornamentation on the other sarcophagi. The façade makes quite an attractive impression, even though the workmanship is inferior, and the carving of the animals is even more primitive than on the other sarcophagi. On the other hand, the right narrow side is merely a conglomeration of motifs, and the incomplete frame spoils the harmony of the composition.

The first question which arises is: What do these aediculae on the front of the sarcophagus represent? In design they are very close to the niche of the Ark of the Law in the synagogue in Dura-Europos,[35] to that of the mosaic in the synagogue at Beth She'an,[36] or to those carved on tombs in catacomb 4.[37] In the opening of one of the Arks in catacomb 4 a menorah is depicted; above the right column of the second Ark a lion was carved; between the columns there is a lulab. Obviously, the artist attempted here to add animals and ritual accessories generally associated with Arks of the Law in Jewish art as, for example, birds, menoroth, lulabim, and shofaroth.[38] Apparently the craftsman of the "shell" sarcophagus had seen examples of Arks of this type and borrowed the lion and the bird in the aediculae from their accompanying repertoire of symbols. Nevertheless, the fact that he carved two aediculae is perhaps evidence that he did not intend them to represent Arks of the Law but only as decoration.[39]

The heraldic portrayal of the two lions and the bull's head appears twice on this sarcophagus — proof of the great popularity of this motif (see above, the discussion on the "eagle" sarcophagus). An interesting innovation in one of the groups is the substitution of the bull's head by the figure of a complete animal, as though the artist revived the original realistic image of the animal from which the symbolic head evolved. Did he have a source from which he copied this version, or is it strictly the product of his own imagination? We have not encountered any parallels except in Assyrian art.[40] The vivid imagination of our village artist is demonstrated by the numerous fish filling up the space in the free composition. It must be admitted that fish are an unusual theme on sarcophagi (except for dolphins), and thus there is no point in trying to guess the artist's intention.[41] However, we would like to make a conjecture: Perhaps the artist attempted to depict at one stroke the birds of the sky, the animals on the earth, and the fish of the sea?

The bird motif must have been one of the artist's favorites[42] since he crammed it into so many places. The birds pecking at a cluster of grapes has a close parallel in the synagogue in Chorazain. The left narrow wall of the sarcophagus, bearing the carving of the four birds, is exceptional for its quiet and balanced composition. The birds are also more attractive, as if they were carved by a different hand.

The vine motif was very common in Jewish decorative art. It is no wonder, therefore, that it appears only on this sarcophagus which is characterized by its local style, in contrast to the other sarcophagi which imitate foreign styles. The vine scroll is devoid of any realism; it is stylized into a lifeless geometric pattern.

The "gable" sarcophagus (Pl. XLIV)

This sarcophagus, no. 103, was discovered in room XXI. It is 2.10 m long, .92 m wide, and .94+ .47 m high.

The central decorative motif on the façade is a relief of a gable enclosing a shell. Even though the two are not attached, it nevertheless seems that this is a stylized version of the well-known architectural feature called "the Syrian gable." This gable is surrounded on three sides by a molded frame horizontal on top and vertical on both sides. There is a Hebrew inscription, painted red, scattered between these architectural features. According to the inscription (no. 25), the daughter of Rabbi Yehoshua was interred in this sarcophagus. On the right acroterium of the lid there are incisions of volute designs. The left acroterium was broken when the sarcophagus was breached.

On the left narrow side of the sarcophagus a rectangular frame was carved, .34 × .49 m in size. At the bottom the frame terminates in a trapezoidal projection in the middle and a triangular edging on either side. Inside the frame there is a long-legged, long-necked bird with wings partly spread —perhaps a heron flapping his wings. A similar bird was found in the left aedicula of the "shell" sarcophagus.

Additional similarities between the two sarcophagi are the bird motif inside the frame, the molding pattern on the projection below the frame on the narrow side, the cornice band above the main decoration of the façade, and the shell as a central motif. It, therefore, seems most probably that both sarcophagi were manufactured in the same workshop.

The "mask" sarcophagus (Pl. XLV)

This sarcophagus, no. 84, was discovered in room XV. It is 2.15 m long, .97 m wide, and .90+ .50 m high.

The lid was well plastered to the coffin. The sarcophagus was plastered onto a platform of stones, .35 m high. It is assumed that placing the sarcophagus on a platform was an indication of particular respect toward the deceased.

The front of the sarcophagus is decorated with three slim columns carved in high rounded relief. Two thin garlands are suspended between the columns. Above each garland a seven-petaled rosette is carved. The leaves of the garlands are molded schematically in two rows. The bases of the columns were set on pedestals, an uncommon feature in local sarcophagi (however, see below, the discussion on the "column" sarcophagus). The capitals are Corinthian, schematically executed. They have several simple leaves, two volutes extending from the leaves, and an abacus.

On the right narrow side of the sarcophagus there are two carved columns, similar to the ones described above, with a heavy garland between them. The ends of the garland are fastened to rings suspended from the capitals of the columns. The garland has a profusion of grooved leaves; the workmanship is more attractive and naturalistic than that of the garland on the façade. Above the garland, there is a carving of a heavily bearded man's head, 20 cm high and 14 cm wide. The carving is quite crude. The curly hair of the head and the beard surround the face like a heavy frame. The dilated eyes without pupils and the thick raised eyebrows are very expressive. The presence of a human head of this type on a Jewish sarcophagus is quite unexpected and will be discussed in full below.

The main decorative components of the façade — the columns and the garlands — are derived from the "column" and the "garland" sarcophagi where each motif appears separately. This composite version is widespread mainly in the East. In Palestine, several sarcophagi decorated in this style were discovered, all of local manufacture. In the sarcophagus under discussion the bipartite division of the façade is typical, i.e., three columns and two garlands, exactly like the sarcophagus discovered in Sebaste.[43] However, tripartite division is even more common, i.e., four columns and three garlands, as exemplified in the sarcophagi in Tulkarem,[44] Gofna,[45] Haifa,[46] and Jerusalem.[47] The exceptional aspects of this sarcophagus are the rounded relief of the columns and their setting on pedestals, undoubtedly in imitation of the Roman "column" sarcophagi.[48] All the other sarcophagi discovered in the country have

pilasters without pedestals. This sarcophagus is also exceptional for its double columns in the corner of the coffin (Pl. XLV, 2, left). The rosettes above the garlands are a common motif in the local sarcophagi and replace the various masks and figures which generally appear on the classical garland sarcophagi. However, as mentioned previously, on the right narrow side of the coffin there is a carving of a bearded head.

Till now, no head of this type had been discovered on sarcophagi found in Palestine. The only coffin of local manufacture which has a carving of a human face is the one discovered in Sebaste: heads appear above the garlands (evidently Gorgonian masks); on the lid, a bust was carved, perhaps a portrait of the deceased.[49] In Tel Barak near Caesarea a lavishly decorated marble garland sarcophagus was discovered, obviously pagan in character. The sarcophagus was certainly imported; it has theatrical masks, heads of Medusae, and busts of goddesses.[50] In the close vicinity of Palestine, near Sidon, locally-made stone sarcophagi were discovered bearing carvings of masks of Pan, Dionysos, and other divinities, with underlying garlands.[51]

These features are all part and parcel of the accepted customs current in the second and third centuries C.E. in the countries throughout the Roman Empire: the decoration of sarcophagi with garlands, above which there were various masks and portraits (for example, comic and tragic masks, Medusa masks, Bacchantes, Silenus, Pan, and Satyr), and sometimes even with a portrait of the deceased.[52] These are the most common figures, frequently exemplified in sarcophagi from the Roman period found in different countries.[53] However, the repertoire of heads decorating the sarcophagi was not limited to these figures only but included other mythological figures as well, among them the main divinities. For example, the Roman sarcophagus in custody of the museum in Copenhagen is decorated with garlands on four sides and has portraits of the heads of Heracles, Medusa, Perseus, Hermes, Silenus, Dionysos, Satyr, and Apollo.[54] Of all these heads, that of Heracles bears the greatest resemblance to the head on the sarcophagus under discussion at present. However, Heracles's hair is short and does not merge with his beard, whereas the head on the Beth She'arim sarcophagus is characterized by the thick hair surrounding it. The only other figure in the Greco-Roman pantheon bearing a close resemblance to this head is the accepted portrait of Zeus-Jupiter-Sarapis. In this connection, it is important to note the extraordinary similarity between the head at Beth She'arim and the statue of the Nabatean god Hadad from Khirbet et-Tannur,[55] which is actually the eastern rendering of Zeus. While it is true that we have not succeeded in finding a portrait of Zeus on another sarcophagus, this is not as yet proof of its absence. On the contrary, it seems likely that the head of Zeus also served as a decorative motif on Roman sarcophagi.[56]

It may safely be assumed, therefore, that the artist who decorated this sarcophagus copied the form of the head of Zeus (Hadad, Sarapis) from an imported coffin, without any intentions of carving a pagan face, since the masks and heads on sarcophagi had long since lost their idolatrous connotation.[57] The alternative theory that the head represents the portrait of the deceased, as found on several pagan sarcophagi (and later also on Christian coffins) is untenable.[58]

The "Nikae" sarcophagus (Pl. XLVI, 1)
This sarcophagus is no. 125; it was discovered in room XXVII. It is 2.20 m long, 1.00 m wide, and .76 m high.

The sarcophagus is made of soft *nari* stone. The front and the right narrow side were decorated with reliefs; the left narrow side was roughed out but the decoration was not completed. The right end of the sarcophagus is broken. The lid is missing.
The front (fig. 64). The entire area of the façade is occupied by a flat relief depicting two flying winged Nikae (victories) holding a wreath. On either side of the Nikae there is a dwarfed column. The carving of the relief is crude and the style is very primitive. The central theme is the wreath; it terminates below in the traditional ribbon tied in a Hercules knot.[59] The sprays of foliage are just awkward clumps. The wreath encloses a pentagonal geometric design which has a circle in the center.

The torso of each Nike is erect and faces forward. The wings are spread on either

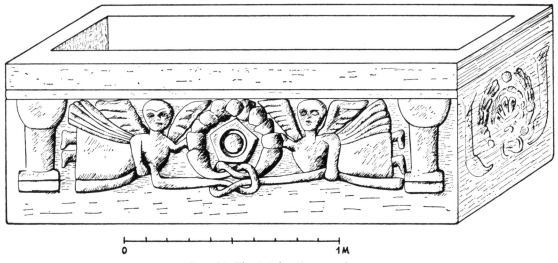

Fig. 64 The "Nikae" sarcophagus

side of the head, thereby emphazing the *en face* appearance. The lower part of the body extends horizontally, at right angles to the upper part. The feet are shown in profile, heel above toe. The Nikae are dressed in long plain gowns, without folds. Behind them their outer cloaks are fluttering, the folds indicated by grooves. The faces of the Nikae are depicted most schematically, without even a trace of hair. In one hand they hold the wreath and in the other the ribbon, which is extended horizontally in a most unnatural way beneath their bodies to the columns. The two columns are schematically indicated as well. Also, since the columns look as though they are suspended in the air, they seem very artificial. Their capitals are shaped like a large convex pillow (echinus), without an abacus. Each base consists of two slabs.

The right narrow side (fig. 65). The right narrow wall of the sarcophagus was broken into several pieces. On it is a carving of a wreath surrounding a shell. The wreath is flanked by two dolphins holding the ends of the ribbon in their mouth.

As a decorative motif, the wreath probably derives from Hellenistic art and most likely originates from the pagan custom of laying wreaths on graves.[60] In Jewish art the wreath first appeared on coins; by the end of the Second Temple period it was already an accepted decoration on Jewish tombs. Thus, it appears on the façade of rock-cut graves, on coffins, and on ossuaries from the end of the first century B.C.E. and the first century C.E. It is also common in the decorative art of the ancient synagogues from the third to the sixth centuries C.E. At first the wreath was depicted without any auxiliary decorations since in itself it signifies victory, peace, and immortality.[61] However, in the course of time it began to serve as a frame for another symbol—for example a menorah.[62] a portrait of the deceased, an eagle, a memorial inscription, or a cross. In decorative synagogal art there are many occurrences of a wreath enclosing an ornamental pattern, e.g., a shell,[63] a rosette,[64] or a geometric design. Since the designs inside the wreath were often deliberately mutilated, they can no longer be discerned.

This is the first time that the motif of Nikae bearing a wreath was discovered in the repertory of ornaments of Jewish sepulchral art in Palestine. On the other hand, it frequently occurs as the central decoration in the Galilean synagogues. The best example appears on the lintel of a synagogue in Rama.[65] The workmanship of the carving on the lintel is superior to that of the sarcophagus in Beth She'arim; however, the faces of the figures were damaged, and the center of the wreath—which apparently also contained a relief of some sort—was deliberately disfigured. From the standpoint of primitive style, a closer parallel may be found in the two fragments of a relief from the synagogue in Ed-Dikke.[66] The wide dissemination of this motif in synagogues is also evidenced by the lintels above the main entrances of the two synagogues in Kefar Bar'am.[67] On these lintels the wreaths are completely preserved; however, the figures were so badly defaced by the iconoclasts that they are no longer distinguishable except in general outline.

The theme of Nikae bearing a wreath has

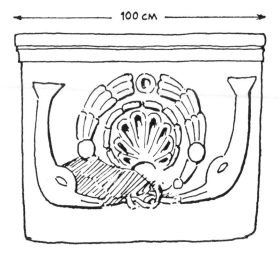

100 CM

Fig. 65 The "Nikae" sarcophagus; narrow side

a long history. The origin of this winged goddess is to be sought in Mesopotamia.[68] Later she became a common concept in the western world and emerged as the Greek goddess of victory, Nike. The Romans adopted her as the goddess of victory, Victoria; and in allegorical art she became the symbol of victory over death.[69] On the Roman triumphal arches the victories appear in pairs, each one holding a wreath in her hands. On the Roman sarcophagi they hold a tablet with a memorial inscription[70] or a round medallion with a portrait of the deceased.[71] On a Jewish sarcophagus from the catacomb in Vinia Randanini in Rome the two Victories are holding a medallion bearing the symbol of a seven-branched candelabrum.[72] In all these cases the victories played only a secondary role. Christian art assigned the winged victory goddesses of the pagans a new function: that of angels of heaven.[73] Apparently the version of two victories holding a single wreath was widespread in the East, especially in Syria and Palestine. The body bent at a ninety degree angle is also one of the indications of oriental style.[74] Sometimes the Nikae are replaced by various animals bearing a wreath, especially eagles. For example, in the keystone of the central arch of the synagogue at Capernaum there is a carving of a wreath containing a shell; two flying eagles, whose outline is blurred, hold the ends of the ribbon in their beaks.[75] This feature is seen even more clearly on a synagogue lintel found in secondary use in a new house in Safed.[76]

The dwarfed pillars on either side of the Nikae seem to be isolated and entirely dissociated from their surroundings, unless we assume that they support the molded rim of the coffin. This would surround the Nikae with an architectural framework similar to that on the "lion" sarcophagus.

On the other hand, on the right narrow wall of the sarcophagus the ends of the wreath ribbon are held in the mouths of dolphins. This is a kind of reiteration of the contents of the relief on the façade of the sarcophagus, with a substitution of figures. The same motif also appears on sarcophagus no. 122 (see below); however, we have found no other exact parallel in Palestine or in the neighboring countries. The closest parallel encountered is a relief of two dolphins bearing garlands on a sarcophagus from Rome, now in Baltimore, U.S.A.[77] On the mosaic floor in catacomb 11 four dolphins fill the corners of a square which encase a circle.[78] With the same function of filling empty space, this motif also appears on the mosaic floor of the synagogue in Yaphia.[79] The dolphin was a favorite design in Greek art and was widespread in the ancient world. It also appears on Roman sarcophagi,[80] on Phoenician lead coffins,[81] and on Nabatean reliefs.[82] First and foremost, it symbolizes the sea. Opinion is divided as to other symbolic meanings, for example, immortality and fertility.[83] The dolphin also appears frequently as a decorative heraldic design.

The "menorah" sarcophagus (Pl. XLVI, 2–3)
This sarcophagus, no. 122, was discovered in room XXVI. It is 2.40 m long, .84 m wide, and .82 + .56 m high.

The front of the sarcophagus is plain except for two small columns carved at the corners. Between these colonnettes two thin red lines were painted: one, from capital to capital; and the other, from base to base. Apparently, these lines were marked in preparation for a carving which was not executed.

On the left narrow side there is a carving in round relief of a menorah with branches made of links. The shaft is short and set on a heavy-looking trapezoidal base. The division and form of the links is asymmetrical: to the right they are alternately round and flat; however, to the left, each of the links is trapezoidal. The height of the menorah is .77 m, and the width of the branches is .74 m.

In Palestine this was the first time that a

149

sarcophagus was discovered bearing the symbol of a menorah, except for the two imported lead coffins, also from Beth She'arim. This is the only coffin in catacomb 20 whose Jewish character is explicit, excluding, of course, those bearing inscriptions. On the other hand, in the catacombs of Rome three sarcophagi were found with carvings of menoroth.[84] It should be noted that none of the numerous coffins and ossuaries found so far from the Second Temple period are decorated with true menoroth, but with stylized menorah-like patterns instead. This phenomenon stems from the tendency among Jews of that time to refrain from decorating tombs with any religious symbols whatsoever.[85] On the other hand, the tombs at Beth She'arim are decidedly influenced by symbols of menoroth;[86] it seems quite certain that if additional Jewish sarcophagi will be discovered, the number of ornamental menoroth will also increase. As a matter of fact, on a Jewish tomb in Tamra in Western Galilee reliefs of menoroth were also found, both on the lintel and on the door wing.[87]

On the other narrow side of the coffin there is a relief of a braided wreath bound by a Hercules knot, with a shell in the center. Two dolphins surround the wreath, their heads down, and their uplifted tails holding the ends of the wreath ribbons. The patterns blend to form a compact, attractive composition, similar almost in every detail to the relief on the narrow side of the "Nikae" sarcophagus (no. 125; see the discussion on this motif).

The "acanthus" sarcophagus A (fig. 66; Pl. XLVII)

This sarcophagus, no. 101, was discovered in room XIX. It is 2.23 m long, .90 m wide, and the restored height is 1.20 m. At present it stands near the eastern wall.

The sarcophagus was found broken, and many pieces are missing. The lower solid part and several fragments of the sides were mainly preserved. It was made of hard stone and comb dressed. The quality of the carving is excellent; the relief is high.

On the rim of the sarcophagus, of which only a few fragments remained, there was a row of egg-and-S pattern, and below it was a row of bead and reel. Along the front, three garlands were carved. The ends of the garlands on each side join up with a large,

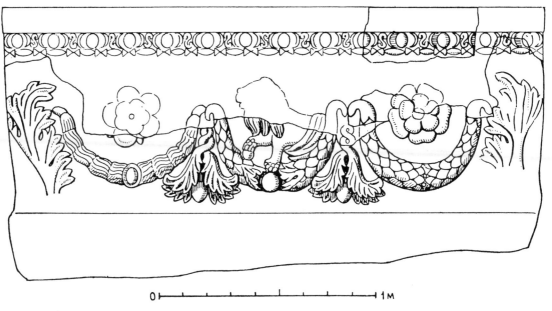

Fig. 66 "Acanthus" sarcophagus A

upright acanthus leaf, whereas in the center the garlands lean on two tassels of suspended acanthus leaves, carved in high hollow relief. The tassels are fan-shaped. Inside each fan, a plain grape cluster was suspended, its details left unfinished. The right and central garlands consist of the usual scale-shaped leaves; however, the left garland is composed of clumps of wavy leaves, difficult to define. A spherical object was carved in the center of the left and middle garlands.

Above the two lateral garlands there are remnants of two superimposed whorls of leaves. Above the central garland the front part of a lion is preserved. Part of the body and the mane and the two front feet are extant. The head is missing. The right foot is raised and is resting on a spherical object. The lion seems to be emerging from the leaves.

The two side walls are only partially preserved. They were decorated with a relief of a wreath which enclosed a crater with a grooved body, the upper part of which is missing. The base of the vase on the right side splits, in unusual fashion, into three parts which merge with the ends of the wreath. We have not found any parallels to these decorations on other sarcophagi (see the discussion on the following sarcophagus).

The "acanthus" sarcophagus B (fig. 67; Pl. XLVIII)

This sarcophagus, no. 97, was discovered in room XVIII. It is 2.06 m long, .73 m wide, and .75 + .38 m high. At present it is standing to the right of the entrance to room XX, replacing sarcophagus no. 96 which was transferred to the Hebrew University in Jerusalem.

The sarcophagus was found broken; many parts of the front and the lid are missing. Nevertheless, its design is readily discernible. It is made of hard, light-colored stone, and is finely comb dressed. There is no question that the quality of workmanship in this sarcophagus is excellent and that the level of execution is unparalleled among the

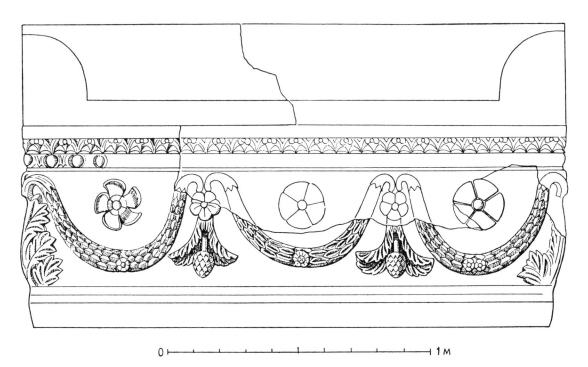

Fig. 67 "Acanthus" sarcophagus B

other stone coffins discovered in this catacomb but quite comparable to the carving on many of the marble sarcophagi. Only the "acanthus" sarcophagus A comes close to it.

The rim is carved with a stylized leaf pattern and a row of egg and dart below. Only the first four eggs were executed. Three garlands are suspended along the length of the sarcophagus. The ends of the garlands in the corners lean against acanthus leaves; however, the junction of the garlands in the middle is missing. The leaves of the two outer garlands are scale shaped, whereas the leaves of the central garland are long and grooved. Between the left and central garlands there is a floral design; in the center of the right garland there are two similar flowers.

Between the garlands, there are suspended tassels of delicate acanthus leaves in very high and hollow relief, similar to those on the previous sarcophagus. They are fan-like in shape with a pendant cluster in the middle. In coffins of this type there are generally clusters of grapes suspended beneath the garlands. The clusters here look more like pine cones; however, that might be quite unintentional. The acanthus tassels are suspended from small rosettes, an attractive motif which has no parallel in the other coffins. The acanthus leaves bulge at both corners of the coffin, thus forming a convex profile. Above each of the two lateral garlands there is a five-petaled rosette. The leaves of the left rosette are bent counterclockwise. It seems very likely that there was also a rosette pattern above the central garland.

On the left narrow side of the sarcophagus there is a single garland with an overlying rosette and an acanthus leaf in the corner. Both the garland and the acanthus leaf were left unadorned. Similarly, the rim of the sarcophagus remained undecorated. Only the carving of the rosette was properly finished.

Most of the right narrow side is missing and only part of a plain garland is preserved. On this side the corner does not have an acanthus leaf.

The two "acanthus" sarcophagi bear a close resemblance to the marble garland sarcophagi which were manufactured in Asia Minor or in other large centers. There is no doubt that they were carved by different artists than those who manufactured the rest of the stone sarcophagi in catacomb 20, since the latter are generally of crude workmanship. The standard of execution is not inferior to that of the stone carvings in the synagogue in Capernaum. This may also account for the smashing of the coffins. Obviously, one cannot help but question why only these two sarcophagi were broken to pieces, while the rest of the decorated sarcophagi (except for the marble coffins which will be discussed later) were left untouched, more or less. It seems likely that the robbers who broke the coffins for the marble thought that these two coffins were also made of marble and therefore began to break them, and only then did they discover their mistake.

The decorations of the two "acanthus" sarcophagi are composed of an unusual mixture of motifs. The three garlands with the lion were apparently copied from the imported marble garland sarcophagi. Other deviant elements, which both sarcophagi have in common, are the acanthus leaves and the acanthus tassels with pendant clusters. Usually garlands are borne by Nikae, figures of Eros, bulls' heads, eagles or columns, and the clusters of grapes are suspended below the garlands.[88] The vases inside the wreaths are also an unusual motif in imported sarcophagi; on the other hand this motif is common in the ancient synagogues of this country.

Another exceptional motif is the lion on sarcophagus no. 101. The front part of his body emerges out of the leaf pattern — a depiction for which we have found no example in the other coffins.[89] This is a Hellenistic theme ("peopled scrolls") which became popular in the decorative art of the Roman Empire,[90] for example, in the stately buildings of Asia Minor and Syria, and of the Nabateans.[91] Generally it appears in acanthus scrolls or as a repeated pattern in decorative friezes, like the frieze on the façade of the synagogue in Capernaum.[92] In the sarcophagus from Beth She'arim, the lion and the leaves are attached to the garland in an unintegrated fashion; thus, this motif does not seem to be in place. It was probably copied from a marble sarcophagus; however, there is also a possibility that it was borrowed from synagogue decorations (e.g., those of Capernaum).

The two acanthus sarcophagi are therefore indigenous productions either from Beth She'arim itself or from the neighboring vicinity. The artist succeeded in executing first-rate work and in attractively blending motifs borrowed from local and foreign art.[93]

The "gate" sarcophagus (Pl. XLIX, 1–2)

This sarcophagus, no. 46, was discovered in room VIII$_2$. It is 2.55 m long, .92 m high, and .97 + .52 m high.

This sarcophagus excels in architectural decoration. The carving is not refined and is sometimes even coarse. The designs were partially effaced. On the front there are four columns: one at each corner and two in the center. They subdivide the surface into three fields. The inner columns are flat and vertically fluted; they have simple bases and capitals with a rounded echinus and an abacus. The style of the capitals is not clear (Doric?). Between these columns a gate with a double door is carved; the door wings are divided into rectangular panels. On the jambs of the gate and on the lintel a sort of string of reels is carved. The two small columns in the corners of the façade are three-quarters round. They have neither bases nor capitals. They are fluted vertically below and obliquely above. The two fields between the corners and the central columns are deeply grooved; the right one

with oblique lines, and the left one with rough curves.

The right narrow side of the sarcophagus has a central column similar to the gate columns on the front (Pl. XLIX, 2). On either side of it, there is a carving of a large rhombus containing a circle. Flanking the rhombi there are small circles and more rhombi. On the left the corner column of the front is visible. The left narrow wall of the coffin is entirely incised with rough curves. The lid, which had been found thrown on the floor, is also outstanding for its unconventional decorations. The two slopes of the gable are partitioned by plain bands into six vertical strips. Each strip contains carvings of various geometric and floral designs, and also a high-necked vase with two handles. The design as a whole looks like an attractive embroidery.[94] Each of the four acroteria is surrounded by a thick rope-like strip. These decorations have no parallel in other sarcophagi. One of the narrow sides of the cover is decorated with a partially broken gable enclosing a shell. The other narrow side is undecorated.

The main architectural element on this sarcophagus, a gate between columns, is very common on Roman burial coffins where it generally symbolizes the gate of the tomb or the entrance to the world beyond. A noteworthy comparison can be made between this sarcophagus and the Roman striated sarcophagi bearing depictions of gates.[95] A sarcophagus of this type served as a model for the artisan from Beth She'arim; however, the result was rather crude. It is of interest to note that the gate design also appears on Jewish ossuaries from the end of the Second Temple period.[96] Therefore, the artist might also have been influenced by Jewish decorative art (see, however, the imitation of the grooves which derive from sarcophagal decoration). Some scholars are of the opinion that the gates on the ossuaries represent the Ark of the Law;[97] even though it is not entirely impossible, this conjecture is not sufficiently well found-

153

ed. To this date, not a single ossuary has been found bearing an object which can be interpreted with absolute certainty as a religious symbol, like the ritual objects so commonly found in the synagogal and sepulchral art of that period.

In summation, the façade of this sarcophagus is very similar to the front of a house with four columns, a gate, and a gabled roof in which the "rafters" are visible. However, the decorative patterns between the "rafters" detract from the architectural impression of the "roof" and make it look more like a carpet.

The "column" sarcophagus (fig. 68; Pl. L, 1)
This sarcophagus, no. 124, was discovered in room XXVI. It is 2.30 m long, .87 m wide, and .85 + .60 m high.

Starting at the right side of the façade and extending for 1.72 m, there is a row of six carved rounded columns. The remaining part is undecorated. Two red horizontal

lines are discernible on the plain surface; they were, apparently, supposed to serve as outlines for additional carvings which, however, were not executed.

The style of decoration is very schematic, and workmanship is crude. The six columns were set on carelessly carved pedestals. Some of the pedestals were not even completed. The capitals of the columns were indicated most schematically. In four of them, the two schematic leaves seem to suggest the Corinthian style; whereas, in the two others, the double circles are reminiscent of Ionic style. The six columns constitute the main architectural decoration of the sarcophagus.

Pedestals are also carved in the spaces between the columns. Flat columns were placed on three of them. These columns are lower than the main ones, i.e., they are free standing and do not support a beam. These secondary columns are fluted vertically and marked with short incisions. Their sche-

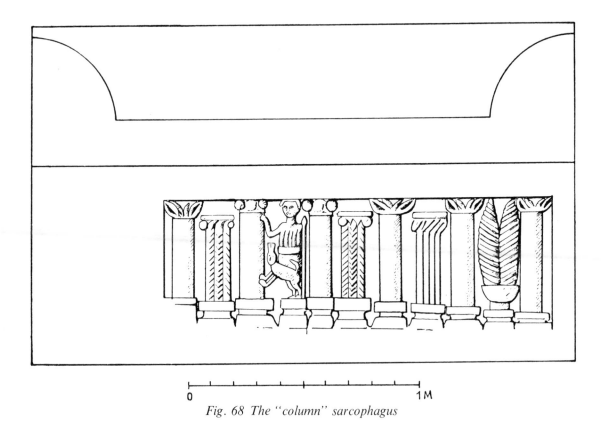

0   1 M

Fig. 68 The "column" sarcophagus

154

matic capitals are suggestive of Ionic style. All the incised lines are painted red.

On the pedestal of the second intercolumniation from the left there is a figure of a man, dressed in a striped shirt, holding a spear in his left hand. In front of him, there is a small animal in a leaping position. The workmanship is crude. It is difficult to identify the animal; it seems to have erect ears (or horns?).

In the first intercolumniation to the right, there is a depiction of a unique article consisting of two elongated bodies of pointed spools, obliquely fluted, standing on a bowl-like object. The bowl has a low stem attached to the pedestal. The pedestal is not an integral part of the stem; rather, it belongs to the row of pedestals.

The main motif—a row of columns on pedestals—is borrowed from the Roman sarcophagi known as the "column sarcophagi."[98] The columns on these sarcophagi generally form a colonnade of arches; however, occasionally they support a horizontal architrave.[99] Between columns of this type figures, also standing on pedestals, are usually sculptured. Of all these figures, only one was carved on the sarcophagus being discussed here: apparently a hunter and his dog—a theme of mythological origin. In Greek sculpture, the figure thus represented is Meleager, the celebrated hero, chasing the Calydonian boar.[100] He usually holds a spear in his hand and is accompanied by his dog. Alternatively, the figures here might represent Artemis and her gazelle. Both of these mythological figures appear on a Roman "column" sarcophagus, each in an intercolumniation.[101]

The three secondary columns apparently served as a convenient device for filling in the space between the columns and replaced the figures which the artisan had seen in the prototype. Obviously, one would doubt whether his model exhibited such a strange architectural combination. The single column served as a decorative motif on ossuaries from the first century C.E.,[102] though

some scholars would assign them a symbolic significance.

The enigmatic object between the two columns to the right is particularly puzzling. This is a most uncommon design. It does not appear on any other sarcophagus, nor in the repertoire of designs from that period. A single spool of this type might have been interpreted as a lulab; however, it is untenable that two such spools represent a double lulab. On the basis of a few parallels, I would like to suggest a tentative interpretation—albeit with some hesitation—which derives both from the source of these parallels and from their early date.

Among the ivory plaques from Megiddo (dating to the thirteenth or the beginning of the twelfth century B.C.E.), there are two which are carved in the form of a crouching female cherub (winged sphinx), holding a chalice in her hands. Standing on the chalice are two joined tall, cylindrical objects, rounded at the top. (fig. 69, 2).[103] A decided Egyptian influence may be detected in the style of the sphinx. In the *Megiddo Excavations Report* this ivory plaque was described as "a sphinx holding a cup," with no additional comment. This chalice and its "contents" bear a close resemblance to the enigmatic object in Beth She'arim, where only the lower part of the high foot of the chalice is missing because of the pedestal of the column (fig. 69, 1).

Since we have mentioned Egyptian influences, led us try to see if there are Egyptian parallels to our object. Among the murals in tombs of the New Kingdom (fourteenth century B.C.E.), where presentations of offerings to the deceased are depicted, some of the bearers of offerings carry in their hands a chalice (fig. 69, 4)[104] or a bowl (fig. 69, 3),[105] which contain two conical pastilles of aromatic fat. The sphinx in the Megiddo ivories also seems to hold an offering chalice of this type. However, it is also possible that the cylindrical objects in the chalice are unusually tall loaves of Egyptian bread.[106]

It is not at all surprising that the Egyp-

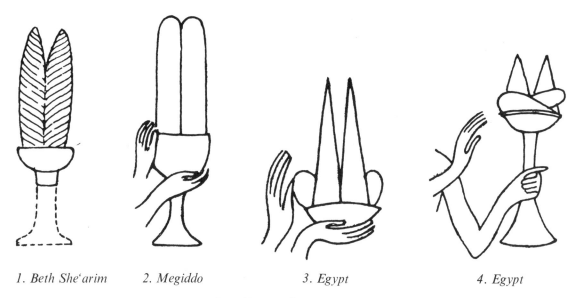

1. Beth She'arim   2. Megiddo   3. Egypt   4. Egypt

Fig. 69 Sacrificial chalices.

tian offering chalice served as a motif for the Canaanite-Phoenician ivories of Megiddo; however, it is difficult to conceive how this motif reached a Jewish sarcophagus from the Roman period. A likely explanation would be that offering chalices of this type were depicted in Egyptian tomb paintings of the Hellenistic period as well,[107] and that on the Hellenistic and Roman sarcophagi it served as a motif associated with the dead. In the course of time this association was probably forgotten, and the artisan at Beth She'arim copied the motif as a purely decorative design, adding the fluting on the cones of his own accord. At any rate, if this interpretation is indeed correct, then we have here an interesting and unusual revival of an ancient motif which had lost its original significance.

The "tabula-ansata" sarcophagi

These sarcophagi are characterized by a tabula ansata as the central motif. They may be divided into two types, A and B.
T y p e A (fig. 70; Pl. LI, 1). Four sarcophagi of this type (nos. 52–55) were found in room XI, and a similar number were found in other rooms. They have almost uniform measurements: length 2.10 m, width .70 m,

and height .70 + .27 m. They are made of hard limestone and finished with delicate comb dressing. They are more neatly worked than the rest of the stone sarcophagi. The decoration on all of them is identical: in the center of the façade there is a plain protruding tabula ansata, with unadorned garlands suspended from either side. Above each garland there is a plain disc, in essence a rosette whose details were not carved. Both the base of the coffin and the rim have a simple molding. The narrow sides are decorated with a garland and a disc. The lid has four acroteria and is exactly fitted to the body of the sarcophagus.

These sarcophagi, which constitute a standard type both in design and in size, were widely disseminated during the Roman period in Palestine, Syria, and other countries.[108] The fact that so large a group was found in one catacomb is evidence of their mass production and popularity. On the other hand, their superb workmanship testifies that they were by no means cheap. The tabula ansata was originally intended for an inscription; however, it was often used as decoration without any inscription.
T y p e B (Pl. LI, 2). Only one sarcophagus of this type was discovered (no. 96); it was

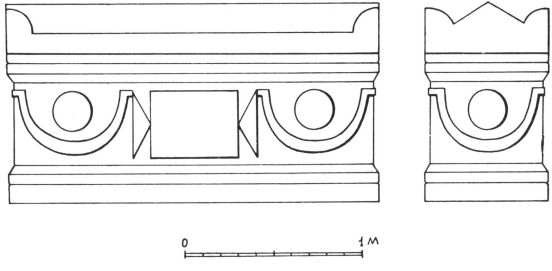

0   1 M

Fig. 70 Sarcophagus no. 54

found in room XVIII. It is 2.12 m long, .80 m wide, and .74 + .44 m high.[109] The sarcophagus was comb dressed, but the stone became corroded. In the center of the façade there is a relief of a tabula ansata flanked by two garlands with carved leaves. The side walls have a single carved garland.

The "rosette" sarcophagi

This group includes the sarcophagi which have a geometric rosette as a main decorative design, including rosettes with carved leaves, plain rosettes (discs), and rosettes incised by compass.

The "circle" sarcophagus (fig. 71; Pl. XLIX, 3)

This sarcophagus, no. 43, was found in room VIII$_1$. It is 2.23 m long, .79 m wide, and .88 + .51 m high.

The cover was mortared to the sarcophagus, the joins being well plastered. On the slopes of the gable four pairs of lines were incised, in imitation of roof rafters. On the

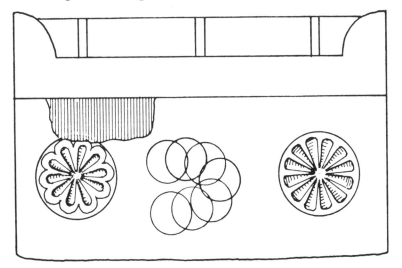

Fig. 71 Sarcophagus no. 43

157

front of the sarcophagus two sunken rosettes were incised. The rosette to the left has ten petals, and the one to the right has twelve. Between the rosettes a group of seven interlacing circles was incised. All the lines are painted red.

On the right side of the sarcophagus, a pattern was incised by compass: an outer circle surrounding four interlacing circlets. Below it is a tiny schematic wreath with suspended ribbons. Double rectangles are incised on both sides of the wreath. The incisions are deep and the lines are painted red. The inside of the "wreath" is also colored. The painted red lines on the white stone still make an impression of freshness.

Sarcophagus no. 94 (fig. 72)
This sarcophagus was in room XVII. It is 2.30 m long, .85 m wide, and .88 + .61 m high.

On the front of the coffin there is an engraving of three rosettes with twelve sunken petals. On the right narrow side there is a relief of a schematic garland with an overlying disc. The two discs below the garland are exceptional.

Sarcophagus no. 87 (fig. 73)
This sarcophagus was in room XVI. It is 2.05 m long, .87 m wide, and .84 + .58 m high.

Four compass-made rosettes are engraved in a row along the front of the sarcophagus. The first rosette to the right is geometrical and has six sunken petals. The second one to the right is a "whirl" rosette with protruding spokes; the background is sunken. The third rosette has six geometric petals, also sunken, their ends connected by additional petals. The fourth rosette was not completed and was only marked out by a circle. This proves that the artisan worked from right to left, a fact also illustrated in other coffins.

The vertical borders of the cover are unusually high. From the section shown (fig. 73) one can get an idea of the smallness of the cavity in relation to the heavy body of the sarcophagus and the massive lid.

Sarcophagus no. 120 (fig. 74)
This sarcophagus was found in room XXVI. It is 2.30 m long, .92 m wide, and 1.02 + .48 m high.

The rim of the coffin has a cyma reversa molding. On the front and back, three plain discs are carved.

On the right narrow side there is a disc with an incised geometric rosette. Along the edges of the wall there is a projecting band, both sides of which culminate in capitals

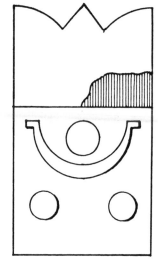

Fig. 72 Sarcophagus no. 94

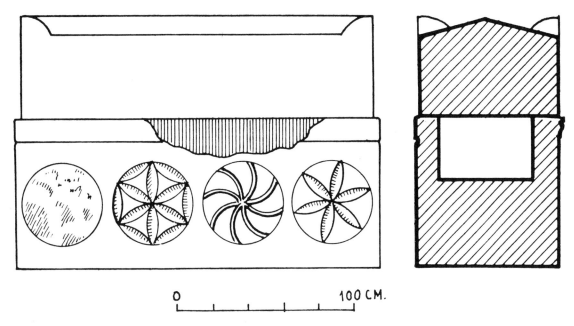

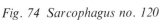

0   100 CM.

Fig. 73 Sarcophagus no. 87

reminiscent of Egyptian *Djed* columns. On the left narrow side there is only one disc.

Sarcophagus no. 119 (Pl. LI, 3)

This sarcophagus was discovered in room XXII. It is 2.28 m long, .80 m wide and .92 m high.

The sarcophagus is broken and the cover is missing.

The central motif is a relief of a "whirling rosette" with two lateral schematic garlands, degenerated into narrow plain bands, above which eight-petaled rosettes are carved. On the narrow side there are a garland and a similar rosette.

Sarcophagus no. 92 (fig. 75)

This sarcophagus was discovered in room XVII. It is 2.30 m long, .97 m wide, and 1.05 + .77 m high.

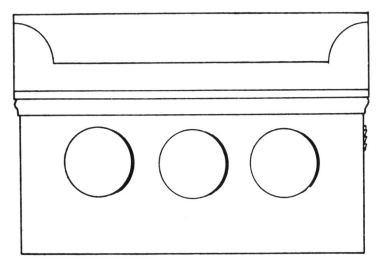

Fig. 74 Sarcophagus no. 120

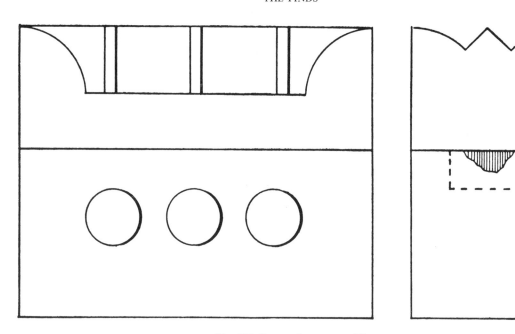

Fig. 75 Sarcophagus no. 92

This is the tallest and most massive of all the stone sarcophagi. It has the smallest cavity (see the figure) and weighs approximately 7 tons. It is made of finely-dressed white stone.

On the front there are three plain discs. The right narrow side is undecorated. On the left there is a large disc. On top of the slope of the lid there are three projecting bands, obviously imitating roof rafters.

The decorations of this group of sarcophagi, which also includes the "hunt" sarcophagus, are particularly interesting. The rosette motif was the most popular decorative design on Jewish ossuaries and sarcophagi of the first century C.E. It, therefore, seems likely that our sarcophagi continue a long tradition of Jewish sepulchral art.[110] Thus at least a few of the "rosette" sarcophagi may be considered to be among the earliest coffins in the catacomb, i.e., they date to the end of the second century or the beginning of the third century C.E.

Miscellaneous sarcophagi

A number of decorated sarcophagi, not classified in the above groups, will be described here.

Sarcophagus no. 27 (Pl. L, 3). This sarcophagus was found in room VII. It is 2.10 m long, and .85 m high.

In the center of the front, there is a protruding vertical band bearing a schematic branch. The band is 17 cm wide. It might be argued that this branch represents a lulab, but it is highly doubtful. At any rate, a band of this type is an unusual decoration for a sarcophagus.

On the back of the coffin a Hebrew inscription of a few lines was painted in red; however, the letters are so blurred that it is illegible.

Sarcophagus no. 60. This sarcophagus was discovered in room XII. It is 2.14 m long, .79 m wide, and .87 m high.

The rim and the base of the sarcophagus are molded. On the front three schematic garlands are carved. Above each garland there is a disc. On the narrow side there is also a garland with an overlying disc. This coffin is of the type found in catacomb 23 (Pl. LIX, 3).

Sarcophagus no. 126 (Pl. L, 2). These are fragments of a sarcophagus found in the courtyard debris. On the walls there are diagonally curved grooves. In one corner

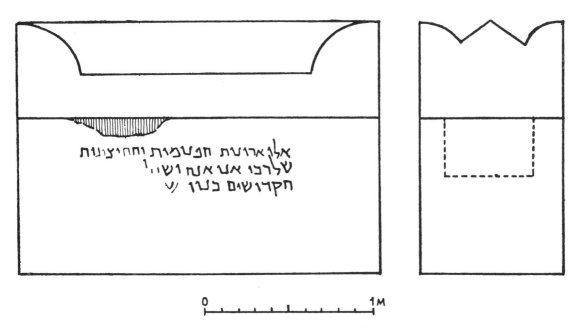

אלו ארונות חפנעמית וחחיצעות
שלרבו אגע א תא ו שי'
חקדושים בגו / / 'ש

Fig. 76 Sarcophagus no. 15

there are carved spirals; in the opposite corner, the carving of the spirals was not executed. This type of striation — though cruder — may also be found on the "gate" sarcophagus (no. 46). On both sarcophagi an attempt was made to imitate the Roman striated sarcophagi.

The inscribed sarcophagi

In catacomb 20 there were ten sarcophagi, six plain and four decorated, bearing Hebrew inscriptions. Following is a list of the sarcophagi, in numerical order, with the name of the deceased:

  no. 15 — The sarcophagus of the Holy Ones; plain

  no. 17 — The sarcophagus of Kyrilla; plain

  no. 25 — The sarcophagus of Atio and Ation; decorated

  no. 27 — The sarcophagus of Kyra; decorated

  no. 89 — The sarcophagus of Rabbi Hillel, the son of Levi; plain

  no. 103 — The sarcophagus of the daughter of Rabbi Joshua; decorated

  no. 114 — The sarcophagus of the three sons; plain

  no. 115 — The sarcophagus of Rabbi Joshua; plain

  no. 116 — The sarcophagus of the lady Mega; plain

  no. 117 — The sarcophagus of Gamaliel, the son of Eliezer; decorated.

The plain sarcophagi are generally very similar in form and size to the decorated sarcophagi described above. We shall briefly comment on two of them since they have inscriptions of particular interest: the first is the coffin of the Holy Ones (no. 15), and the second is the sarcophagus in which "the man who made the catacomb" is interred (no. 89).

Sarcophagus no. 15 (fig. 76). This sarcophagus was found in room III. It is 2.15 m long, .87 m wide, and .90 + .55 m high.

The cover has the usual acroteria. The dressing is smooth. The front of the sarcophagus was breached near the rim. The inscription is painted in red on the long wall of the sarcophagus.

Sarcophagus no. 89 (fig. 77). This sarcophagus was found in the corner of room XVI. It is 2.20 m long, .92 m wide, and .90 + .50 m high.

The sarcophagus was placed on a special

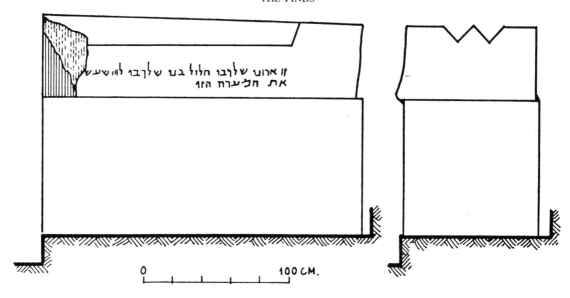

ז ארוני שלובי חלול גב שלקבו ולו שעי
את חלוערת הזו

Fig. 77 Sarcophagus no. 89

platform, .20 m high, hewn in the rock. The workmanship of the coffin is crude and untidy. The lid is irregular and was mortared to the edge of the coffin. The acroteria are flat and wide. The inscription is painted on the vertical margin of the lid.

Summary

The decorated stone sarcophagi of Beth She'arim are an exceptional phenomenon in the decorative art of Jewish tombs since, up to the time of their discovery, no coffins of this type had been found in Jewish tombs anywhere in Palestine. It may even be claimed that a new category of Jewish art emerged, an offshoot of the stone carvings with which we were familiar mainly from the early Galilean synagogues or buildings of similar style, like the mausoleum above catacomb 11 in Beth She'arim. It is difficult to understand what motivated the people of Beth She'arim to decorate the sarcophagi with figurative motifs; however, it seems reasonable to assume that they were strongly influenced by the numerous imported marble sarcophagi which were also deposited in catacomb 20 (see below). Evidently, there was a demand, both by the artisans and by the customers, for a product comparable in some way to the expensive,

elaborate marble sarcophagi that were, however, beyond their means. This desire must have induced local workshops, which mass produced sarcophagi either plain or decorated with simple designs only, to initiate the ornamentation of sarcophagi with other figures and motifs in imitation of the marble coffins.

However, it appears that the local sculptors placed certain restrictions on the subjects which they allowed themselves to copy from the marble sarcophagi. These restrictions were motivated by two factors: *(a)* their limited technical and artistic ability; and *(b)* their desire to avoid, as much as possible, depictions of unmistakably pagan themes. For this reason, the mythological scenes, which are so common on the marble sarcophagi, are absent on the stone sarcophagi. The pagan head on sarcophagus no. 84 and the figure of the hunter on sarcophagus no. 124 were evidently copied without knowledge of their pagan connotation on the part of the local sculptor. The flying Nikae on sarcophagus no. 125 are indubitably a mythological subject; however, this theme became a very integral part of synagogal art and it is, therefore, most likely that the producer of this sarcophagus copied it from a local source. This seems to be the source of the motif of the wreath-bearing dolphins (sarcophagi nos. 122 and 125) as well.

Conventional designs found on Roman sarcophagi are: the garland (sarcophagi nos. 54, 56, 84, 96, 97, 101, 119, and 127); the garlanded columns (no. 84); the eagle and the bull's head (nos. 56 and 127); the tabula ansata (nos. 54 and 96); and the architectural patterns on the borders of sarcophagi nos. 97 and 101. The striated marble sarcophagi certainly must have served as an example for sarcophagi nos. 46 (including the gate) and 126. Sarcophagus no. 126 was probably copied from the general arrangement of columns on marble sarcophagi of the "column sarcophagus" type. It should be noted that the numerous columns and colonettes in the corners (coffins nos. 44, 46, 47, 84, and 122) are conclusive evidence that the basic concept behind this design of the sarcophagi was the wish to represent a house. This feature is particularly outstanding on the lid, an imitation of a gabled roof, which all the sarcophagi have in common.

Despite the schematization of the decoration, all the tabula-ansata sarcophagi similar to type A (e.g., sarcophagus no. 54) are outstanding for accuracy, neat workmanship and quality of stone. Therefore, it is reasonable to assume that they were mass produced in a large workshop outside of Beth She'arim.

Even though the artists of Beth She'arim borrowed motifs from imported sarcophagi or made use of motifs indigenous to the local sarcophagi and to the synagogues, they nevertheless revealed a certain independence and also a degree of imaginative originality in the decoration of some of the sarcophagi. The best example is the "shell" sarcophagus (no. 117), which exhibits an original combination of motifs taken from Jewish art, for example, shells, vines, wreaths, interlacing circles, fish, birds, and lions. Sarcophagus no. 103 was probably produced in the same workshop.

The artist who carved the two "acanthus" sarcophagi (nos. 97 and 101) displayed a relatively high level of craftsmanship. He added a new motif to the conventional garlands: tassels of acanthus leaves with a cluster of grapes suspended between them. For the side walls, he employed a popular design in Jewish art: a crater encircled by a wreath.

Finally, the wide use of the rosette pattern, both schematic and sculptured, should be noted. It is not difficult to trace the schematic rosettes on sarcophagi nos. 57–60 to the traditional, widely prevailing use of this motif on coffins and ossuaries from the end of the Second Temple period. Similarly, the small sculptured rosettes found on many sarcophagi are one of the most common patterns in Jewish decorative art. The "menorah" sarcophagus (no. 122) is, up to now, the only stone sarcophagus found in Palestine bearing any religious symbol whatsoever.

It is noteworthy that the decorations on several sarcophagi were not completed, as for example the left wreath on sarcophagi nos. 25 and 117, the left rosette on sarcophagus no. 59, the egg and dart pattern on the rim of sarcophagus no. 97, and others.

There is nothing particularly impressive or creative in the artistry of the decorations on the sarcophagi of Beth She'arim. On the contrary, they display the low standard and inferior talent of the Jewish artists responsible for the carving. They were obviously provincial, inexperienced craftsmen, who were unable to achieve high artistic standards. There is a large gap between the carving on the sarcophagi and the animal frieze on the mausoleum at Beth She'arim, which is outstanding for its excellent workmanship. Only the two "acanthus" sarcophagi attain this high standard (nos. 97 and 101); they are proof that a workshop of a high level did exist here. The scene of the lion and the gazelle on sarcophagus no. 144 also shows the deft hand of an artist.

Nevertheless, the primitive works of art of Beth She'arim may be viewed as an expression of the folk art of this period and of the Jewish environment from which it sprang. It is noteworthy that the local artists did not always confine themselves to conventional designs in the style current at that time — as craftsmen generally did in other places — but took the initiative to create new patterns by combining motifs borrowed from Hellenistic art with themes current in other branches of Jewish art whose source is the Orient. Beth She'arim, therefore, was a creative factor in the new field of Jewish workmanship and art since it introduced many innovations in what might be called Jewish catacomb art in Palestine.

The primitive style of the figures and the low standard of execution are not surprising since, in this respect, they are similar to the other products of Jewish figurative art of this period — especially in some of the synagogues. A feature of major interest in the sarcophagi from Beth She'arim which caused some surprise is the presence of human and animal figures and pagan motifs on Jewish burial coffins. This is novel, though not entirely unexpected, since it is actually an extension of the custom current in the synagogues of that time. First in-dications of this trend had been discovered previously at Beth She'arim itself. The influence of foreign culture was revealed in many finds, especially in the numerous Greek inscriptions discovered at Beth She'arim; and it was further evidenced by the decorated 'sarcophagi.

The date of the stone sarcophagi cannot be established on the basis of form and decorative style only. A reasonable conjecture might be that the sarcophagi decorated in ossuary style are the earliest, i.e., from the end of the second and the beginning of the third centuries C.E. The sarcophagi decorated in imitation of the imported coffins date approximately to the same period. It is generally accepted that the marble sarcophagi, like those found in catacomb 20, were a common trade article in the world markets of the second and third centuries C.E. (see below); thus, it is probably correct to assume that most of the stone sarcophagi date to the third century approximately. Paleographic considerations concerning the inscriptions on several of the sarcophagi also corroborate this conclusion. If our hypothesis is correct, namely, that catacomb 20 was in use until the middle of the fourth century C.E., then we may well assume that sarcophagi were utilized here during this entire period.

2 THE MARBLE SARCOPHAGI

Aside from the stone sarcophagi discussed above, there were many marble sarcophagi in catacomb 20, as evidenced by the numerous fragments dispersed in various places in the cave, especially in the central hall. Generally, there were shapeless chunks, splinters, and chips, which fell to the ground when the coffins were smashed by tomb robbers. However, while the tomb robbers were satisfied with breaking into the stone sarcophagi and removing their contents, they systematically broke the marble sarcophagi into pieces that could be sold as raw material. The marble might also have been used for burning lime, as was customary in many places; however, this is by no means certain in view of the fact that many pieces which were suitable for this purpose were left in the catacomb. Evidently, the broken marble sarcophagi were transferred from their original locations in the rooms to the central hall where daylight penetrated through the open entrance. The pillagers worked in the front room where they split the marble into the desired shapes and sizes; this is evidenced by the layer of marble dust which covered the entire room right up to the entrance. It is important to note that the sarcophagi breakers did not sit on the rock floor but on a layer of debris approximately 50 cm thick. This proves that the sarcophagi were broken much later than the initial robbing of the catacomb, and that dust had penetrated in the meantime through the open entrance.

The large fragments were removed from the catacomb; however, among several cubic meters of amorphous debris which remained, some fragments were discovered which give us some idea of the general design of the sarcophagi. They were typical Greco-Roman sarcophagi with gable-shaped lids and acroteria. However, a feature of particular interest was the discovery of a number of sculptured and carved pieces of marble. Some of these fragments show that, among the marble sarcophagi, there were also coffins decorated with figures in the finest style of imported sarcophagi. The number of marble sarcophagi is difficult to determine with certainty. However, if we accept the plausible assumption that every empty or partially empty room in the catacomb contained mainly marble sarcophagi (in addition to wooden, pottery, and lead sarcophagi, as indicated by various remains) and if we take into account the large amount of marble residue which was disseminated in many rooms, then an estimate of approximately twenty marble sarcophagi seems reasonable.

A selection of sculptured marble fragments discovered in the catacomb will now be described. These few remains, which the pillagers left as useless, are the silent testimony of the enormous loss to the antiquities of this country caused by the destruction of these sarcophagi.

Three types of marble may be distinguished among the fragments (see Appendix B):

a. Fine, crystalline, pure white marble, with a sprinkling of mica. This is the finest marble.

b. Coarse, crystalline, white marble, with a few discolorations or bluish grey veins.

c. Bluish-grey, coarse, crystalline marble.

The Marble Fragments

The marble fragments will be described according to their numerical order in the photographs.

Plate LII, 1. The upper part of the body of Nike, the goddess of victory, with a garland on her shoulders. She wears a gown tied at the left shoulder. The head is missing. The right breast is bare. A belt is tied below her bosom. She wears a necklace and two bracelets on her right arm. An incipient wing is just visible behind the garland. The workmanship is inferior; the arm in particular was crudely fashioned. The marble is of type "b."

Nikae bearing garlands are a common motif on the corners of sarcophagi.[111] It was not customary to depict Nikae wearing jewellery; such portrayal is oriental in style, like one of the pagan paintings in Dura-Europos from the second century C.E.[112]

An extremely rare parallel of Nikae wearing necklaces may be found in the "garland" sarcophagus from Tarsus in Cilicia, at present in custody of the Metropolitan Museum of Art in New York (no. G.R. 1073). It is attributed to the period between the middle of the second and the third centuries C.E. (fig. 78).[113]

Fig. 78 Nike

Plate LII, 2. A male torso. The man wears a sleeved garment, folded on the abdomen. On his shoulders he wears a *chlamys* most of it in the back and a small part in the front of the body. This might possibly be a figure of a Barbarian (a non-Roman mercenary). The workmanship is excellent. The marble is of type "a."

Plate LII, 3. A fragment of the lower part of a sarcophagus. The lower row of dentils is from the base of the sarcophagus. On the horizontal surface there are traces of a number of figures: on the left side, an erect, naked, slender foot; behind it, apparently the foot of a fallen horse; on the right side, perpendicular to the row of dentils, a recumbent human leg, with folds of a gown visible above the knee. Below this recumbent leg, the toes of another foot are noticeable. A possible interpretation for this fragment will follow shortly. The marble is of type "a."

Plate LII, 4. A winged, headless Eros. To the left, the ends, of his curls are visible. The figure is seated with his hands folded over the right knee — a common depiction of Eros napping, his head resting on his knee (compare with fig. 79).[114] The figure is sculptured in the round. Only the bottom part was attached to the corner of a lid — either above an acroterium or replacing it.

Fig. 79 Eros

The workmanship is fair. The marble is of type "c."

Plate LIII, 1. The hand of a woman (an Amazon), feebly holding the handle of an axe. The anatomical details of the fingers are meticulously rendered. The workmanship is superb. The marble is of type "a."

Plate LIII, 2. A fragment of a woman's head, slightly inclined to the side. Her hair is parted in the middle and hangs down vertically. The tip of her tongue appears between the lips. From the facial expression, we can gather that this is a wounded Amazon bowing her head, dying. The workmanship is excellent. The marble is of type "a."

Plate LIII, 3. A bent leg. The gown of the figure is lifted above the knee. The calf is clasped by the upper strip of a high shoe. This is doubtlessly the leg of an Amazon mounted on horseback. The marble is of type "a."

Plate LIII, 4. A naked foot sculptured completely in the round. The marble is of type "b."

Plate LIII, 5. A fragment of the body of a naked man. The sculpture of the chest and abdomen is excellent. The marble is of type "a."

An interpretation of these fragments is given below.

Plate LIV, 1. A fragment of a man's face. The marble is of type "a."

Plate LIV, 2. A fragment of a man's head. Marble type "a."

Plate LIV, 3. A fragment of a woman's head. A braid hangs from either side of the left ear. The part which protrudes to the right belongs to the sarcophagus itself. It is possible that this fragment is of a Caryatid standing in the corner of a sarcophagus (compare with fig. 84 to the right).[115] The marble is of type "b."

Plate LIV, 4. A hand, probably that of a woman anointing, holding a phial (compare with fig. 80).[116] The marble is of type "b."

166

Fig. 80 Woman libating

Plate LIV, 5. A fragment of a woman's hand, sculptured in the round. The marble is of type "a."

Plate LIV, 6. A hand holding a shield, perhaps Aphrodite writing on a shield (compare with fig. 81).[117] The marble is of type "a."

Plate LIV, 7. A fragment of a bent arm, sculptured in the round. The marble is of type "a."

Plate LIV, 8. A fragment of a flexed leg,

Fig. 81 Aphrodite

carved in the round. The marble is of type "b."

Plate LIV, 9. A small head of a monstrous animal. The mouth is pierced as if for a bit. There seem to be horns (?) on the forehead. It is sculptured in the round out of marble of type "a." For the suggested interpretation of this fragment as the head of a legendary snake, see below.

Plate LIV, 10. A fragment of the front of a horse's head. The hollow section indicates a gaping mouth. The sculpture is in the round, of marble of type "a."

Plate LIV, 11. A fragment similar to no. 10.

Plate LIV, 12. A fragment of a horse's head with a gaping mouth. There is a bit (?) in the mouth. The marble is of type "a."

Plate LV, nos. 1–2. Fragments of a spear sculptured in the round. Marble type "a."

Plate LV, 3. A head of a spear carved in the round out of marble type "b."

Plate LV, 4. A fragment of a spear carved in the round; marble type "b."

Plate LV, 6–7. Fragments of a narrow band with two lines incised along its length. The band terminates in a tiny *pelta* (an Amazon's shield). In all probability this is the sheath of a sword (mistakenly printed upside down in the photograph).[118] The marble is of type "a."

Plate LV, 8. A fragment of a broad, molded, and arched band. This might be part of an architectural arch.[119] The marble is of type "a."

Plate LV, 9. A fragment of a human figure wearing a long toga. The marble is of type "b."

Plate LV, 10. A fragment of a human figure wearing a long toga. The marble is of type "b."

Plate LV, 11. A fragment of a leg (calf). The folds of the garment are fastened on to it with a button. The connection between the leg and the garment is not clear. Marble type "a."

Plate LV, 12. A fragment of an animal

leg sculptured in the round. Marble type "a."

Plate LV, 13. A man's thigh sculptured in the round. Judging by the size of the fragment, the figure must have been about 70 cm high. Marble type "a."

Plate LV, 14. A knee carved in flat relief. The folds of a garment are attached from behind. Marble type "a."

Plate LVI, 1–3. Fragments of a sarcophagus rim molded in cyma reversa.[120] Marble type "a."

Plate LVI, 4. A fragment of a border below the above-mentioned cyma, consisting of part of a row of egg and dart pattern in high relief. The workmanship is superb. Marble type "a."

Plate LVI, 5. A fragment decorated with drilled leaves and a row of dentils. Marble type "b."

Plate LVI, 6. A fragment decorated with drilled leaves. Marble type "b."

Plate LVI, 7. A fragment of a sarcophagus. On the lower part, there is a relief of an animal head (a lion?). The marble is of type "b."

Plate LVI, 8. A fragment of the lower corner of a lid, decorated with leaves and dentils. Marble type "b."

Plate LVI, 9. Part of a cluster of grapes that was probably suspended beneath a garland.[121] Marble type "c."

Plate LVI, 10. A fragment similar to no. 9 above.

Plate LVII, 1. An acroterium from a gabled sarcophagus lid.

Plate LVII, 2. A fragment possibly of a garland tied with a ribbon.

Plate LVII, 3–4. Two fragments of the side of a sarcophagus. The dressing was delicately stippled. Traces of a relief of rounded garlands are visible. Above the lateral garlands there were probably small circles; overlying the central garland was a tabula ansata (see the reconstruction in fig. 82).[122]

Plate LVII, 5. A fragment of a sarcophagus wall, different from those previously described. The wall is thin. The rim is rounded inside and flares outward. Part of the geometric design of the relief (apparently a rhombus inside a square) and a whirl rosette was preserved. This design is not common. See the suggested restoration in fig. 83.

Plate LVII, 6. A fragment of a sarcophagus rim: a Lesbian cyma differing technically in execution from the one in the previous plate.

Plate LVII, 7. A fragment from the capital of a colonnette. The members preserved are the right part of the abacus and part of a decoration of drilled leaves.

Plate LVII, 8. A fragment of a shell, very

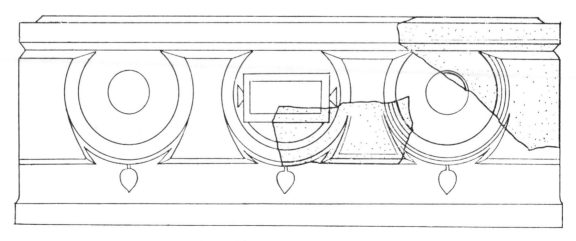

Fig. 82 Marble sarcophagus; reconstruction

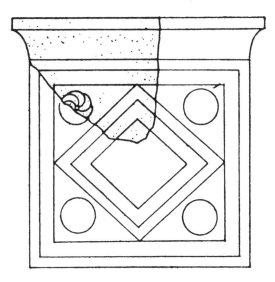

Fig. 83 Marble sarcophagus; reconstruction

likely of the type carved in the arched inter-columniations so characteristic of sarcophagi from Asia Minor.[123]

Plate LVII, 9. A fragment of a flat shell.

Plate LVII, 10. A fragment of a leg (calf), tied with the laces of a high shoe or a sandal (compare with the leg of the Amazon in Pl. LIII, 3).

The Significance of the Marble Fragments

Most of the marble fragments described above come from sarcophagi decorated with figures in very high relief, at times almost three-quarter round; some of the fragments are even sculptured completely in the round. The sculpture is generally of high standard. This technique is usually characteristic of sarcophagi which were in vogue during the second and third centuries C.E. in the large centers of Italy, Greece, Asia Minor, Syria, Alexandria, and North Africa. However, it might be sheer coincidence that such a high percentage of fragments of this type were preserved among the sculptured marble fragments at Beth She'arim. The various types of remains reveal that the fragments come from a number of different sarcophagi. Nevertheless, there are also fragments from plainer sarcophagi of mediocre workmanship.

Several imported marble sarcophagi were discovered earlier in Palestine.[124] Most outstanding among them is a sarcophagus from a Roman mausoleum in Tel Barak (Tell Mubarak) near Caesarea decorated with the depiction of a battle between the Amazons and the Greeks.[125] Another sarcophagus from the same place is decorated with figures and garlands.[126] A sarcophagus from Thurmus-Aya in the vicinity of Nablus is decorated with figures symbolizing the four seasons of the year.[127] Recently a broken marble sarcophagus was discovered in Caesarea; on it there is a depiction of Leda and the Swan.[128] As mentioned above, parts of a superb marble sarcophagus with carvings of Leda and the Swan were discovered at Beth She'arim during the earlier excavations.[129] This was the only marble sarcophagus encountered previously in the necropolis of Beth She'arim. The newly discovered fragments of catacomb 20 are thus a major new addition to the assemblage of imported marble sarcophagi and are of key importance in increasing our knowledge of their use among Jews.

As we have already seen in the previous descriptions, many of these fragments belong to sarcophagi decorated with mythological scenes or with other figures. One fragment (Pl. LIV, 6) apparently belongs to Aphrodite writing on a shield. Another fragment belongs to a woman holding an anointing phial (Pl. LIV, 4). Each of these figures is, of course, part of a larger scene which may be studied from the parallels illustrated here (figs. 78–86).

A number of fragments undoubtedly belong to the scene describing the battle of the Amazons against the Greeks, a popular theme on carved marble sarcophagi from the second and third centuries C.E. Figures 84 and 85 are examples of parts of such scenes from a Greek marble sarcophagus presently in custody of the Louvre Museum.[130] Of the fragments which can unquestionably be attributed to the figure of

Fig. 84 Amazonomachy

Fig. 86 Snake chariots

an Amazon the most noteworthy are, first and foremost, the head of the woman; the hand holding the handle of an axe; and the flexed leg in Plate LIII, 1–3. The flexed leg belongs to an Amazon riding a horse (see fig. 85); the two other fragments are compatible both with this figure and with the figure of Penthesileia, the dying Queen of the Amazons, depicted in fig. 84. The naked foot and body in Plate LIII, 4–5, apparently belong to the figure of a soldier (such as shown holding the hair of the wounded Amazon in fig. 85). The fragments of the horses' heads in Plate LIV, 10–12 are, in all

likelihood, an integral part of the scenes of the battle of the Amazons (fig. 85). All these fragments are components of several different sarcophagi, since many do not match in size, orientation, and type of marble.

The fragment illustrated in Plate LII, 3, may also be interpreted as part of the Amazonomachy. An instructive parallel may be found in the previously mentioned Amazon sarcophagus from Tel Barak near Caesarea[131] (compare particularly the right leg of the bending Amazon on the left side, and the erect leg of the Greek soldier on her left). In the section we are considering there are apparently more figures: a prostrate Amazon, two men standing, and a fallen horse. Other fragments belonging to the same group or to similar scenes are the dressed torso in Plate LII, 2; the fragments of the spears in Plate LV, 1–5; the sheath in Plate LV, 6–7; the heads of the horses; other fragments which are not described here. In view of the finds described above, there is no doubt that several sarcophagi

Fig. 85 Amazonomachy

decorated with scenes of the battle of the Amazons were placed in catacomb 20.

I tend to attribute the small monstrous head in Plate LIV, 9, to another mythological scene. It seems to me that this is the head of one of the two snakes harnessed to the chariot of Demeter, who is searching for her kidnapped daughter, Persephone, a very common theme in classical marble sarcophagi. In figure 86 there are two examples of snake chariots, one from a marble sarcophagus[132] and the other from a Roman coin.[133] A snake with equine teeth is not particularly surprising in an imaginary monster.

The large figures covered with long cloaks (Pl. LV, 9–10), the large thigh (Pl. LV, 13), the fragments with drilled leaves (Pl. LVII, 8), and the fragment of a capital (Pl. LVII, 7) most probably belong to architectural sarcophagi (e.g., column sarcophagi), on which solitary figures are depicted standing beneath arches with overlying conchs. Coffins of this type, called "Sidamara sarcophagi," are attributed to the second– fourth centuries C.E. and originate in Asia Minor.[134]

Fragments of the Nike (Pl. LII, 1), the Caryatid (Pl. LIV, 3), and the cluster of grapes (Pl. LVI, 9–10) are remnants of elaborate garland sarcophagi. Other miscellaneous fragments only add to the variety of the assemblage of the marble sarcophagi that were deposited in catacomb 20.

The Origin and Date of the Marble Sarcophagi

There is no question that the marble sarcophagi of Beth She'arim were imported. The problem is whether the carving and sculpture — entirely or in part — were executed locally or whether the sarcophagi were imported as finished products. It is well known that in the second and third centuries C.E. there was a brisk trade in marble sarcophagi, and many were introduced into the eastern countries of the Roman Empire. While burial in marble sarcophagi was also practiced earlier, now, during the "Golden Age" of Imperial architectural art and sculpture, this usage assumed greater proportions and became widely diffused and popular among the affluent in all countries. As previously mentioned, sarcophagi of this type were also imported into Palestine.

Generally, the artistic aspects of the sarcophagi have been studied quite thoroughly by scholars, whereas the problems of production and marketing have been insufficiently studied. Recently, J.P. Ward Perkins treated this subject in detail;[135] we shall briefly present his principal conclusions here.

Marble quarries and workshops for the manufacture of marble sarcophagi were located at various places in Italy, Greece, and Asia Minor; however, they mainly supplied the local demand. For the export of marble sarcophagi there were two major manufacturing centers: (a) Attica in Greece and (b) the Island of Marmara near the Dardanelles Straits which is culturally attached to Asia Minor. The marble produced in Attica is known as "Pentelic" marble (so called from Mt. Pentelicus where it is quarried); it is pure white and finely crystalline. The marble from Marmara ("Proconnesus") is called "Proconnesian" marble; it is coarsely crystalline and occasionally has bluish-grey discolorations and veins. Ward Perkins discerned that the sarcophagi decorated with Attic themes (like mythological scenes) were generally manufactured of Pentelic marble whereas the garland sarcophagi so widely disseminated in all countries were usually made of Proconnesian marble.

Both these centers perfected their production systems and developed efficient marketing networks; they also competed with each other in the capture of markets. Ward Perkins is of the opinion that these workshops usually roughed out the carving and sent the sarcophagi to subsidiary centers near the point of purchase in the various countries for completion. This was the accepted practice particularly for the Attic sarcophagi whose finished elaborate carvings were most susceptible to damage in shipping. In the large subsidiary centers, like Alexandria and Antioch, there were highly skilled artists who could execute the required delicate sculpture; elsewhere, proficient artists were sent together with the sarcophagi in order to complete the work on the spot. Traveling artists of this type were a common feature in the Roman Empire when large buildings and artistic projects were launched in the various provinces. There are indications that visiting artists even came to Rome itself from Asia Minor in order to carve coffins, a fact which illustrates the enormous oriental influence on Roman sepulchral art.

Close examination of the marble fragments from Beth She'arim confirmed the accuracy of Ward Perkins's analysis of the relationship between the type of marble and the type of sarcophagus. All the delicately sculptured fragments, including those attributable to sarcophagi decorated with Attic scenes like the battle of the Amazons, are carved in fine crystalline pure white marble (our type "a"), which is Pentelic marble from Attica. This is not true of the fragments comparable to the Asiatic sarcophagi of the Sidamara type and the Nike fragment—all sculptured out of white marble with discolorations and grey veins (our type "b"), i.e., the precise characteristics of Proconnesian marble. Only the figure of Eros, the clusters of grapes, and the parts of the coffins decorated solely with geometric designs are made of coarse crystalline grey marble (our type "c"), which might have originated in another quarry in Asia Minor.

Apparently the only marble fragment whose exact origin may be proved is the Nike fragment (Pl. LII, 1). As noted previously,[136] this Nike has a parallel in a sarcophagus from Tarsus, also made of Proconnesian marble. Since Nikae wearing bracelets are such a rare occurrence in marble sarcophagi, we may justifiably assume that this particular sarcophagus was likewise imported from Tarsus. If this conjecture is indeed correct, it may be inferred that other sarcophagi from Beth She'arim were also imported from Asia Minor, the region where the most important centers for the manufacture of marble sarcophagi were located.

On the basis of our scanty material, it is difficult to determine whether the Attic sarcophagi of the type with the Amazon scene were imported into Palestine as a finished product, or whether the carving was completed here. Obviously there was no large auxiliary center in Palestine for the completion of marble sarcophagi similar to those that evidently existed at Tripoli in Syria, or Alexandria in Egypt. Nevertheless, we cannot deny the possibility that in cities like Caesarea or Ascalon there were also adequate — though smaller — workshops. At any rate, in Caesarea itself, there must have been a large demand for many marble products — both for architecture and sculpture — as evidenced by the excavations recently conducted there. Most of the decorated marble sarcophagi found up to now in Palestine were unearthed in the vicinity of Caesarea; and in the recent excavations there many marble statues and fragments of sculpture were discovered. Therefore, it is quite possible that there were workshops of a high standard in Caesarea and that experienced craftsmen from the large centers of art executed the finishing touches on the incomplete imported sarcophagi. The numerous fragments of marble sarcophagi found at Beth She'arim testify that there was a sizeable market for this product in other parts of Palestine as well. While this argumentation is sound, it is nevertheless probable that finished sarcophagi were also imported into Palestine and were sold in centers like Caesarea and Ascalon. The sarcophagi found at Beth She'arim were most probably imported by Diaspora Jews who brought their deceased relatives to Palestine for burial.

In determining the date of the marble fragments, we must bear in mind that our information is only as accurate as the data we have from catacomb 20, all told. This catacomb was apparently in use from the end of the second century to the middle of the fourth century C.E. The fact that we have only small fragments of sarcophagi makes it difficult to compare the artistic and stylistic elements with other sculptured marble sarcophagi. In addition, it must be borne in mind that the dating of marble sarcophagi is not always based on absolute chronological factors but on stylistic criteria as well. Scholars are in agreement as to the date of the "Golden Age" of marble sarcophagi manufacture in the large centers in Greece, Asia Minor, Syria, and Alexandria and as to the period of extensive com-

mercial traffic: the second–third centuries C.E. Many are of the opinion that the manufacture of sarcophagi depicting mythological scenes, as typified by the Attic sarcophagi, terminated in the fourth century C.E.[137] The few marble sarcophagi discovered in Palestine were also attributed to the second and third centuries. Watzinger believes that their import to this country stopped at the end of the third century C.E.[138]

The marble fragments from Beth She'arim are not homogeneous in type; on the contrary, they represent different sculptural styles and various standards of execution. In general, however, it may be concluded that the chronological range to which they were attributed on the basis of circumstantial evidence from Beth She'arim corresponds to the period attributed to the rest of the marble sarcophagi: the Imperial Roman Era.

3 THE LEAD SARCOPHAGI

In the outer tombs discussed above (pp. 125–130), five lead coffins were discovered; they are described here.

Coffin no. 1 (Pls. LXII–LXIII)
This coffin was found in tomb no. 1 (see fig. 35). It was preserved intact except for the bottom which had partly disintegrated. Its cover is 2.06 m long, and .34 m wide; the long wall is 1.96 m long and .31 m high; the narrow wall is .33 m wide and .31 m high; the total height of the coffin, including the lid, is .35 m. This coffin is longer and narrower than the others. The lid was soldered to the coffin at seven points: three on one of the long walls, two on the other long wall, and one on each of the narrow walls. All the joints were still sound, and we severed them in order to open the coffin. The coffin was full of earth with a few stones up to 3 cm in size. This information, plus the fact that the coffin was interred in a hewn shaft entirely enclosed and surrounded by rock, proved that the earth did

not penetrate into the coffin later, but was intentionally introduced before it was sealed. Only bone dust was found in the earth; no teeth were found. The sole archaeological finds in this coffin were gold threads which will be discussed later.

The coffin is decorated with reliefs on all sides but the one narrow side.
The Cover. Two parallel bands of vine scrolls, 7 cm wide and 18 cm apart, are arrayed along the length of the cover. Between them there are intersecting diagonal lines in bead and reel pattern which form nine rhombi and a corresponding number of half rhombi in the interspaces. In six of the rhombi and in all of the triangles were patterns of a flower with eight short petals in a circle.

Each band of vine scrolls is composed of two symmetrical units and is bordered by two lines in rope pattern. The vine proceeds in a regular scroll pattern and gives rise to tendrils, leaves, and clusters of grapes. Between the curves of the vine other motifs were introduced: two heads of women, one to the right and one to the left, facing each other; two ribbed, high-necked vases with two handles; and in the center a broad ribbed bowl, with handles but without a base, with two birds standing on the rim. One bird is bending its head to drink; the other is stretching its head forward. This group of patterns is repeated, as previously mentioned, twice in each band. The decorative pattern is arrayed in a conventional scheme which recurs, with slight variations, in four of the five lead coffins that were found in the outer graves.

In addition to this stereotyped design, there is an exceptional motif on the cover which indubitably establishes the Jewish character of the coffin: in three of the rhombi there is a menorah. It is clearly seen that the menorah were not an integral part of the general design but were added to the original mold before the cover was cast: each menorah is larger than the rhombus and partially covers its surrounding lines of bead and reel. Each menorah is 16.5 cm high and 9.5 cm wide. Each has a tripodal base. The two lateral legs bend toward the outside, and the central one splits into three "fingers." The seven branches are composed of links which culminate in flames. At the sides of the menoroth the traditional ritual vessels are depicted: to the right, a grooved shofar and a rectangular incense shovel with a crooked handle; to the left, a lulab with an ethrog and some other fruit (?) attached to it.

The long walls. The decorative patterns on the two long walls are almost exactly identical to those on the cover. The ends of the two units of vine scroll overlap at their point of junction in the center. Between the rows of vine scrolls there are only seven rhombi. In three of them a menorah was added. It is possible to discern the edges of the tablet which served as the background of the mold for the menorah. The menoroth are different from those on the cover: the branches consist of links in bead and reel pattern, they have only two legs, and there are no accompanying ritual vessels. Each menorah is 12.5 cm high and 7.5 cm wide.

The narrow wall. One of the narrow sides of the coffin is decorated with an architectural design of an arch supported by two pillars. The arch is 22.5 cm high and 19.5 cm wide. Inside the arch there is a menorah identical in every respect to the menoroth on the cover, i.e., it has three legs and ritual vessels at the sides. The arch pillars are fluted, their bases are composed of three fillets, and their schematic Corinthian capitals have two small acanthus leaves from the center of which pairs of tendrils rise up to the abacus. The arch itself is decorated with designs of three schematic laurel leaves and a small rosette in the center. There are a total of ten menoroth on the coffin.

Coffin no. 2 (Pl. LXIV–LXV)
This coffin was discovered in tomb no. 5, whose four sides are stone built. It was preserved in good condition except for the bottom which had rusted a great deal and crumbled. The coffin is 1.87 m long, .34 m wide, and .31 m high. The cover, 1.93 × .43 m in size, was soldered to the body of the coffin at eight points which we had to sever. The coffin was full of earth; its only contents were small particles of bone.

The decorations are generally the same as those on coffin no. 1 except for certain details. The arrangement of the rhombi on the cover was not so well proportioned: although the distance between the vine scrollsbands (27.5 cm) is larger than the distance between the bands on the previous cover, the interspace is, nevertheless, partitioned by the same short (26 cm) row of beads and reels. The menoroth on this coffin are of the second type, i.e., each menorah has two legs and no flanking ritual vessels. There are altogether four menoroth: three on the cover and one beneath the arch on the side wall. On the long walls there are no menoroth; also, there are no flowers in the triangular interspaces. Despite the striking similarities between these decorations, it cannot be maintained that exactly the same stamps were used in the preparation of the molds for these two coffins. There are subtle differences between the various patterns, e.g., the head (different hairstyles), the vases, and the birds (the bird to the left is lifting its head in contrast to the bird on the former coffin which is stretching its head forward), and other examples. However, above the arches one can discern the impressed outlines of the square tablet from which the stamp was made. Both impressions show identical slight defects on the right edge.

Coffin no. 3 (Pl. LXVI)

This coffin was found in tomb no. 6, that is to say, below tomb no. 5. It is 1.84 m long, .38 m wide, and .35 m high. This coffin was also preserved in excellent condition. It, too, was welded and contained only earth.

The Cover. There is considerable difference in the composition of the decorative patterns on this cover in comparison to the previous ones: instead of two bands, there are three parallel bands of vine scrolls running along the length of the cover. Beaded rods divide the area into six narrow rhombi, each containing a rosette. It is noteworthy that the vine scrolls contain no human figureheads but only leaves and clusters of grapes. The bowls upon which the birds are perched have a base and a very broad rim. The rosettes have a knob in the center. Traces of a circle are visible around their petals. It should be noted that in all three bands, the decorations, e.g., birds, vases, are oriented toward the observer; on the other covers, the arrangement is symmetrical.

The Long Walls. These are decorated in the same general layout as the previous coffin, i.e., two bands of vine scrolls (without

human heads), whose interspace is divided into six rhombi and a corresponding number of triangles. In each rhombus and triangle there is a rosette pattern similar to the one described above.

The Narrow Wall. The arch on this side differs from those on the former coffins: the excellent workmanship and the less schematic execution of its members are remarkable. The height of the arch, including the columns, is 23 cm. The lower part of the columns is fluted with narrow, closely-spaced grooves, clearly an attempt to portray the curvature of the columns; the upper part is fluted with broad grooves. This composite fluting is characteristic of certain Roman columns where the change in fluting occurs in the lower third of the column. The craftsman did not retain the correct proportions but made the change at the middle of the column. On the other hand, he faithfully reproduced the classical pattern of concave upper fluting and convex lower fluting.[138a]

The bases of the columns seem to have a raised attic profile. The Corinthian capitals, including leaves, tendrils, and intervening rosettes, were executed in a much superior and more delicate fashion than those on the previous coffin. The archivolt is decorated with garlands of fine laurel leaves, interwoven with ribbons. A small rosette is located in the center of the archivolt. An eight-petaled rosette is placed under the arch.

Coffin no. 4 (Pl. LXVII)

This coffin was found in tomb no. 7. It is 1.87 m long, .40 m wide, and .32 m high. The coffin was preserved intact; only the bottom was slightly damaged. The cover was welded to the coffin at eight points. In this coffin also only earth was found.

The Cover. The composition of the decorative design on this cover is slightly different from the conventional schemes. Two parallel bands of vine scrolls without figureheads run along the length of the cover as usual. Between these bands, there are four intersecting strips of the same vine scrolls which form a large rhombus in the center, bordered by triangular fields. Inside the rhombus and in each of the four wide triangles there are three rosettes; in the triangles at the narrow edges of the lid there is only one rosette. All the patterns are identical with those on coffin no. 3.

The Long Sides. The decorations are similar to those on coffin no. 3, except that there are rosettes only in the rhombi and not in the triangles.

The Narrow Side. The design of the arch and pillars is identical in every respect to that on coffins 1 and 2; however, instead of a menorah below the arch, there is an eight-petaled rosette of the type appearing on coffin no. 3.

Coffin no. 5 (fig. 87)

This coffin was discovered in tomb no. 11. Despite the fact that the construction above the tomb was the most solid of all, the coffin itself was the simplest of the entire group of lead coffins. The cover was welded to the coffin all around, not only at a few points. On the other hand, the soldering material was so poor that during the process of

opening the coffin, the cover came off without difficulty. The lead, too, was of inferior quality and began to disintegrate. Thus, in contrast to the other four coffins, this one broke into pieces when it was removed from the tomb. It is noteworthy that the coffin was only half-filled with earth. However, more particles of bones were found here than in the previous coffins, but no large pieces of bone were extant.

The Cover. The cover is not rectangular but narrows slightly toward one edge: the wide end is .52 m and the narrow end, .38 m; it is 2.05 m long. The only design decorating the lid is a rope pattern: three parallel lines are arranged on the length of the cover; between them, there are diagonal lines forming double rows of rhombi.

The Front. Only one of the long walls of the coffin is decorated. It is 2.00 m long and .30 m high. The parallel and diagonal lines of rope pattern form a frieze of rhombi and triangles. Inside the frieze there are figures of four running animals facing right: two bears and two slender lionesses (or leopards?), as shown in figure 88.

The fact that lead coffins were used in the necropolis of Beth She'arim was known for some time, since many small fragments

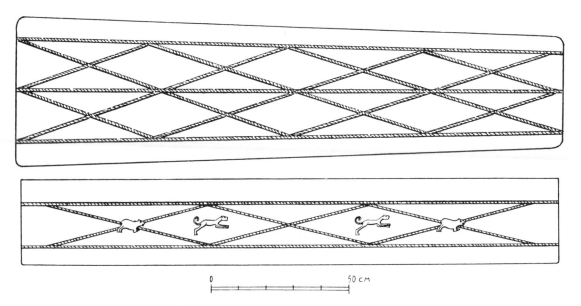

0   50 CM

Fig. 87 Lead sarcophagus no. 5; lid and long side

of lead were discovered in the tombs. These coffins provided the tomb robbers with a very convenient source of valuable raw material. Thus, they did not leave behind any substantial remains from which the form and decoration of these coffins could be deduced. It seems reasonable to assume that the decorations of the coffins exhibited a variety of subjects and styles. Evidence favoring this assumption is furnished by the single, decorated fragment of a lead coffin which was found in catacomb 20 (see Pl. L, 5).[139] Now for the first time complete lead coffins were discovered at Beth She'arim. Despite the small discrepancies between them, these coffins form a homogeneous group with respect to manufacture, decoration, style, origin, and date.

Fig. 88 Animal images

Technique and Decoration

All the coffins were made out of cast lead sheets,[140] about 4–5 mm thick. Usually the two long sides and the bottom were cast as a single unit, whereas the narrow sides were cast separately. Sometimes one long side only was cast together with the bottom (coffin no. 3). The ends of the cast sheets were welded together. The flat cover was made out of one sheet whose edges were bent down and folded at the corners.

For the decorations, the craftsmen used stamps carved in relief out of a hard material which they impressed into a soft mold (apparently clay) in the required order. Since the lead was cast in the sunken mold, the resulting decorations were in relief. Every negative mold could be used for casting only once since it was made out of fragile material; therefore, no two lead coffins are absolutely identical. Even when the same design seals were stamped on new molds, small discrepancies appeared in the composition of the pattern units.

In the decoration of coffins 1–4, the following design units were used: *(a)* a band of vine scrolls, 7 cm wide and 94 cm long. In addition to leaves and clusters of grapes, vases, birds, and human heads also appear. Two impressions of this seal were sufficient to produce a band along the entire length of the coffin; *(b)* a rod of bead and reel pattern, 26 cm long; *(c)* a flower pattern; *(d)* an arch; *(e)* a menorah. In coffin no. 5 three designs only were employed: a rope, a bear, and a lioness.

The workshop made use of several sets of seals for the conventional designs. This is obvious from the subtle differences in the individual designs of the various coffins, despite their close resemblance. These differences arise from discrepancies in the manufacture of the various seals employed for the same design. Thus, it was found that in the decoration of coffins 1–4, three different seals were used for the vine scrolls (fig. 89, 1–3), four seals for the rosette (fig. 89, 4–7), one stamp for the rod of beads

Fig. 89 Designs of ornaments of lead sarcophagi nos. 1–4

(fig. 89, 8), two stamps for the arch (fig. 89, 9–10), and two stamps for the menorah (fig. 89, 11–12).

There is no significant difference in the combination of the conventional designs in the first four lead coffins. On the coffins themselves there is almost no difference whatsoever; however, on covers 1, 2, 3, and 4, there is a discrepancy in the number and arrangement of the long decorative bands. The arrangement of the motifs in the vine frieze, consisting of fruit, vases, birds, and figureheads, is of particular interest[141] since it never appears in Jewish decorative art which is so rich in vine scroll patterns.[142] As will be proved shortly, this particular combination of motifs is restricted to only one group of lead coffins which were imported from Sidon.

The Origin of the Coffins

The use of lead coffins was widespread in many countries, both in the East and in the West. Their origin is conjectured to be in the Hellenistic East. Evidently there was a large center for the manufacture of coffins in Phoenicia and its vicinity, where the largest number of coffins of this type were found. At present they are dispersed in various museums in Europe and the United States, but are found mainly in Istanbul, Beirut, and Jerusalem. Since these coffins received a good deal of attention from various scholars and were carefully studied,

178

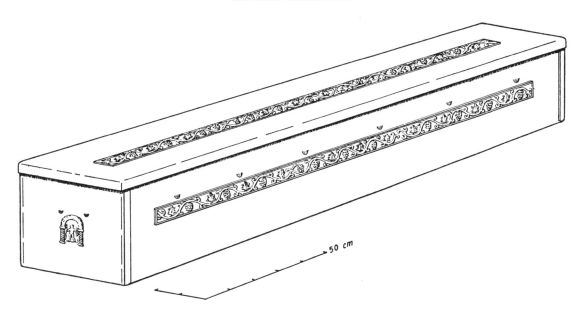

Fig. 90 Lead sarcophagus from Ḥederah

conclusions may confidently be drawn about their methods of manufacture, origin, distribution, and style.[143]

In Palestine, many lead coffins were dis-- covered. A representative group of sixteen. coffins or fragments of these which were found in this country were discussed by M. Avi-Yonah in his thorough study of this subject.[144] On the basis of stylistic analysis, he distinguished between coffins produced locally and coffins produced in a workshop in Tyre in Southern Phoenicia. The coffins were defined as pagan or Christian accord-ing to their decoration, and were attributed to the second–fourth centuries C.E. Since then, several coffins from the Roman period have been added to the list;[145] however, the style of the Beth She'arim coffins was not encountered in any of these groups.

In his survey of the rich material in custody at the National Museum in Beirut, A. M. Chéhab[146] distinguishes three sources of lead coffins in Phoenicia: Tyre, Sidon, and Beirut. Each center had its own par-ticular style, and each workshop used a number of characteristic designs, specific to its product. These distinctive criteria make it possible to identify the center, and some-times even the workshop where a particu-

lar coffin was manufactured. By means of comparison, we were able to ascertain that the first four coffins from Beth She'arim are of the type produced in Sidon. This conclusion is based on a group of lead cof-fins discovered in Sidon and the nearby vicinity, which are now scattered in various collections. Their decorative style bears the closest resemblance to the coffins at Beth She'arim, and at times it is even absolutely identical. Aside from the stylistic similarity of the basic designs, the coffins from Sidon are especially interesting because of the religious symbols they bear. Due to the importance of the comparative material for the subject under discussion, we shall de-scribe it in as much detail as is possible here:

1. In 1864, Renan[147] reported the dis-covery of three decorated lead coffins near Sidon and published his drawing of one of them. While the drawing is not clear in every detail, it is nevertheless possible to discern that, as far as conventional designs are concerned, they are the same as the decorative style of the Beth She'arim cof-fins. In addition, the coffins from Sidon display a mythological motif: a seated mourning figure of a winged Psyche.

2. In 1873, G. B. de Rossi[148] published a description of two lead coffins from Sidon, at present in the Lyklama Collection in Cannes, France. The drawings of one of them were published by Goodenough.[149] This coffin is identical in every detail to coffins 1–2 from Beth She'arim except for the fact that the menoroth are replaced by the Christian monogram ☧ together with the word ΙΧΘΥΣ ("fish") — in the early days of Christianity the fish was used as a secret Christian symbol — and beneath the arch on the second narrow side there is a figure of a man standing. It is noteworthy that the arches on the sides of the coffin are of the type on coffins 1–2 from Beth She'arim, whereas the arches on the cover are of the type on coffin no. 3. The second coffin in Cannes is the same as the first, except that the monogram is missing.

3. In the National Museum in Beirut there are many lead coffins Tyre, Sidon, and Beirut. From the Sidonian group, which is the smallest, the following have been selected for discussion:

(a) A coffin (no. 7)[150] decorated in the typical pattern — two bands of vine scrolls (without vases and other intermediary decorations); the interspace is partitioned into rhombi with enclosed rosettes.

(b) The narrow side of a lead coffin (no. 35)[151] bearing a relief of an arch identical to that of coffins 1, 2, and 4 of Beth She'arim. A figure of a mourning woman and a vase appear beneath the arch.

(c) The cover of a coffin (no. 38)[152] decorated with bands of intersecting vine scrolls which form a rhombus — like coffin no. 4 at Beth She'arim. On this coffin also there are no representations of human heads. Inside the rhombus there is a figure of Silenus playing a double flute.

(d) A fragment of a long wall (no. 39)[153] with bands of vine scrolls, vases, and birds drinking — as in coffin no. 1 from Beth She'arim.

4. In the collection of the American University in Beirut there is a group of fragments of a lead coffin.[154] The patterns of the vine frieze (containing vases, birds, and heads) and the arch are exact replicas of those on coffin no. 1 at Beth She'arim, and there is no doubt that both of them were impressed from the same stamps. Instead of the menoroth, there are Christian monograms. One fragment of the vine frieze[155] is identical to that on coffin no. 2 from Beth She'arim. The left bird standing on the bowl is lifting its head up, whereas the bird on coffin no. 1 is stretching its head forward. On another fragment,[156] there is an arch like the one on coffin no. 3 from Beth She'arim, beneath which there is a figure of a youth holding a shepherd's staff (pedum).

5. In the rich collection of lead coffins at the Antiquities Museum in Istanbul there are, among others, two covers and one coffin which may be classified with the group of coffins from Sidon. One cover[157] is patterned like coffins 1–2 from Beth She'arim, except that the vine frieze contains only floral elements without additional vases and other items. The second cover[158] is decorated with bands of intersecting vine scrolls forming rhombi — like the cover of coffin no. 3 from Beth She'arim. Birds drinking and vases also appear in the vine scrolls. The decorative composition of the third coffin[159] is different: in the center of the long wall there is a single vine scroll band. Nevertheless, the vases and drinking birds are evidence that this coffin definitely belongs to the assemblage from Sidon.[160]

All the coffins reviewed above were discovered, as previously mentioned, in Sidon and the close vicinity; only in a few cases is their provenance at all uncertain. They form a homogeneous group both with respect to selection and combination of motifs and with respect to style and quality of workmanship. They all have two parallel bands of vine scrolls whose interspace is partitioned into rhombi. Apparently there is not even a single coffin or fragment of a coffin of this type whose origin may be attributed to another manufacturing center (i.e., to Tyre or Beirut) since the decorations on the coffins from these centers were generally more heterogeneous and their style was more developed. Their repertoire of motifs is larger and usually includes a row of twisted columns, the façade of a temple with a Syrian gable, medallions, masks sphinxes, mythological figures, floral motifs in a freer style, and others. On the other hand, the Sidon school is characterized by its clarity of composition, simplicity of form restriction in the number of patterns, and decisive execution. While it cannot be inferred that this was the only style employed in Sidon,[161] it seems, nevertheless, that it was the dominant style in the local lead coffin industry or, perhaps, the style of one of the large workshops.

In view of these instructive parallels, there is no question that these coffins and those from Beth She'arim are the product of one and the same workshop in Sidon. Furthermore, even the molds were stamped from the same seals. From the finds described above, the interesting fact emerges that this workshop cast lead coffins in a more or less uniform pattern of conventional designs which were acceptable to an ethnically diversified clientele. Nevertheless, at the request of customer, religious figures and symbols were added before the casting: for pagans, mythological figures; for Jews, a Jewish symbol; and for Christians, a Christian symbol. This fact has far-reaching significance when we come to consider the symbolic implications of the different motifs.

Now a few words about coffin no. 5 whose decorative style is different from that of the other coffins. The closest parallels are two lead coffins from Tyre at present in custody of the National Museum of Beirut.[162] They are characterized not only by the division into rhombi by a rope pattern, but also by the trapezoidal form of the cover which becomes progessively narrower like coffin no. 5 in Beth She'arim. The rhombi of one of the coffins from Tyre

(no. 2) are also interspersed with patterns of a vine growing from a vase. The bears and lionesses on coffin 5 from Beth She'arim are of the type of patterns of lions, sphinxes, and others which were so widely used in the decoration of the coffins from Tyre.[163] Since it is untenable that so large a manufacturing center for lead coffins as Tyre imported coffins from Palestine, and since apparently all the deceased buried in the outer graves at Beth She'arim were brought from Phoenicia, we may well assume that coffin no. 5 was imported from Tyre, in contrast to the four previous coffins, which came from Sidon.

There seems to be no doubt whatsoever that the lead coffins discovered at Beth She'arim were imported from Phoenicia. The next question is: were they imported to Palestine commercially and purchased by local inhabitants, or were they brought together with the bones of Jews from Tyre and Sidon for burial in the necropolis of Beth She'arim? The second possibility seems more likely since there is sound reason to believe that only a few bones — not complete bodies — were deposited in these coffins as previously noted. The epigraphic evidence also testifies to numerous burials of Phoenician Jews, especially from Tyre and Sidon, in the cemetery at Beth She'arim. This would seem to explain the unusual concentration of lead coffins from one source. The fact that three of them were interred at one and the same time (graves 5–7) is intelligible only on the assumption that they were brought simultaneously for burial.

It is obvious that coffins full of earth were not transported great distances, but that they were filled and welded in Beth She'arim. The fact that all the bones disintegrated completely leaving only fine particles and that there were no teeth — which are generally more resistant — is evidence that only a few bones were brought for secondary burial. Similar phenomena have already been discussed (pp. 40, 106).

Another problem ·is the interment of the coffins outside of the catacombs, close to ground surface, instead of the catacomb burial that was customary at Beth She'arim. In the preliminary report I attempted to account for this situation by the conjecture that *(a)* the people from Sidon were brought for burial when catacomb 20 was no longer in use, soon after it was closed (this would have been an additional proof for the relatively late date of the graves); and *(b)* the desire to be buried near catacomb 20 is precisely the reason for the particular location of these burials. At present this interpretation seems no longer tenable, though I have no plausible alternative to offer.

At any rate, we may take satisfaction from the fact that these non-catacomb burials proved to be a great boon to archaeological research. Since these graves were covered with earth, they were not visible on the surface and were not subjected to the plunder of the tomb robbers who pillaged all the tombs of Beth She'arim. Thus, the lead coffins were saved from destruction, and a most valuable heritage was added to Jewish archaeology in general and to the antiquities of Beth She'arim in particular.

The Date of the Coffins

In the non-catacomb graves and lead coffins of Beth She'arim no artifacts whatsoever were found — neither coins nor pottery sherds nor fragments of glass — which

might have been of assistance in determining the date of the coffins. However, we do have other data which may be of help in this respect. First, stratigraphic information: as has already been noted, several of the outer graves were dug into the fill of the second terrace, just west of catacomb 20. This terrace is constructed of debris which very probably originated from the quarrying of the catacomb. In the discussion of this terrace the conclusion was reached that the terrace was built at a late stage in the development of the catacomb which, apparently, was expanded gradually. In our estimate, this terrace was built mainly at the end of the third century C.E. Since the non-catacomb graves were dug even later, it seems reasonable to assume that they date to the first half of the fourth century C.E.

Second, there is internal evidence: the decorations. We have already demonstrated that these decorations are identical to those on the lead coffins from Sidon. Generally, the coffins from Phoenicia are dated to the second–fourth or the third–fourth centuries C.E. on the basis both of stylistic analysis and of the few artifacts contained. The discovery of "Constantine's monogram" in addition to the word ΙΧΘΥΣ on several of the coffins from Sidon justifies their attribution to the beginning of the fourth century C.E.[164]

The coffins found at Beth She'arim doubtlessly date to the same period and, therefore, may be assigned approximately to the first half of the fourth century C.E.

4 CLAY AND WOOD COFFINS

On the use of clay and wood coffins we learn from the Talmud that: "It is forbidden to make further use of a coffin that has been emptied. If it is of stone or clay, it should be shattered; if of wood, burned." (Bab. Talmud Semaḥot 13).

In this connection, it should be noted that in the Talmud the word ארון is used also

for a stone ossuary; the word ארזים, however, is used for a wooden ossuary only.

Clay Coffins

In all the Beth She'arim excavations only one complete clay coffin has been discovered up to now (fig. 91; Pl. XXI, 3). It was found standing in a niche in room V of

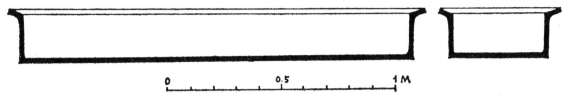

Fig. 91 Clay sarcophagus

catacomb 14. It is 1.87 m long, .54 m wide, and .22 m high. It has a broad rim for supporting cover tiles. The coffin was found without a cover and was entirely empty.

Though fragments of pottery coffins and cover tiles were found in various catacombs, on the whole these coffins were not widely used at Beth She'arim.[165] This is not due to the fragility of clay but rather to the fact that coffins in general were not frequently employed at Beth She'arim except, of course, in catacomb 20.

On the other hand, it is noteworthy that pottery coffins are very widespread in other sites in Western Galilee and on the Syrian coast. It seems, therefore, that the pottery coffins are mainly a Phoenician phenomenon. In note 167 on page 223 there is a list of sites where coffins of this type were discovered in burial caves. From the scanty information published about them, it is evident that they are identical in form to the coffins of Beth She'arim, and that they were found in a context of artifacts from the second–fourth centuries C.E.

The pottery cover with a handle whose fragments were discovered in catacomb 31 (fig. 58) apparently served as a cover for a pottery ossuary. The ossuary itself was not discovered. It seems that the use of pottery ossuaries was not very widespread. Up to now we know of one ossuary which was published,[167] and three ossuaries that have not been published.[168] The pottery and wooden ossuaries seem to have replaced the stone ossuaries which were employed in the Second Temple period.[169]

Wooden Coffins

Wooden coffins were more widely used. This is evidenced mainly by the numerous iron nails found in several tombs (Pl. LXXIII, 4–6). Sometimes, traces of wood were also found on the nails. In addition to the nails, several iron rings were found which had been fastened to the walls of the coffins and were used in carrying them (Pl. LXXIII, 1–3). Fragments of iron plates and iron angles for corners were also found.

From the remains discovered in catacombs 1–4, it was possible to study the form of the wooden coffins and even to reconstruct a complete coffin and ossuary, including the accessories.[170] It emerges that they were mainly ossuaries used for secondary burials. However, there were also regular coffins for primary body interments. Wooden ossuaries, doubtlessly the cheapest type of burial coffin, were occasionally also used in tombs of the Second Temple period in Jerusalem.[171] Usually they were intended for secondary burial. Of these ossuaries, only nails remain. The wooden coffins from the Hasmonean period discovered in the caves at Naḥal David are of a different type.[172]

5 THE LAMPS (figs. 92–93; Pls. LXX–LXXI)

Among the scanty artifacts found in the catacombs, the lamps are the most numerous, but even these do not number more than forty-two, complete and fragmented, excluding the lamps from catacomb 20. Because of the systematic robbing of the tombs, these lamps were found scattered in the catacomb rooms and in the debris (except for the lamps in the cache of vessels discovered in catacomb 12). We, therefore, have no means of determining whether they served as funerary gifts for the deceased or whether they were used by undertakers and visitors, or both.

The disturbed condition in which the lamps were found does not enable us to establish their exact date or even a reasonable chronological classification. Actually, we possess only one chronological criterion for dating the assemblage of finds from the catacombs, i.e., the supposition that the catacombs were not used regularly for burial after the destruction of Beth She'arim in 352 C.E. Obviously, it is quite possible that isolated burials did take place later, since a small settlement continued to exist in Beth She'arim even after the destruction. However, the fact remains that in none of the catacombs we excavated, except for catacomb 20, were there Byzantine lamps or other artifacts attributable with certainty to this period or to the Arab period. This means that the tomb robbers did their work in a hurry, removing their booty quickly without leaving behind any traces of their belongings. This implies that all the lamps discovered in the catacombs (except those of catacomb 20) date to the period before the destruction of the city, and that the middle of the fourth century C.E. should be considered the *terminus ante quem*.

The situation is entirely different in catacomb 20, where the largest number of lamps was found. Aside from the types familiar to us from the other catacombs, new, different types of lamps were discovered here which may be dated with certainty to the end of the Byzantine period and to the Arab period. It seems likely that a few of these lamps are associated with intrusive burials from the late Byzantine period; this may be deduced from several glass vessels of this period which were found in the catacomb (see the discussion on glass vessels). However, the explanation for the large number of late lamps is that they served the tomb robbers in their work.

Therefore, the collection of lamps presented in Plates LXX–LXXI and in figures 92–93 may be divided into two main groups: *(a)* Nos. 1–33: Lamps in this group, discovered in the different catacombs, including catacomb 20, date to the time when the catacombs were regularly used for burial, i.e., up till 352 C.E. (about no. 32, see below). *(b)* Nos. 34–53. These lamps, discovered in catacomb 20 only, were used later, i.e., at the end of the Byzantine period and at the beginning of the Arab period.

In the aforementioned plates, we have tried to present the selected lamps in chronological and typological order. There may be a few slight inaccuracies in the order of some of the individual lamps in the sub-groups; however, this in no way affects the general picture.

Lamps from the "burial period" of the catacombs

1. Registration no. 54–145. Catacomb 16, hall A. Brown clay, gray core. Spatulated nozzle, knife-trimmed at the bottom and sides. This is generally classified as a Herodian lamp, which was common in the first century C.E. and persisted with slight variations until the first half of the second century.[173] It is doubtful whether this lamp was used in the catacomb; more likely, this fragment infiltrated from the outside with the debris.

2. 54–216. Catacomb 17, hall B. Part of a round lamp. Buff ware; red slip above and driblets of paint below. The place of the spout is in the upper right-hand break. Around the shoulder, oblique lines in relief. On the disc, a relief of a running lion (or dog?).[174] Above, a raised tail of a second animal. In the center, a small filling hole. Third century C.E.

3. 55–287. Catacomb 20. Part of a round lamp. Light brown clay; red slip above and below. Semicircular impression around the

disc. On the lower left side, part of a double spiral. On the disc, remains of an erotic scene in relief showing a man kneeling and the back of a kneeling woman's body. Circles on the base. Second century C.E. (see discussion below).

3a. 55–56 (not shown on plate). Catacomb 20. Part of a lamp similar to no. 3. Traces of an erotic scene. Two double spirals. On the shoulder, a "double-axe" pattern. Second century C.E.

4. 55–71. Catacomb 20. Light brown clay; red slip on top and underneath. Semicircular impressions encircle the disc. On the shoulder to the right, a "double-axe" pattern. Near the nozzle, two double spirals. On the disc, a relief of a rosette. In the center, part of a filling hole. In the base, incised circles. On either side of the nozzle, two oblique lines. Second century C.E. (see discussion below).

5. 53–959. Catacomb 12, hall A, room VI. Yellowish clay. Broken disc. Short grooves around the shoulder. On the nozzle, a row of short lines and four small circles. On the base, inscribed circles; near the small central circle, the potter's mark H is inscribed.[175] Third century C.E.

6. 54–190. Catacomb 16, hall A. Reddish-brown ware. On the broken disc, traces of decoration in relief. On the left side, a small filling hole. On the flat shouldder, a circle in rope pattern surrounding the disc.[176] On the nozzle, two small circles. On the base, an incomplete circle near the nozzle. Inside the circle, a row of three small circles. Third century C.E.

7. 55–67. Catacomb 20. Red clay. Broken disc surrounded by a circle in ladder pattern. On the shoulder, interlacing semicircles. On the nozzle, a pattern of two ladders and dots. All the decorations are in relief. The nozzle is broad and longer than those previously discussed. Concave base with knob in center. Third century C.E.[177]

Lamps 2–7 are classified as Roman lamps typified by a round body, the absence of a handle, a short round nozzle, a disc decorated in relief, and a small filling hole in the center. This type of lamp first appeared in the countries of the Roman Empire in the first century C.E. and became widespread in the second century. As a local product, these lamps appeared in Palestine at the beginning of the second century but were common mainly in the third century.

Lamps 3–4 are characterized by the double spiral on either side of the nozzle. This type was found in the workshop at Gerasa and was attributed to the beginning of the second century C.E.;[178] in the cave of Naḥal Ḥever (from the time of Bar Kochba);[179] and in a Jewish burial cave in Lifta, near Jerusalem,[180] for which the Bar Kochba period seems a reasonable *terminus ante quem*. In Samaria, disc lamps attributed to the first-third centuries were also found, among which one had a double spiral, a "double-axe" pattern, and a disc with a rosette.[181] In the city of Beth She'arim (Beth Seid), lamps with double spirals were found in a context attributed to the third century.[182]

Lamps decorated with erotic scenes were widely disseminated during the Imperial period. For example, lamps of this type from the first century were found in Vindonesia;[183] from the second century, in Corinth;[184] and from the third century, in Dura-Europos.[185] In Palestine, they are very rare. In Gerasa,[186] scenes of this type are depicted on lamps very similar to those under discussion here from Beth She'arim (beginning of the second century).

In view of these examples, it appears that lamps 3–4 date to the end of the second century C.E. Lamps 2 and 5 retained the traditional form, whereas lamps 6 and 7 are unusual variants. All four should probably be attributed to the third century C.E.

8. 55–193. Catacomb 20. Round body. Very thick brown clay. Large filling hole surrounded by rings. Elongated nozzle. High, flattened knob handle with two grooves. On the shoulder, alternate globules

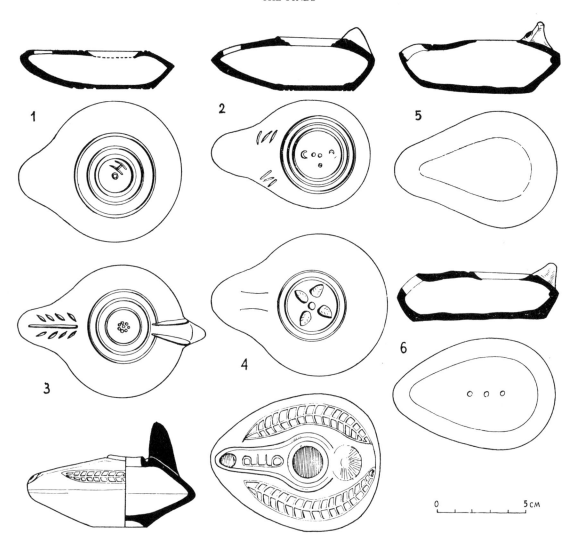

Fig. 92 Selection of bases and sections of lamps

and impressed rosettes. Between the filling hole and the nozzle, a group of three short lines. On the base, a group of inscribed small circles. Under the nozzle, a branch pattern is incised (fig. 92, 3). It is difficult to find an exact parallel to the decorations on this lamp. While globules on round Roman lamps are common,[187] they occur without impressed rosettes. The group of short lines on the nozzle is similar to that on lamp no. 5. Approximately third century C.E.

9. 53–957. Catacomb 12, hall A, room VI. Reddish-brown clay. Pear-shaped body. Elongated nozzle. Elongated knob handle. Inside a group of concentric circles, a sunken

filling hole — apparently cut from a disc before firing; the workmanship of the cutting is inferior. Small circles stamped along the shoulder. Lines on the nozzle are a characteristic ornamentation of this type: near the wick hole, one line is longitudinal (splitting at the end) and one is horizontal; at the joint of the nozzle to the body of the lamp, the lines proceed in a series of diagonal pairs. On the base, three concentric circles; in the center, four tiny circles and a horseshoe pattern are impressed (fig. 92, 2). On either side of the nozzle, a group of three diagonal lines.

10. 53–1024. Catacomb 12, hall B, room

186

V. Light buff clay. Broken disc. The decorations on the shoulder and nozzle as well as its shape are similar to no. 9.

11. 53–958. Catacomb 12, room VI. Brown clay. Broken disc. Plain shoulder. Shape and nozzle decoration like no. 9. Found together with two additional lamps of the same type: one (53–961) with a plain shoulder; and the other (53–960) with a perpendicular line pattern on the shoulder. A lamp similar to the latter was also discovered in catacomb 20 (55–253).

Lamps nos. 9–11 form a distinct, uncommon type. In room VI of catacomb 12, lamps like these were found together with a lamp of type 5 which is characteristic of the third century. In the pit found on the Seid estate in the city area, similar lamps were also discovered together with types 4–5.[188] A lamp of this kind was also uncovered in a Byzantine context[189] in a tomb from Gush Ḥalav; however, it may reasonably be assumed that this tomb, of the kokh type, was also in use at an earlier period. On the Syrian coast, additional lamps of type 9–11 were found with a complete disc. A number of lamps from the vicinity of Tyre[190] were attributed to the first and second centuries C.E.; however, this date is too early. On the other hand, two similar lamps with an undecorated shoulder, which were discovered in Antioch in an unclear context, were tentatively attributed to the fifth century,[191] which would seem to be too late a dating.

Lamps of this type, not published as yet, were found in tombs at Makher, Naharia and Ḥanita in the Galilee, in a tomb at Lahav in the southern part of the country (together with round lamps from the second and third centuries),[192] and in the excavations of the synagogue at Caesarea.[193] Thus, the geographic distribution of these lamps is very broad indeed. Apparently they should be dated to the middle of the third century C.E.

12. 54–213. Catacomb 17, in the debris of the western room. Light brown clay; pear-shaped body. Conical, fluted handle. Broken disc. Horseshoe-like impressions on the shoulder. On the base, two circles with four palmettes in the center (fig. 92, 4).

13. 55–231. Catacomb 20. Brown clay. Pear-shaped body. Disc decorated with small circles. In the center, a small filling hole which was enlarged. Disc surrounded by a ring. On the shoulder, horseshoe-like (scalloped) patterns; on the nozzle, a branch design. Base flat and narrow.

Lamps nos. 12–13, which form a transition to the next group, may be attributed to the beginning of the fourth century.

14. 53–1040. Catacomb 12, room VIII. Brown clay. Pear-shaped body. Conical handle. Broken disc. On the shoulder, patterns of rhombi with a circle in the center. On the nozzle, designs of lines and circles. Flat, narrow base with a hexagon stamped in the center.

15. 54–197. Catacomb 17, hall A. Light brown clay. Pear-shaped body. Broken pierced handle, conical in shape. On the shoulder, groups of stamped rosettes inside triangles. Flat, wide base.

16. 54–36. The courtyard of catacomb 13, in a niche opposite hall L. Brown clay. Pear-shaped body. Broken disc. On the shoulder, semicircular lines and dots. On the sides of the nozzle, dots and oblique lines. Flat, narrow base.

17. 55–02. Catacomb 20. Brown clay; pear-shaped body. The handle is missing. Disc decorated with a pentagon. Filling hole in the center. Disc surrounded by a circle which extends onto the nozzle in the shape of a "light bulb." On the shoulder, palmettes and small circles are alternately impressed. Flat, narrow base.

18. 55–284. Catacomb 20. Brown clay. Pear-shaped body. Broken disc surrounded by a circle. On the shoulder, round impressions. Base flat and narrow. In the center, a rounded impression.

19. 54–32. The courtyard of catacomb 13. Pear-shaped body. Conical, fluted handle. Disc broken; surrounded by a

"bulb" as above. On the nozzle, a herringbone pattern. On the shoulder, stamped palmettes. Flat, broad base.

20. 55–14. Catacomb 20. Brown ware. Pear-shaped body. Pierced handle. Disc broken; surrounded by a "light bulb" incision. On the shoulder, impressions of circles. Flat, narrow base.

21. 55–99. Catacomb 20. Brown clay. Ovoid body. Broken disc surrounded by a "bulb." On the shoulder, a herringbone pattern and impressions of palmettes. Flat, broad base.

22. 55–978. The courtyard of catacomb 12. Light brown clay. Pear-shaped body. Small filling hole. Around the disc and on the nozzle, round impressions. Herringbone pattern on the shoulder. Flat, broad base with a row of seven small circles.

23. 54–196. Catacomb 17, hall A, in the debris near the entrance. Brown clay. Pear-shaped body. The Christian monogram ☧ is incised on the handle. Narrow channel on the nozzle; herringbone pattern on the shoulder. Flat, broad base with two stamped circles.[194] The use of a lamp bearing a Christian monogram in a Jewish tomb is surprising. Evidently the Jewish buyer of this lamp did not notice the symbol or did not understand its significance. At that time, the first half of the fourth century C.E., this symbol was still relatively new[195] and perhaps did not disturb the sensibilities of Jews as the sign of the cross would later on.

24. 55–103. Catacomb 20. Brown clay. Pear-shaped body. Broken disc. Herringbone pattern on the shoulder and nozzle. Base flat and broad.

25. 43–214. Catacomb 17, in the debris of the western room. Brown clay; pear-shaped body; broken disc. On the shoulder and nozzle, a pattern of triangles enclosing blurred impressions of palmettes. Base flat and broad.

26. 54–207. Catacomb 17, hall A, room III. Light reddish-brown clay. Pear-shaped body. Small filling hole. Herringbone pattern and stamped circles on the shoulder and nozzle. Flat, broad base with three stamped circles (fig. 92, 6).

Lamps 14–26 constitute a homogeneous family with the following characteristics: pear-shaped (pyriform) body; conical handle; small disc, sometimes with a small filling hole which was generally broken on purpose; flat elongated base; and, in particular, impressed decorations of several patterns: a palmette, a rosette, circles, rhombi, and various combinations of lines. Frequently the filling hole is surrounded by a frame in the shape of a "bulb" which extends to the nozzle. The workmanship of these lamps is not very good, neither from the point of view of design nor firing. Nevertheless, there is quite a variety in the repertoire of decorations. The clay is light to reddish-brown without slip; the quality is inferior.

In this group of lamps, two variants may be distinguished according to the type of base and to the construction of the body: (a) lamps with a flattened base, pyriform shape, and sloping sides (fig. 92, 5). This variant includes lamps nos. 14, 16–18, and 20, and (b) lamps with a flat base and elongated ovoid shape (fig. 92, 6). This group comprises nos. 15 and 21–26; perhaps no. 31 as well. Nos. 21–24 differ from the rest in having a herringbone pattern. No. 23 is exceptional in having a channel on the nozzle. These differences in form are chronologically significant since group (a) is relatively earlier than group (b).

The lamps with the stamped decorations became known as the "Beth She'arim type" because they were so common there. They were first distinguished as a characteristic group in the earlier excavations at Beth She'arim. Mazar assumes that they were locally produced[196] and attributes them to the end of the third and the first half of the fourth century C.E. Lamps of this type were not found in earlier or later contexts. It should be noted that in the cistern discovered on the Seid farm in the city area, twenty-nine third-century lamps were discovered, but not a single one was of this type.

Lamps of the Beth She'arim type have been found at several sites. For example, in el-Bassa in western Galilee, a grave was discovered containing a number of lamps of this type together with coins from the end of the fourth century C.E.[197] In a tomb in Gush Ḥalav a similar lamp was found.[198] At Gadot in Upper Galilee, a group of lamps similar to those of Beth She'arim was unearthed, except that they were larger in size.[199] They most closely resemble our lamp no. 17. Together with this group triangular lamps with seven wick holes were discovered; they too had stamped decorations. According to the report, the lamps from Gadot bore no traces of soot and had never been used; it may be assumed, therefore, that they were locally manufactured.

In the Department of Antiquities and the Museums of the Ministry of Education and Culture, there are lamps and fragments of lamps of the type under discussion which were discovered in tombs in Naḥaf, Makher, and Manawat — all three in Galilee.[200] The two lamp fragments from Naḥaf were found in association with a coin from the beginning of the fourth century C.E.[201] Lamps of this type were also uncovered in graves at Nahariya and Ḥanita which were excavated on behalf of the Department of Antiquities by Dan Barag. According to the coins, the excavator dated these lamps to the end of the third and the beginning of the fourth century C.E. (private communication). A number of lamps of this type were also found in a tomb near Yeḥiam in Galilee together with coins from the fourth century C.E.[202]

A Beth She'arim-type lamp very similar to our no. 19 and a fragment of a triangular lamp of the Gadot type were discovered in the excavation of the synagogue in Caesarea but have not as yet been published.[203] All this evidence testifies that the distribution of these lamps was restricted almost entirely to the northern part of the country. They are indisputably a Galilean product which apparently was manufactured in a number of major workshops. It seems almost certain that the lamps discovered in Caesarea were brought from the north; they should be attributed to the first half of the fourth century C.E.

27. 55–199. Catacomb 20. Light brown clay; round body. On top, dark red slip; on bottom, trickles of paint. Short nozzle merging with body. Conical, hollow handle, extending horizontally from the body of the lamp. Stamped decorations. Around the filling hole, a ring and a rope pattern. On the shoulder, rhombi with pairs of dots between them (compare with lamp no. 14). Along the handle and around the mouth, a ladder pattern. A row of four short lines on the nozzle (cf. with lamps nos. 5 and 8). The nozzle is not sooty. Rounded base.

28. 55–95. Catacomb 20. Similar to no. 27. On the shoulder and nozzle, a pattern of circles. Another fragment of a lamp of this type was also found (55–68).

29. 54–206. Catacomb 17, hall A, room II. Brown clay; dark red slip. A small lamp of the previous type, decorated with herringbone pattern. Sooty nozzle.

Lamps nos. 27–29 are of a rather rare type. Two lamps of this type were discovered in Beth She'an[204] together with lamps of the first half of the fourth century C.E. An additional lamp was discovered in the excavations of the church at Beth Yeraḥ in an unclear stratigraphic context.[205] Most of this material is late; however, since it also includes several lamps from the fourth century, it seems reasonable to attribute this type also to the first half of the fourth century C.E.

30. 53–1038. Catacomb 12, hall B, room IV. Dark brown clay; ovoid form. Broken handle. Decorated with globules. Circa fourth century C.E.

31. 54–108. Catacomb 14, in the collapsed material of the built tomb. Fragment. Light brown clay. Knobby handle. Com-

pletely flat surface with stamped circles. Small filling hole. Flat, broad base. We have encountered no parallel to this lamp; however, it should apparently be classified with the previously mentioned type of stamped lamps from Beth She'arim.

32. 54–195. Catacomb 17, hall A, in the debris near the entrance. Light brown clay; dark red-brown slip. Round body. Vertical, triangular handle. Spatulated nozzle. On the shoulder, a linear guilloche in relief. Flattened base. This lamp is not common and its date is uncertain. Some characteristics, for example the handle and the nozzle, would seem to indicate a late date. We have included it in this group because it was discovered in catacomb 17; however, it might well be an intrusion since it was found in the debris near the entrance. In the cache of lamps unearthed in catacomb 24 a similar lamp was discovered in a sixth-century context.[206]

33. 55–286. Catacomb 20, in the eastern entrance corridor. Brown clay; smooth red-brown slip on the back of the lamp. On the shoulder radial lines. Flat base. Circa fourth century C.E.

The Late Lamps from Catacomb 20

All the lamps discussed here were found in catacomb 20. They were assembled during the excavations and during the clearing operations of the catacomb which continued intermittently for several years. They were found scattered in various places in the accumulations of debris which covered the catacomb floor. Occasionally, lamps were found in the narrow spaces between the sarcophagi or inside an empty sarcophagus, proof that the lamps had fallen out of the robbers' hands while they were at work. Sometimes a lamp was even discovered in the dust below a coffin, evidence that the coffin had been moved from its original place either during the pillage of the catacomb or when the catacomb was inhabited.

A total of about 142 lamps (complete and fragmentary) were discovered in this catacomb, of which twenty may be classified with group A (early lamps) and the rest with group B (late lamps). Of the latter, fifty-six are Byzantine lamps, represented here by lamps nos. 34–44; and sixty-four are Arab lamps, exemplified by lamps 45–53. Fragments of two medieval lamps were also found.

Byzantine Lamps (nos. 34–44)

34. 55–195. Brown clay; pyriform. Around the filling hole, a ring and groove. Narrow channel on nozzle. Arcaded pattern on shoulder. Oblique lines on nozzle. Ring base. This lamp is unique at Beth She'arim. It is a degenerate version of the so-called "candlestick lamp." Earliest possible date, sixth century C.E.[207]

35. 55–281. Brown clay. Pear shaped. Broken filling hole. Small knob handle. On the shoulder, a herringbone pattern. Vague resemblance to lamp no. 34.

36. 55–44. Yellowish-brown clay. Elongated oval body. Small knob handle. Broken filling hole. The disc was horseshoe shaped but is now broken. Patterns of circles and rhombi in relief on the shoulder. This lamp is unique in its class.

37. 58–182. Yellowish-brown clay; red slip. Traces of a small triangular handle are discernible. Round filling hole. Decorated channel. Net pattern on the shoulder. Flat base, parallel to the outline of the body. Five additional lamps of this type were found.

38. 55–247. Light yellow clay; red slip. Same shape as no. 37. Small triangular handle. Patterns of circles and leaves. On the channel, a branch pattern. Four other lamps of this type were discovered plus fragments of an additional four lamps.

39. 55–192. Light brown clay; red-brown slip. The same form as no. 37. Decorated in vine-scroll pattern. In the channel, a row of rhombi. Four more lamps of this type and a fragment of a fifth lamp were found.

40. 55–200. Light brown clay without slip. Same shape as no. 37. On either side of

the shoulder, a pattern of two birds flanking "the sacred tree." Two additional lamps of this type were discovered; however, their ornamentation is different (cf. with the bird-decorated lamps from catacomb 24).[208]

41. 55–86. Thin brown clay. On the back of the shoulder, geometric designs. On the front, a herringbone pattern of fine lines in relief. One more lamp of this type was discovered.

42. 55–101. Fine brown clay. Horseshoe-shaped disc with small filling hole. On the shoulder, designs of branches and circles in a relief of fine lines.

43. 55–40. Fine brown clay. Broken horseshoe-shaped disc. Designs of branches in fine lines on the shoulder.

44. 55–273. Fragment of lamp of the previous type. Light brown clay. The shoulder is decorated with the letter M below which the letter Δ is suspended. A lamp of this type which has the letter M on its channel was among the group of lamps discovered in catacomb 24.[209] On the shore of Caesarea a fragment of a lamp was found, decorated with impressions of Byzantine coins with the letter M.[210] Below one of the letters, the sign Δ was also suspended. The coins used for these stamps date to the first half of the seventh century C.E.

Lamps nos. 36–44 constitute a large group with the following characteristics: ovoid body, slightly pointed at the end of the nozzle; tiny knob handle, pyramidal in shape; channel terminating in a straight line near the filling hole; geometric designs and decorations in relief of plants or birds; elongated base, parallel to the outline of the body. Three subtypes may be distinguished in this group:

(a) No. 36. Thick ware. Broad, plain channel. The filling hole was irregularly perforated by breaking the disc after firing. Only one example of this subtype was discovered.

(b) Nos. 37–40. Thick ware. The channel is narrower and decorated. The filling hole

is round and was perforated before firing. Generally, red slip.

(c) Nos. 41–44. Thin ware, decorated with fine lines. The disc, horseshoe-shaped because of the straight line at the beginning of the channel, was irregularly broken after firing.

The date of these lamps is very significant for determining the dates when catacomb 20 went out of use and when it was robbed. If there is no time gap between these lamps and those attributed to the first half of the fourth century, then these lamps could be attributed to a burial period which continued without interruptions after the first half of the fourth century; however, if there is a discrepancy in date between them, this would infer that the pillage of the cave took place at a later date.

Opinions are divided as to the date of lamp types 36–44. For our discussion, let us consider the lamps found in a tomb at el-Bassa in Western Galilee.[211] In this tomb fifteen lamps, glass vessels, and more than fifty coins from the end of the fourth century were discovered. On the basis of the numismatic evidence, Iliffe propounds that these lamps be dated to the fourth century. By viewing them as a homogeneous group, he attempts to contradict the generally accepted opinion that most of these lamps date to a later period. However, the truth of the matter is that this group is not homogeneous and apparently contains lamps from various periods.

Florence E. Day proved[212] that the earliest date to which lamp no. 2 in the el-Bassa group may be attributed is the seventh century C.E., since a lamp of the identical type was discovered in Gerasa with an Arabic inscription from the eighth century. Likewise, lamp no. 12 of the same group (the "candlestick" type) is later than the fourth century,[213] and so is lamp no. 14.

The lamps from el-Bassa which are pertinent to our discussion are nos. 3 and 5–7. They all have the same properties as those of lamps 36–43 from Beth She'arim.

Iliffe does not go into detail about these lamps; instead he merely mentions a parallel to no. 3 from the Museum in Beirut, which is customarily attributed to the fourth-seventh centuries C.E. Lamps of this type do not appear in the catacombs of Beth She'arim (except for catacomb 20), nor in any other tomb in the northern part of the country which contains material from the fourth century. It may, therefore, be concluded that they are later than the fourth century.

In a grave in Sidon[214] a large group of lamps was found of the previously mentioned type from el-Bassa. These lamps were attributed to the fourth century on the basis of Iliffe's dating of the el-Bassa lamps. A number of lamps of this type were also found in the excavations of the church at Beth Yeraḥ.[215] Even though they were not discovered in a clear-cut stratigraphic context, nevertheless, since most of the material was late (Byzantine and Arabic), it seems quite reasonable to assume that the lamps too are late.

The search for additional parallels from other sites excavated in the country revealed that these lamps never occur in the southern or central parts, but only from Beth She'arim northward. In 1956, during the excavation of catacomb 24 (which once served as a water reservoir), Mazar discovered a large cache of glass vessels and lamps from the second half of the sixth century C.E. — a dating based on the numismatic finds.[216] Among the lamps, a large group was found to be of the type under discussion. Since this material has not been published as yet, the parallels cannot be illustrated. However, since the numerous artifacts from catacomb 24 differ entirely from the finds in the rest of the catacombs, they must belong to the period when the catacombs were no longer used for burial. It thus seems that the latest findings from Beth She'arim corroborate the contention that the group of el-Bassa lamps is not homogeneous.

From a typological point of view as well, a later date for our lamps seems to be more suitable. There is a striking general resemblance between the lamps of type 37–40 and between the Arabic lamps of type 49–50. Comparisons between the decorative patterns are also instructive:

(a) The vine-scroll design found on lamp no. 7 from el-Bassa also occurs on our Arabic lamp no. 51 and on lamps of the Khirbet et-Mafjar type from the eighth century C.E.

(b) The net pattern on lamp no. 37 is also characteristic of the Arabic lamp from Khirbet el-Mafjar and other places.

(c) Lamp no. 45 (to be described below) is generally attributed to the beginning of the Arab period and is doubtlessly a direct development of lamp types 41–43.

(d) There is a great similarity between the floral designs and the geometric patterns of lamp no. 38 and those on lamp no. 50.

These examples suffice to prove that Byzantine lamps nos. 36–43 are closer in time to Arabic lamps 45–52, which succeed the Byzantine lamps chronologically, than to lamps nos. 14–26, which precede them considerably. The conspicuous similarity between these first two groups of lamps precludes their attribution to the end of the fourth century.

Finally, a decisive chronological proof may be ascribed to the fragment of a lamp found on the coast of Caesarea. The fragment is decorated with impressions of coins from the beginning of the seventh century C.E. Indeed, the similarity between this fragment and the lamps of the type discussed from el-Bassa as well as from Beth She'arim has been convincingly demonstrated by A. Kindler.[217]

It may, therefore, be concluded that lamps of the type 36–44 are indigenous (to the extent that conclusions may be drawn from the published material) only to the northern part of the country and that they should be dated to the end of the sixth and the beginning of the seventh century C.E.

Arabic Lamps (nos. 45–53)

45. 55–243. Brown clay. Oval, elongated body. Flat "tongue" handle, Horseshoe-shaped filling hole. The steep shoulder is decorated with net and line design, and herringbone pattern. In the channel, a pattern of a menorah-like branch. Flat, long base. The influence of lamps of types 41–43 is obvious on this lamp; however, while the latter were discovered only in the north of the country, this lamp was encountered frequently in many excavations all over the country.[218] It dates approximately to the end of the seventh century.

46. 55–194. Thick brown ware; traces of straw discernible; black core; poor firing. Coarsely hand made. The handle is similar to that on the previous lamp.

47. 55–212. Brown clay; red slip. Serrated outline. Broken conical handle. Decorated with oblique lines. Rounded base with star pattern.

48. 55–260. Light brown clay. Conical handle. Shoulder decorated with lines and dots. Floral design on channel. Ring base with star pattern. Two other lamps of this type were discovered as well as fragments of two additional lamps.[219]

49. 55–244. Red brown clay. Conical handle. Decorated with semicircles. Concave base. Between base and end of nozzle, a ridge. Sixteen additional lamps of this type as well as fragments of another five lamps were discovered.

There are several variations in motifs of branches, bands, triangles, lattice pattern, etc.; the ring bases have patterns of a star, a branch, bands, and dots (fig. 93).[220]

50. 55–16. Red-brown clay. Patterns of a wheel, rosettes, and animals. Upright tongue-like handle.

51. 55–196. Light buff clay. Tongue-like handle. On the shoulder, a vine scroll; near the wick hole, designs of birds. The base is parallel to the outline. A ridge connects the lamp to the end of the nozzle. Five more lamps and fragments of another five were discovered.[221]

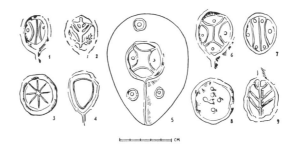

Fig. 93 Decorations on bases of Arab lamps. In the middle, lamp no. 49

52. 55–48. Light yellowish clay. Similar to no. 51. On the shoulder there is an Arabic inscription which has not yet been deciphered.

53. 55–325 (fig. 92, 7). Lamp of type no. 48. Inside the channel there is a stylized Arabic inscription which should be read علله ("Allah"). Lamps of this type were recently found in the excavations of the synagogue at Ḥammath-Tiberias in its last phase of building attributed to the seventh century C.E.[222]

Lamps nos. 48–53 may be divided into two main groups according to the shape of the handle, the decorations, the base, and the type of clay:[223]

(a) Nos. 48–49 and 53. These lamps date to the Umayyad period (seventh and eighth centuries C.E.).

(b) Nos. 51–52. From the Umayyad and Abbasid periods (eighth and ninth centuries C.E.). No. 50 is classified with type *(a)* but has a handle like type *(b)*.

In contrast to the late Byzantine lamps whose distribution is restricted to the North, the Arabic lamps are widely disseminated over the whole country.

Fig. 93 illustrates a selection of decorations found on bases of type no. 49 lamps. They are very common on lamps of the Arab period.

Thus, while the occupation of catacomb 20 began earlier, it continued into the Early Arab period. We may reasonably assume that during their protracted operations, the tomb robbers made use of lamp types 45–53.

From the Middle Ages, when the catacomb was occupied by Arab shepherds and others, only two fragments of lamps were discovered.[224] This implies that the pillage of the tombs and the fracturing of marble coffins, which extended over a lengthy period and which required many sources of light, did not occur during this era.

6 POTTERY

The amount of pottery discovered during our excavations of the catacombs was extremely meagre. To make matters even worse, this pottery was not discovered in the tombs but in the debris which accumulated in the rooms and in the courtyards. A likely reason for the paucity of vessels is that the graves were very thoroughly robbed. However, it is also possible that the deposition of ordinary pottery vessels as funerary gifts in tombs was not customary in Beth She'arim, and that the pottery discovered was used by undertakers and visitors. A similar picture also emerges from the report of the earlier excavations of the catacombs, though, apparently, slightly more vessels were discovered. Nevertheless, even among these vessels, only one juglet was found in a tomb.[225] In the debris which accumulated in the courtyard, many shards were found which were not indigenous: they had rolled down the slope of the hill and were in no way associated with the tombs.

The pottery may be classified into two main groups. One group (fig. 94) includes vessels from the Roman period, i.e., vessels from the period when the various catacombs were still in regular use. The second group (figs. 95–96) consists of Arabic vessels and shards from the Middle Ages, i.e., vessels belonging to people who temporarily occupied catacomb 20. Since these vessels were not discovered in a stratigraphic context, their classification is strictly typological.

Late Roman Pottery (fig. 94)
The vessels in this group are utilitarian and consist mainly of jugs and other closed containers. Several of them are common; however, a few are quite rare. Most of them are characterized by a ribbed body.

Vessel no. 1 is one of the common jars of this period. Close parallels were found in the city area, in the cisterns on the Seid farm.[226] All the vessels discovered there date to the third or the first half of the fourth century C.E.

Jug no. 2 is typified by a small spout at right angles to the handle. Vessels of this type were prevalent mainly during the Byzantine period; however, they began to appear in the Late Roman period.[227]

Jug no. 3 is distinguished from the rest of the vessels by its smooth body. Since the rim in the figure is only a reconstruction, it is by no means certain that the suggested shape is accurate. A somewhat similar jug was discovered in one of the graves on the Mount of Olives.[228] Another possibly closer parallel may be found among the Byzantine vessels from Beth She'an.[229] It is noteworthy that our jug was discovered in catacomb 20 where lamps from the end of the Byzantine period were also unearthed.

Vessel no. 4, whose handle is missing, is a squat bottle which is quite rare. A close parallel is a third-century bottle discovered in a Roman tomb in Amman.[230]

Jug no. 5 is not common; no. 6 is identical to it, except for its narrower neck. They are characterized by a concave ribbed base (Pl. LXXII, 6–7). The lower part of a jug of this type, which served as a container for paint, was discovered in catacomb 13 (see above, p. 41). We have not encountered an exact parallel to these jugs in other excavations. Somewhat similar vessels were found in the earlier excavations at Beth She'arim; they are attributed to the third

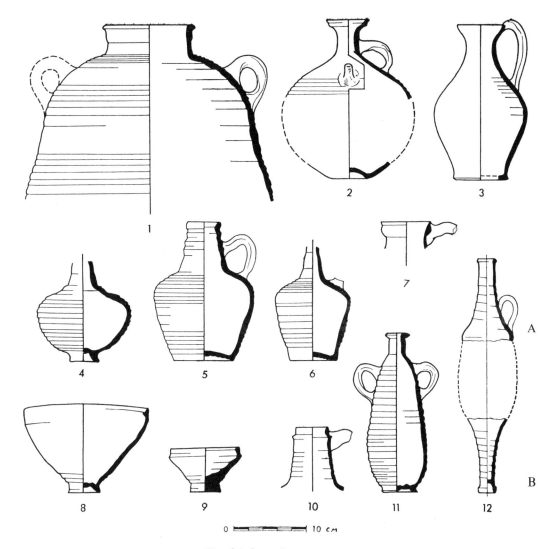

Fig. 94 Late Roman pottery

Serial Number	Object	Registration Number	Locus	Plate	Description
1	Jar	54–40	Catacomb 13, hall C		Light reddish-brown
2	Jug	54–98	Catacomb 14, hall C, arcosolium 3		Brown-red
3	Jug	55–73	Catacomb 20, room II		Light reddish-brown
4	Jug	56–233	Catacomb 20		Brown
5	Jug	55–10	Catacomb 19, near central entrance	LXXII, 6	Brown-red
6	Jug	55–12	Catacomb 19, hall B	LXXII, 7	Brown-red
7	Rim of Jug	54–53	Catacomb 13, hall H		Brown
8	Bowl	55–72	Catacomb 20, room II		Brown; gray core
9	Small bowl	55–159	Catacomb 20, room XVII		Brown
10	Jug	54–54	Catacomb 13, hall H		Brown
11	Amphoriskos	53–554	Catacomb 13, Hall L, room II	LXXII, 3	Light brown
12a	Jug	54–52	Catacomb 13, hall H		Brown
12b	Jug	54–41	Catacomb 13, hall C		Yellowish gray

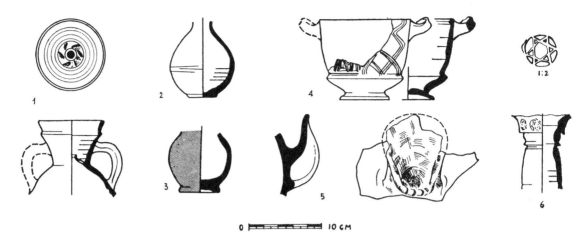

Fig. 95 Plain Arab pottery

Serial Number	Object	Registration Number	Locus	Description
1	Small jar with strainer in neck	55–28	Catacomb 20	Greenish yellow ware; red core
2	Bottle	55–214	Catacomb 20	Brown clay; gray core
3	Bottle	55–215	Catacomb 20	Brown clay; reddish-brown slip; burnished
4	Deep bowl	58–257	Catacomb 20	Red-brown; incised decoration
5	Handle of cooking pot	55–80	Catacomb 20	Gray; dark gray core
6	Neck of jug	55–209	Catacomb 20	Yellowish-gray; pinkish core; impressed patterns of "Star of David"

century and the first half of the fourth century C.E.[231]

Bowl no. 8 became distorted in the kiln. It is characterized by a disproportionately small base, which makes the vessel unstable. A similar type was found elsewhere at Beth She'arim.[232]

Vessel no. 9 is illustrated here as a small bowl, but it is more likely a cover, as evidenced by the raised wheel marks on the interior.[233]

The neck of jug no. 10 has a characteristic molded rim. A similar neck was found in the city area of Beth She'arim.[234]

No. 11 is an amphoriskos, one of five of this type discovered in the catacombs (see Pl. LXXII, 1–5).[235] These vessels are particularly interesting because of their unique shape: they have a tall, ribbed body which narrows toward the top; two oversized earlike handles protrude from the shoulder. These amphoriskoi, with narrow mouths and elongated bodies, are convenient for storing oil (and other liquids) used for burial. We have not encountered a single parallel in any of the other excavations in Palestine. On the other hand, jars of this type were discovered in a tomb from the Roman period in Jal el-Amed near Tyre.[236] It seems, therefore, reasonable to assume (see above, pp. 41–42) that these jars were brought to Beth She'arim from Phoenicia

Fig. 96 Painted Arab pottery

Serial Number	Object	Registration Number	Locus	Description
1	Jar handle	55–75/1	Catacomb 20	Light brown; brown decoration
2	Shard from jug	60–319	Catacomb 20	Red-brown; purple-brown decoration
3	Shard from jug	55–75/2	Catacomb 20	Red-brown; purple-brown decoration
4	Shard from jug	55–76	Catacomb 20	Brown to yellowish-brown; purple-brown decoration
5	Shard from jug	60–318	Catacomb 20	Red-brown; purple-brown decoration
6	Shard from jug	60–317	Catacomb 20	Yellowish-gray; brown decoration

together with the deceased who were interred in catacomb 13.[237] The graduated heights of the five amphoriskoi (Pl. LXXII) may be evidence of standard sizes.[238]

Jug. no. 12 was assembled from two parts of the same type of vessel which were discovered in catacomb 13. Its restoration was patterned after complete jugs of this type, as yet unpublished, which were found in catacomb 26.[239] This vessel, with its fusiform contour, handle, particular type of spiral ribbing, and high concave base, is quite rare. A somewhat similar jug was found in tomb 157 at Gezer.[240]

Plain Arabic Pottery

All the vessels in this group (fig. 95) were found in catacomb 20, except for no. 4 which apparently dates to the beginning of the Arab period. All of them should be attributed to the Middle Ages (eleven–thirteenth centuries C.E. approximately).

Small jar no. 1 is characterized by the strainer in its neck. Vessels with a strainer of this type are common in Arabic pottery.[241]

Bottles nos. 2–3 and 5 are handmade; this is also typical of the decorated pottery discussed below. The strange handle of no. 5 is characteristic of Arabic cooking pots from the Middles Ages to present days.[242]

The shape of bowl no. 4 is unusual; however, the decoration technique and the type of clay are typical of Early Arabic pottery.

The neck of jug no. 6 is particularized by the stamped decorations encircling it. The hexagon pattern ("Star of David") is very prevalent in Arab decorative art. Necks of vessels with stamped patterns of pentagons, octagons, and other designs are widespread in Arabic pottery of the Middle Ages.[243]

Decorated Arabic Pottery

In catacomb 20 many pottery fragments decorated with geometric designs were dis-

197

covered. A few examples are presented in fig. 96. They have a light brown or yellowish slip; the designs are painted in brown or purple on a light background. The clay is generally gray; the firing is only fair. As far as we can determine, all these shards seem to belong to closed vessels, jugs for instance. All are handmade.

Pottery of this type is very widely disseminated in Arab strata and sites in Palestine. It is generally attributed to the eleventh–thirteenth centuries C.E. Brief discussions of this subject are provided in the excavation reports from Samaria,[244] Abu Ghosh,[245] and Afula.[246] A rich variety of this pottery was also found in the Arab stratum of the excavations at Hama in Syria.[247]

7 GLASS VESSELS, by Dan Barag

In catacombs 12–20 nineteen glass vessels and several hundred fragments of glass were discovered; most of them were free blown, and only a minority were mold blown. The dominant colors are light bluish-green and light green. Only a few vessels are made of colorless glass with a greenish tinge. Three vessels are made of blue glass, and only one of greenish-brown glass. The quality of the glass is generally quite good, but the workmanship is only medium and sometimes even poor. On most of the vessels iridescence can be distinguished; however, in a number of cases the traces of iridescence are only slight.

The vast majority of the vessels are small- and medium-sized receptacles for liquids, salves, etc. The same is also true for the fragments found in these catacombs. A complete lamp beaker, fragments of lamps, two fragments of chalices, and a plate were also discovered. No remnants of cups or bowls were found.

The small quantity of finds is due to the thorough robbing of the catacombs: most of the vessels were pillaged or broken and their fragments scattered. Only in catacomb 15, where a rock fall occurred in antiquity, was a group of vessels discovered in its original location (see p. 24, fig. 9). In catacomb 12, an intact glass vessel was unearthed (no. 26) together with five pottery lamps, a cosmetics spoon, and several beads. The largest number of artifacts was found in catacomb 20. There is almost no resemblance between the finds in this catacomb and those in catacombs 12–19; however, this is probably due mainly to the paucity of the finds in the other catacombs.

The vessels are of common Palestinian and Syrian types and there is no doubt that they were produced locally. There are no means of determining exactly where the vessels were manufactured but, if indeed there was a glass industry in Beth She'arim as Mazar maintains,[248] then at least some of the vessels could have been manufactured at Beth She'arim itself.

1. 55–326 (fig. 97, 1; Pl. LXVIII, 5). Catacomb 20. Bottle with conical body and slightly concave base. Long cylindrical neck; constriction at base of neck. Pushed-out ridge below rim. Light bluish-green with small and large bubbles. Height: 230 mm.

2. 55–202, 205 (fig. 97, 2). Catacomb 20, room X. Bottle similar to no. 1 but narrower. Pontil mark on base. Light bluish green with only a few bubbles. Coarse workmanship. Height: 205 mm.

3. 55–230 (fig. 97, 3). Catacomb 20, room V. Neck of a bottle similar to no. 2. Light bluish-green.

4. 55–142 (fig. 97, 4). Catacomb 20, room VII. The upper part of a bottle similar to no. 1, except that the neck is shorter. Light bluish-green, with a small number of elongated bubbles. The upper part of the body is surrounded by a horizontal coil of the same color.

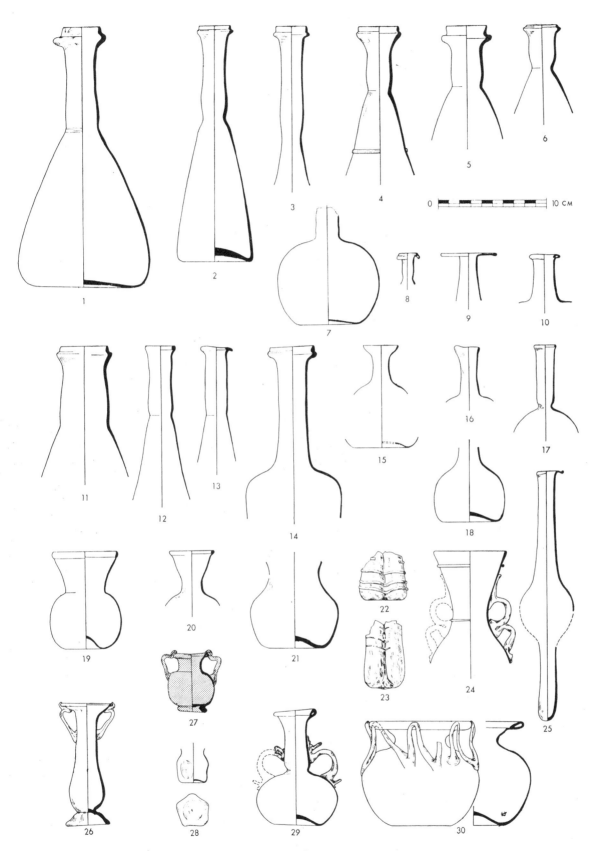

Fig. 97 Glassware

5. 55–226 (fig. 97, 5). Catacomb 20, room III. Upper half of a bottle similar to no. 1. Short neck. Bluish-green with spherical bubbles.

6. 55–224 (fig. 97, 6). Catacomb 20, room III. As above, but without a vertical lip. Greenish with a few elongated bubbles.

7. 55–278 (fig. 97, 11). Catacomb 20, room XXI. As above. The neck is short and wide. Greenish with elongated bubbles.

8. 55–288 (fig. 97, 12). Catacomb 20, room XVI. The upper part of a bottle similar to no. 2. The rim is folded inward. Light green with elongated bubbles.

9. 55–135 (fig. 97, 13). Catacomb 20, room XV. Like no. 8. The rim is folded both outward and inward. Light bluish-green.

10. 55–276 (fig. 97, 14). Catacomb 20, room XXI. The upper part of a bottle with rounded shoulders. Long, cylindrical neck. Pushed-out ridge below. Green with a few rounded bubbles.

Bottle no. 1, subtype no. 2, and bottle fragments nos. 3–9 constitute a single typological group. All of them were found in catacomb 20; no fragments of bottles of this type were discovered in any of the other catacombs discussed in this book. In addition to the examples described here, twelve necks, nine bases (the majority with pontil marks), and many body fragments of similar bottles were unearthed in catacomb 20.

A bottle similar to nos. 8–9 was discovered in Tomb E 220 I at Samaria.[249] The excavators attributed this tomb to the third century C.E.; however, the rest of the finds seem to indicate that this tomb was in use at the beginning of the fourth century C.E. as well.[250] The upper part of a bottle of this type was also found in Tomb 23 at Gezer which, according to the other finds, should be dated to the third–fourth centuries C.E.[251] An additional bottle was discovered in a tomb at Silwan; however, its date cannot be determined with certainty.[252] Fragments of a bottle of this type were also

found in a tomb on the Mount of Olives.[253] At Karanis in the Fayyum, two bottles similar to our no. 2 were discovered; in Harden's opinion, they should be attributed to the fourth–fifth centuries C.E.[254] The neck and rim of no. 10 are similar to those of nos. 1–9; however, the body has a different shape, characteristic of glass vessels from the Late Roman and Byzantine periods.

11. 53–968 (fig. 97, 8). Catacomb 12, hall A, room VI. The neck of a small bottle. Rim folded outward, downward, and upward. Constriction at base of neck. Light bluish-green with elongated pinprick bubbles.

12. 55–133/2 (fig. 97, 9). Catacomb 20, room I. Neck of a bottle. Rim folded inward. Light bluish-green.

A bottle like no. 11 was discovered at Azor in a tomb from the Late Roman period.[255] Harden dates this type, also familiar from the finds at Karanis, to the second–fourth centuries C.E.[256] The complete original form of nos. 12–13 is uncertain. The form of no. 13 may resemble two bottles from Gerasa which were attributed to the Byzantine period;[257] However, it seems more likely that nos. 12–13 date to the Early Arab period.

14. 58–328 (fig. 97, 7; Pl. LXVIII, 8). Catacomb 20. Bottle with a spherical body. Concave base and cylindrical neck; the upper part of the neck is missing. Both on the shoulder and on the lower part of the vessel there are two groups of thin incisions, coarsely executed. (These groups of incisions were not shown in the drawing and are scarcely discernible on the photograph.) Colorless. Height: 104 mm.

15. 54–217 (fig. 97, 15). Catacomb 17, the eastern room. Upper part of a bottle with rounded shoulders. Short neck. Rounded flaring rim. Light green.

At the same spot, fragments of a concave base were found which might belong to the same vessel.

16. 58–256/3 (fig. 97, 16). Catacomb 20,

room XIII. Neck of a bottle. The rim is thickened and distorted. Light green.

17. 55–140 (fig. 97, 17). Catacomb 20, room XII. Upper part of a bottle with rounded shoulders. Long, cylindrical neck; constriction at base of neck. Thickened rim. Very light bluish-green.

18. 54–151 (fig. 97, 18; 27, 7). Catacomb 15, hall B, room I. Bottle with a wide, low body and rounded shoulders. Concave base with pontil mark. Cylindrical neck; the upper part of it is missing. Green. Height: 64 mm.

The shape of no. 14 is typical of the Later Roman and the Byzantine periods. Thin abrased lines also were commonly used as a decoration in the Late Roman period.[258] Nos. 15 and 18 belong to a type which was very widespread in Palestine at the end of the Late Roman and during the Byzantine periods. A bottle of this kind dating to the third century C.E. was found in a tomb at Amman.[259] Bottles of this type from the first half of the fourth century were discovered in Samaria (Tomb E 220 I),[260] and on the Mount of Olives together with a coin of Constantine.[261] Several additional bottles of this type found in Palestine, also from the Late Roman and Byzantine periods, are likewise worthy of note.[262] A fragment of a bottle of this type was unearthed at Karanis.[263] Two bottles similar to our no. 17 were discovered at Amman in a tomb from the third century C.E.[264] Despite the slight differences in the form of the neck, there is certainly a typological association between this bottle and the type with the spherical body and cylindrical neck which was so common during the third–fourth centuries C.E., particularly in the West.[265] In the Byzantine period, various types were developed from this prototype, all of them characterized by long cylindrical necks usually decorated with horizontal glass threads.[266]

19. 55–327 (fig. 97, 19; Pl. LXVIII, 7). Catacomb 20. Jar with a spherical body, concave base, and a wide flaring neck. Rim folded inward. Light bluish-green bubbly. Height: 87 mm.

20. 58–256/2 (fig. 97, 20). Catacomb 20, room XIII. Upper part of a bottle with rounded shoulders and a short funnel-shaped neck. Rim folded inward. Light bluish-green.

21. 54–64 (fig. 97, 21). Catacomb 13, hall IX. Bottle with a low and broad body. Concave base with a pontil mark. Short and wide neck. The rim is missing. Green, bubbly. Height: 79 mm.

Glass vessels similar to no. 19 were discovered in Beth She'an in a fourth-century tomb,[267] and on the Mount of Olives in a tomb from the same period.[268] The shape of no. 20 is characteristic of the Late Roman Period. The shape of no. 21 is similar to that of no. 19.

22. 54–152 (fig. 97, 22; 27, 4). Catacomb 15, hall B, room I. Lower part of a double tubular flask with a flat base. Light green. A horizontal glass thread of the same color is coiled around the vessel. There is a pontil mark on the base. In one of the tubes, a residue of black material was preserved.

23. 54–201 (fig. 97, 23). Catacomb 17, the central hall, in the debris near the entrance. A fragment similar to no. 22. Light bluish-green.

Another fragment resembling no. 23 was found in the debris of the courtyard of catacomb 15 (no. 54–168).

Nos. 22 and 23 belong to a very common class of vessels typical of Palestine and Transjordan. In this class there are many types which were frequently found containing residues of cosmetics and bronze kohl-sticks. These vessels first appeared at the beginning of the fourth century,[269] and continued to appear throughout the fifth and sixth centuries C.E. No. 22 apparently belongs to the type in which the thread coiled around the body ends at the top in a zigzag pattern. Vessels of this kind were found in Meggido,[270] and in Tiberias.[271] This type is evidently one of the earliest in this class of vessels.

24. 55–206 (fig. 97, 24). Catacomb 20, room X. Upper part of a bottle with a wide flaring neck. Thickened rim and rounded shoulders. Near the rim and also at the base of the neck, there is a glass thread decoration of the same color as the vessel. The handle consists of two loops, one above the other; the lower end of the handle is ledge shaped but was broken. Bluish-green with pinprick bubbles.

No close parallel among the glass vessels from excavations in Palestine is known to this writer. The form of the bottle is typical of the Late Roman period. Horizontal glass threads decorating the necks of jugs and bottles and handles consisting of two or more loops with ledge-shaped ends (see also no. 29) are, however, characteristic of glass vessels from the Late Roman and Byzantine periods.

25. 54–39 (fig. 97, 25). Catacomb 13, the niche in the corridor opposite Hall M. Upper and lower parts of a spindle-shaped bottle. Rim folded inward; coarse workmanship. Light bluish-green with many elongated bubbles. Pontil mark on the base.

Fragments of two additional bottles of the same type were found together with no. 25.

Spindle-shaped bottles were very widespread in the West during the fourth century C.E.[272] A bottle of this type was discovered in Dura-Europos as well,[273] in Cyprus,[274] and Egypt.[275] According to Harden, it is typical of Syria.[276] Only a few bottles unearthed in excavations in Palestine have been published. At el-Maker similar bottles were found, except that they have a bulbous end.[277] Bottles of the same type were found in a tomb in Wadi Badhan and in a tomb at Nahariya.[278] It is noteworthy that no. 25 is identical in shape to the western specimens of this type.

26. 53–966 (fig. 97, 26; Pl. LXVIII, 4). Catacomb 12, hall A, room VI. Elongated flask with a concave/tubular base made by blowing out and pushing upward (the base is mistakenly drawn with a solid rim). The body narrows toward the top. Flaring rim, folded inward. Two handles with a fold below the rim extend from the rim to the body. Light bluish-green with a few elongated bubbles. On the base, a pontil mark, 9 mm in diameter. Height: 167 mm.

A bronze cosmetics spoon was found together with this vessel (see Pl. LXXIII, 15).

This type, in all its variants, was very widespread in Palestine, especially in tombs from the third–fifth centuries C.E.[279] The finely-worked bottle from Beth She'arim is among the earliest examples of this type. The lamps found in conjunction with it (see p. 24) lead us to conclude that it should be dated to the middle of the third century C.E.[280] Since this type is also known from Dura-Europos, its initial appearance cannot be dated later than the middle of the third century C.E.[281]

27. 55–132 (fig. 97, 27; Pl. LXVIII, 3). Catacomb 20, room VIII. Amphoriskos with a spherical body, a pad base, a short wide neck, and an inward-folded rim. Two handles from the rim to the shoulders. The handles terminate on top in an out-turned fold. The vessel is distorted. Dark blue and very bubbly. Height: 55 mm.

Somewhat similar amphoriskoi were found in Egypt[282] and Cyprus.[283] Two amphoriskoi, of different types, were discovered at Amman in a third-century tomb[284] and at Beth Fajjar in a tomb from the fourth–fifth centuries C.E.[285] The shape of this amphoriskos resembles that of the amphoriskoi common in Jewish art. It differs in color from all the other glass vessels discovered in catacombs 12–20. The only other vessel made in bubbly blue glass is no. 49, which dates to the end of the Byzantine period.

28. 52–967 (fig. 97, 28). Catacomb 12, hall A, room VI. Small flask with five indentations pressed into the wall, lending it a pentagonal shape. The rim is missing. Colorless with many pinprick bubbles. Height: 20 mm.

Flasks of this type[286] and similar ones were found in this country in tombs from the Late Roman Period.[287]

29. 56–523 (fig. 97, 29; Pl. LXVIII, 6). Catacomb 20. Bottle with a wide low body and rounded shoulders. Concave base with pontil mark. Elongated neck constricted at the base. Rim folded inward. Two handles with ledge-like ends between the shoulders and the middle of the neck. The body is made of good quality, greenish-brown glass with few bubbles; the handle is dark bluish-green with numerous bubbles. Height: 101 mm.

Similar bottles were found at Karanis in Egypt.[288] The body of one of them is made of brown glass whereas the handle is formed from green glass.[289] Harden attributes these vessels to the fourth-fifth centuries C.E.; however, he notes that some of them were discovered in houses from the period of Constantine.

30. 55–141 (fig. 97, 30). Catacomb 20, room VIII. Jar with a low, wide body. Concave base with pontil mark. Short neck. Broad rim folded inward. Colorless. Between the rim and the shoulders, a coil of the same kind of glass. Height: 90 mm.

This is one of the most characteristic types of glass vessels found in Palestine. Two such jars were found in the cemetery on the Mount of Olives, one of them with a coin of Constantine the Great.[290] A vessel of this type was also found in Bethany in a tomb dating to the second half of the third or the beginning of the fourth century C.E.[291] A vessel of this type from Amman should also be attributed to the middle or the second half of the third century.[292] Additional vessels were discovered in Meggido[293] and Samaria.[294] These finds show that this type should be assigned to the end of the third and the fourth centuries C.E. A similar type was prevalent in Egypt during the fourth and fifth centuries C.E.[295]

31. 54–34 (fig. 98, 1). The corridor of catacomb 13. Bottle with a spherical body. The long neck widens toward the top.

Thickened rim. The body is decorated with vertical ribs. The base is missing. Light bluish-green. Height: 202 mm.

An almost identical bottle, dated to the third/fourth centuries C.E.[296] was found in a tomb near Ḥuqoq.[297] Similar bottles were also found in Cyprus.[298] Bottles with a spherical body and a long neck widening toward the top were rather common all over the Roman Empire during the third/fourth centuries C.E.[299]

32. 54–149 (figs. 98, 2; 27, 5). Bottle with a wide body and broad rounded shoulders. Concave base. Wide neck broadening toward the top. The rim is missing. A horizontal thread the color of the vessel is coiled around the neck. Light green with a few bubbles in the neck. Height: 213 mm.

33. 54–148/1 (figs. 98, 6; 27, 3). Catacomb 15, hall B, room I. Neck of a bottle like nos. 32 and 34. A horizontal thread is coiled twice around the neck. Light green with a few elongated bubbles.

34. 54–148/2 (figs. 98, 7; 27, 2). Catacomb 15, hall B, room I. Shoulder and neck of a bottle similar to no. 32. The neck widens toward the top and has horizontal threads of the same color glass coiled around it; three rows of threads remained. Light bluish-green with a few bubbles. Fragments of the base are identical to the base of bottle no. 32.

Fragments of two addtional vessels of this type were found in catacomb 14 (54–49 and 54–100).

The shapes of the body and neck of bottles nos. 32–34 and their thread decorations are typical of the Late Roman and Byzantine periods. Nevertheless, only a small number of bottles of this sort have been published in the excavation reports from Palestine.[300]

35. 55–132 (fig. 98, 3). Catacomb 20, room VIII. Bottle with a conical body and concave base. Neck widens toward the top. Thickened rim. Light bluish-green with a few spherical bubbles. Height: 202 mm.

36. 54–211/1 (fig. 98, 9). Catacomb 17,

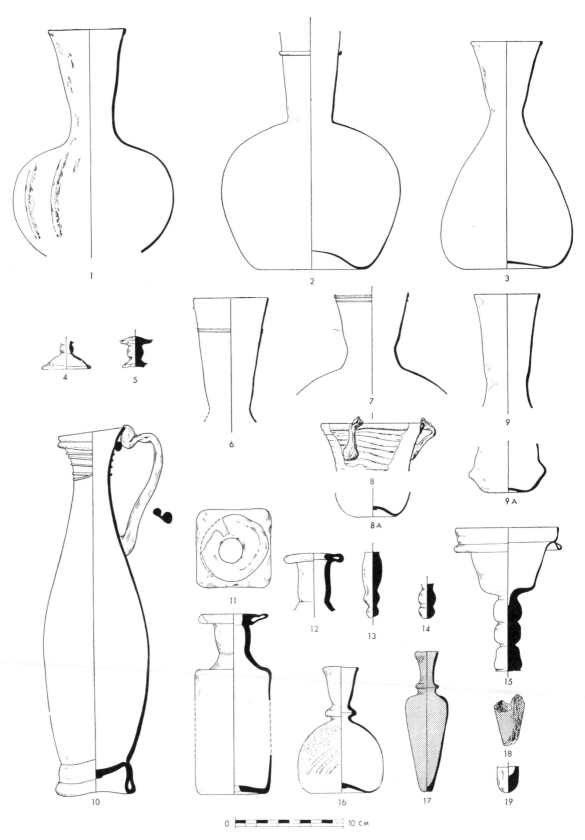

Fig. 98 Glassware

hall A, room II. Neck of a bottle like no. 35. Light green with deformed bubbles.

This type of bottle was fairly common in Palestine, especially during the fourth century C.E. A bottle from Jerusalem (Rockefeller Museum site) very similar to no. 35, may probably be assigned to the second half of the third or the beginning of the fourth century.[301] Bottles of this type from the first half of the fourth century have been found in tombs from the Mount of Olives[302] and Samaria.[303] A bottle of this type from Gezer may tentatively be dated to the fourth century.[304] The type also occurs in Egypt[305] and Cyprus.[306]

37. 54–211/2 (fig. 98, 9a). Catacomb 17, hall A, room II. The lower part of a bottle (or a cup). The vessel is carinated near the base. Light green.[307]

38. 54–167 (fig. 98, 4). Catacomb 16, in the debris of the courtyard. Concave base and hollow stem of a wine cup. The rim of the base is folded inward. Beaded stem. Green.

39. 54–210 (fig. 98, 5). Catacomb 20, room XVIII. Broken stem of a wine cup. The stem is solid and beaded. Light bluish-green with deformed and pinprick bubbles.

To date no parallel for no. 37 has been found in Palestine. Nos. 38 and 39 belong to a class of vessels which was very wide-spread in Palestine during the Byzantine period. For example, vessels of this type were discovered in Beth Yeraḥ, Beth She'an, Samaria, Jerusalem, Gerasa, and Mount Nebo.[308] Since no. 38 was found in the courtyard of the catacomb, its date cannot be determined; likewise, the date of no. 39, found in catacomb 20, cannot be accurately fixed. Wine cups of this sort, including their various subtypes, were especially common in the Levant (Egypt, Cyprus, Syria, and Asia Minor),[309] but are also known from Italy.[310]

40. 55–133/1 (fig. 98, 8). Catacomb 20, room XVIII. Upper part of a lamp. The rim is folded outward. A handle—apparently one of three—from the rim to the

wall. Shallow diagonal corrugations on the body. Light green with deformed bubbles; the handle has black impurities.

41. 55–138/1 (fig. 98, 8a). Catacomb 20, room VIII. Concave base of a lamp bearing pontil mark. Light bluish-green with many bubbles.

Three additional bases similar to no. 41 and fragments of rims and handles of another five lamps were also discovered in catacomb 20.

Glass lamps began to be used in the Late Roman Period and are still used up to the present.[311] Their handles served as suspension loops. Lamps of types similar to nos. 40–41 were found in many places in Palestine, for example at Beth She'an, Samaria, Jerusalem, 'Ain Karim, Gezer, Gerasa, and Mount Nebo.[312] These lamps, dating to the Byzantine period, may be divided into two groups: (a) lamps with a vertical tube attached to the bottom inside the vessel;[313] (b) lamps without a tube of this kind.

No traces of tubes of this type were discovered on the lamp bases from catacomb 20; nor were any unattached, separate fragments of tubes found. It should, however, be pointed out that among the decorations of bowl no. 49 there are suspended squares which probably depict glass lamps (see p. 163). Till now, lamps of this type are mainly known from Palestine; however, according to Isings, they were also used in Sicily and Italy from the fourth century C.E. onward.[314]

42. 54–153 (figs. 98, 15; 27, 6; Pl. LXVIII, 2). Catacomb 15, hall B, room I. Wine cup or lamp shaped like a wine cup. Rounded, convex rim; below it a cut-out fold. The solid stem is beaded; three beads were preserved. The lower edge of the vessel is broken. Light green glass of good quality with a few deformed bubbles. Height: 127 mm.

43. 55–138/2 (fig. 98, 14). Catacomb 20, room VIII. Lower part of a stem, as above (no. 42). At the end of the stem, a pontil mark. Light bluish-green with a few bubbles.

44. 55–137 (fig. 98, 13). Catacomb 20,

room XVIII. Similar to no. 43. The workmanship is coarse. The end of the stem bears a pontil mark. Green with numerous bubbles.

Many lamps and fragments with a beaded stem were discovered in Gerasa, dating to the Byzantine period.[315] Fragments were found in other places as well.[316] Lamp no. 42 and these lamps have a beaded stem in common. The shape of the upper part has no parallel as yet. This vessel — which might be either a lamp or a wine cup — was discovered in catacomb 15 with a large group of glass vessels (see p. 69) which apparently cannot be dated later than the destruction of Beth She'arim (352 C.E.). Therefore, this vessel is the earliest example of its kind known up to now.[317] The shape of fragments nos. 43–44 bears a close resemblance to that of the lamps from Gerasa.

45. 58–256/4 (fig. 98, 11). Catacomb 20, room XIII. Upper part and base of a square mold-blown bottle. Cylindrical neck with a constriction at its base. Rim folded outward, downward, and inward and flattened on top. The bottle did not have a handle. Light green glass of poor quality with many pinprick and medium-sized bubbles. At the same spot, fragments of a similar bottle were found.

46. 58–256/5 (fig. 99a). Catacomb 20, room XIII. Fragments of the base of a square, mold-blown bottle. The base is decorated with circles; a knob juts out of each corner. Light green.

47. 55–203 (fig. 98, 12). Catacomb 20. Neck of a bottle, like no. 45. Colorless with a greenish tinge and pinprick as well as medium-sized bubbles.

Fragments of two additional bottles similar to no. 47 were also found in catacomb 20. Nos. 45–47, despite the absence of the handle, are subdivisions of a type of square jug which was common over the whole Roman Empire from the first to the fourth centuries C.E.[318] In a tomb at Jerusalem (Rockefeller Museum site) a square bottle was found (also without a handle) dating to the Late Roman period.[319] Numerous bases, like no. 46 in type, were discovered elsewhere, for example in Dura-Europos.[320] The coarse workmanship of nos. 45–47 and other fragments doubtlessly justifies a dating to the Late Roman period.

48. 54–154 (figs. 98, 10; 27, 1; Pl. LXVIII, 1). Catacomb 15, hall B, room I. Tall jug with an elongated ovoid body. The high ring base was made by blowing out and folding inward. Flaring neck with rounded rim. Strap handle with a groove in the center extends from the rim to the body.

Fig. 99a Base of glass bottle

Fig. 99b Fragments and reconstruction of glass juglet

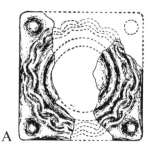

A

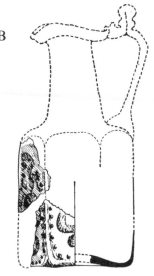

B

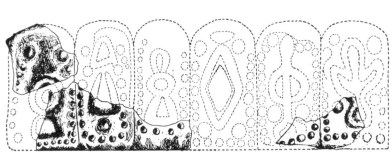

The vessel is unstable since the base is deformed. Light green. A coil of the same glass is wound around the neck. Thick band applied below the rim. In the handle and the decorative coils, a little brown glass was intermixed. In the handle there are a few black impurities and numerous deformed bubbles, both medium and large. On the base, a pontil mark. Poor workmanship. Height: 326 mm.

Similar jugs were found in tombs near Shoval[321] and Kfar Dikhrin.[322] Additional jugs are preserved in various collections in Israel.[323] A photograph of a similar jug appears in Kisa's book.[324] Various kinds of elongated jugs were widespread during the fourth century over the entire Roman Empire; however, the type under discussion was particularly characteristic of the Eastern Roman Empire.

49. 54–155 (fig. 100; Pl. LXIX). Catacomb 15, hall B, room I. Large shallow plate with cut-out tubular ring base. Broad rim folded downward and inward. At the edge, there is an additional outward fold. On the lower exterior side of the plate intricate decorations were incised (see p. 209). Light green with deformed bubbles arrayed concentrically. Pontil mark. Diameter: 509–520 mm; height: 53 mm.

Two plates, identical in shape, dating to the fourth century C.E., were discovered in a tomb at el-Bassa.[325] The diameter of one of these plates is 44 cm. Fragments of a similar plate were also found in the church at Shavei Zion.[326]

50. 55–210 (fig. 99b). Catacomb 20, room XVIII. Three fragments of a hexagonal mold-blown jug. The base is concave. The shoulders are rounded and the sides, slightly concave. The intaglio decorative designs were surrounded by a frame of dots. Of side no. 1 the remnants preserved are: the upper part — depicting the top of an amphora; and the lower part — showing the right side of its base. Side no. 2 describes the lower part of an unidentified object. On side no. 3, only the lower dots of the frame were preserved. In the lower right corner of side no. 5, there are dots from the frame. Of side no. 6, only the lower part of an unidentified object was preserved. Nothing was left of side 4. Light turquoise-blue;[327] bubbly, with a few black impurities.

Three glass fragments of the same color were found together with these fragments, two of them belonging to a mold-blown vessel.

The fragments of this juglet belong to a well-defined group of hexagonal or octagonal mold-blown jugs and bottles, dating to the Late Byzantine period. This group is characterized by its intaglio designs, proving that the body of the vessel was blown in a mold of hammered metal with protruding patterns which emerged as sunken designs on the sides of the vessel. The vessels of this group occur in various shades of brown, greenish, or blue glass.

This group may be classified into three subgroups according to the symbols on the vessels: *(a)* vessels whose designs also include Jewish symbols, e.g., a menorah; *(b)* vessels which also have Christian symbols among their decorations, e.g., a cross; *(c)* vessels with the same designs as the previous two subgroups but without obvious religious symbols whatsoever.

Quite a large number of vessels of this type are in different museums and collections all over the world.[328]

While very little has remained of the designs on our vessel, it is nevertheless possible to reconstruct the patterns on the basis of vessels blown into the same mold, familiar to us from various collections. Up till now, five jugs of this type are known.[329] In the Museum of Toledo, Ohio, there is a jug of the same type made of turquoise-blue glass.[330] Since it bears no decisive Jewish or Christian symbols, the patterns of this mold must be assigned to subgroup *(c)*, i.e., the "neutral" group.

All the vessels of this group whose origin is known were found in Palestine or Syria except for one in the Collection of Cypriot Antiquities in the Metropolitan Museum of New York. The large number of hexagonal and octagonal bottles and jugs of this type that were preserved intact is evidence that the practice was to deposit them in tombs.[331]

Up to 1970 the generally accepted date for these vessels was the fourth century C.E.;[332] however, already in 1962, Ross published a jug of this type which, in his opinion, should be attributed to the sixth century C.E.[333] Further proof for this dating may be deduced from the fact that a fragment of a similar vessel was found at Gerasa in Passage 30 between the Church of St. Theodore and the Baths of Placcus.[334] The baths were built in 454/5 C.E. and the church, between 494 and 496 C.E. The passage is marked in the plan as a later addition to the church. Therefore, the heap of glass fragments found in this corridor cannot be earlier than the end of the fifth century. It seems reasonable to assume that it dates close to the final stage of the church, i.e., the period of the Persian conquest (614 C.E.), or even later during the second half of the seventh century and the first half of the eighth century C.E. Typologically speaking, the rest of the finds in this heap also date to the end of the Byzantine period. Therefore, the fragments of jug no. 50 show that burials took place in catacomb 20 at the end of the Byzantine Period also.

51. 55–156 (fig. 98, 19). Catacomb 20, room XI. Base of a cylindrical vessel or lamp. Colorless with a greenish tinge.

52. 55–227 (fig. 98, 18). Catacomb 20, room II. Lower part of a square bottle which tapers toward the bottom. The vessel is mold blown. Light turquoise, with a large quantity of deformed bubbles.

53. 55–155 (fig. 98, 16). Catacomb 20, room VIII. Bottle, body broadest near the bottom. Concave base with pontil mark. The shoulder is rounded and diagonally corrugated. The neck widens toward the top, and it has a fold near the base. The rim is rounded. Light green with a large quantity of deformed bubbles. Estimated height: 112 mm.

54. 55–225 (fig. 98, 17; Pl. LXVIII, 9). Catacomb 20, room II. Bottle with an elongated body tapering toward the bottom. The neck widens slightly toward the top; fold near the base. Rounded and slightly thickened rim. Brown and bubbly. Height: 124 mm.

Nos. 52–54 constitute a separate group, differing entirely from the other glass finds listed here. Nos. 53–54 have parallels among the finds at Ḥama in Syria, dating to the eleventh–thirteenth centuries C.E.[335] Nos. 51–52 may be a little earlier.

From the parallels of the glass vessels from catacombs 12, 13, 15, and 17, it emerges that all the vessels from these catacombs date to the Late Roman period, i.e., the second half of the third, or the fourth, century C.E. If it is correct to assume that burial in these catacombs ceased after the Gallus rebellion, then these vessels should be attributed to the second half of the third or the first half of the fourth century C.E.; In any case, they cannot be dated later than circa 352 C.E. It seems likelier that most of the glass vessels date to the first half of the fourth century. The lamps found with no. 26 leave no doubt that this vessel dates to the second half of the third century; by stylistic inference, no. 31 may also be assigned to this period.

The finds from catacomb 20 are in a different category altogether. The fragments of the hexagonal jug (no. 50) prove that this catacomb was used for burial at the end of the Byzantine period as well; therefore, the artifacts from this catacomb may derive from either the Late Roman or the end of the Byzantine periods. Thus the exact date of these vessels may be determined only by comparison with parallels whose date has been established. While most of the finds from this catacomb may be attributed to the Late Roman period, there is nevertheless a possibility that some of them should be assigned to the Byzantine period (e.g., nos. 13, 16–17, 40–41, 43–44, 50). Nos. 52–54 date to the Arab period.

Generally speaking, the glass vessels from Beth She'arim are later than the glass vessels which were prevalent all over the Roman Empire during the first and second centuries C.E. [336] The distribution of these types is restricted mainly to Palestine and Syria,[337] and to a certain extent also to Egypt, Cyprus, and perhaps even to Asia Minor. Only a small minority of these types, like no. 25, were also found in the western part of the Roman Empire.

It seems very reasonable to conjecture that these vessels were produced by Jewish craftsmen; at any rate, they were used by Jews. The vessels from catacomb 15 are doubtlessly funerary gifts. As to the rest of the vessels, it is difficult to determine their exact function, i.e., whether they were burial articles or not. The fact remains that almost all of them are small or medium-sized closed receptacles, radically different in character from the rich group of vessels characteristic of several tombs discovered in Northern Palestine (e.g., el-Manawat, el-Maker, Nahariya, Yeḥiam, Ḥanita),[338] which contained open vessels mostly, such as cups, plates, and bowls.

Another point is noteworthy: not a single fragment of a "candlestick" bottle, so common during the first–third centuries in Palestine and the rest of the Roman Empire, was discovered among the Beth She'arim finds.[339] This fact implies that the use of these bottles in Palestine was restricted to the first–third centuries C.E. and seems to have ceased approximately in the middle of the third century C.E.

8 THE DECORATED GLASS PLATE (fig. 100)

The technical and chronological aspects of the large glass plate have been already discussed by Dan Barag (see p. 207). Here we shall deal with the decorations on the plate, actually its most important feature. The plate, 52 cm in diameter and 5.3 cm high, was found broken into many fragments. Since its initial publication,[340] several additional pieces were discovered; at present, only a few parts have not been retrieved.. As a result, more details of the decorations have become clear and have enabled us to correct some of the interpretations suggested previously. The decorations are engraved on the outside of the vessel but are to be viewed from the inside — the accepted practice for open glass vessels. In figure 100 the plate is drawn from the engraved side, i.e. from the bottom; however, in Plate LXIX, the plate is photographed from the inside. This explains the reverse ordering of the designs in the two illustrations.

The engraving was evidently done with a rotating wheel of hard crystalline stone.[341] The incisions are shallow. The short lines are wide in the center and pointed at the ends. The artisan did not always have full control of his instrument: the lines frequently cross the pattern margins thus causing the formation of fine scratches around the designs. He also did not manage to draw a perfect circle and executed the designs schematically. Nevertheless, he did produce a work of art. His rendition of a rich variety of motifs, pleasingly arranged on thin glass, is most praiseworthy, from the technical and artistic points of view. He endowed us with a rare and valuable specimen of ancient Jewish glass art.

The thirteen arches on low pillars which encircle the plate form a rhythmic pattern of an arcade. The capitals and bases of the pillars and the archivolts are emphasized by hatching. Below the arches various objects are incised; they will now be described individually.

In arch no. 1, there is a representation of a gate flanked by two high, narrow pillars.

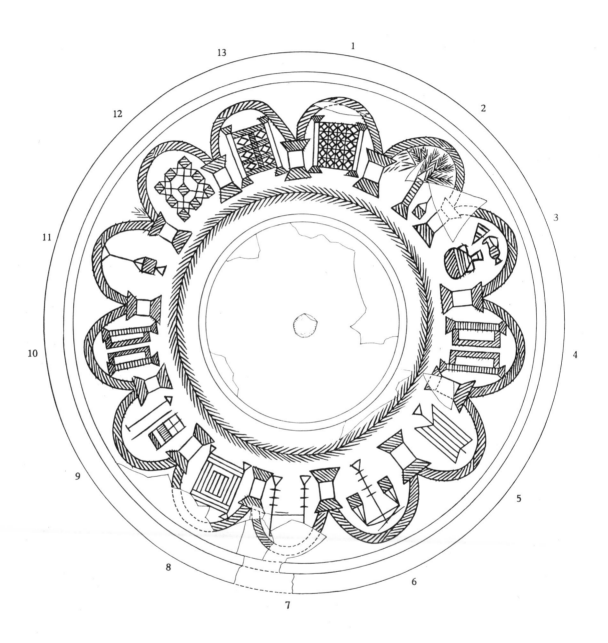

Fig. 100 Glass plate

The wings of the gate are divided into panels inscribed with rhombi.

Arch no. 2 contains a tree, apparently a palm, with a square object suspended from one of its branches. In view of the other figures on the plate, this object may possibly be a glass lamp shaped like a deep bowl with vertical sides,[342] schematically depicted here and elsewhere in the form of a square.

In arch no. 3 three glass objects are portrayed. The triangular object is a glass lamp in the shape of a conical cornet, examples of which were found at el-Bassa in Galilee in a tomb dating to the fourth century C.E.[343] The second object is a jug with one handle, very common among the glass vessels of this period. A similar jug was found in conjunction with the conical-shaped lamps discovered in the above-mentioned tomb at el-Bassa.[344] An analogous jug was also discovered together with the plate under discussion here. (cf. fig. 98, 10; Pl. LXVIII, 1). The third object is probably a glass flask; a parallel to this flask was found in a tomb in Gezer.[345] However, the engraver could not depict the object in a perfectly circular form. He also added decorations which are generally not encountered in vessels of this type.

In arch no. 4 the gateway flanked by two pillars appears again — only this time the two doors are open and undecorated.

The object depicted in arch no. 5 is particularly noteworthy. In our first publication it was interpreted as a menorah whose upper part was missing. However, now that the upper part has been found, the earlier interpretation is doubtful since the shape in which the upper part terminates is unparalleled in a menorah. Nevertheless, for want of a more plausible explanation, it should be observed that this object bears a closer resemblance to a schematic menorah than to any other article.

Arch no. 6 evidently contains a depiction of a candelabrum from which two square lamps like those in arch no. 2 are suspend-

ed.[346] The interpretation of this engraving as a balance scale is untenable since balance pans are generally flat and wide.

I can offer no acceptable interpretation of the object depicted in arch no. 7. It is composed of two vertical bars standing on triangular bases, with a connecting horizontal bar between them, and probably an additional horizontal bar at the top where the plate is broken. The small discrepancies between the photograph and the drawing of this segment are due to the fact that additional fragments were inserted *after* the photograph was taken.

A gate is apparently portrayed in arch no. 8, similar to that in arch no. 1, but more schematically executed.

It is difficult to identify the objects in arch no. 9: they are not decorative designs, nor is there reason to assume that they are abstract drawings. The following interpretation of the objects (from left to right) is offered most tentatively: a builder's plumb line, a builder's rope, and the schematic plan of a building (?).

In arch no. 10 there is a repetition of the open gate motif, similar to that in arch no. 4.

The object suspended below arch no. 11 is doubtlessly a glass lamp, apparently an eternal flame. Lamps in the form of a wine cup with a high base are prevalent in the synagogue mosaics of the Byzantine period: one is suspended above the Ark of the Law in the mosaic at Beth Alpha;[347] others are suspended from menorah branches in the mosaic at Na'aran.[348] Lamps suspended from arches are depicted on pottery lamps from the third/fourth centuries,[349] and in a mosaic at Gerasa (Church of St. John).[350] An instructive comparison may be drawn between our lamp and the schematic, round lamp suspended from the Holy Ark drawn in catacomb 1 at Beth She'arim: even the way it is attached to the gable — in the form of a V — is similar to our lamp.[351]

Arch no. 12 differs from the others. It contains neither objects nor insignia but only a geometric pattern of squares.

Arch no. 13 completes the arcuated circle. The motif of arch no. 1 is repeated here, i.e., a gate flanked by pillars. The gate is divided into two paneled doors which are decorated with rhombi.

Below the arcade, a branch pattern encircles the bottom of the plate.

The ornamental composition on the plate is based on the well-known arcade motif in which various objects are depicted within the constituent arches. Generally, the arches furnish only the decorative framework whereas the main themes appear in their bays. For example, this motif is common on Roman sarcophagi where various figures or scenes are portrayed within the arches.

The arcade would seem intrinsically to be most suitable for decorating glass plates. However, the fact remains that we have not yet encountered an earlier example which could have served as a source of inspiration for the Beth She'arim artisan. Incidentally, at the Louvre in Paris there is a Christian glass plate from the second half of the fourth century C.E. which is decorated with an arcade of schematic trees below which biblical scenes are portrayed.[352] Obviously, the latter composition was derived from an architectural motif with which the artisan was familiar. During and subsequent to the Byzantine period, the circular arcade served as a decorative pattern for many nations but never became conventionalized.[353]

Granted this assumption, from what source then did the Beth She'arim artist derive the motifs for decorating the plate? During the Second Temple period, the arcade was already a common motif in Jewish decorative art. One of the earliest depictions of a colonnade with eight arches may be found on an ossuary lid from Jerusalem dating to the first century C.E. approximately (at present in custody of the British Museum).[354] Some scholars were of the opinion that this arcade was a portrayal of one of the stoae surrounding Herod's Temple, and that these very stoae inspired the creator of the ossuary.[355] However, even if we do not accept the specific contention about the Temple, which has not been proved, we may, nevertheless, assume that the beautiful arcade on the ossuary was inspired by the buildings existing in Jerusalem at that time and that, in the course of time, arches became a conventional motif.

I tend to believe that the artist from Beth She'arim also borrowed the arcade design from his surroundings, i.e., from the arcaded façades of the Beth She'arim tombs which were doubtlessly one of the most impressive features of the local landscape. The circular arcade results simply from the application of this recurring motif to a round plate. Perhaps the most convincing proof of this hypothesis lies in the fact that so many gates are depicted inside the arches of the plate. In a free-standing arcade surrounding a building or an internal hall there are usually no doors. If the arcade generally furnishes a mere framework for symbolic themes, it is indeed suspect that symbols should be replaced by doors. The contention that the gate represents the Holy Ark is untenable in view of the fact that there are no less than five gates on the plate. Thus, the doors depicted here are really an organic part of the panorama of arcades and single arches, the prevailing view in the Beth She'arim tombs. Quite likely the three arches (1, 13, and 12) were the starting point from which the artist attempted to portray the trio of arches from catacombs 14 or 20 (see figs. 20 and 36). With a little imagination, we can even conjecture that he tried specifically to portray the façade of catacomb 14 which is located directly below the tomb where the plate was discovered.[356] This façade has doors in only two of the three arches. The plate, likewise, originally had doors incised in only two arches (nos. 1, 13), the third (no. 12) being empty. However, since the empty arch disturbed the general harmony of the design, the artist added a trivial geometric design which he did not use in any of the other arches. Moreover, if we look at the plate from the inside

(Pl. LXIX), as it was always viewed, we shall notice that the "empty" arch (no. 12) was placed to the right of the arches with the doors, exactly like the original façade of catacomb 14 (see fig. 20).

It is difficult to determine the criteria by which the artist chose the rest of the motifs for filling in the arches. However, they also seem to be an integral part of the atmosphere of Beth She'arim which, according to our hypothesis, was the artist's source of inspiration in choosing his main motif. This applies first and foremost to the three glass vessels which are so originally depicted on the glass plate. Very probably the artist wanted thereby to give an expression of his own craft. We have already noted that vessels of this type served as funerary gifts in the tombs and that two of these vessels were even found in conjunction with the glass plate itself. The eternal lamps appearing in three of the arches are clearly associated both with tombs and with synagogues. The combination of the lamp and the tree is not intelligible except if given a far-fetched symbolic interpretation from the world of symbols: for example, the tree as the Tree of Knowledge and the lamp as the Source of Light. The menorah (if indeed it is a menorah) is one of the most prevalent symbols at the Beth She'arim tombs. The function of the builder's symbols here is more difficult to comprehend; however, we should bear in mind that all the various arcades and arches were the proud achievements of the Beth She'arim masons.

If the above interpretation is correct, we must also assume that the designs on the plate and perhaps even the plate itself were produced at Beth She'arim proper. While this conjecture seems very probable, it does not preclude the possibility that a visiting artist could have been duly impressed by the place and could very well have executed the order in a workshop outside of Beth She'arim. At any rate, according to the different remains discovered at Beth She'arim, there is a sound basis for maintaining that glass manufacture was a local tradition.

Wherever the plate may have been manufactured, one point is clear: the plate is unique among the glass vessels of Palestine and of the entire Near East. Engraved glass vessels are very rare in the Syro-Palestinian region which is generally prolific in glass products. In a tomb at el-Bassa a glass bowl was discovered, decorated only with circles and a cross.[357] Another glass bowl originating in Palestine or Syria and dated to the fourth century C.E. is at present in custody of the Ashmolean Museum in Oxford.[358] At Gerasa in Transjordan a richly-decorated Christian glass wine cup was discovered; it is attributed to the sixth century C.E.[359]

In the West, on the other hand, decorated glass vessels were much more common. The themes of the decorations, whether engraved by hand or by wheel, are usually figurative. Decorated vessels appeared in relatively great abundance during the fourth century C.E. Particularly relevant to our discussion are several glass vessels decorated with rare architectural motifs derived from public buildings of that era. We refer specifically to a group of bottles depicting the public buildings of Putioli near Naples, i.e., buildings of a commercial city which was also an important center for glass manufacture in the fourth century C.E.[360] Even though no connection of themes is being sought here, it is nevertheless interesting to note that at this very same period there was an artist at Beth She'arim who also followed the same trend: he, too, employed motifs from local buildings to decorate a glass plate. This means that artists working in glass at that period were well aware of tendencies of this type.

From the above discussion it emerges that, despite its unique decorations, our glass plate is quite at home in the fourth-century world of glass art. The circumstances of its discovery at Beth She'arim point to a mid-fourth century C.E. dating for the decorated glass plate.

9 MISCELLANEOUS ARTIFACTS

Bronze Articles (fig. 101)

All the articles in this group, except no. 4, were found in catacomb 20. The only complete object is a cylindrical box (no. 3), closed with a dome-like cover. It is 4.2 cm in diameter and 4.5 cm in total height. At the top of the cover there is a bronze wire loop which was inserted from the top via a perforation and bent underneath. Apparently a chain was attached to this loop, similar to the one on lid no. 5; lid no. 5 closely resembles the cover on article no. 3, except that it is much smaller. Chain no. 2[361] is attached to the loops of two covers at either end. No. 6 might also be a cover of this type, and not a bell similar to those found in tombs at other places.[362] A black powder of carbonized organic material was found inside box no. 3.[363] This object is certainly a cosmetics box which was placed in a woman's grave.[364] All the other articles in this group, including the broken cylinder (no. 1), are apparently associated with cosmetics vessels, except for no. 4 which is a rather uncommon type of glass bead.

Iron Objects (fig. 102; Pl. LXXIII, 1–6, 25)

All the objects appearing in fig. 102, except no. 10, were discovered in catacomb 20. No. 10 is an iron plate into which four nails were driven. It evidently served as an iron fitting on a wooden coffin. The chisels (nos. 1–2) might have been used by the hewers and masons of the catacomb or by tomb robbers. The scissors (no. 3) and spur (no. 11) seem to be late in date. The other articles

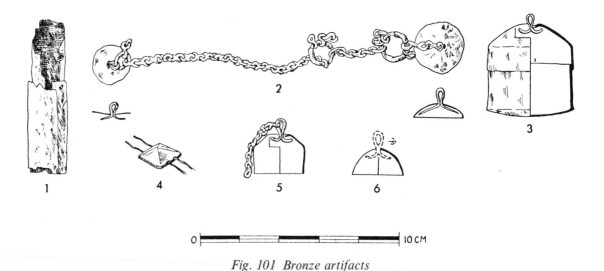

Fig. 101 Bronze artifacts

Serial Number	Registration Number	Locus	Description
1	55–146/3	Catacomb 20, room XXI	Fragments of a hollow bronze cylinder
2	55–146/4	Catacomb 20, room XXI	Bronze chain
3	55–146/1	Catacomb 20, room XXI	Bronze box closed with a cover
4	53–964	Catacomb 12, hall A, room VI	Flattish pyramidal glass bead, opaque blue in color; perforated with two holes
5	55–146/2	Catacomb 20, room XXI	Bronze cover with chain
6	55–153	Catacomb 20, room XXI	Bronze cover (?)

in figure 102 cannot be precisely dated.

Nos. 1–6 of Plate LXXIII illustrate iron accessories from wooden coffins: three rings used for transporting the coffins and a selection of twenty nails of various sizes that were found in different coffins. The nails range from 3 to 8 cm in length; there are thick and thin ones, square and round, and wide- and narrow-headed ones.[365] The rusty rings and several of the nails still have traces of attached wood. The double-pointed iron pickaxe (Pl. LXXIII, 25), 28 cm long, was apparently used either by the catacomb hewers, or by the tomb robbers for breaking into the stone coffins.

Jewelry and Associated Objects
(Pl. LXXIII, 15–24)

These are burial gifts and personal jewelry belonging to women. The paucity of objects

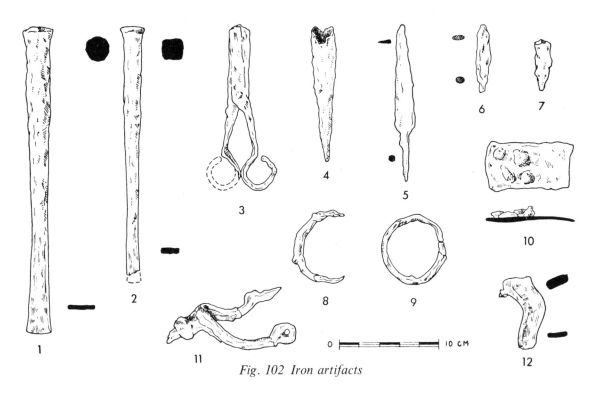

Fig. 102 Iron artifacts

Serial Number	Registration Number	Locus	Description
1	55–220	Catacomb 20, room V	Iron chisel
2	55–219	Catacomb 20, room V	Iron chisel
3	55–222	Catacomb 20, room X	Iron scissors
4	55–151/2	Catacomb 20, room I	Hollow iron point
5	55–228	Catacomb 20, room X	Iron knife blade
6	55–148/1	Catacomb 20	Iron arrowhead
7	55–148/2	Catacomb 20	Iron point
8	55–147/2	Catacomb 20, room XXI	Iron bracelet (?)
9	55–147	Catacomb 20, room VIII	Iron bracelet
10	54–42	Catacomb 13, room III	Iron plate with nail heads
11	55–151/1	Catacomb 20, room I	Iron spur (?)
12	55–145	Catacomb 20, room XVI	Lead handle (?)

215

DETAILS OF PLATE LXXIII

Serial Number	Registration Number	Locus	Description
1–3	60–300	Catacomb 20	3 iron rings
4	60–300	Catacomb 20	8 iron nails
5		Various places	7 iron nails
6		Various places	5 iron nails
7		Catacomb 20, room IX	Iron chisel
8	54–35	Catacomb 13	Iron nail
9		Catacomb 20, room IX	Iron chisel
10	55–250	Catacomb 20, room VIII	Iron pick with handle
11	56–148	Catacomb 20, room I	Iron chisel
12	54–35	Catacomb 13	Iron hook
13	56–298	Catacomb 20	Iron arrowhead
14	54–35	Catacomb 13	Iron ring
15	53–963	Catacomb 12, hall A, room VI	Bronze toilette spoon
16	55–148/1	Catacomb 20	Bronze kohl-stick
17	55–148/2	Catacomb 20	Bronze kohl-stick
18–20	54–101	Catacomb 14, tomb 5	3 bronze rings
21	54–150/1	Catacomb 15, hall B, room I	Blue glass bracelet
22	54–150/2	Catacomb 15, hall B, room I	Fragments of glass bracelets
23	53–962	Catacomb 12, hall A, room VI	Necklace of shell beads
24	54–105	Catacomb 14	Bone handle
25	55–316	Catacomb 20	Iron pickaxe

of this type in so large a number of tombs may be attributed first and foremost to the systematic looting of the tombs. Secondly, it was probably not customary to inter jewelry together with bones brought for secondary burial. The cosmetics spoon (no. 15) has a flat blade and a handle with a thickened end; this type was common in the Late Roman period.[366] This bronze spoon was discovered together with a glass amphoriskos (see fig. 9) which apparently contained the cosmetics. Bronze kohl-sticks (nos. 16–17) are more frequently encountered.[367]

Three bronze finger rings (nos. 18–20) were discovered in one tomb. They are plain and are round in section. The glass bracelets (nos. 21–22) were common in the Late Roman period. Similar bracelets have been found in tombs throughout the country.[368] The string of beads (no. 23) was part of the cache which also contained

other personal effects belonging to a woman (fig. 9). The cylindrical bone handle (no. 24) is decorated with incised lines.

Gold Threads (fig. 103; Pl. LXXIV)
The only artifact discovered in the earth contained in lead coffin no. 1 was a small quantity of thin, crumbled gold threads, grouped in bands on the bottom of the coffin. These threads are the remnants of gold embroidery — a few tiny pieces of which were found among the disintegrated threads (Pl. LXXIV). The embroidery threads were found just as they had been sewn originally onto the cloth, one beside the other in straight, close rows. Obviously, nothing remained of the cloth itself. The threads themselves come apart at the slightest touch. The threads look like tubes, but actually they are made out of flat gold strips, coiled like a spring (fig. 103). Twisted threads of this sort break and crumble

Fig. 103 Gold threads

easily. Only a small percentage of them could be collected from the earth. They weighed 17.02 grams.

The manufacture and embroidery of these gold threads may be reconstructed thus: the threads were made of thin flat strips of pure gold (about .32 mm wide) which were twisted spirally around a thread of cotton or silk. These spun gold threads were then placed on the cloth in straight close rows and were sewn to the cloth with fine silk or cotton thread, a technique called "couched embroidery." The cloth, the threads enclosed in the gold, and the sewing threads have disintegrated completely, leaving only the hollow coils of gold threads.[369]

Gold threads and embroidery of this type are known since the Roman period and are still produced today. In both eastern and western countries a few examples from the third century C.E. have been found.[370] In Palestine these are the first examples of gold embroidery from the Roman period that have been encountered.

It thus transpires that a gold-embroidered cloth or prayer shawl was placed on the floor of the lead coffin, upon which the bones brought for secondary burial were deposited. This practice in a Jewish burial arouses particular interest. From the Talmudic sources we know that wealthy Jews customarily laid out the dead in costly clothes. There is an explicit verse which testifies that even gilded clothes were used for burial and that the less affluent would go deeply into debt in order to observe this custom. In order not to embarrass the poor, Rabbi Gamaliel the Second instituted a regulation prohibiting this practice, and he himself willed that he be laid out in plain linen cloth.[371] Prof. S. Lieberman has written me the following on this subject: "In chapter 4 of Mourning Laws II, the Rambam says: burial in silk shrouds or gold-embroidered clothes is forbidden even to the Patriarch (Nassî) of Israel because it is an arrogant, degenerate, and heathen practice. The commentator of *Migdal 'Oz* referred to *Ebel Rabbati*. In the tractate *Semaḥot* no mention is made of this ruling; however, several baraithoth from this tractate have been lost. Higger[372] has correctly included this baraitha in his edition (p. 246). This prohibition implies that the custom was common practice among the wealthy, especially prior to Rabban Gamaliel's regulation for burial in simple shrouds. One can understand that Rabban Gamaliel's decree probably did not immediately stop the former custom."

As previously noted, the deceased in the lead coffin was almost certainly a Sidonian Jew. Both the coffin and the gold threads testify that he was wealthy. His family was probably not aware of Rabbi Gamaliel's regulation; or at any rate, they did not observe it.

NOTES

1 D. H. Vincent, *Jérusalem et l'Ancien Testament,* I, Paris, 1954, pp. 345–361; Goodenough, *Symbols,* III, pp. 232–239.

2 *Dominus Flevit,* Pls. 13–18. Apparently the sarcophagi that were found in these tombs are just unusually large ossuaries, since they are too small to hold an entire adult body.

3 Two coffins were found in a tomb that was discovered in 1967 on the grounds of the Hebrew University on Mount Scopus. One of them was decorated with vine scrolls, leaves, and clusters of grapes. See N. Avigad, "The Burial Vault of a Nazirite Family on Mount Scopus," *IEJ,* XXI (1971), pp. 185*ff.,* fig. 5, Pls. 38–39.

4 A few sarcophagi of unusual dimensions and elaborate decorations were found not far from the ruins of the Roman temple at Kadesh in Upper Galilee. They have not yet been fully published. For a short description see: C. R. Conder & H. H. Kitchener, *Survey of Western Palestine: Memoirs,* I, London, 1881, p. 228. A relatively rich find was discovered at Samaria: nine sarcophagi were found in the Roman mausoleum, and ten were found in Tomb 220-E. See: R. W. Hamilton, "The Domed Tomb at Sebastya," *QDAP,* VIII (1938), p. 64, fig. 1, Pl. XXXIX; *Samaria-Sebaste,* I, fig. 61. For sarcophagi from a number of different places in the country see: Avi-Yonah, *QDAP,* XIII (1948), Pl. XLVII, 2–3, 6; XIV (1950), Pls. XIX, 7–12; XX, 4–5, 8–9; XXI, 1–2, 4. And see also: Goodenough, *Symbols,* I, pp. 133–139; III, nos. 240–250, 453. For more recent sarcophagi that were discovered see: Y. Kaplan, *Eretz-Israel,* VIII (1967), p. 104, Pl. XVI (Hebrew). A name in Hebrew letters is inscribed on the sarcophagus. A. Eitan, *ibid.,* p. 114, Pl. 18 (Hebrew). A sarcophagus belonging to the Beth She'arim type, also decorated with garlands, was discovered a few years ago in the vicinity of Jerusalem. It now stands at the entrance of the Rockefeller Museum in Jerusalem. Lately a mausoleum with elaborately decorated sarcophagi was discovered near Nablus: *IEJ,* XXII (1972), p. 174, Pl. XXXVI.

5 Goodenough, *Symbols,* I, p. 139.

6 On the wreath pattern, see below the discussion on the Nikae sarcophagus.

7 On the significance of this subject see: Goodenough, *Symbols,* VII, pp. 67*ff.*; figs. 59–60, 64–66, 68; XII, pp. 133*ff.*

8 Cf. the sarcophagus from Athens: Robert, *Sarkophagreliefs,* III, 2, fig. 161b; Pl. LXX, 216c. See also the posterior side of the "sarcophagus of columns and muses," which is exhibited in the National Museum in Rome. According to the sketches which I made on the spot, a vase is depicted flanked by two lions, their forelegs raised toward the vase. On both ends the sarcophagus is engraved with columns and leaved capitals, very similar to those on the lion sarcophagus from Beth She'arim. This vase symbolizes, apparently, a fresh water source. This conclusion emerges from the Rome sarcophagus where the lions' mouths touch the rim of the vessel and, especially, from another sarcophagus in which a lion and a lioness (similar to the pair of lions from Beth She'arim) are standing with open mouths at the sides of a vase from which water is flowing, See: F. Matz & F. V. Duhm, *Antike Bildwerke in Rome, II: Sarkophage,* Leipzig, 1881, nos. 267, 2668, 2671.

9 Goodenough, *Symbols,* III, no. 509; Kohl & Watzinger, *Synagogen,* figs. 139, 142.

10 Goodenough, *Symbols,* III, no. 460.

11 *Ibid.,* no. 536.

12 *Ibid.,* no. 43.

13 See the Byzantine lintel at Avdat: A. Negev, *Cities in the Desert,* Tel Aviv, 1966, pp. 84–85 (Hebrew).

14 Goodenough, *Symbols,* III, no. 523.

15 See the relief from the third millenium B.C.: A Parrot, *Sumer,* 1960, fig. 162. See also the sealing ring from the Israelite period: Y. Aharoni, *Excavations at Ramat Raḥel,* Rome, 1964, Pl. 40, 7.

16 See the sarcophagus from the Torlonia Catacomb: Goodenough, *Symbols,* III, no. 831. And cf. a depiction similar to ours on the sarcophagus lid from Rome: Robert, *Sarkophagreliefs,* II, Pl. XIV, 25.

17 According to a photograph from the excavations at Kurnub, which Dr. A. Negev showed me.

18 After the excavations the sarcophagus was transferred to room X, in order to make it possible for the public to view it from all sides.

19 Contrary to what was mistakenly stated in the first publication of the excavation.

20 Kohl & Watzinger, *Synagogen,* figs. 139, 142; Goodenough, *Symbols,* III, no. 509.

21 *ZDPV,* XXIX (1906), p. 199, fig. 14. The lintel is exhibited in the Rockefeller Museum in Jerusalem.

22 C. H. Kraeling, *The Excavations at Dura-Europos,* VIII, 1: *The Synagogue,* New Haven, 1956, Pl. XXXVII, p. 245, n. 979.

23 H. Frankfort, *The Art and Architecture of the Ancient Orient,* 1954, Pl. 171.

24 Kohl & Watzinger, *Synagogen,* p. 198.

25 W. Altmann, *Architektur und Ornamentik der antiken Sarkophage*, Berlin, 1902, pp. 62, 66.

26 Goodenough, *Symbols*, III, no. 548; Avi-Yonah, *QDAP*, XIII (1948), Pl. XLII, 9.

27 Goodenough, *Symbols*, III, no. 45. On the symbolic significance of the bull see: *Ibid.*, VII, pp. 3*ff.*; XII, p. 132.

28 Robert, *Sarkophagreliefs*, II, Pls. X, 22c; XXIX, 69c; III, 2, Pl. XLIV, 144c; J. B. Ward Perkins, "Roman Garland Sarcophagi from the Quarries of Proconnesus (Marmara)," *The Smithsonian Report for* 1957, Pl. 1; idem, "Four Roman Garland Sarcophagi in America," *Archaeology*, XI (1958), p. 98.

29 *BBSAJ*, VI (1924), Pl. V, 2.

30 J. B. Peters & H. Thiersch, *Painted Tombs in the Necropolis of Marissa*, London, 1905, frontispiece; Goodenough, *Symbols*, III, no. 12.

31 Goodenough, *Symbols*, III, nos. 522, 531, 993; N. Avigad, "Remains of Ancient Jewish Art in the Galilee," *Eretz-Israel*, VII (1954), p. 19; Pl. II, 1–2 (Hebrew).

32 N. Avigad, *Archaeology*, VIII, 1955, p. 240.

33 For the discussion on the symbolic meaning of the eagle see: Goodenough, *Symbols*, VII, p. 122; XII, p. 149.

34 Goodenough (*Symbols*, VII, no. 1, p. 4) exchanged it by mistake with the eagle sarcophagus from Beth She'arim.

35 Kraeling, *Dura Europos*, Pl. LI; Goodenough, *Symbols*, XI, Pl. II.

36 N. Zori, "The Ancient Synagogue at Beth She'arim," *Eretz-Israel*, VIII (1968), Pl. 29, 5 (Hebrew).

37 *Beth She'arim*, I, Pls. XXXII and XXXIV.

38 E. L. Sukenik, *The Ancient Synagogue at Beth Alpha*, Jerusalem, 1932, Pl. VIII (Hebrew); Goodenough, *Symbols*, III, no. 639.

39 Cf. the architectural motif similar to this on the sarcophagus from Hammath-Tiberias: Goodenough, *Symbols*, III, no. 247.

40 For two lions attacking a gazelle see: A. Parrot, *Nineveh and Babylon*, 1961, fig. 33.

41 On symbolism in the decoration see: Goodenough, *Symbols*, V, pp. 31*ff.*

42 On birds in art see: Goodenough, *Symbols*, VII, pp. 22*ff.*

43 Hamilton, *QDAP*, VIII (1938), Pl. XXXIX, 5.

44 Avi-Yonah, *QDAP*, XIV (1950), Pl. XXI, 1.

45 *Ibid.*, XIII (1948), Pl. XLVII, 6 (Goodenough, *Symbols*, III, no. 249).

46 *Ibid.*, XIV (1950), Pl. XX, 9.

47 C. Clermont-Ganneau, *Archaeological Researches in Palestine*, II, London, 1896, p. 157.

48 See below, the discussion on the "column" sarcophagus (no. 124).

49 See above, n. 43.

50 See above, n. 29; Watzinger, *Denkmäler*, II, fig. 75.

51 E. Renan, *Mission de Phénicie*, Paris, 1864.

52 Altmann, *Architektur*, pp. 74–80, 98.

53 *Ibid.*, figs. 22–23; J. B. Ward Perkins, *Archaeology*, XI (1958), pp. 98, 102–103.

54 *Antike Kunstvaerker*, I, Ny Carlsberg Glyptotek, Copenhagen, 1907, Pl. LXVIII, 791.

55 Avi-Yonah, *QDAP*, X (1942), Pl. XXII, 12.

56 M. Avi-Yonah, "Lead Coffins from Palestine," *QDAP*, IV (1934), Pl. LV, 1 (ii). See there the masks and figures on other sarcophagi.

57 Goodenough expresses another opinion; see the extensive discussion on the masks: Goodenough, *Symbols*, VII, pp. 202*ff.*; XII, p. 152. The head from Beth She'arim is interpreted as the sun-god Helios.

58 Nevertheless, a Jewish tombstone was found in the Roman province of Panonia in Hungary; it bears the profiles of a father, mother, and child. The engraved menoroth and the child's name indicate that the tombstone is of Jewish origin.

59 *QDAP*, XIII (1948), pp. 156*ff.*

60 Kohl & Watzinger, *Synagogen*, p. 189.

61 On the distribution and on different opinions regarding the symbolic meaning of the wreath see: Goodenough, *Symbols*, VII, pp. 148*ff.*; XII, p. 139.

62 Goodenough, *Symbols*, III, nos. 518, 571, 576, 584, 592.

63 *Ibid.*, nos. 465, 490, 622.

64 *Ibid.*, nos. 467, 510.

65 *Ibid.*, no. 555.

66 *Ibid.*, nos. 524–525.

67 *Ibid.*, nos. 510–511.

68 G. Contenau, *Manuel d'archéologie orientale*, II, Paris, 1931, p. 775.

69 On the Nike motif see: Goodenough, *Symbols,* VII, pp. 135–148; XII, p. 138.

70 Cumont, *Symbolisme funéraire,* Pl. XXIII; Robert, *Sarkophagreliefs,* III, 1, Pl. XIV, 49.

71 Cumont, *Symbolisme funéraire,* Pls. VII, 2; XLVII, 2–3.

72 Goodenough, *Symbols,* III, no. 789.

73 For angels on a Christian tomb in Palestine see: C. Schick, *PEFQSt.,* 1887, p. 54.

74 Avi-Yonah, *QDAP,* XIII (1948), p. 132.

75 Kohl & Watzinger, *Synagogen,* fig. 25; E. L. Sukenik, *Ancient Synagogues in Palestine and Greece,* London, 1934, Pl. IIIa.

76 Avigad, *Eretz-Israel,* VIII (1964), p. 19; Pl. II, 11 (Hebrew).

77 Goodenough, *Symbols,* V, no. 10.

78 Goodenough, *Symbols,* III, nos. 84–85.

79 *Ibid.,* no. 992.

80 A. Rumpf, Die Meerwesen auf antiken Sarkophagen, apud: Robert, *Sarkophagreliefs,* V, 1, 1939, pp. 97 *ff.*

81 N. Glueck, *Deities and Dolphins,* New York, 1965, Pl. 24a.

82 For an extensive discussion of dolphins see: Glueck (note 81 above).

83 Goodenough, *Symbols,* V, pp. 12, 22 *ff.*

84 See: Goodenough, *Symbols,* III, nos. 788–789, 818.

85 Except for a few grafitti of menoroth by visitors in the corridor of the tomb of Jason in Jerusalem; see: L. Y. Raḥmani, *IEJ,* XVII (1967), p. 72, Pl. 21B.

86 See: *Beth She'arim,* I, p. 228. On the menorah forms that were found in our excavations see below.

87 Avigad, *Eretz-Israel,* VII (1964), p. 20; Pl. I, 1 (Hebrew).

88 J. B. Ward Perkins, *Archaeology,* XI (1958), pp. 98–103.

89 For winged lions or griffins upon garlands see: Robert, *Sarcophagreliefs,* II, 1, Pl. X, 22c; III, 2, Pl. XLIV, 144c.

90 For an extensive discussion on this subject see: J. M. C. Toynbee & J. B. Ward Perkins, "Peopled Scrolls — A Hellenistic Motif in Imperial Art," *Papers of the British School in Athens,* XVIII (1950), pp. 1–43; Pls. I–XXVI.

91 Glueck, *Deities and Dolphins,* p. 244; Pl. 169a–b.

92 Kohl & Watzinger, *Synagogen,* pp. 16–17, 153; Pl. III.

93 Prof. Ward Perkins wrote me the following concerning sarcophagus no. 97: "My impression is that this sarcophagus is rather a personal creation of a local sculptor who was influenced by two distinct sources: (1) The familiar gable-lidded garland sarcophagi, based ultimately on the imported Proconnesian type but with elements of personal fantasy — notably the curious pendant leaf framing. (2) An architectural entablature, again probably in marble style, which would explain the two architrave-like architectural mouldings along the upper border; also the gentle S-curve (as on an architectural frieze element) which is apparent at any rate at the angles."

94 Avigad, *IEJ,* VII (1957), Pl. 22b.

95 B. Ashmole, *A Catalogue of the Ancient Marbles at Ince Blundell Hall,* Oxford, 1929, Pl. 47:396; Morey, *Sarcophagi,* figs. 41, 98–99.

96 Goodenough *Symbols,* III, nos. 216, 219.

97 Goodenough sees the depiction of an Ark on only one ossuary (Goodenough, *Symbols,* III, no. 215) and he is probably right.

98 Morey, *Sarcophagi,* figs. 55, 61–62, 65, 87.

99 *Ibid.,* figs. 92, 103.

100 Reinach, *Statuaire,* I, p. 484.

101 Cumont, *Symbolisme funéraire,* Pl. XXXV, 3; cf. Robert, *Sarcophagreliefs,* III, 1, Pl. V, 21a–b; III, 2, Pl. LXXIX, 231b.

102 Goodenough, *Symbols,* III, nos. 160, 165, 170. Goodenough also attributes a symbolic meaning to these columns: the single column symbolizes a complete cultic building; see: *ibid.,* I, pp. 121 *ff.*

103 G. Loud, *The Megiddo Ivories,* Chicago, 1939, Pl. 7, 21–22; K. M. Kenyon, *Archaeology in the Holy Land,* London, 1960, Pl. 46B.

104 N. de Garis Davies, *Seven Private Tombs at Kurnach,* London, 1948, Pl. XXX (tomb of Nakhtamun).

105 *Idem, Tomb of Nefer-Hotep at Thebes,* I, New York, 1933, p. 61, Pl. L.

106 Lucienne Epron *et al., Le tombeau de Ti,* Fasc. I, Cairo, 1939, Pls. LXI *ff.*

107 The late Y. Leibowitz informed me that similar figures also appear in Egyptian tombs from the Ptolemaic period.

108 *Syria,* I, 1920, p. 152, fig. 53; G. Contenau, *La civilisation phénicienne,* Paris, 1926, fig. 105. For tabulae

ansatae see: *PEFQSt.*, 1887, p. 86; Avi-Yonah, *QDAP*, XIV (1950), Pls. XX, 8; XXI, 1–2, 4; Goodenough, *Symbols*, III, nos. 243–244, 246–247; A. Eitan, *Eretz-Israel*, VIII (1968), Pl. 18 (Hebrew).

109 The sarcophagus is now kept at the Hebrew University.

110 Typologically it is possible to compare sarcophagi nos. 92 and 120 to the sarcophagus of "Tzida Malketa" in the tomb of Queen Helena in Jerusalem (Goodenough, *Symbols*, III, no. 237). Sarcophagi nos. 42 and 49 may be compared to the sarcophagi decorated with developed rosettes from the same catacomb (Goodenough, *Symbols*, III, no. 236). For another sarcophagus decorated with rosettes in the Jewish style, see: Goodenough, *Symbols*, III, no. 248.

111 This motif is very widespread. See, for example, the Nikae in the corners of one of the sarcophagi found at Tel Barak near Caesarea: *BBSAJ*, VI, 1924, Pl. V, 2; Watzinger, *Denkmäler*, II, fig. 75.

112 P. V. C. Baur & M. I. Rostovtzeff (ed.), *The Excavations at Dura-Europus — Preliminary Report*, 1928–1929, New Haven, 1931, frontispiece; Pl. I, 1.

113 It is impossible to distinguish any bracelets on the photographs of the sarcophagus that were published. See: J. B. Ward Perkins, "Four Roman Garland Sarcophagi in America," *Archaeology*, XI (1958), p. 102. The sketch in fig. 78 depicting an Amazon wearing two bracelets was prepared by the author from the original.

114 B. Ashmole, *A Catalogue of Ancient Marbles at Ince Blundell Hall*, Oxford, 1929, Pls. 26, 83d. And cf.: Reinach, *Statuaire*, I, Pl. 644 A, no. 1459 D.

115 See also: Robert, *Sarkophagreliefs*, II, Pl. III.

116 *Catalogue of Sculptures in the Department of Greek and Roman Antiquities of the British Museum*, 1931, Vol. I, Part 2, fig. 79.

117 Morey, *Sarcophagi*, figs. 40, 114.

118 Cf. a similar sheath in relief on the narrow side of a marble sarcophagus from Athens: Robert, *Sarkophagreliefs*, II, Pl. L, 138a.

119 *Ibid.*, Pls. XX, 40; XXIV, 51a.

120 Cf. Morey, *Sarcophagi*, fig. 138.

121 Clusters of grapes are common on most of the developed garland sarcophagi; cf. Ward Perkins, "Roman Garland Sarcophagi…," pp. 98, 102–103; Watzinger, *Denkmäler*, II, fig. 75.

122 Cf. the sarcophagus from Nablus: *QDAP*, XIV (1950, Pl. XXI, 2; the sarcophagus from Samaria: *QDAP*, 1938, Pl. XXXIX, 2; and the sarcophagus from Istanbul: G. Mendel, *Catalogue des sculptures grecques, romaines et byzantines*, I, Constantinople, 1914, p. 113 and Robert, *Sarkophagreliefs*, III, 2, Pl. XLVI, 191c, p. 177. See also the posterior side of the sarcophagus from Tarsus mentioned in n. 3, *ibid.*, p. 102. The primary carving of the garlands was done in the quarries, but the details were added in the workshops. Often, however, the rough shape of the garland remained unfinished, sometimes becoming an independent decorative style, as in the present case.

123 Morey, *Sarcophagi*, figs. 41–42, 54–55, 61.

124 Watzinger, *Denkmäler*, II, pp. 102–103.

125 The Amazon sarcophagus is attributed to the second century C.E. or the beginning of the third century and is thought to have been brought from Athens; see: *BBSAJ*, V, (1923), p. 55, Pl. IV; Watzinger, *Denkmäler*, II, fig. 74.

126 See above, n. 111.

127 This sarcophagus is attributed to the second century C.E.; see: R. Savignac, *RB*, NS X, 1913, pp. 106–111.

128 This sarcophagus has not yet been published. It now stands in the courtyard of the Israel Museum.

129 Goodenough, *Symbols*, III, no. 456; M. Avi-Yonah, *Eretz-Israel*, VIII (1967), p. 143; Pl. 25, 1 (Hebrew).

130 Robert, *Sarkophagreliefs*, II, Pls. XXVIII, 69; XXIX, 69a; Reinach, *Statuaire*, I, Pls. 117 A, 117 B.

131 See above, n. 125.

132 Robert, *Sarkophagreliefs*, III, 3, Pl. CXX, 363; pp. 450 *ff*.

133 *Ibid.*, p. 456.

134 Morey, *Sarcophagi*, pp. 79–89.

135 J. B. Ward Perkins, "Roman Garland Sarcophagi from the Quarries of Proconnesus (Marmara)", *Smithsonian Report for 1957*, pp. 455–467.

136 See above n. 114.

137 G. Rosenwaldt, "Sarkophagenprobleme," *Mitteilungen des deutschen archäologischen Instituts, Römische Abteilung*, LVIII, (1943), pp. 1–26.

138 Watzinger, *Denkmäler*, pp. 102 *ff*.

138a For a description of the method see: D. S. Robertson, *A Handbook of Greek and Roman Architecture*, Cambridge, 1943, *s.v. cabling*. Cf. also the pillars fluted in similar manner on Asian sarcophagi from the third century C.E.: Morey, *Sarcophagi*, figs. 72–73; M. Lawrence, "Season Sarcophagi of Architectural Type," *AJA*, LXII (1928), Pl. 72, figs. 7, 11. This method is commonly found in monumental architecture of the second–third centuries C.E.; see: F. Noack, *Die Baukunst des Altertums*, Pls. 149, 151.

139 Depicted on this lead coffin fragment is a soldier holding a lance. The fragment was discovered when cleaning catacomb 20, a long time after the excavations.

140 For the analysis of the type of lead see: R. H. Brill & J. M. Wampler, "Isotope Studies of Ancient Lead," *AJA*, LXXI (1967), p. 71; p. 76, n. 191.

141 A vine scroll with intervening animals and human faces was found on the Roman temple lintel at Kadesh in the Galilee. See: *Survey of Western Palestine, Memoires*, I, the plate facing p. 227. The motif of birds drinking from a bowl is common on Roman mosaics; see, for example, the mosaic from Tivoli which is kept in the Capitoline Museum in Rome: H. P. l'Orange & P. J. Nordhagen, *Mosaics*, London, 1966, Pl. 12a; and the mosaics from Malta and Naples: E. Pernice, *Pavimente und figürliche Mosaiken*, Berlin, 1938, Pls. 1:4; 64–66.

142 On the vine-scroll motif see: Avi-Yonah, *QDAP*, XIII (1948), pp. 159–162; *idem., Oriental Art in Roman Palestine*, Rome 1961, p. 23, Pl. II. Stylized vine scrolls with leaves and bunches of grapes, forming regular horizontal bands, appear among the decorations of the synagogues at Kfar Bar'am (Goodenough, *Symbols*, III, no. 511), Capernaum (*ibid.*, n. 460), and Eshtemoa (*ibid.*, no. 616).

143 Lead coffins from the eastern coast of the Mediterranean (mainly the Syro-Phoenician and Palestinian coasts), now found in various collections, were published and summarized in the following studies (see additional bibliography there): A. Müfid, "Die Bleisarkophage im Antikenmuseum zu Istanbul," *AA* (1932), Cols. 389–446, figs. 1–47; M. Avi-Yonah, "Three Lead Coffins from Palestine," *JHS* (1930), pp. 300–312, Pl. XII; *idem*, "Lead Coffins from Palestine," *QDAP*, IV (1934), pp. 87–99, 138–153, Pls. LV–LX; E. M. Chéhab, "Sarcophages en plomb du Musée national libanais," *Syria*, XV (1934), pp. 337–350, Pls. XLI–XLVIII; XVI (1935), pp. 51–72, Pls. XII–XVIII; E. v. Merklin, "Untersuchungen zu den antiken Bleisarkophagen," *Berytus*, III (1936), pp. 51–75, Pls. IX–XVI; V (1938), pp. 27–46, Pls. V–XIII; VI (1939), pp. 27–61, Pls. V–XVII; J. Hajjar, "Un hypogée romain à Deba'al dans la région de Tyr," *BMB*, XVIII (1965), pp. 61–104, Pls. I–XVI (see there short summaries of previous discoveries). See also: Watzinger, *Denkmäler*, II, pp. 103–105.

144 Avi-Yonah, "Three Lead Coffins...".

145 A. On one that was discovered in Ḥadera, only a short article was published: E. L. Sukenik, *QDAP*, IV (1932), p. 185. I believe that this is a good opportunity to publish a photograph and also a sketch of this sarcophagus (fig. 90, Pl. LXXIV) whose vine scrolls and arches bear some relation to the patterns on the Beth She'arim sarcophagus (see n. 160 below). The sarcophagus from Ḥederah was also discovered in a rectangular tomb built of stone and covered with stone slabs.

B. For a lead sarcophagus found in Jerusalem see: L. Y. Raḥmani, "Roman Tombs in Shmuel Hanavi Street in Jerusalem," *Eretz-Israel*, VI (1961), p. 68, Pls. 8–9 (Hebrew).

C. On a richly decorated sarcophagus found in a Roman mausoleum in Kfar Gil'adi see: Y. Kaplan, "The Mausoleum in Kfar Gil'adi," *Eretz-Israel*, VIII (1967), p. 104, Pls. 15–17 (Hebrew).

146 Chéhab, "Sarcophages en plomb...".

147 E. Renan, *Mission de Phénicie*, Paris, 1864, pp. 427*f*; Pl. LX, 1.

148 G. B. de Rossi, "Saida in Fenicia," *Bulletino di Archeologia Cristiana*, Ser. 2 IV (1873), pp. 77–80; Pls. IV–V; figs. 1–4.

149 Goodenough, *Symbols*, V, no. 59.

150 Chéhab, "Sarcophages en plomb..." Pl. XLII, 7.

151 *Ibid.*, 1935, p. 56, n. 35.

152 *Ibid.*, Pl. XVII, 39.

153 *Ibid.*, p. 58, n. 38.

154 Merklin, "Untersuchungen..." 1939, Pl. XIV, 3–6.

155 *Ibid.*, Pl. XV, 1.

156 *Ibid.*, Pl. XIII, 3.

157 Müfid, "Die Bleisarkophage...," fig. 12.

158 *Ibid.*, fig. 16.

159 *Ibid.*, fig. 13.

160 A simple and beautiful single band of vine scrolls in the center of a sarcophagus also appears on a lead coffin from Ḥadera (see n. 8, A; fig. 90; Pl. LXXIV). On the strength of this parallel, it may be possible that the sarcophagus from Ḥadera was also imported from Sidon. The arch on the narrow wall lends support to this assumption, despite the fact that it is somewhat different from the arch on the sarcophagus from Sidon. Avi-Yonah, however, attributes the sarcophagus from Ḥadera to an Ashkelon workshop (*QDAP*, IV [1934], p. 149).

161 Cf.: *Syria*, XV (1934), Pls. XLII, 8; XLIII, 9–10.

162 *Ibid.*, p. 341, nos. 2–3.

163 *Ibid.*, Pl. XLIV, 12.

164 Chéhab, "Sarcophages en plomb…," 1935, pp. 71–72.

165 In the earlier Beth She'arim excavations as well only fragments were found. See: *Beth She'arim*, I, p. 135.

166 In kibbutz Alonim: B. Mazar, *BIES*, XXI (1957), p. 164 (Hebrew). In Khirbet Uzza: A. Ben-Tor, *'Atiqot*, III (1961), p. 23; Pls. I, 6; IV, 5–6 (Hebrew). In Tiv'on: Ruth Amiran, *Bulletin of the Department of Antiquities*, I (1949), p. 9; Pl. I, C (Hebrew). In Nahariya: M. Avi-Yonah, *BIES*, VIII (1941), p. 93 (Hebrew); D. Barag, *Archaeological News*, IX (1964), p. 17 (Hebrew). In Nesher: *Bulletin of the Department of Antiquities*, IV (1953), p. 5. In Ibelin: *PEFQSt.*, 1886, p. 80. In Shefar'am: *Ibid.*, 1889, p. 104. In el Bi'na and Yagur, together with the lead coffins from the third fourth centuries: *QDAP*, IV (1934), pp. 91, 93. In Sidon: *Syria* I (1920), pp. 150*f.*, figs. 48, 50. In Amasa in Syria: *Ibid.*, XXX (1953), p. 14, Pl. VIII, 1.

167 The ossuary was discovered in a burial cave in Jerusalem from the second century C.E. See: E. L. Sukenik, *Tarbiz*, I (1930), p. 122; Pl. 2, 3 (Hebrew).

168 Two clay ossuaries and several lids with two handles were discovered in a tomb at Umm-Kalkh near Ramle. They are now kept in the Rockefeller Museum (nos. 32–2682 and 32–2683). From the report it transpires that they were found together with stone ossuaries, but these have not been traced. One clay ossuary, now in the storerooms of the Department of Antiquities (83.808), was found at Khirbet Uzza. At this site several clay sarcophagi were also found. See: A. Ben-Tor, *'Atiqot*, III (1961). My thanks to Y. L. Raḥmani for this information.

169 N. Avigad, *Sefer Yerushalayim*, ed. M. Avi-Yonah, Jerusalem, 1959, p. 330 (Hebrew).

170 *Beth She'arim*, I, pp. 222–223, Pl. XXX, 5.

171 For a bibliography see: *Ibid.*, p. 228, no. 1; see also: N. Avigad, *Eretz-Israel*, VIII (1967), p. 124 (Hebrew).

172 N. Avigad, *IEJ*, XII (1962), p. 182, Pl. 22A.

173 For a detailed discussion on this type see: P. Kahana, *'Atiqot*, III (1961), pp. 135–139. For a short summary see: N. Avigad, *IEJ*, XII (1962), p. 177, n. 12 (see there for additional bibliography).

174 This motif is rare; cf. M. Ponsich, *Les lampes romaines en terre cuite de la Maurétanie Tingitane*, Rabat, 1961, Pls. XVII, 203; XXV, 339; XXXI, 479.

175 The potter's mark HZ appears on two other lamps from Beth She'arim. One lamp was found in the 1936–1940 excavations and is now in the Rockefeller Museum in Jerusalem (PAM 42-474), while the second was discovered in the 1954 excavation (54–270). See the letter H on the base of a similar lamp from the vicinity of Tyre: *BMB*, XVIII (1965), p. 48, fig. 11:3.

176 The wide and flat shoulder around the disc resembles several similar types from Beit-Natif. Cf.: *QDAP*, V (1935), Pls. VI, 1–3; VII, 2–8.

177 This type is not common. For a closely related form see: *QDAP*, I (1931), Pl. XXXII, 2. And cf. also: F. O. Waagé, apud: *Antioch-on-the-Orontes*, III, Princeton, 1941, type 48, pp. 65*f.*, fig. 78:48, 133 (the lamp there is dated to the second–third centuries C.E.).

178 J. H. Iliffe, "Imperial Art in Trans-Jordan," *QDAP*, XI (1944), Pl. VIII, 140.

179 Y. Yadin, *The Finds from the Bar-Kokhba Period in the Cave of the Letters*, Jerusalem, 1963, fig. 42:12.II.

180 E. L. Sukenik, "A Jewish Tomb Northwest of Jerusalem," *Tarbiz*, I (1930), p. 124; Pl. 3, 14 (Hebrew). However, the date suggested there for the lamps is much too early.

181 *Samaria-Sebaste*, III, fig. 88:8; Pl. XXII, 5.

182 *IEJ*, V (1955), p. 210, fig. 3:1.

183 S. Loeschke, *Lampen aus Vindonesia*, Zürich, 1919, Pl. VIII; and see especially no. 402.

184 O. Broneer, *Corinth*, Vol. IV, *Part II: Terracotta Lamps*, Cambridge, 1930, pp. 102–114, 257; Pl. XVII, 1198–1199.

185 P. V. C. Baur, *The Excavations at Dura-Europos*, IV, *III: The Lamps*, New Haven, 1947, nos. 313–321.

186 Iliffe, "Imperial Art," Pl. VIII, 140–143.

187 Cf. the lamps from a Roman tomb at Amman: L. Harding, *QDAP*, XIV (1947), Pl. XXV, 51, 54, 65.

188 *IEJ*, V (1955), p. 210, fig. 3:3. On the Seid estate other lamps of this kind were found but have not been published yet.

189 N. Makhouly, *QDAP*, VIII (1938), Pl. XXX, 1d.

190 M. Dunand, *BMB*, XVIII (1965), p. 48, fig. 11:1–2, 5; J. Hajjar, *ibid.*, Pls. XX F 373–374; XXI F 454.

191 Waagé, *Antioch-on-the-Orontes*, III, Type 50, p. 66, fig. 79:144–145.

192 The tombs were excavated by R. Gofna under the auspices of the Department of Antiquities.

193 Excavated by Prof. M. Avi-Yonah.

194 For a discussion on this type see: Marguerite Mendrac, "Une sépulture chrétienne à Sidon," *Berytus*, IV (1937), pp. 130–143; Pl. XXV, 3.

195 At first the ☧ monogram was an abbreviation with various connotations. The accepted opinion is that Constantine the Great introduced it as a Christian symbol after his decisive victory in 312 C.E. Since it does not appear as a symbol on coins prior to 320 C.E., this date is generally accepted as a *terminus post quem* regarding finds bearing the Constantinian monogram. In this connection see: D. B. Harden, *JGS*, II (1960) p. 72, no. 69; M. A. Frantz, *AJA*, XXXIII (1929), pp. 10*ff.*; F. L. Cross (ed.), *The Oxford Dictionary of the Christian Church*, London, 1957, *s.v. Labarum*. Recently an attempt was made to update the appearance of the monogram as a Christian symbol to the first century C.E. on the basis of its discovery on an ossuary in Jerusalem. See: *Dominus Flevit*, pp. 178*f.* See, however, Avi-Yonah's opinion on the matter: *IEJ*, XI (1961), p. 94.

196 *Beth She'arim*, I, p. 213, fig. 24, 4–5.

197 J. H. Iliffe, "A Tomb at el-Bassa of c. A.D. 396," *QDAP*, III (1933), pp. 81–91, figs. 11, 13, 16. The group of lamps in this tomb is not homogeneous, as Iliffe claims. He based his date of the end of the fourth century on coins found in the tomb. On this subject see below, the discussion on lamps nos. 36–44.

198 *QDAP*, VIII (1938), Pl. XXX, 1a.

199 Varda Zussman, "Some Lamps from Gadot," *BIES*, XXIII (1963), pp. 192–194, Pl. 8 (Hebrew).

200 I wish to thank the Department of Antiquities and its employees for making it possible for me to examine the lamps from different tombs that have not yet been published.

201 According to Varda Zussman (n. 27 above), p. 194, n. 7.

202 Personal communication from Dan Barag, who researched this find.

203 I wish to thank Prof. M. Avi-Yonah for making it possible for me to examine the material.

204 G. M. Fitzgerald, *Beth Shan Excavations 1921–1923, III: The Arab and Byzantine Levels*, Philadelphia, 1931, p. 41; Pl. XXXVI, 15–16.

205 P. Delougaz & R. C. Haines, *A Byzantine Church at Khirbet al-Karak*, Chicago, 1960, Pl. 44:15–16.

206 The lamp is not yet published. On the discovery of the cache see: B. Mazar, *BIES*, XXI (1953), p. 163 (Hebrew). Mazar attributes too early a date for the hoard. Subsequently, decisive numismatic evidence was found for a later dating.

207 O. Sellers & J. Baramki, *BASOR, Supplementary Studies*, XV–XVI (1953), pp. 47*ff.*, type XV.

208 A. Kindler, "A Seventh-Century Lamp with Coin Decoration," *IEJ*, VIII (1958), Pl. 24 D.

209 A. Kindler, *IEJ*, VIII (1958), Pl. 24 D.

210 *Ibid.*, pp. 106–109, fig. 1; Pl. 24 C.

211 Iliffe, "A Tomb at el-Bassa...".

212 Florence E. Day, "Early Islamic and Christian Lamps," *Berytus*, VII (1942), pp. 74*f.* Pl. XIII.

213 *Ibid.*, p. 77; Sellers & Baramki, *BASOR, Supplementary Studies*, XV–XVI (1953), p. 47. See also the discussion on lamp no. 34.

214 Mendrac, "Une sépulture chrétienne...," Pls. XXV–XXIX.

215 Delougaz, *Khirbet al-Karak*, Pls. 44:10, 16–17.

216 See above, n. 206.

217 See above, n. 210.

218 Macalister, *Gezer*, III, Pl. CVIII, 5; Fitzgerald, *op. cit.* (n. 32), *Beth Shan*, III, Pl. 36:17; *Samaria-Sebaste*, III, fig. 89:8; Delougaz, *Khirbet al-Karak*, Pl. 44:13. For a lamp of this kind with a Samaritan inscription see: L. A. Mayer & A. Reifenberg, *Journal of the Palestine Oriental Society*, XVI (1936), pp. 44*f.*; Pl. III.

219 Identical lamps were found at Khirbet el-Mafjar and in other places. See: *Berytus*, VII (1942), Pl. XI, 2; *QDAP*, X (1942), Pl. XVII, 7; Macalister, *Gezer*, III, Pls. CIV, 4; CX, 5; Delougaz, *Khirbet al-Karak*, Pl. 44:11.

220 Cf.: Delougaz, *ibid.*, Pl. 44:12.

221 For the lamp types from Khirbet el-Mafjar see: *QDAP*, X (1942), Pls. XVII–XVIII; *Berytus*, VII, Pl. XII, 2; B. Bagatti, *I monumenti di Emmaus el-Qubeibeh*, Jerusalem, 1947, Pl. 36:87.

222 According to a personal communication from Dr. M. Dothan.

223 On this class of lamps see: Day, "Early Islamic and Christian Lamps," pp. 65–79; Pls. IX–XII.

224 Macalister, *Gezer*, III, Pl. CIa; *QDAP*, III (1933), Pl. LVII, 1c.

225 *Beth She'arim*, I, pp. 210–211.

226 N. Avigad, *IEJ*, V (1955), p. 210, fig. 3:6–7.

227 *QDAP*, VIII (1938), Pl. XXX, 2a, d; *Dominus Flevit*, fig. 30:3.

228 *Dominus Flevit*, fig. 29:7.

229 G. M. Fitzgerald, *A Sixth-Century Monastery at Beth Shan*, Philadelphia, 1939, Pl. III, 3 (at bottom right).

230 *QDAP*, XIV (1950), Pl. XXV, 18.

231 *Beth She'arim*, I, p. 211, figs. 20, 23:4.

232 N. Avigad, *IEJ*, V (1955), p. 210, fig. 3:13.

233 For a similar lid cf.: *AASOR*, XXIX–XXX (1955), p. 30, no. 102, Pl. 25 X 91.

234 N. Avigad, *IEJ*, V (1955), p. 210, fig. 3:20.

235 Jars nos. 1 (54–48), 2 (54–47), 3 (53–554), and 5 (54–46) were found in different places in catacomb 13, whereas no. 4 (55–11) was found in catacomb 19.

236 Denyse le Lasseur, "Mission archéologique à Tyr," *Syria*, III (1922), p. 20, fig. 11a, c.

237 After these lines were written, a jar of this type was discovered in the excavations at Kurnub (Mampsis). The vessel was found inside a tomb together with coins from the third and the beginning of the fourth centuries C.E. (verbal communication from the excavator, Dr. A. Negev). This single discovery cannot as yet be used to disprove the above-mentioned theory as to the possible origin of this type of vessel.

238 Cf.: J. L. Kelso & J. P. Thorley, apud: W. F. Albright, "The Excavation of Tell Beit Mirsim, III," *AASOR*, XXI–XXII (1943), p. 122, fig. 4.

239 Their necks are shorter. Catacomb 26 was excavated by Prof. B. Mazar in 1956.

240 Macalister, *Gezer*, III, Pl. CIX, 1.

241 R. de Vaux & A. M. Steve, *Fouilles à Qaryet el-'Enab (Abū Gôsh)*, Paris, 1950, Pl. D 18; Fr. Sylvester & J. Saller, *Excavations at Bethany*, Jerusalem, 1957, figs. 48:3202, 3974; 62:2441.

242 Sylvester, *ibid.*, p. 215, fig. 42:1453; *Samaria-Sebaste*, III, p. 362, fig. 84a:12; Macalister, *Gezer*, III, Pl. CLXXXIX, 5 (the sketch is not good).

243 P. B. Bagatti, *I monumenti di Emmaus el-Qubeibeh*, Jerusalem, 1947, fig. 28:6–9; Pl. 24, fot. 52:1, 5; Sylvester & Saller, *Excavations at Bethany*, Pl. 129b; de Vaux, *Qaryet el 'Enab*, Pl. G 27–29.

244 *Samaria-Sebaste*, III, pp. 362 *ff*.

245 De Vaux, *Qaryet el 'Enab*, pp. 133–137. De Vaux attributes too long a period of use to these vessels (twelfth–fifteenth centuries).

246 M. Dothan, *'Atiqot*, I (1957), pp. 23–24, figs. 5–6 (see there additional bibliography) (Hebrew).

247 P. J. Riis & V. Poulsen, *Hama*, IV, 2, Copenhagen, 1957, pp. 270 *ff*.

248 B. Maisler (Mazar), *BIES*, IX, pp. 16–17 (Hebrew); *Beth She'arim*, I, p. 218.

249 *Samaria-Sebaste*, III, p. 409, no. 6, fig. 96:6.

250 *Ibid.*, I, pp. 81–88; III, pp. 409 *f*., 403–434.

251 Macalister, *Gezer*, I, p. 311; III, Pl. 72:18.

252 J. Saller, *Excavations at Bethany* (1949–1953), Jerusalem, 1957, p. 169, fig. 34:21; pp. 328 *f*.

253 *Dominus Flevit*, p. 143, no. 11, fig. 33:11.

254 Harden, *Karanis*, pp. 221, 226, nos. 686–687, Class X A; Pl. 19:686.

255 The tomb was excavated in 1955 by Dr. M. Dothan and Sarah Ben-Arieh. The excavation reports have not yet been published. The bottle is in custody of the Department of Antiquities (no. 55–253). It is 80 cm tall. The glass is colorless. Five very thin lines are incised across the width of the body. According to the other finds in the tomb, the bottle can be ascribed to the second half of the third century or to the fourth century C.E.

256 Harden, *Karanis*, pp. 186, 203 *f*.; Pls. 7:562, 568; 17:562; 18:568.

257 *Gerasa*, p. 540, nos. 84, 86, fig. 29:790; Pl. 140.

258 See, for example, the bottle in custody of the Cairo Museum: C. C. Edgar, "Graeco-Egyptian Glass," *Catalogue général des antiquités égyptiennes, du Musée du Caire*, Cairo, 1905, p. 50, no. 32.579; Pl. 6. For a general discussion see: Harden, *Karanis*, p. 193.

259 G. Harding, *QDAP*, XIV (1950), p. 91, no. 352; Pl. 29:352.

260 *Samaria-Sebaste*, III, p. 410, no. 9, fig. 94:9.

261 *Dominus Flevit*, p. 23 (tomb 230); p. 143, no. 18, fig. 33:18.

262 Macalister, *Gezer*, I, pp. 378 *f*.; Tomb 201; III, Pl. 123:1; Harden *Iraq*, XI (1949), p. 154, W 2, fig. 2:2; Pl. 49:4; *Gerasa*, p. 532, no. 55, fig. 28:231; and the tomb in Azur (see n. 255).

263 Harden, *Karanis*, p. 215, no. 636; Pl. 18:636.

264 Harding, *QDAP*, XIV (1950), pp. 91 *f*., nos. 370, 376; Pl. 29:370, 376.

265 C. Isings *Roman Glass from Dated Finds*, Groningen, 1957, pp. 121 *f*., Form 103; C. W. Clairmont, *The Excavations at Dura-Europos — Final Report*, Vol. IV, *Part V: The Glass Vessels*, New Haven, 1963, nos. 540–554.

266 See, for example: N. Makhouly, *QDAP*, VIII (1939), Pl. 33. For a bottle that was found in a tomb from the second half of the sixth century C.E., see: P. Delougaz & R. C. Haines, *A Byzantine Church at Khirbet al-Karak* (= Al-Karak), Chicago, 1960, p. 62, no. 44, Pl. 59:22.

267 G. M. Fitzgerald, *PEFQSt.*, 1932, p. 148; Pl. V:10. The first vessel on the bottom line to the left. The date was determined on the basis of the coins found in the tomb.

268 *Dominus Flevit*, p. 23, Tomb 228; p. 147, no. 2, fig. 35:2.

269 Harden also supports this opinion. See: Harden, *Karanis*, p. 270 (g); *Iraq*, XI (1949), p. 156.

270 G. Schumacher, *Tell El-Mutesellim*, I, Leipzig, 1908, pp. 189*f.*, fig. 292b; P. L. O. Guy & R. M. Engberg, *Megiddo Tombs*, Chicago, 1938, Pl. 175:7.

271 P. P. Kahane, *Antiquity and Survival*, II, 1957, p. 215, fig. 20. Since the tomb has not yet been published, the basis for its third century dating is unknown. The majority of the glass vessels there (nos. 18–22) are types attributed to the fourth century C.E.

272 Isings, *Roman Glass*, p. 125, Form 105.

273 Clairmont, *Dura-Europos V: The Glass Vessels*, pp. 132*f.* (Type K); Pl. 36:736.

274 O. Vessberg, *Opuscula Archaeologica*, VII (1952), p. 141; Pl. 9:31.

275 Edgar, "Graeco-Egyptian Glass," p. 61, no. 32.693; Pl. 8.

276 Harden, *Karanis*, pp. 268*f.*, 270 (f).

277 *Bulletin of the Israel Antiquities Department*, II (1950), p. 24; III (1951), Pl. 8, 6 (Hebrew).

278 This tomb served for burial a number of times between the first and seventh centuries C.E. See: A. K. Dajani, *ADAJ*, II (1953), p. 81, no. 24; Pl. 9:89. Hypothetically, we can assume that the bottle dates to the same period as the lamp published in *ADAJ*, III (1956), p. 87, fig. 22:7. The bottle from burial cave no. 1 at Nahariya has not yet been published. The bottle is at the Department of Antiquities and Museums (no. 64–504).

279 See, for example: D. C. Baramki, *QDAP*, I (1932); Pl. 8:4 (cf. Pls. 7–8, 10); C. C. McCown, *Tell En-Naṣbeh*, I, Berkeley-New Haven, 1947, p. 107, fig. 22:26; *Dominus Flevit*, pp. 145*f.*, nos. 12–13, 18; fig. 34:12–13, 18.

280 In the excavations at Lahav and Reḥovoth that were organized by the Department of Antiquities several vessels of this type were discovered in tombs from the third and fourth centuries C.E. They have not yet been published.

281 Clairmont, *Dura-Europos V: The Glass Vessels*, p. 132 (Type O); p. 140, nos. 742–743; Pls. 16:743, 36:742–743.

282 Harden, *Karanis*, pp. 255, 263, nos. 789–790; Pl. 20:789–790; Edgar, "Graeco-Egyptian Glass," p. 35, no. 32.556; Pl. 5.

283 Vessberg, *Opuscula Archaeologica*, VII, p. 146 (A IV); Pl. 4:32.

284 Harding, *QDAP*, XIV (1950), p. 91, no. 339; Pl. 29:339.

285 S. A. S. Hussaini, *QDAP*, IV (1935), Pl. 85:7.

286 D. C. Baramki, *QDAP*, I (1932), Pl. 5:22; O. R. Sellers & D. C. Baramki, "A Roman-Byzantine Burial Cave in Northern Palestine, *BASOR, Supplementary Studies*, 15–16 (1953), fig. 11, no. 229; *Dominus Flevit*, p. 143, no. 14; p. 151, fig. 33:14.

287 Hussaini, *QDAP*, IV (1935), Pl. 85:5; C. C. McCown, *Tell En-Naṣbeh*, p. 126, fig. 22:22; *Samaria-Sebaste*, III, p. 408, no. 5, fig. 94:5.

288 Harden, *Karanis*, pp. 254*f.*, 262; nos. 783–786; Pls. 10:783.

289 *Ibid.*, p. 262, no. 284.

290 *Dominus Flevit*, p. 148, nos. 7–8, fig. 35:7–8 (nos. 7–8 were found in Tomb 230, p. 23).

291 Saller, *Bethany*, pp. 327*f.*, no. 4029, fig. 34:20.

292 According to the lamps that were found in it, it appears that the tomb was in use during the first–third centuries C.E.; see: *ADAJ*, I (1951), p. 31, no. 21, Pl. 9:21 (upper row, in the center).

293 Guy & Engberg, *Megiddo Tombs*, Pl. 175:6.

294 *Samaria-Sebaste*, III, p. 413, no. 17, fig. 95:17; Pl. 25:1.

295 Harden, *Karanis*, pp. 174*f.*, 179*f.*, nos. 493–496; Pls. 6, 17.

296 B. Ravani, *'Atiqot*, III (1961), p. 125, fig. 4:3; Pl. 19:7.

297 P.P. Kahane, *ibid.*, p. 141.

298 Vessberg, *Opuscula Archaeologica*, VII, p. 133; Pl. 7:17.

299 See: Isings, *Roman Glass*, pp. 123–125, Form 104b.

300 A similar bottle was found in Tomb I 220 E at Samaria: *Samaria-Sebaste*, III, p. 409, no. 7, figs. 94:7, 95:10.

301 Baramki, *QDAP*, I (1931), Pl. 12:4.

302 *Dominus Flevit*, p. 143, no. 7, fig. 33:7 (Tomb 230, p. 23 fig. 10).

303 R. W. Hamilton, *QDAP*, VIII (1939), p. 68, fig. 2d. The bottle was found in stone sarcophagus F. This is one of three sarcophagi dating, apparently, to the first half of the fourth century C.E. A similar bottle

decorated with longitudinal ribbing was also found at Samaria: *Samaria-Sebaste,* III, p. 412, no. 7, fig. 95:7.

304 Macalister, *Gezer,* I, pp. 373*f.* (Tomb 185); Pl. 115:5.

305 Edgar, "Graeco-Egyptian Glass," p. 42, no. 32.591; Pl. 7.

306 Vessberg, pp. 131, 134; Pl. 7:32.

307 Cf.: G. Eisen, *Glass,* I, New York, 1927, p. 347; Pl. 89 (above to the left).

308 *Al-Karak,* p. 49; Pls. 50:16; 60:14–18, 21–23; G. M. Fitzgerald, *Beth-Shan Excavations,* 1921–1923 (= Beth Shan), *III: The Arab and Byzantine Levels,* Philadelphia, 1931, III, p. 42, Pl. 39:16, 23; *Samaria-Sebaste,* III, p. 415, no. 7, p. 416, no. 11, fig. 96:7, 11; *PEFA,* V, Pl. 21:13; *Dominus Flevit,* p. 146, nos. 23–24; *Gerasa,* pp. 524*f.* (Type F), figs. 19–21; S. J. Saller, *The Memorial of Moses on Mounte Nebo* (= Saller, *Mt. Nebo*), Jerusalem, 1941, pp. 318*f.*; Pl. 140:30–39.

309 Harden, *Karanis,* pp. 167–172, Pls. 6:479, 482, 484, 16:479–484; Vessberg, p. 124, Pl. 4:17–18; Hanfman, *JGS,* I (1959), p. 53, fig. 2; A. v. Saldern, *AJA,* LXVI (1961), pp. 9*f,* Pl. 9:10a–f.

310 Isings, *Roman Glass,* pp. 139*f.,* Form 111.

311 On glass lamps see: G. M. Crowfoot & D. B. Harden, "Early Byzantine and Later Glass Lamps," *JEA,* XVII (1931), pp. 196–208; Pls. 28–30.

312 *Beth-Shan,* III, Pl. 39:4; *Samaria-Sebaste,* III, p. 418, nos. 2–3, fig. 99:2–3; *Dominus Flevit,* p. 148, nos. 11*ff.,* pp. 152*f.,* fig. 35:11*ff.*; P. B. Bagatti, *Il santuario della visitazione ad 'Ain Karim* (= 'Ain Karim), Jerusalem, 1948, p. 77, fig. 34:1; Macalister, *Gezer,* I, pp. 362*f.,* Fig. 189; *Gerasa,* p. 526, no. 29, fig. 22:380, p. 528, no. 37, fig. 23:381 F, p. 531, no. 49, fig. 21:382, etc.; Saller, *Mt. Nebo,* pp. 315*f.,* Pl. 140:1–15.

313 *Samaria-Sebaste,* III, p. 418, nos. 2–3.

314 Isings, *Roman Glass,* p. 162, Form 134.

315 *Gerasa,* pp. 515*f.,* 519, nos. 1–3, fig. 17:368–369, Pls. 104a, 141a; Crowfood & Harden, "Glass Lamps," p. 198, Pl. 29:21–23.

316 See, for example: Saller, *Mt. Nebo,* p. 314, no. 244, Pl. 140:28.

317 A wine cup similar to that from catacomb 15 was discovered at Stein in Holland on a stone sarcophagus from the third century C.E. The wine cup from Stein has a concave base and zigzag lines join the top to the base. See: F. Fremersdorf, *Germania,* XIV (1930), pp. 214–218, fig. 2.

318 A. Kisa, *Das Glas im Altertume,* Leipzig, 1908, II, pp. 323*f.*; III, pp. 777*ff.*; Harden, *Karanis,* pp. 237*f.,* 248–251, nos. 749–764; Pls. 9:757; 20:757, 761, 763 (Class IX C); Vessberg, pp. 125*f.*; Pl. 4:4; Isings, pp. 66*f.,* Form 50b.

319 Baramki, *QDAP,* I (1931), Pl. 10:3.

320 Clairmont, pp. 121–127, nos. 600–640; Pls. XIV–XV.

321 The finds from the tombs discovered near Shoval have not been published. They are dated to the Late Roman period. The jug is at the Department of Antiquities (no. 51–180). The photograph was presented by Kahane, p. 216, fig. 23.

322 L. Y. Rahmani, *IEJ,* XIV (1964), pp. 53*f.,* fig. 2:7, Pl. 15G.

323 For example: In the collections of the Institute of Archaeology of the Hebrew University (Museum for Jewish Antiquities, no. 933).

324 Kisa, *Das Glas…,* II, p. 431, fig. 93.

325 J. H. Iliffe, *QDAP,* III (1934), pp. 88*ff.,* figs. 19, 20. This is not the place to discuss this tomb in detail. Contrary to Iliffe's opinion that the tomb dates to the end of the fourth century C.E., we believe that it dates to a longer period, from the fourth-seventh centuries C.E. According to the plate from Beth She'arim, there are good grounds for assuming that the two above-mentioned plates date to the fourth century C.E.

326 D. Barag in: M. W. Prausnitz, *Excavations at Shavei Zion,* Rome, 1967, p. 67, fig. 16:13–14.

327 The color of the glass is similar to the blue of the modern glass vessels produced in Hebron.

328 On vessels of this kind see: Kisa, III, pp. 803*f.,* figs. 331, 331a; Goodenough, *Symbols,* I, pp. 168–173; III, nos. 338–432, 435; R. W. Smith, *Glass from the Ancient World,* Corning, 1957, pp. 205*f.,* nos. 404, 410–412.

329 Toledo (Ohio), no. 355.705–706; Leiden (Holland), no. B 1948/4–1; The Jewish Museum, New York, no. F. 4677; The Field Museum Chicago, no. 158616.

330 No. 355.705.

331 Goodenough, *Symbols,* I, p. 173.

332 The use, origin, and meaning of the symbols of these vessels will be discussed in a separate article by the present writer.

333 M. C. Ross, *Catalogue of the Byzantine and Early Mediaeval Antiquities in the Dumbarton Oaks Collection,* I, Washington, 1962, pp. 82*f.*; Pl. 53.

334 *Gerasa,* pp. 544*f.,* no. 101; Pl. 141a.

335 P. J. Riis & V. Poulsen, *Hama*, IV, 2, Copenhagen, 1957, no. 52; p. 41, fig. 81, no. 53; p. 36, fig. 46.

336 Prof. Mazar also attributes the glass vessels from his excavations in 1936–1940, to the third fourth–centuries. See: *Beth She'arim*, I, p. 218.

337 It is noteworthy that until now only a very small amount of material of this kind has been published from Palestine and even less from Syria, a fact that makes it difficult to reach any definite conclusions.

338 They have not been published, except for one tomb at Nahariya. On this tomb see: M. Avi-Yonah, *BIES*, VIII (1941), pp. 91–94 (Hebrew).

339 On vessels of this kind see: Harden, *Karanis*, pp. 265*ff.*; *idem*, *Iraq*, XI (1949), p. 155; *idem*, "Roman Tombs at Vasa: The Glass," *Report of the Department of Antiquities, Cyprus* 1940–1948, Nicosia, 1958, pp. 56*ff.*; fig. 24, Pl. VI. However, it should be noted that Prof. Mazar mentions this type among the finds in his excavations. See: *Beth She'arim*, I, p. 218.

340 *Eretz-Israel*, IV (1956), p. 99, fig. 12 (Hebrew); *IEJ*, V (1955), p. 230, fig. 12.

341 On the techniques of glass engraving see: D. B. Harden, "The Wint Hill Hunting Bowl and Related Glasses," *JGS*, II (1960), pp. 47, 51, 65; Gladys D. Weinberg, "A Parallel to the Highdown Hill Glass," *ibid.*, V (1963), pp. 25–27; F. Fremersdorf, *Figürliche geschliffene Gläser*, Berlin, 1951.

342 Fragments of bowls with vertical sides such as these, that were used as hanging lamps, were also found at Beth She'arim. See Dan Barag's discussion on p. 205 and fig. 98–8A. Cf. also: *Gerasa*, Pl. CXLa; fig. 22:380.

343 J. H. Iliffe, "A Tomb at El-Bassa," *QDAP*, II (1934), p. 89, figs. 21–22.

344 *Ibid.*, p. 88, fig. 18. Cf. there also figs. 19–20, where plates similar in form to the plate from Beth She'arim are cited.

345 Macalister, *Gezer*, III, Pl. CXXIII, 5.

346 Cf. O. Seyffert, *A Dictionary of Classical Antiquities*, London, 1891, p. 114, fig. 3.

347 E. L. Sukenik, *The Ancient Synagogue at Beth-Alpha*, Jerusalem, 1932, Pl. 8; Goodenough, *Symbols*, III, no. 639.

348 Sukenik, *ibid.*, fig. 27; Goodenough, *Symbols*, III, no. 646.

349 Goodenough, *Symbols*, III, no. 304–305.

350 *Gerasa*, Pl. LXVIIb. On Pl. CXLIc a glass lamp with a tall stem is cited.

351 *Beth She'arim*, I, pp. 110–111, fig. 11, 1.

352 *JGS*, II (1960), pp. 32, 70. A fragment of a bowl on which arcades and a herringbone pattern are engraved was found at Corinth. See: Gladys R. Davidson, *Corinth, XII: The Minor Objects*, Princeton, 1952, p. 95, fig. 6:593.

353 For different objections that have been expressed concerning the arcade motif on the plate from Beth She'arim and for the literature on this motif in later periods see: *Carnuntum Jahrbuch*, 1959, Römische Forschungen in Niederösterreich, Beiheft 5, pp. 9*f.*

354 Goodenough, *Symbols*, III, no. 211.

355 R. D. Barnett, "Reminiscences of Herod's Temple," *Christian News from Israel*, XII, 3 (1961), pp. 14–20.

356 This, in our opinion, provides indirect confirmation for our theory that the façade of catacomb 14 is earlier than that of catacomb 15.

357 *QDAP*, III (1933), p. 88, fig. 17.

358 D. B. Harden, "Tomb-Groups of Glass of Roman Date from Syria and Palestine," *Iraq*, XI (1949), pp. 156*f.*; Pl. L; fig. 3.

359 *Gerasa*, Pl. CXXXIXb.

360 *Glass from the Ancient World, The Ray Winfield Smith Collection, A Special Exhibition*, 1957, New York, 1957, pp. 172–174, no. 353; A. Kisa, *Das Glas im Altertume*, Leipzig, 1900, pp. 640*ff.*, fig. 244. I thank Dr. Dan Barag for this reference.

Miscellaneous Artifacts

361 Similar chains were also found in other tombs from the Late Roman period. Cf.: *BASOR Supplementary Studies*, XV–XVI (1953), fig. 23: 262, 266, 278.

362 Cf.: *QDAP*, XIV (1950), Pl. XXVIII, 266–267; *Samaria-Sebaste*, III, fig. 100:22; *Dominus Flevit*, fig. 36:37–38.

363 I wish to thank Prof. B. Kirzon and Dr. Yeshayahu Barzilai from the Hebrew University, who examined the powder.

364 A box containing a black powdery substance was also found in a tomb from the Late Roman period near Jerusalem: S. J. Saller, *Excavations at Bethany*, Jerusalem, 1957, pp. 334–335; Pl. 58a–b1. For another cylindrical box see: *QDAP*, IV (1936), Pl. LXXXVI, 1–2.

365 Cf.: nails of different kinds: *Beth She'arim*, I, p. 223, fig. 27.

366 Cf.: *QDAP*, I (1931), Pl. XI, 11; *Samaria-Sebaste*, III, p. 437, fig. 101a; Macalister, *Gezer*, II, fig. 291:13.

367 Cf.: *QDAP*, I (1931), Pls. IV, 9; X, 13.

368 *QDAP*, I (1931), Pls. VI, 10, 14; XI, 4; XIV, 5; XV, 2–3. For a stamped bracelet, see: *Ibid.*, Pl. VI, 13.

369 I am indebted to the laboratory of the Department of Biological Chemistry of the Hebrew University for the initial treatment of the gold threads and for their photographs; to the Institute for Fibres and Forest Products affiliated with the Department of Commerce and Industry for the examination of the threads; and to Mrs. Aviva Lancet-Moller of the Israel Museum for determining the type of embroidery and for appending the bibliography below (n. 370).

370 M. Braun-Ransdorf, "Gold and Silver Fabrics from Medieval to Modern Times," *CIBA Review*, 1961–1963, Basle, pp. 2 *ff.*; photo p. 2.

371 Ketuboth 8b; Mo'ed Qatan 27b.

372 M. Higger, *Tractate Semahot*, New York, 1931, p. 81, 246.

CHAPTER IV

THE HEBREW AND ARAMAIC INSCRIPTIONS

The necropolis of Beth She'arim is endowed with a wealth of inscriptions. This rich epigraphic find is one of the most important contributions that the excavations at Beth She'arim have made to the research on Jewish culture of the Talmudic period. These inscriptions are especially informative about Beth She'arim itself and about the cemetery: they give a vivid account of its dwellers, their names, languages, occupations, and origin; their attitude toward death and their belief in resurrection.

The most prominent feature is the profusion of Greek inscriptions in contrast to the paucity of Hebrew inscriptions. It emerges that Greek was the tongue spoken by many Palestinian Jews and by all the Diaspora Jews, except for a small group of Palmyrene Jews who also wrote in Palmyrene. Of the inscriptions published from the 1936–40 excavations 150 were Greek, ten Palmyrene, and twenty-two Hebrew. This implies that a maximum of 15 % of the total inscriptions were in Hebrew. The Greek inscriptions are not only more numerous, but also generally longer and more heterogeneous in content. It is they, therefore, that furnished most of the information about the deceased of the earlier discovered catacombs. The Hebrew inscriptions, on the other hand, were short and meager in content: most of them contained one or two words (the word *shalom* and/or a name); only two were longer.[1]

In the catacombs published here, ninety-seven inscriptions were discovered: twenty-four in Hebrew, three in Aramaic, one in Greek but in Hebrew transliteration, and the rest in Greek.[2] The difference between this and the former group of inscriptions does not lie only in the larger percentage of Hebrew inscriptions but also in their length, content, and distribution in the different catacombs. Nevertheless, in most of our catacombs as well, the number of Hebrew inscriptions is small in comparison to the number of Greek inscriptions: in catacomb 12 there are three Aramaic versus fifteen Greek inscriptions; in catacomb 13, three Hebrew versus twenty-six Greek inscriptions; and in catacombs 15–19, not a single Hebrew inscription was found though a few Greek inscriptions were discovered in each of them.

The crucial difference lies in catacombs 14 and 20. In catacomb 14, three Hebrew and two bilingual (Hebrew/Greek) inscriptions were found, but not a single entirely Greek inscription. In catacomb 20 sixteen Hebrew inscriptions[3] were found on the walls and on some of the sarcophagi, as well as another three which are so blurred that they are illegible; however, only six Greek inscriptions were discovered. Of these six, only one is a proper epitaph (on a child's pit grave in the floor of room VIII_2); the remaining five (three of which consist of only one word) were inscribed by visitors: one inside the cave, three in the corridor, and one outside. It is evident, therefore, that there were almost no Greek burial inscriptions in catacomb 20.

The Hebrew and Aramaic inscriptions mainly record the names of the tomb owners, innovations in wording and additions of various details make them quite unusual and add new interest to them. These inscriptions are especially important because of the meager Hebrew epigraphic material from this period discovered so far in the country.

Another interesting fact is noteworthy: all the men referred to in the Hebrew inscriptions have Hebrew first names (except for one whose name is Greek in form:

230

Aniana); whereas all the women have Greco-Roman names (except for one: Miriam). The Greek cultural influence may also be detected in the title *Kyra* by which several of the women were designated. One of them, Kyra Mega, was the wife of Rabbi Joshua ben Levi. On the other hand, the only title by which the men were designated is *Rabbi*.

The terms for a grave are משכב ("bed," "couch," "resting place") and מנוחה ("rest," "resting place"). The latter is new in Palestinian Hebrew epigraphy. The coffins are called ארונות; the word appears both in the masculine and in the feminine. It should be noted that the term ארון was not encountered previously in the burial inscriptions of Palestine. A grave is referred to twice by the demonstrative זו ("this") alone, without the subject.

The Hebrew inscriptions supply some unusual information about the deceased: two are called "the holy ones"; one is mentioned as "he who made the cave"; and one is described as "having died a virgin." The age of three persons is recorded on their tombs.

Blessing formulae are few. One occurs twice:

זכר צדיקים לברכה

"May the memory of the righteous be blessed."

Another formula which is incomplete may be reconstructed thus:

עמידתן [עם הצדיקים]

"May their resurrection be [with the righteous]."

Both "plene" and "defective" spellings are used in the Hebrew inscriptions: Examples of plene spelling are the words לווי, הלילי, חודשים; examples of defective spelling are the words כן (=כאן) and מנחות (=מונחות). Phonetic spelling appears once: שולם instead of שלום. In general, it may be stated that the language of the Hebrew inscriptions in catacombs 14 and 20 is pure Mishnaic Hebrew.

The two complete Aramaic inscriptions and the fragments of a third inscription discovered in catacomb 12 all have the same contents: a warning and a curse. Their innovation lies in the wording of the curse, ימות בסוף ביש ("He shall die of an evil end"), a formula unknown from other sources. No other Aramaic inscriptions were found at Beth She'arim except for a few scattered Aramaic words.

The fact that almost all the burial inscriptions in catacomb 20 are written in Hebrew is a most remarkable point and requires careful consideration. Since the cemetery at Beth She'arim consistently exhibited an overwhelming majority of Greek inscriptions, this is an exceptional and problematic phenomenon which cannot be explained away as "accidental" or "insignificant." This phenomenon may have bearings on other questions as well.

As previously noted, the inscriptions from catacomb 20 refer preponderantly to rabbis or their families. It has likewise been shown that all the inscriptions in catacomb 14 pertain to rabbis. Thus, there appears to be a connection between the social class to which the deceased belonged and the exclusive use of Hebrew in their epitaphs. Perhaps it is also significant that both catacombs are the products of the same peculiar architectural concept, and that both probably date to the time of Rabbi Judah Ha-Nassî — end of second to beginning of third centuries — as already explained.

It seems therefore, that catacombs 14 and 20 served as burial centers for rabbinical families which still continued to use the Hebrew language. Such a situation could only have existed at the end of Rabbi Judah Ha-Nassî's lifetime and in the period immediately subsequent to his death, since, according to the accepted assumption, Hebrew ceased to be spoken at the end of the second century C.E. and was replaced by Aramaic and Greek.[4]

It is noteworthy that in catacombs 14 and 20, alongside the relatively numerous Hebrew inscriptions, not a single Aramaic inscription was discovered, though Aramaic was the dominant language among the Jewish population at that time. Perhaps it is not at all accidental that Hebrew was used in the tombs of rabbis who lived during Rabbi Judah Ha-Nassî's lifetime and were perhaps his colleagues. Rabbi Judah's saying, "What has the Syrian tongue (i.e., Aramaic) to do in Palestine? Speak either Hebrew or Greek"[5] (Bab. Talmud, Sotah 49b) proves that he himself spoke Hebrew, not Aramaic. As is well known, even the maids in Rabbi's household knew Hebrew so well that scholars used to request their assistance in interpreting obscure Hebrew words. From this we may confidently infer that at Beth She'arim there was a circle of scholars and their families who remained fluent in Hebrew at a time when the general populace spoke Aramaic or Greek. It seems to me that this particular state of affairs is reflected in the Hebrew burial inscriptions discovered in catacombs 14 and 20.

Objections to this conclusion, both verbal and written,[6] have been voiced by some scholars. They contend that the Beth She'arim Hebrew inscriptions do not in any way reflect the spoken language of the deceased, but they were written in Hebrew because of the traditional holiness generally associated with epitaphs. For confirmation of their argument, they point to the Hebrew epitaphs of many generations of Jews in the European Diaspora, Jews who certainly did not speak Hebrew. On the whole, this opinion is correct, especially in regard to recent periods of the Diaspora when special historical and religious circumstances were conducive to the development of the custom of writing epitaphs in Hebrew. However, there is no evidence of a similar development in the ancient Diaspora. On the contrary, in the largest Jewish cemeteries from the Roman period — at Tell el-Yehudiyeh (Leontopolis) in Egypt, at Cyrene in North Africa, and in the catacombs at Rome — the language on the tombstones is Greek, not Hebrew.[7]

The epigraphic finds in Palestine testify that, during the time of Beth She'arim, there was no tradition whatsoever of writing sepulchral inscriptions in Hebrew. Besides, from what source would such a tradition have been derived? Even by the end of the Second Temple period, the majority of epitaphs were written in Aramaic or Greek, and only a small minority were written in Hebrew.[8] In the Jewish cemetery at Jaffa which is more or less contemporary with the cemetery at Beth She'arim, of the sixty-six inscriptions discovered, sixty were written in Greek and only six were written in Aramaic or Hebrew.[9] Three epitaphs, dating to circa 500 C.E., from Zo'ar near the Dead Sea, are all written in Aramaic.[10] These findings and others are evidence that no tradition of writing epitaphs in Hebrew existed in Palestine.

Furthermore, traditional burial inscriptions inherently tend to become conventionalized into standard, fixed formulae. For example, the inscription of Rabbi Joshua son of Rabbi Hillel (no. 16) seems to be stereotyped in character; the wording זכר צדיקים לברכה ("May the memory of the righteous be blessed"), though not encountered previously on tombs, became ultimately conventionalized. This does not apply to the inscriptions of the two daughters (no. 15), the holy ones (no. 17), the three sons (no. 22), of Rabbi Hillel "who made this cave" (no. 28), and others, each of which is conspicuous for its individuality. These inscriptions seem to have been written by people who spoke Hebrew from birth, and pure Mishnaic Hebrew at that. If the opening phrase כן הן מנחות ("Here they lie") in inscription no. 15 is indeed a translation from the Greek as we have assumed, then our conclusion is only corroborated, since it may scarcely be presumed that the writer of the inscription would have translated the phrase into a non-spoken language. Most likely, the use of Hebrew in the cemetery of Beth She'arim was a locally established tradition which continued after Rabbi's death also. This may account for the paucity of Aramaic inscriptions.

There is, of course, no direct evidence as to the identity and the origin of the people mentioned in the Hebrew inscriptions. We have ventured to identify the rabbis from catacomb 14 with Rabbi Judah Ha-Nassî's family; however, this identification remains hypothetical. Judging by the composition and the language of the inscriptions, we must conclude that the rabbis and their

families who were interred in catacomb 20 were local inhabitants, especially since one of them is designated as "he who made this cave." In our opinion, these people were not brought for burial from the Diaspora. Up to now, there is no proof that the Diaspora Jews wrote Hebrew inscriptions of such complexity. All the inscriptions from Beth She'arim which mention a foreign origin are written in Greek, except for the word שלום ("peace"). Nevertheless, we obviously must not preclude the possibility that Jews from the Diaspora were also buried in catacomb 20, especially in the marble coffins which were subsequently destroyed.

1 THE ARAMAIC INSCRIPTIONS IN CATACOMB 12

1. Hall A, room III, the back wall of arcosolium 3.

Four lines painted in red. The inscription is partly blurred. It is 22 cm long; the letters are circa 2.5 cm high (fig. 104; Pl. III, 3)

כל מן דיפתח
הדה קבורתה
על על מן דבגוה
ימות בסוף ביש

"Anyone who shall open this burial upon whomever is inside it shall die of an evil end."

הדה קבורתה — The definite article is written here with a he instead of an aleph as in הדה קבורתא which appears in the burial inscriptions of the Jewish cemetery in Jaffa.[11]

על מן דבגוה — The word על occurs twice, due either to a mistake or to a flaw in the rock. The inscription is written in the third person and does not mention the name of the deceased: מן דבגוה means "whosoever is inside the grave." This expression also appears in an Aramaic inscription on an ossuary of the Second Temple period from the Kidron Valley. It warns against second-

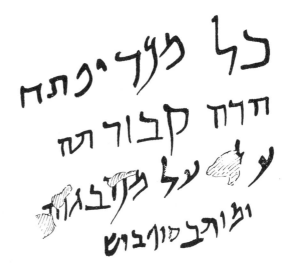

Fig. 104 Inscription no. 1

ary use of the ossuary:[12] כל די אנש מתהנה בחלתה דנה קרבן אלה מן דבגוה "All that a man may find to his profit in this ossuary (is) an offering to God from him who is within it."[13]

ימות בסוף ביש ("shall die of an evil end") —Before the first word, there seem to be traces of a letter, but it is indecipherable. This expression is unique and has no parallel whatsoever in Aramaic or Hebrew epigraphy.

This warning was intended for Aramaic-speaking people. However, it apparently was not sufficient for the writer who added another warning above the same arcosolium (no. 3), worded somewhat differently, for readers of Greek (see above, p. 23).

2. Hall A, room VIII, above the opening of the right kokh in the southern wall.

Six lines painted in red on the rock which was roughened by a hewer's axe. Excellently preserved. The inscription is 18 cm high, and the letters are 1.5–2 cm high (fig. 105; Pl. IV, 4).

דקביר בהדין
שמעון בר יוחנן
ובשבועה דכל
4 דיפתח עלוי יהי
מאית בסוף
ביש

"He who is buried here is Shim'on the son of Yoḥanan; and on oath whoever shall open upon him shall die of an evil end."

Fig. 105 Inscription no. 2

The inscription deals with two subjects: the identity of the deceased and the curse upon whomever disturbs his rest.

דקביר בהדין — This opening phrase refers to the deceased and not to the grave, unlike the conventional formulas found in the inscriptions e.g., ...הדה קבורתה ד "this is the burial of..." or ...קברא דנא די "this grave belongs to..."

שמעון בר יוחנן — We have not been able to identify him with a particular person in the literary sources.

ובשבועה — The wording of the curse is similar to that of the previous inscription except for one small change: It begins with an oath in the sense of a "sworn curse," שבועת הָאָלָה (Baba Metzia 5, 21). In the Bible, a sworn curse is usually associated with a death penalty: כי השבועה הגדולה היתה לאשר לא עלה אל ה' המצפה לאמר מות ימות (For they made a great oath concerning him that came not up to the Lord to Mizpeh, saying, He shall surely be put to death. Judges 21:5); or והנחתם שמכם ('And ye shall leave your name for a curse unto my chosen: for the Lord God shall slay thee... Isaiah 65:15); and compare also with וישבע יהושע בעת ההיא לאמר ארור האיש (And Joshua adjured them at that time saying, cursed be the man before the Lord... Joshua, 6:26).

עלוי — upon him, i.e., upon Shim'on bar Yoḥanan. Instead of the third person "upon whomever is inside," על מן דבגוה of the former inscription, the name of the deceased is referred to here. On the combination of the verb פתח ("open") with the impersonal reference עלוי ("upon him") see below.

יהי מאית — the composite future instead of the simple future ימות as in the previous inscription. This may be compared to Targum Onkelos, Genesis 50:5 אנה מאית בקברי in contrast to Targum Yonathan אנא מיית בקברי.

The wording of this inscription may also be compared with that of the Greek inscription (no. 129) from catacomb 11, which in translation reads: "I, Hesychios, lie here with my wife; whoever dares to open upon us shall not have a share in eternal life."[14]

Both these inscriptions, written in Palestinian Aramaic, are of the type that were devised to warn people against touching the grave and disturbing the rest of the deceased and to threaten them with punishment otherwise.[15] At Beth She'arim additional inscriptions of this type were found, all in Greek.[16] They threaten offenders with God's judgment or exclusion from eternal life. The two Aramaic inscriptions are the only ones threatening a death penalty.

Curses and warnings against tomb robbers or against secondary use of the tomb are common in epitaphs throughout the ancient Near East in all languages.[17] A noteworthy example from the Phoenician inscriptions is that of Tibnat, the King of the Sidonians (fifth century B.C.), part of which runs thus:

מי את כל אדם אש תפך אית הארן ז אל אל
תפתח עלתי ואל תרגזן... ואם פתח תפתח
עלתי ורגז תרגזן אל יכן לך זרע בחים תחת
שמש ומשכב את רפאם

"Whatever person you may be who shall turn over this coffin, do not open it upon me and do not anger me... and if you shall open it upon me and if you shall anger me, may you not be bestowed with offspring in this life under the sun and may your resting place be with the shades."[18]

Special interest is aroused by the wording of a curse in a Hebrew burial inscription at Silwan near Jerusalem, from the First Temple period: ארור האדם אשר יפתח את זאת "Cursed be the man who shall open this (i.e., burial)."[19] In Jewish tombs from the end of the Second Temple period, a short Aramaic formula was customary: ולא למפתח ("not to be opened");[20] or ולא למפתח עליהון ("not to be opened upon them"),[21] i.e., a request that the bones in the ossuary or kokh not be moved again. A similar epitaph from Palmyra dating to the second or third century C.E. reads:
ואנש לא יפתח עלוהי גומחה דנה עד עלמא

("And let no man open over him this niche forever").[22] There are many other similar examples.

The Aramaic inscriptions from Beth She'arim apparently date to the third century C.E. Because of the exceptional wording of their curses, they are unique in Aramaic epigraphy.

3. Hall A, room VIII

The first three words of an inscription painted in red on a fragment of a stone slab. The inscription is 12 cm long, and the letters are 1–2 cm high (fig. 106)

כל מן דיפתח

"Anyone who shall open..."

Fig. 106 Inscription no. 3

These are also the opening words of inscription no. 1. The stone slab possibly served to close one of the kokhim or to cover one of the trough graves in this room.

4. Hall A, room II, the northern jamb of the entrance.

One word incised in fine lines; following it, there is an engraving of a small menorah (fig. 8).

עאיק[ס]ו

This word is a Hebrew transliteration of the first word of the Greek inscription AEKCO EΦ, incised on the opposite jamb[23] and also followed by an engraved menorah. For the interpretation of this inscription, see p. 22; the writer seems to have left out the letter *samekh* or to have merged the letters *kof* and *samekh* (see fig. 8).

2 THE HEBREW INSCRIPTIONS FROM CATACOMB 13

5. Hall B, room I, the interior western jamb of arcosolium 3.

Ten lines painted in red in an elliptical, irregular framework, also painted red. The inscription is 28 cm high; the letters are 1.5–2 cm high. The script is slipshod. It has thick and thin lines, quickly drawn. The letters are not uniform in type. The area inside the frame is partitioned by a very thin crack in the rock; the writer tried, therefore, to divide the contents into two groups on either side of the crack. The lines are not homogeneous in size, density, or orientation (fig. 107; Pl. X, 2).

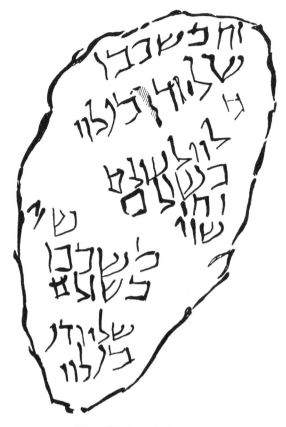

Fig. 107 Inscription no. 5

זה משכבו
שליודן בן לוי
לוי לעולם
4 בשולם
יהי
שוי שוי
משכבו
8 בשולם
שליודן
בן לוי

The writer obviously repeated the words לוי and שוי twice by mistake. Leaving out the superfluous words, we may translate the inscription thus:

"This is the resting place of Yudan son of Levi forever in peace. May his resting place be set (?) in peace. Of Yudan son of Levi."

This inscription is divided into two parts, each expressing a different version of the same ideas: the name of the tomb owner, and a prayer or request for the peace of the resting place. The word לעולם ("forever") reflects the anxiety that the tomb might be desecrated or that it might be used for secondary burial at some future date.

משכבו —This term, which also appears in inscription no. 15, is commonly en-countered in burial inscriptions from various periods. In a Phoenician inscription from Cyprus we read: על משכב נחתי לעלם ("on the couch of my rest [on my resting place] forever").[24] In the Eshmunezer in-scription from the fifth century B.C. the word משכב ("resting place," "couch," "bed"), is used synonymously with the term קבר ("grave," "tomb"): שכב אנך בחלת "ז ובקבר ז...אל יפתח אית משכב ז "I lie in this tomb and in this grave...may no one open this grave ("resting place").[25] On the façade of a tomb in Jerusalem from the end of the Second Temple period, this term occurs at the beginning of the inscription: ...המשכב הזה של ("this tomb belongs to...").[26] On a Jewish tombstone from the second or third century C.E., after a Greek inscription beginning with the word PABBI, the following Hebrew words are engraved:

236

[שלום ע]ל מישכבך ("peace upon your tomb").[27] On a Hebrew tombstone from Italy dating to the ninth century C.E. the inscription runs: יבוא שלום (על) משכבו ("may peace come upon his grave").[28]

שליודן — The contiguity of the preposition של ("of") and the succeeding word is a regular feature of the Beth She'arim inscriptions; for example: שלקירה, שלרבי, and שלשלשת, שלכוהנים. This way of writing occurs only once in the Bible מטתו שלשלמה: (Song of Songs, 3:7). However, in the manuscripts of the Mishnah, this usage is widespread (see the Kaufmann manuscript). It was generally accepted that this contiguous writing was regularly pursued in the Mishnaic and subsequent periods; however, the discovery of the Bar Kochba letters in which the word של always appears detached[29] has shown that writing practices varied during the same period.

בשולם — Instead of בשלום ("in peace"). This is not an erroneous exchange of letters, since this particular spelling occurs twice here. Very probably the writer of this inscription wrote בשולם just as he pronounced the word. We may instructively compare this pronunciation of the word with that of the Ashkenazi and Yemenite Jews. Another exceptional spelling was found in the catacombs at Rome: שאלום.[30]

שוי — This is a problematic word. Apparently it should read שְׁוֵי משכבו from the word שְׁוָיָה, meaning in Aramaic cradle, bed, couch, or pillow. Thus it could be interpreted as יהי ערש משכבו בשלום ("may the couch of his tomb be in peace"). This interpretation may be compared to ערש יצועי ("nor go up into my bed" Psalms 132:3).

During a visit to Beth She'arim, Professor Saul Lieberman suggested an interesting alternative interpretation for the word שוי ("immediately," "without delay"). Lieberman has shown[31] that in Palestinian Aramaic, the meaning of this word is "immediately," and that it also appears in the Akdamoth prayers of the Palestinian Rabbinical literature: שוי דלא בששתא, i.e.,

"immediately," "without delay." The word שוה also appears in this sense in one of Shim'on Bar Kochba's letters.[32] According to this interpretation our inscription should be rendered יהי מיד משכבו בשלום ("may his tomb be in peace immediately"). Prof. Lieberman has added a further explanation for this wording: according to a legend, a soul which has died wanders for twelve months until it enters paradise or hell. The author of the Beth She'arim inscription therefore expressed his wish that peace may come upon Yudan ben Levi's tomb immediately, without delay.

6. Three lines painted in red below the same arcosolium (no. 3). The inscription is 15 cm long, and the letters are 2–3 cm high (fig. 108).

זה משכבו
שליודן בן
לווי לעום

"This is the resting place of Yudan son of Levi forever."

Fig. 108 Inscription no. 6

The writer of the previous inscription apparently thought that one double inscription was inadequate and therefore added a second inscription, identical to the beginning of the first. He omitted the lamed in the last word which should read לעולם ("forever").

לווי — The same scribe who wrote לוי in

the previous inscription with one waw wrote it here with two. Paleographically, the reading לווי is absolutely certain since the two waw are very long and the yod is very short. This also solves the problem of the reading of these names in inscriptions nos. 24 and 28, previously given a different interpretation (see the discussion on these inscriptions). Even though we have not found an epigraphic parallel to this spelling of the name לוי, the principle of using two waw to indicate a consonant is very common in the literature: for example, כִּנּוּן גְוִיָּה, לְוִיָה, לִוְיָה, לְוִי שִׁיוִיּיא, שָׁוֶוה and others (see dictionaries as well).

7. Hall D, room II, below arcosolium no. 2.
   One word, coarsely painted in red. The

inscription is partly blurred. It is 18 cm long, and the letters are 3.5–5 cm high (fig. 109).

טבלה

"Tablah"

Fig. 109 Inscription no. 7

This name may be compared with that of the Amora, R. Tabla.

3   THE HEBREW INSCRIPTIONS IN CATACOMB 14

8. Hall A, room I, a sealing stone in situ in niche 1.

Two lines painted in red. The length of the inscription is 13 cm, and the letters reach a height of 2.5–5.5 cm (fig. 110; Pl. XXII, 3).

רבי
שמעון

"Rabbi Shim'on"

Fig. 110 Inscription no. 8

The inscription is written with quite a flourish. The ligature of the last three letters עון is noteworthy.

רבי — This title is frequently encountered in the Beth She'arim inscriptions (see below). It also occurs in a Hebrew inscription discovered in the earlier excavations of Beth She'arim and in Hebrew epitaphs at Jaffa and in the synagogue at Na'aran.

9. Hall A, room VI, above kokh 4

A bilingual inscription, one line in Hebrew and one line in Greek, painted in black. It is 31 cm long, and the letters are 2.5–3 cm high (fig. 111; Pl. XXII, 4).

זו שלרבי גמליאל מ

PABI ΓAMAΛIHΛ

"This [is the tomb of] Rabbi Gamaliel (M) Rabbi Gamaliel."

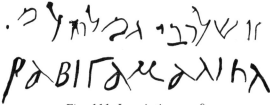

Fig. 111 Inscription no. 9

זו ("this [is the burial of].") — This abbreviated form, used also in inscription no. 10, has its origin in early Hebrew usage.[33]

שלרבי — On the contiguous spelling of this word, see the discussion on inscription no. 5.

גמליאל — A name of Tannaim and Amoraim (see below, inscriptions nos. 15 and 26). The form of the aleph is unusual; a similar aleph also appears in the name אלעזר ("El'azar") on an ossuary from Jerusalem.[34] The purpose of the letter *mem* at the end of the line is obscure. The Greek transliteration ΓΑΜΑΛΙΗΛ also occurs in the Septuagint.

PABI — The Greek transliteration ʿΡαβί is of particular interest. The pronunciation of the title רבי has been extremely controversial, due to the numerous forms in which the word is rendered: בירבי, רבי, רב, בירבי, ʿΡίβ, ʿΡιββί, Βηρέβι.[35] In inscription no. 10 and in the Greek epitaph mentioned in note no. 16, the transliteration is also commonly used in the New Testament. Therefore, it seems that the common and original pronunciation was רַבִּי and that all the other forms were just variants.[36]

10. Hall A, room I, on a sealing slab found in the corner of the room near grave no. 3

A bilingual inscription, two lines in Hebrew and two lines in Greek, painted in red. The Hebrew script is very coarse. The inscription is 26 cm long; the Hebrew letters range from 3.5–6 cm in height (fig. 112; Pl. XXII, 6).

זו שלרבי

אניאנא

PABBI ANIANOY
TOY NANOY´

"This is Rabbi Aniana's (tomb).
Of Rabbi Anianos the Little
(lit: the dwarf)"

The Hebrew wording is the same as that of inscription no. 9.

אניאנא — Cf. with the name אניאנה in inscription no. 17. In the Greek version the

Fig. 112 Inscription no. 10

name takes the Greek form ʾΑνιανός, as found in catacomb 13. The name אניאנא is a variant of the name חנינא or חנניה. On the transliteration ʿΡαββί, see above, inscription no. 9.

The second line of the Greek inscription is especially interesting. In the first publication of the inscription,[37] just the word νάνου was included, since the preceding letters were unintelligible; thus, no interpretation was offered for this line. Lately, B. Lifshitz[38] has suggested the reading τοῦ νάνου in the sense of "of the little" (more precisely: "of the dwarf"). This reading is also justifiable from the paleographic point of view. In Lifshitz's opinion, Aniana was dubbed "the dwarf" because of his diminutive stature. We shall return to this point in our discussion of inscription no. 11 because it has turned out that these two inscriptions are mutually associated. It appears that the stone bearing the inscription does not belong to grave no. 3, as was assumed immediately after its discovery, but very probably to grave no. 2 in the opposite corner, above which the inscription אנינא/הקטן (no. 11) was found.

11. Hall A, room I, above niche 2 in the southern wall.

Two rows of coarse letters that were painted in red on the rough rock face. The inscription was 15 cm long, and the letters 4 cm high. The first word was perfectly clear; the second was partially blurred;

however, this did not affect the certainty of the reading. Since the discovery of the inscription, the rock has crumbled and the inscription has disappeared (fig. 113; Pl. XXII, 5).

אנינא

הקטן

"Anina the Little"

Fig. 113 Inscription no. 11

When it emerged that there was a close relationship between this inscription and no. 10, it also became evident that אנינא is only an abbreviation of אניאנא. It may be instructively compared with the name אנינא in Palmyrene script beside the name 'Αννιανός on a Jewish burial inscription from Carthage in North Africa.[39] The designation "the Little" — corresponding to the Greek νάνος in the previous inscription — requires special attention.

In the Beth She'arim inscriptions, the title "the Little" appears a number of times, once in Hebrew and twice in Greek: יהודה הקטן "Judah the Little,"[40] ΙΩCHΦ O MIKKOC ("Joseph the Little"),[41] and ΔOMNIKA H MIKPA ("Domnika the Little").[42] In all these cases there is reason

to assume that the title *little* means a young boy or girl.

When the "Anina the Little" inscription was discovered, I proposed a different interpretation. I suggested that "the Little" was the designation an important sage chose for himself out of modesty. Evidence for this interpretation is readily found in the literature: "Yonatan ben haqqatan" (Avodah Zarah, 8, 12), and "Shmuel haqqatan," a contemporary Tanna of R. Gamaliel, who was renowned for his charity, modesty, and virtue (Mishnah Avoth 4, 19; Tossephet Yom-Tov explains the designation *the Little* "since he made little of himself"). Thus I arrived at the conjecture — which I have not been able to prove — that "Anina the Little" does not refer to a child but to one of the Rabbis who were interred in this catacomb. This assumption received additional corroboration from the fact that "Anina the Little" is the same as "Rabbi Anina," even though the Greek word νάνος proves that the reason for being called *the Little* lies in his small stature, as stated above.

12. Hall A, room III

Four letters in two rows, engraved deeply on a small flat surface formed by a rock fracture in the western wall. The inscription is not associated with a particular grave (Pl. XXII, 1):

אב

על

The aleph may be compared to that in the name אנינא, and the 'ayin, to that in the name שמעון ("Shim'on"). We have no explanation for this inscription, except if we interpret it as the personal name אבעל ("Avi'al") which is hardly acceptable for this period.

4 THE HEBREW INSCRIPTIONS OF CATACOMB 20

13. Hall, A, the western entrance corridor (fig. 114)

One word incised in the southern wall:

אחיה

"Her brother"

Fig. 114 Inscription no. 13

This is probably the anonymous signature of someone visiting his sister's tomb.

14. Room I, the eastern wall

The beginning of an incised inscription. The continuation is faded.

...שלום ע[ל]...

"Peace up[on]..."

This inscription does not belong to a specific grave and is probably the handiwork of a visitor. It might also be part of the customary blessing שלום על ישראל ("peace upon Israel"). Another possibility is that the writer wanted to bless the deceased of the cave in the spirit expressed in the Greek inscriptions engraved in the eastern entrance corridor (see p. 95).

15. Room V, the "daughters" sarcophagus (fig. 115; Pl. XXXIX).

Eight lines engraved on the cover of the sarcophagus. This is the longest Hebrew inscription discovered to date at Beth She'arim. Its total length is 120 cm; the height of the letters is circa 4 cm. Seven lines are incised on the slope of the cover; the last line is engraved on the vertical edge of the cover. The script is monumental, in contrast to that of the rest of the inscriptions. The letters are deeply engraved and are square in shape. They resemble the script commonly encountered in the Galilean synagogues of the third century C.E. There are traces of evidence that originally the letters were also painted in red. At present the cover is on display in room I near the main entrance of the cave.

כן הן מנחות אטיו בתו שלרבי
גמליאל בן נחמיה שמתה
בתולה בת עשרין ושתים
4   שנה ואטיון בתו שלרבי
יהודה בנו שלרבי גמליאל
שמתה בת תשע
שנים
8   וששה חודשים עמידת[ן עם הצדיקים]

"Here they lie, Atio, the daughter of Rabbi Gamaliel, son of Nehemiah, who died a virgin at the age of twenty-two years, and Ation, the daughter of Rabbi Judah, the son of Gamaliel, who died at the age of nine years and six months. May their resurrection [be with the righteous]."

Line 1 — כן (=כאן) A defective spelling often found in the literary sources as well.

מנחות—The opening כן הן מנחות ("here they lie") is new to Hebrew sepulchral inscriptions. It might very well have been borrowed from the Greek epitaphs which generally begin with the phrase ἐνθάδε κῖτε.

אטיון—An abbreviation of the name אטיו ("Ation")—see below—.

שלרבי—The preposition של is contiguous, in the accepted manner, with the word רבי.

Line 2—The name *Gamaliel* appears four times in this cave. We have not been able to identify Rabbi Gamaliel ben Neḥemiah with a specific individual in the literary sources. Neḥemiah is the only person mentioned in the inscriptions of this catacomb who is not entitled "Rabbi."

Line 3 — עשרין ("twenty"). The use of

241

וישׁח חודשׁים עׁ עׁ ורם

Fig. 115 Inscription no. 15

nun instead of mem is customary in Mishnaic Hebrew.

Line 4 — אטיון. In Lifshitz's opinion,[44] this name is derived from the Roman name Attius; in the masculine it assumes the form Ἀττίων.

Line 8 — חודשים. Plene spelling, in contrast to the defective spelling in line 1.

[עמידת]ן עם הצדיקים] ("their resurrection with the righteous"). The end of the inscription is missing because the stone was damaged. It may also be completed as: [עמידת]ן עם הכשרים] ("their resurrection with the worthy"). This proposed completion is based on the wording of a Judeo-Aramaic epitaph discovered near Tiflis in the Caucasus:[45]

הד[א] קבר[א] דאבא יק[ירא] יהודה
דמתקרי גורק משכבה עם הצדיקים
עמידתו עים הכשרים.

"This is the grave of dear father Judah known as Gurk. May his resting place be with the righteous, his resurrection with the worthy."

Chwolson, who published this inscription, attributes it to the fourth or fifth century C.E. עמידה ("standing," "to stand up") in the sense of standing up from the grave (i.e., resurrection of the dead) is used in this sense at a later period in the Gaonic literature. In one of the documents from the Cairo Genizah (twelfth/thirteenth centuries) which contains a prayer for the dead, we find: תהא עמידתם בקרוב יטה עליהם השלום "May their resurrection be soon, may He extend peace upon them."[46] Compare also Daniel 12:13: ותעמד לגרלך לקץ הימין ("...and thou...shalt stand in thy lot at the end of the days.") This belief in resurrection was also expressed in a Greek inscription engraved in the entrance corridor to the cave (see above, p. 95) and in other inscriptions.

Behind this inscription lies a tragic story of the untimely death of a young aunt and her still younger niece who apparently died at the same time and were buried together in one coffin. Here the problem arises as to the use of a single coffin for two bodies. On the matter of multiple burial, the Halakhah states: "One must not bury two bodies one beside the other, or a body alongside bones, or bones alongside a body."[47] However, there is no injunction against burying the bones of more than one person together. In fact, we have found ossuaries in Jerusalem from the Second Temple period which contained the bones of at least two people. It seems likely, therefore, that the child Ation and her aunt Atio were first buried in separate graves (perhaps even in the same cave), but that later on their bones were collected and interred in a single coffin. On collective burial see also inscriptions nos. 21–22 below.

The genealogy of the members of the family mentioned in the inscription would thus be:

Nehemiah
|
Rabbi Gamaliel
|
Atio (22)   Rabbi Judah
|
Ation (9½)

16. Room II, above the arcosolium to the right of the entrance leading to room III (fig. 116)

Three lines painted in red with a thin stick and partially incised. Since most of the paint was washed away by the water, several letters are discernible only by the thin lines incised in the rock. The inscription is 47 cm long and the letters are 3–5 cm high.

רבי יהושע בירבי הלל
בן אטיון מש[כבו]
בשלום

"Rabbi Joshua, son of Rabbi Hillel, son of Ation (may his) res(ting place be) in peace."

יהושע — The waw was suspended between the shin and the 'ayin, proving that the author intended to write יהשוע. On the other hand, compare with the plene spelling of the name יהושע in the other inscriptions.

בירבי — This word, coming as it does here between two names, obviously means בן רבי ("the son of Rabbi"). Cf. with

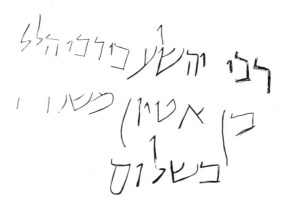

Fig. 116 Inscription no. 16

ר' יוסי ברבי חנינא and ר' יוסי בירבי אבין and others in the Talmudic literature. Generally the designations ברבי and בירבי were prestigious titles attributed to scholars who were pupils of Rabbi Judah Ha-Nassî, or students in schools of other famous sages. In the inscriptions of Beth She'arim and Jaffa, the titles בירבי, בריבי, and Βηρέβι[48] always appear *after* the name: e.g., רבי טרפון בירבי,[49] יצחק בן יוסף בירבי[50] and תנחום בירבי.[51]

אטיון ("Ation") — In inscription no. 13, this was a woman's name. Would it be correct to conclude, therefore, that Rabbi Hillel bore the surname of the maternal side of his family? Though there are such cases in Talmudic literature,[52] the masculine name 'Αττίων. has also been noted previously.[53]

מש... should be completed מש[כבו]. Compare this to the wording משכבו בשלום in inscription no. 5, and note the discussion there.

17. Room III, sarcophagus no. 15 (fig. 117; Pl. XXXVIII, 3)

Three lines painted in red on the long walls of this plain sarcophagus. The inscription is 125 cm long; the letters are 5 cm high. The right part was well preserved; however, the left part was blurred due to dampness and mud. The cover had been slightly moved by the tomb robbers and its edge projected over the right side of the inscription thus protecting it against the winter rains which penetrated through the ceiling.

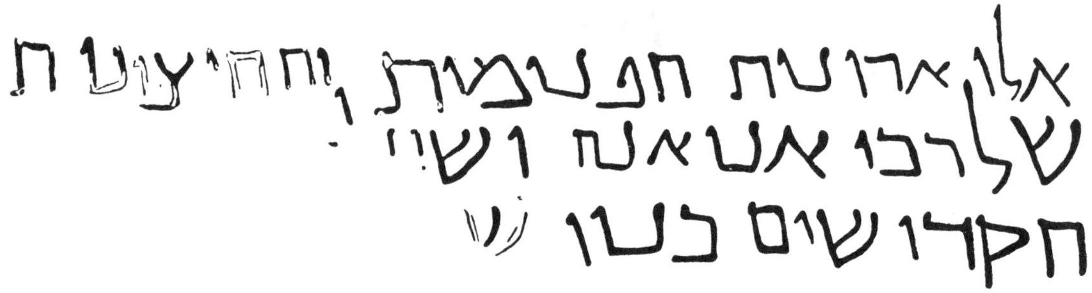

אלו ארונות חפנימית וחיצעות
שלרבי אניאנה ושי[
חקדושים בנו עי

Fig. 117 Inscription no. 17

אלו ארונות הפנימית והחיצונית

שלרבי אניאנה וש[לרבי........]

הקדושים בניו ש[רבי........]

"These sarcophagi, the inner and the outer are of Rabbi Aniana and of ... the holy ones, the sons of ..."

אלו ארונות — ארון as a term for a sarcophagus is found in Phoenician inscriptions,[54] but this is the first time it appears in Hebrew epigraphy. In Talmudic literature, the term applies both to a sarcophagus for a body burial and to an ossuary for the collecting of bones.

הפנימית והחיצונית ("the inner and the outer") — The first word is clear; the second is badly effaced but can be read with certainty from the context. The text of the inscription refers to sarcophagi nos. 15 and 16 which were placed directly one behind the other. No. 15, upon which the inscription was written, was apparently termed "the inner one" since it stood close to the scribe, whereas no. 16 was referred to as "the outer one" since it was farther away. However, this is not perfectly certain.

Apparently, two individuals (or their bones?) were simultaneously interred in the two coffins. However, since the front coffin concealed the back one, an unusual method was devised of writing a joint inscription on one sarcophagus for both burials. The word ארון is frequently used in the feminine in Mishnaic Hebrew.[55] (See also the next inscription.)

שלרבי אניאנה — Compare with the discussion on רבי אניאנא in inscription no. 10. This name is not specifically mentioned in the sources; however, it is possible that it appears in the Talmud with a different spelling, e.g., רבי גמליאל בר איניגא[56] and רבי אניני בן סוסי, who lived at the time of Rabbi Judah Ha-Nassî and whom, we are told, knew the correct pronunciation of the divine name.[57]

וש...... — This should probably be completed as ושל plus the effaced name of Rabbi Aniana's brother, though the traces of the letters after the shin as illustrated in fig. 117 leave this interpretation open to doubt.

הקדושים ("the holy ones") — This is the first time in Hebrew epigraphy that this term is applied to a person. Attempts have been made to interpret this word as a reference to sages who died a martyr's death, like the Ten Martyrs. In our opinion, this interpretation seems improbable, though we have no proof to the contrary. It seems more likely that the phrase "the holy ones" should be taken literally, i.e., as just, observant, righteous, pure-hearted, and God-fearing people. It would seemingly appear that "whoever observes the ordinances of the Sages is called holy";[58] however, in fact, very few people in our ancient literature were endowed with this title.

Rabbi Judah Ha-Nassî was called "our holy rabbi (teacher)" because of the loftiness of his spiritual stature.[59] This title was also bestowed upon Rabbi Naḥum bar

Simai because of his extreme puritanism: "Why was Naḥum called the 'holy· of holies' man? The answer given was: because never in his lifetime did he look upon the image on a coin."[60] The reason for this behavior was to avoid seeing the face of the emperor which was stamped on the coin. Urbach has already noted on this point: "There are thus grounds for presuming that those of the Sages buried at Beth She'arim who earned the title "holy ones" regarded statues and images in much the same way as Rabbi Naḥum. It is, therefore, most surprising that, side by side with sarcophagi bearing inscriptions of this kind, we find others adorned with reliefs not only of animals but also of the human face..."[61]

בניו ש.... — This should be completed as [בניו ש]ל רבי[...]; the name of the father of the "holy ones" was effaced.

18. Room III, sarcophagus no. 17 (Pl. XXXVIII, 2)

A single word engraved in large, nicely shaped letters in the center of the plain front of the sarcophagus. It is 30 cm long, and the letters are 3 cm high.

קירילא

This is a transliteration of the Greek name Κύριλλα which was found in catacomb 12, hall B (see p. 74). The masculine form Κύριλλος appears in Hebrew transliterations in different forms: קרלוס,[ק]רילס.[62] Paleographically, this script resembles that of inscription no. 17.

19. The left jamb of the entrance to room IV (fig. 118)

Three lines of a red dipinto. The paint blurred due to the dampness. Each line apparently consisted of a single word. The height of the inscription is 25 cm and the height of the letters is 5–6.5 cm.

קירה
ש..ל.ל
שלום

"The lady Sh..l.l. Peace."

Fig. 118 Inscription no. 19

קירה — For a discussion of this Greek title, meaning "lady," see below, inscriptions nos. 20 and 24. The name in the second line is blurred.

שלום — This word of blessing is very commonly encountered at the end of Jewish epitaphs, though it appears only a few times in our inscriptions.

20. Room XI, the arcosolium in the southern wall (fig. 119)

The inscription is painted in thin red lines below the arcosolium on the left side. The rough rock was smoothed in preparation for the inscription, an exceptional feature for this catacomb. There were originally four lines to the inscription; today, only the top one is barely legible. Apparently the inscription was deliberately obliterated. The inscription is 51 cm long and the letters are 2.5–4 cm high.

מנוחתה שלקירא דומנה

"The resting place of the lady Domna...."

מנוחתה — Literally "her rest" signifies a

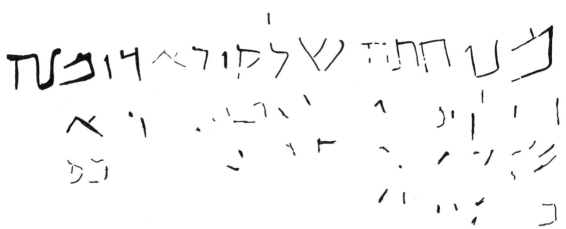

Fig. 119 Inscription no. 20

grave here. Actually it is an abbreviation of משכב מנוחתה or מקום מנוחתה; it may be compared to the Phoenician inscription על משכב נחתי לעלם, which is equivalent to על משכב מנוחתי לעולם ("on my resting place forever").[63] This term has not been encountered in other inscriptions in Palestine though it is frequently found on Jewish epitaphs in Italy: יהי שלום; שלום על מנוחתך על מנוחתו.[64]

קירא — קירא דומנה ("the lady Domna") with an aleph instead of the customary he. This is the first time that the name Domna appears in a Hebrew inscription. Compare with Κυρὰ Δόμνα in a Greek inscription attributed to the synagogue in Ashkelon.[65] The name Δόμνα also appears in a Greco-Jewish inscription found near Shechem.[66] See also the name Δόμνικα on the child's grave in room VIII₂.

21. Room XI, to the right of inscription no. 20, beneath the same arcosolium and above the niche hewn at floor level (fig. 120; Pl. XXXVIII, 1).

Two rows painted in thick red lines. The inscription is 61 cm long and the letters are 3–6 cm high. Because of the deep grooves in the rock, the resulting script is coarse and untidy. Though many letters are blurred, the inscription is still readily decipherable. It runs thus.

מרים בתו שלרבי יונתן
עם שתי בנותיה

"Miriam the daughter of Rabbi Jonathan with her two daughters"

An unusual feature for an inscription of this type is the use of the preposition עם ("with") instead of the conjunction *and*. The most puzzling aspect of this inscription is its location near the previous inscription: Both are written beneath the

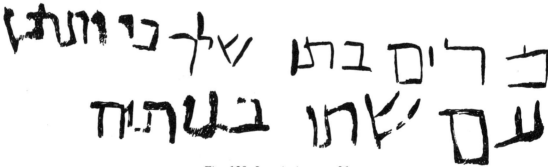

Fig. 120 Inscription no. 21

arcosolium, though it is hardly conceivable that Miriam and her daughters and Kyra Domna were all buried in one and the same grave. The niche at floor level below the arcosolium might offer a possible solution to this problem. Presumably, Domna was first buried in the trough grave inside the arcosolium; later, the grave was emptied and the bones interred in the underlying niche. Miriam and her two daughters were then buried in the empied grave;[67] and, while their epitaph was being written, the previous inscription of Domna was deliberately erased, leaving only faint traces of the first line.

The circumstances leading to the emptying of the grave and the subsequent triple burial are unknown. Quite possibly the mother and her twin daughters died during childbirth; thus, their burial in one grave was permitted. Or perhaps all three died under exceptional circumstances, for example in an epidemic, and were buried secondarily in a common grave. It seems to us that a similar interpretation holds for the inscriptions on ossuaries from the Second Temple period discovered in Jerusalem, for example אתת מתיה ובריה ("the wife of Mathiah and her son");[68] שלום ובנה ("Shalom and her son").[69] In this connection see also the following inscription.

22. Room XXI, sarcophagus no. 114 (fig. 121)

One line painted in red on the plain sarcophagus. The inscription is 74 cm long and the letters are 2 cm high. It was difficult to distinguish the small, fine letters since they were covered by sticky dust. Despite this handicap, the inscription was legible at first sight, except for the last name which is damaged in part. The script is nice; it is

similar in style to that of inscription no. 17. The inscription runs:

זוא ארונן שלשלושת בניו שלרבי יודן
בנו שלרבי מיאשה

"This is the sarcophagus of the three sons of Rabbi Judan the son of Rabbi Miasha..."

זוא —This is a plene spelling, similar to that used in some of the Dead Sea Scrolls; cf. לוא, זאת,זאת, and other examples from manuscript A of the Isaiah Scroll.[70] Alternatively, this might be a case of dittography. On other coffins, the normal spelling זו ארונו is encountered (see also below). On the use of the word ארון in the feminine, compare inscription no. 17.

ארונן ("their coffin") — The nun at the end of the word is accepted usage in Mishnaic Hebrew (cf. with the word עשרין in inscription no. 15).

שלשלושת ("of the three") — The customary contiguous writing of the Beth She'arim inscriptions.

מיאשה —Only the last two letters are perfectly clear. The suggested reading is based on the traces of the first letters. The name Miasha is familiar from the literary sources; the grandson of the Amora Rabbi Joshua ben Levi is called Miasha.[71]

Here again we have a case of a triple burial in a single coffin. Since it cannot be presumed that three adults (nor even three youths or children) were buried in a single sarcophagus, both because of lack of space and because of the injunction against a multiple body burial in one grave, we must assume that here, too, we have another instance of a secondary bone burial. We may reasonably infer that the deceased

Fig. 121 Inscription no. 22

יאַרונ שלרם וושו ־ ד

Fig. 122 Inscription no. 23

were three children who died at the same time — perhaps in an epidemic — and that they were anonymously buried, as was apparently the custom for infants (see inscription no. 21). Similar inscriptions, which do not even mention the number of children, appear on ossuaries discovered in Jerusalem: בני אלעזר ("the sons of El'azar");[72] בני חנן ("the sons of Ḥanan").[73] Since the contents of the "sons" sarcophagus and of the grave of Miriam and her daughters had been removed, we could not determine the age of the deceased.

23. Room XXI, sarcophagus no. 115 (fig. 122)

The inscription is painted in red on the front edge of the gabled cover. The inscription seems to continue on the plain body of the sarcophagus; however, this contention cannot be verified since this sarcophagus is concealed by sarcophagus no. 114. The latter, in turn, is cracked and cannot be moved since it might fall apart. At any rate, the letters in the continuation seem to be very blurred. The letters of the inscription are large and coarse; they are 6–10 cm in height. The preserved length of the inscription is 95 cm.

זו ארונו של רבי יושוע ה...

"This is the sarcophagus of Rabbi Joshua the..."

The spelling יושוע instead of the customary יהושוע found in the rest of the Beth She'arim inscriptions, is noteworthy. The subsequent letter *he* is the beginning of a word which was effaced, perhaps a title.

24. Room XXI, sarcophagus no. 116 (fig. 123; Pl. XXXVIII, 5)

Three lines engraved on the wide vertical front edge of the coffin lid which was found broken. The sarcophagus itself is undecorated. After the excavations, it was trans-

Fig. 123 Inscription no. 24

ferred from its original place (see the plan) to a spot near the opposite wall. The inscription is 80 cm long; the letters are 4–5 cm high.

זו ארו[נ]ה שלקירה מגה
אשתו שלרבי יהושע
בן לווי שלום

"This is the coffin of the lady Mega,
the wife of Rabbi Joshua son of Levi.
Peace."

זו ארו[נ]ה — The nun is missing because of the fracture in the cover. שלקירה ("of the lady") — The Greek title κυρά, meaning "lady," was popular among Jewish women and is quite common in the Greek inscriptions at Beth She'arim.[74] It also appears in an Aramaic inscription from the synagogue in Ḥamat Gader.[75] However, in Hebrew it was found for the first time at Beth She'arim (see also inscriptions nos. 19–20).

מגה — The name is not known. It apparently derives from the Greek titles μέγας, meaning large.[76]

יהושע — The plene spelling of Joshua, customary both in the Beth She'arim inscriptions and in the sources.

לווי ("Levi") — In the first publication of this inscription and of inscription no. 28, the reading of this name was not certain since it was impossible to distinguish clearly between the waw and the yod.[77] It was suggested at that time that the name be read as לוַיי corresponding to the pronunciation בר לואי or בר ליואי, which was synonymous to the names of the Amora Rabbi Joshua ben Levi and Rabbi Zabdi ben Levi.[78]

The late President of the State of Israel, Mr. Itzhak Ben-Zvi, during a discussion, suggested the plene spelling reading לִיוַי, as exemplified by the word הליל in inscription no. 28. Yehoshua Brand, on the other hand, suggested the reading לווי.[79] This, indeed, seems to be the correct reading since it is also corroborated in inscriptions nos. 5 and 6: in one of them the spelling is לוי, and in

the other, לווי, despite the fact that both inscriptions refer to the same person.

Rabbi Joshua ben Levi, one of the outstanding Amoraim, lived in Lod at the end of Rabbi Judah Ha-Nassî's lifetime. The name of his wife is not preserved, nor is her place of burial known. At any rate, the similarity of name alone is insufficient basis for determining whether there is any connection between the Amora and the Rabbi Joshua ben Levi mentioned in this inscription. On the other hand, there seems to be a good basis for assuming that Kyra Mega's husband was interred in the adjacent sarcophagus (no. 115) since it also bears the name רבי יושע ("Rabbi Joshua").

25. Room XXI, the "gable" sarcophagus, no. 103 (fig. 124; Pl. XLIV, 2–3)

Four lines painted in red on the decorated façade of the sarcophagus. The lines of the inscription are not regular and the letters are not uniform in size since they are dispersed among the architectural designs of the gable and the shell. It is difficult to understand the purpose of cramming in the inscription so carelessly when there was adequate empty space on the lower surface of the coffin. The breach in the sarcophagus made by the tomb robbers also destroyed the end of the first line. The inscription is 160 cm long; the letters are 3–8 cm high. It runs:

הארון הזה [של......]
בתו שלרבי יהושע [....]
זכר
צדיקים לברכה

"This sarcophagus (belongs to ...)
the daughter of Rabbi Joshua ... (May)
the memory of the just be blessed."

Line 1. הארון הזה, the masculine form, in contrast to the feminine form found in the previous inscriptions. The continuation of the line to the left of the gable was obliterated.

Line 2. The end of this line was also to

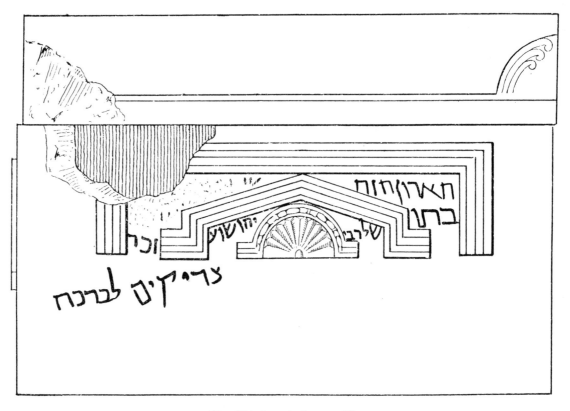

Fig. 124 Inscription no. 25

the left of the gable. In this small area there was room only for a short word, probably the name of Rabbi Joshua's father (Levi?).

Lines 3–4 זכר צדיקים לברכה — This wording, taken from Proverbs 10:7 ("the memory of the just is blessed") appears here for the first time in an ancient Hebrew epitaph in Palestine. (It also appears on sarcophagus no. 26; see below.) This seems to be the earliest example of the use of this phrase as a blessing for the dead. It is also encountered in Hebrew burial inscriptions from Venosa in Italy, dating to the ninth century.[80]

Professor Lieberman was of the opinion that Palestinian Jews did not customarily use the title צדיק for a person, neither in life nor in death.[81] This view was based mainly on the absence of this title from the inscriptions discovered in the earlier excavations at Beth She'arim. He noted that in the Diaspora, on the contrary, this custom

was quite prevalent. In Zunz's estimation, the blessing "may the memory of the just be blessed" is very late.[82]

The name of the daughter buried in this coffin has been obliterated. However, the father's name, Rabbi Joshua, is preserved. It seems very likely that he may be identified with the Rabbi Joshua mentioned in inscriptions nos. 24 and 25. The short words בן לוי could just have fitted into the limited space after the name *Joshua*. If this conjecture is correct, then there must have been at least three sarcophagi belonging to one family in this room: the father, Rabbi Joshua ben Levi (sarcophagus no. 115); his wife, Kyra Mega (sarcophagus no. 116); and their daughter, whose name is unknown (sarcophagus no. 103).[83]

26. Room XXI, the "shell" sarcophagus (no. 117, fig. 125)

Four lines inscribed on the plain surface, between the two niches of the decorated

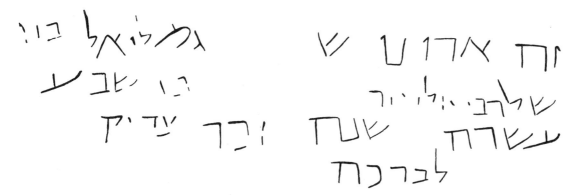

Fig. 125 Inscription no. 26

façade of the coffin. During the process of removing the dirt from the coffin, it was still possible to distinguish the thin red lines of the letters; however, they have since disappeared entirely. The inscription is 61 cm long; the letters are 2–3 cm in height.

זה ארונו ש[לרבי] גמליאל בנו
שלרבי אליעזר [שמת] בן שבע
עשרה שנה זכר צדיק
לברכה   4

"This is the sarcophagus of [Rabbi] Gamaliel the son of Rabbi Eliezer [who died] at the age of seventeen years. (May) the memory of the just be blessed."

Line 1 — The gap in the word in the middle of the line was completed as [לרבי]ש in accordance with the conventional phrasing in the other inscriptions. The question arises whether a young man of seventeen could indeed have been a rabbi, or whether the title *rabbi* could also have been conferred posthumously as a sign of respect. I put this question both to Prof. Lieberman and to Prof. Urbach, and both ruled out the second possibility. They maintain that it is perfectly conceivable that a brilliant young scholar of this age could have been endowed with the title *rabbi*. Nevertheless, we cannot preclude the possibility that Gamaliel might have had a different title, even though we cannot suggest a reasonable alternative. This is the third time that the name Gamaliel appears in our inscriptions.

Line 2 — The suggested introduction of the word שמת in the middle of this line seems quite likely in view of the context of the inscription; compare also with inscription no. 15. However, it should be noted that there is more space in the line than is required for this word. Therefore, it is very possible than the word was longer, for example שנפטר ("who passed away"). In any case, this remains an open question.

Lines 3–4 — On the phrase זכר צדיק לברכה see inscription no. 25.

27. Room XV, on a fragment of rock.

Traces were found of an inscription of at least three lines which were originally painted in red on one of the walls (fig. 126). At present, only one word is complete; its letters are 4 cm high (fig. 126).

יהודה

Judah

28. Room XVI, sarcophagus no. 89 (fig. 127; Pl. XXXVIII, 4)

Two lines painted in red on the vertical edge of the undecorated coffin cover. The inscription is 134 cm long; the letters are 3–5 cm high.

זו ארונו שלרבי הליל בנו שלרבי לווי שעשה
את המערה הזו

"This is the coffin of Rabbi Hillel, the son of Rabbi Levi, who made this cave."

Fig. 126 Inscription no. 27

זו ארונו — In catacomb 20, the term ארון ("sarcophagus") appears seven times altogether: five times in the feminine, and twice in the masculine.

הליל — The plene spelling of הֲלֵל (cf. with inscription no. 16).

לווי — For a discussion of this spelling of Levi, see above, inscriptions nos. 6 and 24.

שעשה את המערה הזו ("who made this cave") — This ending is unique among the Beth She'arim inscriptions. It is particularly noteworthy since this is the first time that the name of a person directly associated with the hewing of the cave is mentioned. This phrase may be explained in several ways, depending upon the specific interpretation of the words עשה and מערה.

(a) עשה — in the sense of made with his own hands, executed the work, initiated the work, or was responsible for the work, on the one hand; or in the sense of donated or contributed, on the other.

(b) מערה — could mean the whole cave or catacomb, one of its branches, or only the single burial room in which the sarcophagus was found.

In the ancient Palestinian synagogues, there are many inscriptions similarly worded, which refer to people who "made" עשו (in Aramaic, עבדו,פעלו) one part or another of the synagogue. Most scholars believe that these inscriptions should be interpreted as donation inscriptions, i.e., as acknowledgements. S. Klein [85] proved decisively that in the Talmud the words עשה and עבד were used as technical terms meaning a contribution for a building component of a synagogue. E.L. Sukenik[86] and others followed suit. They attributed all the inscriptions of this type to benefactors and classified them as inscriptions commemorating donations of money or valuables.

At this point, a new epigraphic discovery came as a warning against sweeping generalizations. This is the story behind it: In the nineteenth century, a Hebrew inscription was discovered on the lintel of the small synagogue at Kfar Bar'am (part of the inscription is presently at the Louvre in Paris). It runs: יהי שלום במקום הזה ובכל מקומות ישראל יוסה הלוי בן לוי עשה השקוף הזה תבא ברכה במע[ש]יו שלו[ם] "May there be peace in this place and in all the places of Israel. Jose the Levite, son of Levi, made this lintel. May blessing come upon his works. Peace."[87] Jose the Levite was customarily viewed as the donator of the lintel whose name was publicly commemorated for this reason.[88] At the beginning of this century, a fragment of a lintel from a synagogue was discovered at 'Alma in Upper Galilee. It bore the first part of an inscription: יהי שלום על המקום הזה ועל כל מקומות עמו ישראל "May there be peace upon this place and upon the places of his people Israel."[89] Surprisingly enough, in 1957 the second half of this lintel was discovered, bearing the continuation of the inscription in Aramaic: ...א[מן סלה, אנה

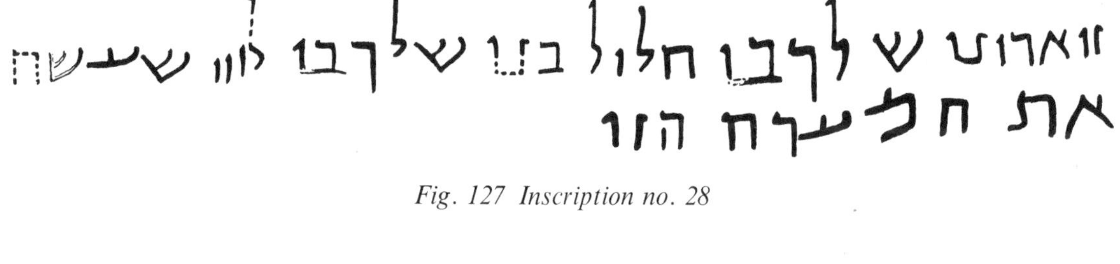

וזאורו ש לרבו חלול בז שלדבו לווי ששה את חלערה הזו

Fig. 127 Inscription no. 28

יוסה ברלוי האומנה דעבד ה[דה שקופה]
"...Amen selah! I, Jose son of Levi, am the artisan who made [this lintel]."[90]

From the contents of this inscription, it emerges that the man who "made" the lintel in Kfar Bar'am and the man who "made" the lintel at 'Alma are one and the same person, the difference being that in the 'Alma inscription he speaks of himself in the first person and appends the title *artisan* to his name. Therefore, the man who commemorated his name in both these inscriptions was the actual builder of the lintels and not the contributor, as was formerly maintained. The fact that the inscriptions were so conspicuously placed above the entranceway is evidence that the artisan, and the whole community, took great pride in his achievements.

In view of this discovery, other inscriptions bearing this formula should be re-examined. Such an investigation might reveal that several of the purported contributors were in reality craftsmen who commemorated their names — as did the artisans Marinos and his son Ḥanina in the Greek inscription on the mosaic floor at Beth Alpha, where it is clearly stated that they carried out the work.

For our purposes, particular importance is attached to the interpretation of the inscription from the synagogue at Umm el 'Amed in Galilee: יועזר חזנה ושמעון אחוי עבדו הדן תרא דמרי שומיא "Yo'ezer the Ḥazan and Shim'on his brother made this gate of the Lord of Heaven."[91]

Since the inscription is engraved on a stone which is in no way associated with the gateway, "the gateway of the Lord of Heaven" was interpreted as a synonym for "synagogue."[92] The cantor was obviously not a builder; nor can a synagogue official be assumed to have built the synagogue with his own money. It seems, therefore, that the two brothers were leading figures in the synagogue and that they were the initiators of its construction.[93]

In all probability, the inscription from Beth She'arim should be similarly interpreted. The word עשה in this inscription cannot mean "contributed" or "donated" since the hewing of catacombs at Beth She'arim was not a charitable, but a commercial, enterprise based on the sale of burial places to Jews from Palestine and from the Diaspora. Rabbi Hillel cannot have been the artisan who hewed the cave with his own hands or even the contractor for this project since he was a rabbi, the son of a rabbi. It seems far more likely that Rabbi Hillel was a leader of the community or one of the heads of the burial society, and that he initiated the hewing of the cave which later became one of the most important public catacombs at the necropolis of Beth She'arim.

What is the connotation of the words המערה הזו ("this cave")? Do they refer to the whole large and ramified catacomb, or to a part of it? In the Mishnah (Baba Bathra, 6, 8) there is a description of the method of hewing burial caves: "And makes a courtyard at the entrance of the cave ... opening on to the courtyard two caves, one on one side and one on the other. Rabbi Shim'on says — four caves, in each of the four directions. Rabbi Shim'on ben Gamaliel says — it all depends upon the rock." It appears, therefore, that the word מערה refers to the particular part of the catacomb which we call a "hall," i.e., the unit of the catacomb into which one of the entrances leads from the courtyard. In our specific, case, this is the entire catacomb. Thus, Rabbi Hillel should be credited with the execution of the entire catacomb, including all its component branches.

It is quite possible that the use of the term מערה was not so unequivocal and that one of the branches of the central hall which consisted of a few rooms (in this case, rooms XV–XVII) might also be called a "cave." Perhaps the author of the inscription referred only to room XVI (where the sarcophagus stands), which may have been hewn at the request of Rabbi Hillel ben

Levi as a family tomb. Rabbi Hillel himself was buried in the simplest of coffins; his dignity was stressed only by the placement of the coffin on a hewn pedestal. This proves that the location for the coffin was deter-mined in advance since the pedestal was doubtlessly hewn contemporaneously with the floor. All the other pedestals encounter-ed were built out of stone, *after* the hewing of the rooms.

5   THE PALEOGRAPHY OF THE INSCRIPTIONS (fig. 128)

The inscriptions discussed here are impor-tant not only for their texts but also for their paleography. This is the largest group of Hebrew inscriptions from the early centuries following the destruction of the Second Temple which were found at one site in Palestine (except, of course, for the Bar Kochba documents and letters which were discovered in the Judean Desert). Though written by different hands, they illustrate the various writing styles custom-arily employed during this period.

Of the twenty-eight Hebrew and Aramaic inscriptions described in this chapter, three are engraved on stone sarcophagi (nos. 15, 18, and 24), three are incised in the rock (nos. 4, 13, and 14), and one is inscribed on the soft rock with a thin stick dipped in paint (no. 16); all the rest are dipinti, i.e., they were written with a brush and paint on the rock walls or on the sarcophagi. The technique of writing obviously affects the form of the script. Inscriptions engraved with a chisel are lapidary in character, whereas inscriptions brushed on with paint are cursive to various degrees. Other factors influence the script as well, e.g., the use of a thick or a thin paint brush, or a smooth or rough background. Finally, the idiosyn-cracies of each individual's handwriting have a predominant effect on the style of the script. It should also be borne in mind that most of the inscriptions were probably not written by professionals but by members of the family, undertakers, and others.

A professional scribe must have executed the deep engraving of inscription no. 15 since the script is lapidary, i.e., the letters are straight, square, and uniform. The only exception is the wavy shape of the final nun. Lapidary script is intrinsically conservative in character and retains its forms over a long period of time. Thus, most of the letters in this inscription do not differ from letters in first-century inscriptions (e.g., on ossuaries). Comparisons with second-century lapidary inscriptions cannot be made since none have been discovered. Only in the third-century script (from syna-gogues and tombs) do certain changes begin to appear. The most noteworthy alteration occurs in the he where the left vertical stroke rises above the horizontal line.[94]

Inscription no. 18 is also a fine example of lapidary script. No. 24, despite the fact that it is engraved on stone, is not purely lapidary but incipiently cursive in character.

Special attention should be paid to the refined script of inscription no. 22: the letters are relatively small and are written with a fine brush. The slant of the script in the direction of the writing, the ligature of the waws and yods with the preceding bet and nun, and the regular cursive script are all evidence of a trained scribe's hand. This script bears a strong affinity to the formal or semi-formal script commonly encountered in the Judean Desert scrolls of the first century C.E., except that the execution of the Beth She'arim inscriptions is simpler. We have already discussed the connection between the spelling הוא in inscription no. 22 and the identical spelling in the scrolls. Paleographically speaking, this inscription could be attributed to the first century C.E.; the context, however, calls for a late second-century dating, at the earliest. In-scription no. 17 is similar in style, except

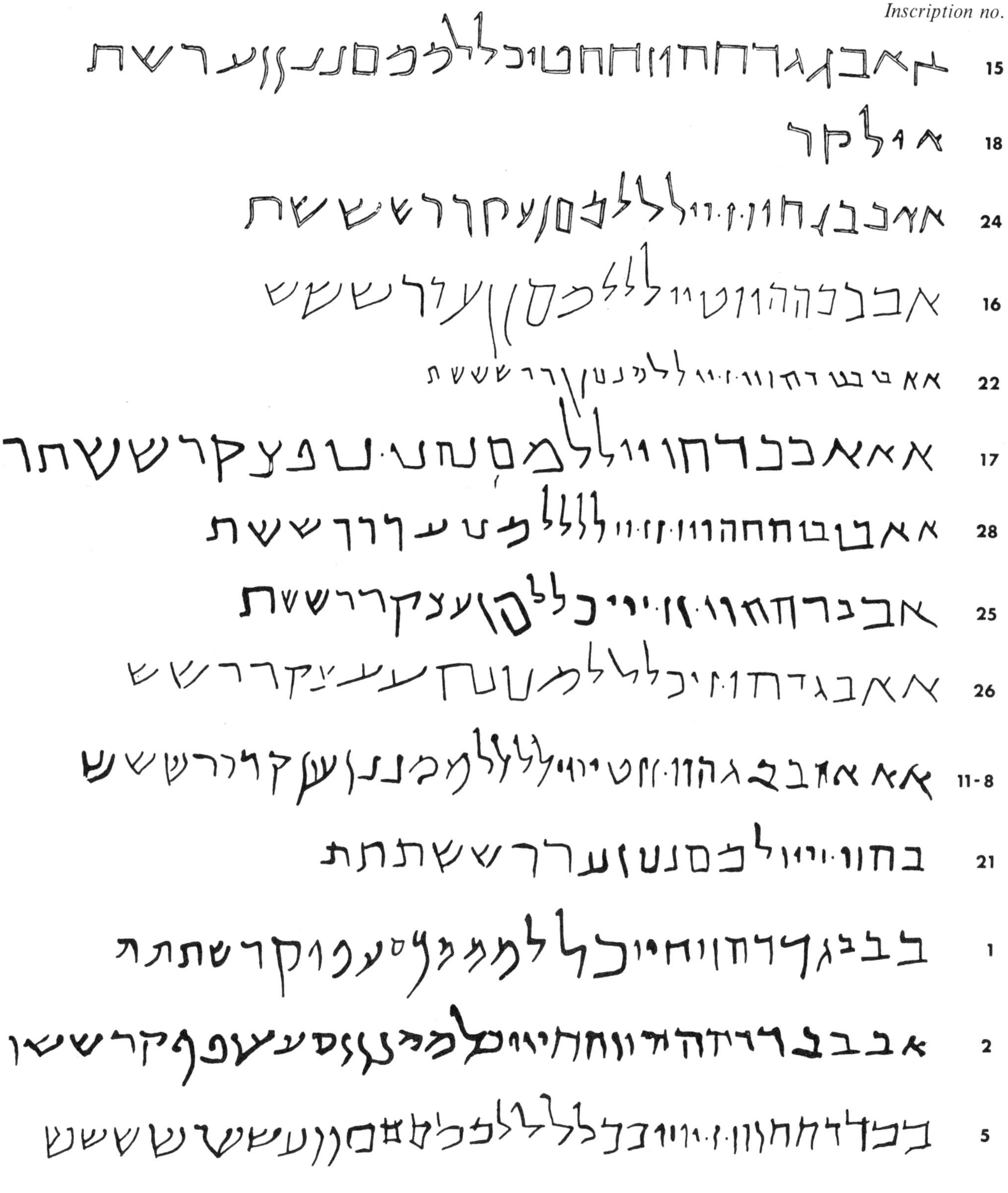

Inscription no.

	Inscription no.
תארשצנסמכללכיוטחהחזוהדגבאת	15
קרלוא	18
תשרשקרקנעסבזללויוחנזבבצא	24
ששרלעכןסכללטיוההזכבא	16
תשש רדקנגילללויוידוחדזעטאא	22
תרשיקפצטטעמסמללויוחדרבבכאאא	17
תששרעטעכללולויזוחההורטבאא	28
תשרקעןבוללכייוחדחרבגבא	25
ש רקעצ עטעמללויכיוחדגבאא	26
ששרירקעשנזמללעיולליויטיוההזבבאא אא	8-11
תתששרעןטסמכלויוווחב	21
תתשרקועעסמגמללכייוחדדגבבב	1
ושרקפפעעסנגנמלטסוייוחחחדהדיורבבא	2
ששששענמטבלללויווחדחחחלדבבב	5

Fig. 128 Alphabetical chart of the inscriptions

that it has much larger letters. These two inscriptions appear to be the earliest of this group. Inscription no. 28 still bears some resemblance to the two previous inscriptions, except that its letters have a vertical stance, like those of nos. 20, 25, and 26. All these inscriptions may be attributed to various periods in the third century C.E.

Different forms of semi-cursive script may be discerned in the rest of the inscriptions. This applies particularly to inscriptions nos. 1, 2, 8, and 9. Though their script is similar to that of several second-century documents and letters discovered in Wadi Murabba'at, they should be attributed to various phases of the third century.

Among the individual letters, the following are noteworthy: *(a)* the special form of the aleph in inscription no. 9, an example of which was also found on an ossuary from the first century C.E.;[96] *(b)* the hooked 'ayin in the third line of inscription no. 2, which has a parallel in one of the second-century C.E. documents from Wadi Murbba'at;[97] *(c)* the zayin of inscription no. 10 with the characteristic right turn of its head; and *(d)* the archaic nun of inscription no. 1, which apparently has no parallel in the inscriptions of this period.

It is more difficult to classify inscriptions nos. 5 and 6 because of careless writing. As the forms of the letters seem more developed, they are the latest and probably date to the first half of the fourth century C.E.

NOTES

1 *Beth She'arim*, I, pp. 193–209.

2 For a detailed discussion on the Greek inscriptions discovered in catacombs 12–21, see: *Beth She'arim*, II, pp. 121–186. Only four of the inscriptions that appear here are not included there: catacomb 13, the lintel of hall F (p. 37); catacomb 13, hall G, room I (p. 38); catacomb 19, the marble tablet (p. 82; Pl. XXIX, 5); the courtyard of catacomb 20, the marble tablet (p. 83; Pl. L, 4).

3 B. Lifshitz (*Beth She'arim*, II, p. 221) uses incorrect statistics in claiming that only seven Hebrew inscriptions were found, thereby understimating their value.

4 Y. Kutscher, "Lashon Ḥazal," *Ḥanoch Yalon Jubilee Volume*, Jerusalem, 1963, p. 249 (Hebrew).

5 Baba Qama, 83a; Sotah, 49b.

6 For the most recent criticism see: *Beth She'arim*, II, pp. 183–221.

7 See: *CIJ*, I–II.

8 Y. Kutscher, *Sefer Yerushalayim*, pp. 349–357 (Hebrew).

9 *CIJ*, II, nos. 892–960.

10 E. L. Sukenik, "Jewish Tombstones from Zo'ar," *Kedem*, II (1945), pp. 83–88 (Hebrew).

11 *CIJ*, II, no. 892.

12 J. T. Milik, "Trois tombeaux juifs," *Liber Annus*, VII (1956–57), p. 235.

13 The translation follows the revised interpretation by Fitzmayer: J. A. Fitzmayer, "The Aramaic Qorban Inscription from Jebel Ḥallet et-Turi and Mark 7:11; Matt. 15:5," *Journal of Biblical Literature*, LXXVIII (1959), pp. 60–65.

14 *Beth She'arim*, II, p. 112, no. 129.

15 The desecration of tombs for the purpose of plunder or secondary usage was a very frequent occurrence in ancient times. The amount of harm that it caused during the Roman period is made evident by the Imperial law enacted to prevent the desecration of tombs and the removal of bones from tombs in order to bury other bodies instead. See: *Supplementum Epigraphicum Graecum*, III (1929), p. 13.

16 *Beth She'arim*, II, nos. 129, 134, 162.

17 See: A. Parrot, *Malédictions et violations de tombes*, Paris, 1939.

18 See: G. A. Cooke, *A Text-Book of North-Semitic Inscriptions*, Oxford, 1903, no. 4, ll. 3–8.

19 N. Avigad, The Epitaph of a Royal Steward from Siloam Village, *IEJ*, III (1953), pp. 137–152.

20 *CIJ*, II, nos. 1334, 1359b.

21 *Ibid.*, no. 1300.

22 G. A. Cooke, *A Text-Book of North-Semitic Inscriptions*, Oxford, 1903, no. 145, ll. 3–4.

23 And not above the inscription ו[ס]קיאֵﬠ as mistakenly stated in *Beth She'arim*, II, p. 121, no. 133.

24 Cooke, *NSI*, no. 16.

25 *Ibid.,* no. 5, ll. 3–4.

26 *CIJ,* II, no. 1413.

27 *Ibid.,* no. 1414.

28 M. D. Cassuto, "The Ninth Century Hebrew Inscriptions at Venosa," *Kedem,* II (1948), p. 105 (Hebrew).

29 Y. Yadin, *IEJ,* II (1962), p. 256; also see there, note 50, a reference to H. Yalon on this problem in his introduction to *Sefer Mo'ed, Six Books of the Mishnah,* Jerusalem–Tel Aviv, 1952, p. 26 (Hebrew).

30 Goodenough, III, no. 725.

31 S. Lieberman, *Greek in Jewish Palestine,* New York, 1924, pp. 176*f.*

32 Y. Yadin, *IEJ,* XI (1961), p. 44: תשלחון לי ית אלעזר בר חלה שוה קדם שבת "Send…just before the Sabbath."

33 See the inscription אשר על הבית from the First Temple period, which concludes with the words אשר יפתח את זאת (see above, n. 19).

34 *CIJ,* II, no. 1288.

35 In the previous excavations at Beth She'arim, the term *Rabbi* was found only once. Mazar (*Beth She'arim,* I, pp. 199–201) then tried to interpret it as the shortened form of "Ribi" because he found the terms ʽΡιβ and ʽΡιββί several times in the Greek inscriptions (*Beth She'arim,* II, nos. 41, 45, 61, 202, 208); in Hebrew he found ביר'ב' (Biribi), but not once did he find ʽΡαβί. Now Mazar has suggested that there may be a substantial difference between the titles ʽΡαββί and ʽΡιββί.

36 Cf.: Y. Kutscher, *The Language and Linguistic Background to the Complete Scroll of Isaiah from the Dead Sea Scrolls,* Jerusalem, 1959, p. 48 (Hebrew).

37 *Eretz-Israel,* IV (1956), p. 93 (Hebrew).

38 *Beth She'arim,* II, no. 175.

39 Goodenough, *Symbols,* II, no. 65; III, no. 871.

40 *Beth She'arim,* I, p. 200.

41 *Beth She'arim,* II, no. 28.

42 See p. 103.

43 *Eretz-Israel,* IV (1956), p. 95 (Hebrew).

44 B. Lifshitz, *ZDPV,* LXXVIII (1962), p. 71.

45 D. Chwolson, *Corpus Inscriptionum Hebraicarum,* St. Petersburg, 1882, no. 36, pp. 134*f.* The late President, Mr. Itzhak Ben-Zvi, who visited the Beth She'arim excavations close to the time of the discovery of the inscription, was the first to suggest a completion for it and drew my attention to the inscription from Tiflis.

46 J. H. Greenstone, "Two Memorial Lists from the Genizah," *Jewish Quarterly Review,* NS I, 1910–11, p. 48.

47 Semaḥoth 13, 8.

48 *CIJ,* II, no. 951.

49 *Ibid.,* no. 892.

50 *Ibid.,* no. 893

51 *Beth She'arim,* I, p. 200.

52 Sages bearing matriarchal names: R. Mari bar Rachel (Bab. Talmud *Shabbat,* 154a), Abba Shaul ben Miriam (Bab. Talmud *Ketuboth,* 7a), etc.

53 B. Liftshitz, *ZDPV,* LXXVIII (1962), p. 71.

54 H. Donner-W. Röllig, *Kanaanäische und aramäische Inschriften,* Wiesbaden, 1962, nos. 1, 9, 11, 13.

55 ותהא ארוני נקובה (Jer. Talmud, Kelaim 9, 32a). ארון שהיא רחבה מלמטן וצרה מלמעלן והמת בתוכה (Oholoth 9, 15)

56 Pesaḥim, 1a.

57 See also: E. E. Urbach, *IEJ,* IX, pp. 149–165, 229–245.

58 Yebamoth, 20a.

59 For the tradition explaining the term "holy" see: Urbach, *IEJ,* IX.

60 Jer. Talmud Avodah Zarah 3, 42b; Koheleth Rabba 9, 10.

61 *Eretz-Israel,* V, p. 190 (Hebrew).

62 *Beth She'arim,* I, pp. 197–199.

63 Cooke, *NSI,* no. 16.

64 *CIJ,* II, nos. 558, 622, 630.

65 *Ibid.,* no. 964.

66 *Ibid.,* no. 1169.

67 On the evacuation of tombs the Talmud states: "Come and hear! Thus we see that there are three kinds of graves: A grave that has been found; a known grave; and one which injures the public. A grave that has been found may be cleared; when cleared, the place thereof is (levitically) clean and permitted for use. A known grave may not be cleared; if it has been, the spot is unclean and forbidden for use. A grave which injures the public may be cleared; if it has been, the place thereof is clean but may not be used." (Bab. Talmud Sanhedrin, 47b; Semahoth 14). It is surprising that in the Baraitha (Semahoth 13) it is asserted that כוך שפינהו אסור בהנאה ("A vacated kokh should not be reused"). This ruling opposes one of the main reasons for bone collection, i.e., the evacuation of bones from the kokhim and their deposition in ossuaries in order to allow the continued burial in the small family kokh cave.

68 *CIJ*, II, no. 1362a.

69 *Dominus Flevit*, no. 9.

70 Kutscher, *Scroll of Isaiah...*, p. 509.

71 A. Hyman, *Toledoth Tannaim Ve-Amoraim*, Jerusalem, 1964, p. 881 (Hebrew).

72 *CIJ*, II, no. 1357.

73 *Ibid.*, no. 1360.

74 *Beth She'arim*, II, nos. 39, 57, 70, 191.

75 *CIJ*, II, no. 858, I, 1.

76 Cf. the masculine name Μεγάλος (*CIJ*, II, no. 889) that M. Schwabe interprets as Μέγας and even cites it in the Hebrew transliteration of מיגס as in the Hebrew literature, *BIES*, II (1934), pp. 55–57 (Hebrew).

77 *Eretz-Israel*, VI (1960), p. 62 (Hebrew).

78 Hyman, *Toledoth Tannaim Ve-Amoraim*, p. 379.

79 "Haaretz," 12.2.1961, p. 10 (Hebrew).

80 *CIJ*, I, nos. 625, 629, 635.

81 Lieberman, *Greek in Jewish Palestine*, pp. 69–70.

82 In his book, *Zur Geschichte und Literatur*, Berlin, 1845, L. Zunz comments on the phrase "may the memory of the righteous be blessed": "Es hat lange gedauert bevor aus dieser Bibelstelle eine stehende Formed wurde. Sie tritt zuerst im zehnten Jahrhundert auf." I thank E. E. Urbach for drawing my attention to this source.

83 The genealogy that B. Lifshitz (*ZDPV*, LXXVIII [1962], p. 71) reconstructed seems doubtful since he incorporated names from inscriptions found in other rooms.

84 Cf.: Y. Kutscher, "Lashon Hazal," *Hanoch Yalon Jubilee Volume*, Jerusalem, 1963, p. 257 (Hebrew).

85 S. Klein, "Inscriptions from Ancient Synagogues in Palestine," *Bulletin of the Institute of Jewish Studies*, II, Jerusalem, 1925, pp. 23–48. On p. 34 Klein quotes from the Jerusalem Talmud, Shekalim 5, 49b: רבי אבון עבד אילין תרעייה דסדרא רבא ("Rabbi Abun made these gates of the Great Beth Midrash"). He also cites the story of Antoninus who "made" a menorah to the synagogue: "Rabbi heard and said: Blessed be the Lord who planted the desire in his heart to donate a menorah for the synagogue." There is also an additional epigraphic evidence that the Jews used this phrase in Greek. In the Nikanor inscription engraved on an ossuary, the name of Nikanor who "made" (ποιήσαντος) the doors (of the Temple) is mentioned, and the meaning is of course "donated."

86 Sukenik, *Ancient Synagogues*, pp. 69 *ff*.

87 *Ibid.*, p. 71; Klein, "Inscriptions...," p. 28.

88 Klein, "Inscriptions...," p. 30, suggested that Jose the Levite was a professional artist; nevertheless, he interprets the word עשה as "charitable donation".

89 Klein, "Inscriptions...," p. 30; *CIJ*, II, no. 973.

90 Ruth Hestrin, "A New Aramaic Inscription from 'Alma," *BRF*, III, pp. 62 *ff*.

91 N. Avigad, "An Aramaic Inscription from the Synagogue at Umm el-'Amed in Galilee," *BRF*, III (1960), pp. 62 *ff*.

92 Cf. also in Genesis 28:17: "This is none other than the house of God, and this is the gate of Heaven."

93 On the construction of a synagogue under the auspices of the leaders of the congregation, see the inscription from Nabratein (Kefar Naburiyeh): N. Avigad, *BRF*, III (1960), pp. 49 *ff*.

94 Cf., for example, the he in the synagogue inscriptions at Dura-Europos, attributed to the third century C.E.: C. H. Kraeling, *The Excavations at Dura-Europos, VIII, 1: The Synagogue*, New Haven, 1956, Pl. XLI.

95 P. Benoit, J. T. Milik, & R. de Vaux, *Discoveries in the Judean Desert*, II, Oxford, 1961; *idem, La Grotte de Murabba'at*, Pls. XLV–XLVI; nos. 42–43.

96 See above, n. 34.

97 Benoit, Milik, de Vaux, *La Grotte de Murabba'at*, fig. 23; N. Avigad, "The Palaeography of the Dead Sea Scrolls and Related Documents," *Aspects of the Dead Sea Scrolls*, Jerusalem, 1957, p. 83, column XXX.

CHAPTER V

THE TYPOLOGY AND CHRONOLOGY OF THE CATACOMBS

The data available which could be of assistance in establishing the dates of the catacombs discussed here is quite inadequate, both in respect to absolute dates and to relative chronology. The systematic pillage of the tombs; the scarcity of vessels and their discovery in a disturbed context; the consequent lack of a characteristic section of all the phases of the catacomb use; inscriptions with no indications of date and the absence of coins or other artifacts of chronological value; and the total lack of any external evidence which might be of assistance in dating, all contribute to the difficulty of establishing precise chronological conclusions. In our analysis of the chronology of the catacombs, therefore, we must rely on two other sources of information: *(a)* the typology and architectural style of the tombs; *(b)* the results of the earlier excavations at Beth She'arim which yielded several important chronological data.

(a) Before discussing the typology of the Beth She'arim tombs, we should briefly review the development of tomb types in Palestine, since they are the product of a long historical evolution of which the Beth She'arim tombs are an inseparable component.

In the second century B.C.E., due to foreign influences, burial tombs with kokhim hewn into the walls began to appear in Palestine. They resulted from the desire to make burial procedures as economical and convenient as possible. In a room only 4×4 cubits (circa 2×2 m) in size, nine kokhim could be hewn: three in each wall, except for the entrance wall. The kokh room became the typical form of a Jewish family tomb in the centuries immediately prior, and subsequent, to the destruction of the Second Temple. For Jews the use of the kokh is associated with the custom of bone collecting for secondary burial. The bones gathered from kokhim were usually deposited in stone ossuaries; however, sometimes they were placed in small niches specially hewn into the wall. The combination of several adjacent kokh rooms resulted in the formation of a catacomb which belonged to large, wealthy families.[1]

Arcosolia began to appear sporadically during the first century B.C.E. The deceased was placed on the arcosolium bench, sometimes in a coffin or in an ossuary. Frequently a room with three arcosolia, one in each wall, was hewn as part of a kokh cave; occasionally, arcosolium rooms were cut out separately. A room of this type was more expensive because it contained only three burial places instead of six or nine loculi; it was, therefore, considered more dignified.

During this period, the idea arose of interring the deceased in a trough grave hewn in the arcosolium instead of in a coffin deposited on the bench. Sometimes the wall of the trough was decorated like a coffin, thus creating a "coffin" contiguous with the rock wall. Examples of this kind are rare, but the idea caught on, and in the course of time the number of trough graves increased. From the third century C.E. on, the trough grave became the prevalent type of burial, although kokhim were still used intermittently.

At this point of development, each arcosolium still contained only a single trough grave. However, since such utilization was uneconomical, people began to think of more efficient methods of exploiting the available wall area. Thus, two or three trough graves were hewn in each arcosolium, one behind the other. With experience, it became obvious that it was better to cut out the three trough graves perpendicular to the arcosolium since it ensured access to each grave. Often a fourth trough grave was added behind them, parallel to the arcosolium. In an arcosolium of this type — where another one or two trough graves could be added — the area was utilized to best advantage: In a room only 2×2 m in size, it was possible to hew at least twelve graves, four in each wall. Tombs of this type were frequently used even in the Byzantine period.

(b) The first excavations at Beth She'arim enabled Mazar to reach important conclusions about the chronology of the buildings in the city and the catacombs in the necropolis.[2] Mazar discerns five main building periods:

Period I. From the Herodian period to the first half of the second century C.E. Only one kokh cave belonging to this period was discovered.

Period II. From the second half of the second century to the beginning of the third century C.E. This period, consisting of Rabbi Judah Ha-Nassî's lifetime and the following generation, was the "Golden Age" of Beth She'arim. Attributed to this period are the public buildings, outstanding for their high quality of construction, and the mausoleum above catacomb 11, considered one of the finest examples of Jewish architecture.

Period III, Phase A. From the middle of the third to the beginning of the fourth century. The synagogue was erected during this phase.

Period III, Phase B. From the first half of the fourth century up to the destruction of Beth She'arim in 352 C.E. This date was established on the basis of a cache of 1,200 coins, found in one of the buildings, which does not contain a single coin later than the middle of the fourth century C.E.

Most of the catacombs are attributed to Period III.

Period IV. The Byzantine period: a time of decline and retrenchment.

Period V. The Arab period: temporary settlement.

This basic classification has stood the test of later excavations conducted by Mazar in 1956 in the southern part of the city.[3] They also proved that Period II was an era of extensive construction. Remains of a basilica, 40 m long, were unearthed. The building was constructed of excellent drafted stone and was built in the same style as the public buildings in the northern part of the city. This excavation also brought to light new information on two early periods in the occupational history of Beth She'arim: Iron Age II (the ninth–seventh centuries B.C.E.) and the Persian period. In our discussion, we shall not be concerned with these data — interesting as they may be in their own right — or with periods IV and V.

The *terminus ante quem* of the catacombs is the date of the destruction of Beth She'arim in the year 352 C.E. This assumption is corroborated by the fact that, in general, none of the finds discovered in the tombs was attributable to a later date. However, in the early excavations of the catacombs, an important point of absolute chronology was revealed which provides us with a *terminus ante quem* for certain tombs from the period prior to the destruction of Beth She'arim, i.e., tombs in which Jews from Palmyra were interred. There is reason to believe that after 272–73 C.E., when Palmyra was destroyed by the Roman armies, the burial of Palmyrene Jews at Beth She'arim doubtlessly came to an end.

In catacomb 1, halls E, G, and K contain graves of Palmyrene Jews.[4] In hall G, the inscriptions testify that a Palmyrene family was buried there for four generations.[5] In Mazar's opinion, if the latest possible date for the burial of a Palmyrene Jew was 272 C.E., this implies that the hall was hewn before the middle of the third century C.E. In a private conversation, Mazar suggested 230 C.E. as a tentative date.

This and other halls in which Palmyrene Jews were interred are laid out[6] according to the stereotyped Beth She'arim plan: a row of rooms containing arcosolia with four trough graves, three longitudinal and one transverse. Thus, it is evident that this plan—characteristic of most of the Beth She'arim catacombs—had already been initiated by the first half of the third century C.E. However, it is impossible to differentiate between early and late arcosolia since they persisted at Beth She'arim until the end of the burial period in the catacombs.

On the basis of structural considerations, it can be established that hall M[7] antedates the tombs of the Palmyrene Jews, and that it was the first hall to be hewn in catacomb 1. Mazar attributes it to the beginning of the third century and assumes that its hewing[8] began at an even earlier date, approximately 220 C.E. The same date is assigned to halls N and O.[9] These halls have a characteristic plan consisting of central rooms from which secondary arcosolium rooms branch off. Among these arcosolia, both kokhim and single trough graves are also commonly found. Mazar contends that these spacious halls were hewn before it became necessary to save space, but otherwise they have no significant differences from the later style and are similar to hall K of this catacomb and hall A of catacomb 4, both connected to Palmyrene families.

Catacomb 11, above which the remains of the mausoleum were found, is attributed to Period II, i.e., the beginning of the third century. The plan of this catacomb is entirely different from that of the above-mentioned catacombs.[10] Its spacious rooms were intended mainly for sarcophagi; sometimes they contain no hewn graves whatsoever. Occasionally they have only arcosolia with a single grave or kokhim. The more advanced arcosolium with several trough graves is completely absent here. The architectural style also is definitely an early element.

The earliest type of tomb is the kokh cave, attributed to the Herodian era (first century C.E.). This cave, located near catacomb 1 was partially destroyed during the hewing of hall N in the first half of the third century C.E.[11]

Catacombs 12—23 and 31

To what extent can we establish a chronological framework for our catacombs in view of the development of tombs in Palestine just described above? Also, what relation do these catacombs bear to the typological/chronological classification evinced by the report of the early excavations at Beth She'arim?

There is no doubt that the earliest catacomb, attributed to circa the Herodian period, is kokh cave no. 31, since it has all the characteristic properties of a tomb from this period. At that time, tombs of this type were regularly used by the small community at Beth She'arim. As previously mentioned, one of these tombs was discovered near catacomb 1, but similar ones are also located on the slopes of the hills north of Beth She'arim.[12]

A second tomb retaining the first century style of burial caves is catacomb 21, which has kokhim with heavy sealing stones. It has a small entrance closed by a heavy sealing stone with a projecting boss in the center. This tomb dates to the same period as the former tomb (catacomb 31); however, in view of the considerations mentioned above, it probably can be attributed to the beginning of the second century C.E. Both these kokh caves belong to building Period I of Beth She'arim.

The kokhim per se are not always a reliable chronological criterion, since they also occur sporadically throughout the country during the early centuries after the destruction of the Second Temple. Thus, for example, kokh graves from the third and fourth centuries C.E. are encountered in the Jewish cemetery at Jaffa. At Beth She'arim the kokh grave was apparently supplanted very quickly by the arcosolium grave, though not all at once. There is no doubt that hall A of catacomb 17 was originally a typical kokh room having an entrance without a hinged stone door; later it was refashioned in a composite style of kokhim and single trough graves. The hewing of this catacomb was probably begun in the second century C.E., more precisely at the end of the century. On the other hand, hall B cannot be assigned a date earlier than the third century. Normally the main hall in the front wall was hewn first whereas the side halls were cut out later, often after a considerable lapse of time.

Catacomb 22 may be categorized as a second transitional type, consisting of only one room with loculi, an arcosolium, and a niche. However, it also displays a new feature: a hinged stone door, one of the earliest examples at Beth She'arim. Since its conventional pattern is typical of most of the doors at Beth She'arim, it cannot provide us with a chronological criterion. Catacomb 22 should apparently be attributed to the end of the second or the beginning of the third century C.E., except for the room with arcosolia on the western side. As previously mentioned, this room is really just a kokh that was extended at some time during the first half of the third century C.E.

The various aspects of the problem of dating catacomb 20 have already been discussed. The architectural details of the façade call for a dating to the end of the second century; however, since exact limits to their range of time cannot be specified, an early third-century date for the building of the façade is equally possible. Some measure of confirmation for these dates is provided by two of the lamps (nos. 3–4) found in the catacomb, by the style of the marble fragments, and by the paleography of the inscriptions. The plan of the catacomb itself also seems to support this dating.

The large size of catacomb 20 is not a determining factor in our chronological considerations since this size was determined by the need for sufficient space to accommodate numerous sarcophagi. The important point is that the rooms of this catacomb are *not* like the type of kokh rooms that were formerly used, nor even like the advanced arcosolium rooms which constituted almost the only type used during the third and fourth centuries at Beth She'arim. This is also attested by the catacombs discovered in the previous excavations. Of the approximately two hundred burial places in catacomb 20, the majority are of the single grave arcosolium type (the few exceptions resulting from extensions of the arcosolia), niches for bone collection, and sporadic kokhim. Aside from these types of burial, there are spacious chambers with no, or very few, hewn graves. In general, it may be stated that the absence of a unified plan is conspicuous not only in the general layout, which lacks organization and proportion, but also in the individual rooms, each different from the other. This phenomenon can also be seen in catacomb 14: an irregular plan, unexploited space, single grave arcosolia, niches for bone collections, and kokhim. Catacomb 11 is also characterized by spacious rooms without graves (probably intended for sarcophagi), arcosolium rooms of the above-mentioned type, and a kokh room. All three catacombs display an elaborate architectural façade.

The excavations in the city area revealed that Period II (second half of the second century and beginning of the third century) witnessed the erection of large public buildings which were remarkable for their high standard of construction. This peak was never reached again at Beth She'arim. It seems reasonable to suppose that monumental building of this quality would also be reflected in the cemetery. Indeed, it is to the end of this period that Mazar attributes catacomb 11 with its overlying mausoleum and also catacomb 6, outstanding for its excellent construction and original plan.

Now, catacombs 14 and 20 may also be added to the list of important architectural projects of this period. There are good grounds for assuming that catacomb 20 was hewn before catacomb 14 (see below).

It is immaterial whether catacomb 20 is dated to the end of the second century or to the beginning of the third century since it emerges that this huge burial enterprise was executed during the lifetime of Rabbi Judah Ha-Nassî, who came to Beth She'arim during the last third of his life, and who is conjectured to have died in the second decade of the third century C.E. In addition to the archaeological testimony to the extensive public construction work of this period, there are also references in the Talmud to the magnificent buildings of Beth She'arim: רבי מתיר אקסדרה בבית שריי. כמה עמודין היו בה׳ ("Rabbi permitted an exedra at Beth She'arim, how many columns were these? etc...”). Apparently Rabbi Judah was not only a teacher of the Law, but also the main driving force behind the erection of public buildings in the style which was fashionable at that time. This was one of the means of raising the prestige of the small seat of the Sanhedrin and of enhancing the reputation of its leadership. Rabbi Judah is reported to have been highly respected by the Roman authorities and to have allowed regal pomp and elegant manners to prevail in his court.[14] It is not surprising, therefore, that he emulated the secular rulers in permitting "ostentatious" building operations. Rabbi Judah Ha-Nassî was "the great builder" of Beth She'arim; it was he who adorned the city with magnificent edifices and the necropolis with monumental memorials.

Catacomb 20 is singular for its exceptionally large dimensions. Its numerous graves and sarcophagi are indicative of a public cemetery and not of a family burial cave. Were only local inhabitants buried here or were outside residents from Palestine and the Diaspora also brought for interment? The generally accepted opinion is that Beth She'arim became a large burial center for Jews from Palestine and the Diaspora *after* the death of Rabbi. This process, however, probably began even during Rabbi's lifetime and assumed large scale proportions only after his death. In this connection, we should note the Talmudic tradition that the coffin of Rabbi Huna — the leader of Babylonian Jewry — was brought to Eretz Israel during Rabbi Judah's lifetime.[15] Since the coffin is said to have been sent directly to Rabbi's home, it seems reasonable to assume that Rabbi Huna was buried at Beth She'arim.

If it is indeed true that catacomb 20 was hewn during Rabbi Judah's lifetime, this would shed light on several related matters. Since the discovery of this catacomb, we have constantly been asking the question: why were stone and marble sarcophagi lodged only in this catacomb and not in other catacombs as well (apart from a few individual contemporary coffins)? How can we explain the fact that Hebrew was used for inscriptions more in this particular catacomb than in any other cave?

These phenomena seem to be the circumstantial products of that era. The catacomb was planned on a broad scale in the time of Rabbi Judah, in keeping with the trend for public construction operations of that period. Just as exedrae and basilicas were built in the spirit of the times, so were attempts made to inaugurate burial in large decorated sarcophagi, according to the prevailing fashion. However, this system apparently proved to be unfeasible. Burial in sarcophagi was very expensive, and the enormous weight of the sarcophagi made them very awkward to handle. The hewing of large catacombs deep into the rock entailed enormous difficulties and expenses, and there was the constant danger of collapse. Perhaps the experience of catacombs 14 and 20 even proved that the use of large doors was impractical because their hinges were so readily broken. At any rate, immediately after the death of Rabbi Judah, burial in catacomb 20 seems to have continued as before. However, with the introduction of large scale commercialized catacombs, the hewing of catacombs for sarcophagi came to an end.

We have already attempted to explain the exclusive use of the Hebrew language (see above) by the well-known fact that Rabbi Judah frankly preferred Hebrew to Aramaic, the language used by the general populace. Justos, the Hellenized resident of Beth She'arim who was buried in the mausoleum above catacomb 11, could have his death mourned in poetic Greek; however, the members of the rabbinical families who were buried in catacomb 20 and who may even have been close colleagues of Rabbi Judah doubtlessly preferred Hebrew. This usage seems to have become a custom in catacomb 20.

Catacomb 14 exhibits the same characteristics as catacomb 20: a large courtyard, a catacomb, and an overlying open-air assembly place with benches. The unfinished triple entrance indicates that its plan was borrowed from catacomb 20, and not vice-versa. This catacomb also displays the same monumental architecture, irregularity of plan, lack of conventionality, and the same types of graves as catacomb 20. Also, the built internal arches are a characteristic only of these two catacombs. We have already emphasized that, in contrast to catacomb 20 which was a public enterprise, catacomb 14 was a family burial vault; we have even tentatively attempted to ascribe it to the family of Rabbi Judah Ha-Nassî. There is no point in repeating our argument in favor of this interpretation because it can never be more than any assumption. In any case, it would certainly be in keeping with the tenor of our previous comments on the characteristic monumental building of Rabbi's time and about Rabbi as the instigator of large construction projects to impute catacomb 14 to Rabbi's initiative as well.

The Talmud relates that Rabbi Judah prepared his tomb during his lifetime.[16] In doing so, he followed the example of other leading figures. This tomb would probably have been a customary family burial vault and not a separate, individual grave. Perhaps Rabbi's daughter, whose death is recorded in the Talmud, had already been buried there. Assuming that a person prepares his tomb in his old age and that Rabbi Judah died circa 220 C.E. (as is generally accepted), we may confidently attribute catacomb 14 to the beginning of the third century C.E. From the point of view of the façade architecture and the catacomb layout, this dating is quite plausible.

The interrelationships between catacomb 14 on the one hand and catacombs 15 and 22 on the other have not yet been satisfactorily established.

Hall A of catacomb 15 is typologically exceptional. If this catacomb was indeed hewn after catacomb 14, as it most probably was, then it is also later than the adjacent assembly place of catacomb 14. It is difficult to understand why the courtyard of catacomb 15 was so anomalously included within the bounds of the assembly place of catacomb 14. Its location outside the boundaries of the assembly place would have yielded a more harmonious solution since the niche in the upper wall could then have been fixed slightly eastward, thus retaining a more symmetrical position.

From a typological point of view, catacomb 22 seems very possibly to be earlier than catacomb 14. If this catacomb were cut by the courtyard of catacomb 14, there would be no problem. However, since the room which was cut is a late extension of catacomb 22, and since the plan of the room seems to be typologically later than catacomb 14, it is difficult to explain the chronological relationship between these two catacombs. Despite the apparent contradiction of the structural evidence as explained in the description of the catacomb, the most plausible assumption is, nevertheless, that the courtyard wall of catacomb 14 was cut during the hewing of the western room of catacomb 22, and not vice-versa. Otherwise, we would have to presume that this type of room, also customarily encountered in the early halls of catacomb 1 and attributed to the beginning of the third century (see above), is earlier than we originally estimated.

Catacomb 23 is similar to catacombs 14 and 20 in its general conception: it, too, has a relatively large courtyard, an architectural façade, a cave with a large room, and an overlying structure. Its location between catacombs 14 and 20 created a group of three catacombs with overlying structures which were paramount in the architectural landscape of Beth She'arim. Since this catacomb was originally intended for sarcophagi only, the multi-troughed arcosolia are conjectured to be a later addition. An interesting connecting link between this catacomb and catacomb 22 is the group of two pilasters flanking the inside of the entrance. Thus, it appears that this catacomb should also be dated to the beginning of the third century.

It emerges, therefore, that catacombs 14, 20, 21, 22, and 23 constitute a closely-related group of early catacombs. Later on, the hewing of the catacombs was extended eastward and westward.

The tremendous expansion of the Beth She'arim cemetery took place after the death of Rabbi Judah. Of the catacombs that have been discovered, the vast majority date to this period. At this point, the necropolis became a huge burial center for Jews from Palestine and the neighboring countries. Such a large-scale enterprise naturally required organization and planning. The matter of burial at Beth She'arim turned into a commercialized public enterprise directed, apparently, by the Burial Society (Hevrah Kadishah) which was responsible for hewing the catacombs and selling burial places to any purchaser.

In contrast to the earlier catacomb plans,

a new, rational plan was now instituted. However, this standardized plan still allowed for a variety of grave types from which the client could choose. The determining factor was social and economic status: beautiful, spacious catacombs for the wealthy; crowded, small catacombs for the less well-to-do. Nevertheless, space was probably distributed generously at first, and only later did it become necessary to economize and exploit the available area to the maximum.

If indeed this was the course of development, then catacomb 12 was the first to be hewn after the death of Rabbi Judah Ha-Nassî. It has a well-organized plan: hall A consists of central passage rooms and groups of burial rooms with single trough-grave arcosolia; in hall B, the more advanced arcosolium with 3–4 trough graves is dominant. The plan of central rooms serving as a passageway to burial chambers has its parallel in the early halls of catacomb 1 and in Mugharet el-Jehennem,[18] halls which Mazar attributes to the first half of the third century C.E. In catacomb 12, this principle is clearly demonstrated by its symmetrical, generously-proportioned plan. The graves of hall A, doubtlessly very expensive, testify to the wealth of their owners. Since the finds in the pit of the floor of hall A date to the middle of the third century, the hewing of this hall should apparently be dated to the first half of this century.

In contrast to the spaciousness and convenience encountered in catacomb 12, catacomb 13 is characterized by the congestion of its halls and rooms. This is a typical public catacomb in which the calculated density reaches its highest peak. The objective of this split-level plan (cf. also catacomb 1) was to obtain a maximum number of burial places in a minimum of space and to make graves available at the lowest possible price. The numerous inscriptions in this catacomb indicate that Jews from Phoenicia were also interred

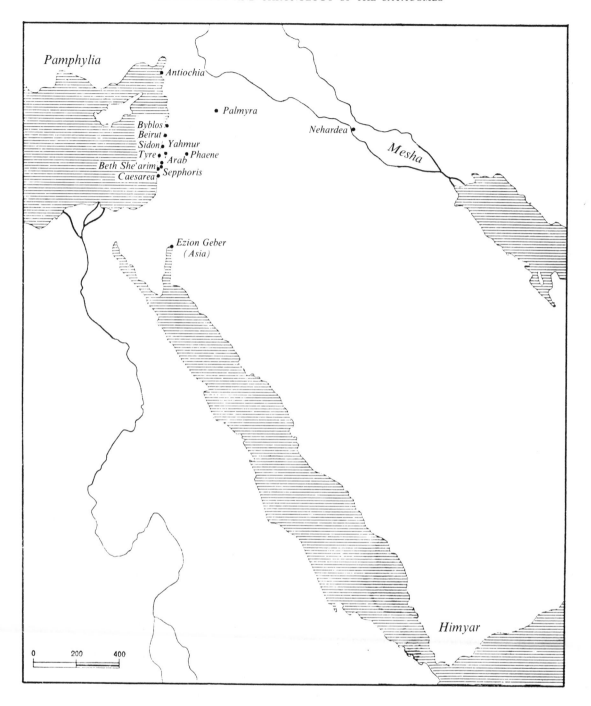

Fig. 129 Origins of those interred in Beth She'arim

here. Hall B, in which a large group of Jews from the Syrian coast were buried, was hewn after hall A. In general layout it is the same as hall A, but it is smaller in size and has more advanced arcosolia. We obviously cannot determine how much time elapsed between the hewing of these two halls.

The rest of the catacombs (15–19) are relatively small. All of them (except their earlier parts which were mentioned previously) have a more or less uniform plan consisting of a small room, or a row of small rooms, with advanced arcosolia. Of course, each catacomb may also contain other types or graves — for example, arcosolia with single graves or kokhim. The small niches (bone depositories), so common in the earlier catacombs, are almost completely absent here. In general, these catacombs are comparable to the halls in catacombs 1–4 which Mazar attributes to the period between the middle of the third century and the first half of the fourth century C.E. This means that for approximately a hundred years the tomb builders of Beth She'arim continued to use the same standardized plan for the hewing of catacombs. The catacombs East of catacomb 20, discovered by Mazar in 1956, also conform to this scheme. (These catacombs are not included in this report but appear in the general plan of the site, fig. 131.)

It is, of course, hazardous to base our chronological conclusions on the typological classification of the catacombs. Nevertheless, under the circumstances, this is the only means of arriving at any understanding whatsoever of the historical development of the Beth She'arim tombs. It should also be noted, however, that this classification is supported by certain objective historical considerations and chronological data. As a rule, the results of our excavations corroborate the general conclusions reached by Prof. Mazar in his earlier excavations. In fact, they are mutually complementary and are instrumental in achieving a certain degree of understanding about the typological and historical evolution of the Beth She'arim tombs. Further excavation would doubtlessly reveal new information and correct previous misapprehensions.

NOTES

1 For plans of the tombs see: Watzinger, *Denkmäler*, pp. 59–76; K. Galling, "Die Necropole von Jerusalem," *Palästina Jahrbuch*, 1936, pp. 73–101; N. Avigad, "The Necropolis of Jerusalem During the Second Temple Period," *Sefer Yerushalayim*, 1956, p. 320–327 (Hebrew).

2 *Beth Shea'rim*, I, pp. 14 *ff.*

3 B. Mazar, *BIES*, XXI (1957), pp. 153 *ff.* (Hebrew).

4 *Beth She'arim*, I, p. 141.

5 *Ibid.*, p. 86.

6 *Ibid.*, p. 47.

7 *Ibid.*, p. 49.

8 *Ibid.*, p. 115.

9 *Ibid.*, p. 52.

10 *BIES*, IX (1942), p. 20 (Hebrew).

11 *Beth She'arim*, I, p. 25.

12 *Ibid.*, p. 22.

13 Jer. Talmud 'Eruvin 1, 18c.

14 Bereshit Rabba 33, 15, and others.

15 Jer. Talmud Ketuboth 1, 35a; Genesis Rabba 33, 3.

16 "Rabbi lies (sick) at Sepphoris and a (burial) place is prepared for him at Beth She'arim." (Ketuboth 103b).

17 "And it happened that the daughter of Rabbi died at Beth She'arim, and Rabbi entered the Beth Midrash and lectured all the day." (Mo'ed Qatan 21a, according to manuscripts).

18 *Beth She'arim*, I, p. 227. The position of the cave is marked in our general plan as no. 32 (see fig. 1).

CHAPTER VI

THE MENORAH AND OTHER RITUAL OBJECTS

The menorah is a very deeply-rooted symbol in Jewish religious and national consciousness. The first graphic representation of this phenomenon appeared on a coin of Matityahu Antigonus (40–37 B.C.E.).[1] The infrequent use of this symbol in the Second Temple period may apparently be ascribed to the extreme holiness in which the menorah was held. In any case, no representations of the menorah or of any other ritual objects have been found in the numerous burial caves or on the decorated ossuaries and coffins antedating the destruction of the Temple, almost as though such representations were prohibited. Otherwise, it could be assumed that the menorah, despite its holiness, had not yet achieved the distinctive symbolic value which it was to receive later on in Jewish national consciousness, and that on the coin of Matityahu Antigonus it appears just as one of a group of the usual ritual objects — like the lulab, the shofar, or the goblet — which are depicted on other coins. It is precisely for this reason that particular importance should be attached to the "casual" graffiti discovered recently in Jerusalem on the corridor wall of Jason's tomb, erected prior to the Herodian period.[2] These graffiti include several very crudely and schematically executed menoroth at the entrance of the tomb, which were probably sketched by members of the family who wished to express their feelings for the deceased in this manner, in contrast to the accepted custom. Such an act can only be explained by the profound symbolic significance in which the menorah was held by the family. The same interpretation applies to the menorah from the Herodian period recently discovered in the excavations at the Jewish quarter of the Old City of Jerusalem.[3] This menorah also does not belong to the original painted mural decorations but was engraved by someone who apparently viewed the Temple menorah as a symbol of profound significance. Not in vain did the builders of Titus's Arch in Rome choose the Temple menorah as the symbol of their victory over Judah: the menorah indeed represented not only the Temple but the entire nation of Israel as well.

After the destruction of the Second Temple, as the menorah came to be extensively used in many synagogues, the symbolism attached to it became enhanced even further. This development was expressed, first and foremost, in synagogal art where the menorah occupied an important place.

The symbolic meaning of the menorah is open to many interpretations.[4] The origin of its form probably derives from the sacred tree motif of the ancient Near East.[5] To many scholars, the menorah symbolizes Light, Knowledge, and Eternity, especially when it is displayed in public.

The attitude of the individual toward the menorah may be deduced from the fact that he affixed it symbolically to tombstones. A menorah on a grave doubtlessly retained its original profound significance; however, it primarily represented affiliation and identification with the Jewish people. This conclusion is supported by the fact that in the Jewish cemeteries of the Diaspora, like the Jewish catacombs in Rome from the second–fourth centuries C.E., the menorah is infinitely more common than in the Jewish cemeteries of the same period in Palestine.[6] Evidently, Diaspora Jews felt a stronger need to display their Jewish identity on tombstones than did Palestinian Jews who lived among their own people in

Fig. 130 Various types of menoroth and ritual objects

their own country, and whose national identity did not require supplementary affirmation. This might explain the seemingly unwarranted phenomenon that at Beth She'arim the menorah symbol is relatively common, especially in catacombs 1–4.[7] It should be borne in mind that Beth She'arim served mainly as a burial center for Diaspora Jews, who were usually Hellenized. Upon their death, these Jews, Greek speaking and bearing Greek names, doubtlessly wanted to stress their national affiliation by appending a distinctively Jewish symbol to their tombstones. At least nine of the fourteen menoroth found in our excavations may be attributed with absolute or reasonable certainty to Jews of this type (see below, the discussion on menoroth nos. 2–6, and 12–14). It is noteworthy, nevertheless, that in a cemetery as large as Beth She'arim, the total number of graves bearing a menorah is not very large. In addition, it should be noted that in our excavations, menoroth were found on three marble tablets with Greek inscriptions which were apparently brought from the Diaspora together with the deceased.

In catacombs 12–20, fourteen representations of seven-branched menoroth were found. These menoroth may be classified into two groups: *(a)* Menoroth which were carved, engraved, or cast on movable objects such as coffins or marble plaques. There are seven examples in this group, two of which are duplicated a number of times. *(b)* Menoroth which were carved or engraved on the walls of tombs. This group also consists of seven menoroth.

We shall now describe the menoroth and other symbols illustrated in figure 130:

1. Menorah carved on sarcophagus no. 22, catacomb 20 (Pl. XLVI, 2). Height, 77 cm; width, 74 cm. The branches of the menorah are semicircular and carved in rounded relief. They are composed of links, asymmetrical both in shape and distribution: to the left of the central branch, the links have a cup-like, trapezoidal shape; to

the right, the links are alternately rounded and somewhat flattened. The central branch has links of both types. The uppermost links look like bases for lamps. The short thick shaft stands on a trapezoidal, cumbersome-looking base,[8] which is 47 cm wide and 20 cm high. This menorah differs both in form and dimension from all the others at Beth She'arim.[9]

2. A menorah cast in relief on lead coffin no. 1 (Pl. LXIII). There are four replicas of this menorah. It is 16.5 cm high and 9.5 cm wide. The branches consist of semicircles and culminate in flames. They are composed of alternate rounded and cylindrical links. The menorah is tripodal. The two side legs are bent outward, whereas the central leg, viewed frontally, is divided into three finger-like prongs. This "leg" bears somewhat of a resemblance to the lions' paws of the menoroth in the mosaic floor of Hammath-Tiberias[10] (the beginning of the fourth century C.E.), and in the mosaic of the synagogue at Ma'on (Nirim), dating to the sixth century C.E.[11] On either side of the menorah the traditional ritual objects are depicted: to the right, a grooved shofar and a square incense shovel with a crooked handle; to the left, a lulab and an ethrog.

3. A menorah cast in relief on lead coffins nos. 1–2 (Pl. LXV). There are six replicas of this menorah on coffin no. 1, and four on coffin no. 2. There are only a few discrepancies in detail between this and the previous menorah: it has only two legs; it is not flanked by ritual objects. Its branches consist of links in astragal pattern (bead and reel).[12] The menorah is 13 cm high.

4. A menorah carved in sunken, flat relief, on a marble tablet in catacomb 18 (Pl. XXVI). It is 12.5 cm high and 18 cm wide. Its wide semicircular branches terminate in a horizontal band running along the entire width of the menorah. The shaft is extremely short. The legs resemble the three prongs of a trident. This menorah is schematic, in contrast to the "realistic"

menoroth described up till now. To the left, a shofar and an incense shovel are engraved; to the right, an ethrog is loosely tied to a lulab. For some obscure reason, the workmanship of the lulab and ethrog is very careless, while that of the shofar and incense shovel is excellent. The shofar has a concave aperture which lends it a realistic look. The incense shovel, open at the end, is also characterized by its realistic appearance.[13] The dots in the shovel apparently symbolize the embers.[14]

5. A menorah incised in simple lines on a marble tablet in catacomb 13 (Pl. XI, 4). It is 7.8 cm high and 9.5 cm wide. The shaft does not have a base. To the left there is a shofar; to the right, a lulab and a square incense shovel, schematically executed.

6. A small menorah incised on a marble tablet, between the lines of a Greek inscription above the entrance to hall C of catacomb 19 (fig. 33, above; Pl. XXIX, 5). The menorah is 4.6 cm high. Its branches are rounded and connected on top by a horizontal line. The menorah has three stepped legs. The execution is schematic.

7. A menorah (?) incised on the decorated glass plate from catacomb 15 (fig. 100). It is 6.3 cm high. The definition of this object as a menorah is by no means certain since it is so unconventional in shape; however, it seems closer in form to a stylized menorah than to anything else. The branches are erect and parallel. They are connected at the bottom by two oblique "branches" since the perpendicular branches are not joined to the central branch in the customary fashion. The sloping lines above, connecting the tops of the branches, are easier to explain (see below).

8. A menorah carved in high relief on the wall of room XXIII in catacomb 20 (Pl. XXXV, 1). It is 1.90 m high, 1.25 m wide, and protrudes 12–36 cm from the wall. The plain branches were badly mutilated and the shaft, which was not attached to the wall, broke and disappeared. Part of the amorphous base is still attached to the floor. A well-preserved example of a tall menorah of this type was discovered in catacomb 3.[15]

9. A menorah carved in relief on one of the walls of room I in hall B of catacomb 12 (Pl. V, 2). It is 1.35 m high and 0.83 m wide. The branches are oblique. Most of the shaft is broken; it is, however, clear that it had no base. The top of the shaft is decorated with two horizontal bands, above which a pattern of two ovals is engraved. Menoroth of this type are common in catacombs 1–4.

10. A menorah carved in relief on one of the walls of room I in hall A of catacomb 19 (Pl. XXVIII, 4). It is 26 cm high. The workmanship is rough and the design schematic. It has a flat columnar shape, gradually widening toward the top. The upper part is partitioned into crude branches by oblique, irregular grooves. The shaft is tall and has a low base.

11. A menorah incised on one of the walls of room II in hall L of catacomb 13 (Pl. X, 3). It is 28 cm high and 33 cm wide. The entire menorah is schematically delineated by small notches. The side branches consist of straight lines issuing obliquely from the central branch. A horizontal line connects them on top. The shaft is very short; the base is high and is shaped like a tripod constructed out of triangles. This menorah has exceptional, enigmatic hooks on either side, both on top and near the base. The notch technique in which the menorah is executed is also unique at Beth She'arim.

12. A menorah incised on an archway between room I and room II of hall A in catacomb 12 (see also fig. 7). It is 12 cm high. The sketch is very schematic. A horizontal line connects the branches. The shaft does not have a base.

13. A menorah incised as above on the opposite jamb of the archway (see also fig. 8). It is 18 cm high. The tops of the branches are graduated, i.e., the height of the branches decreases from the center toward the sides. The shaft does not have a base.

14. A menorah engraved on the lintel of hall C in catacomb 19 (Pl. XXVII, 2). It is 15 cm high. The workmanship is schematic and careless. The branches are oblique and slightly rounded. The shaft is very short. The base is rectangular. This is the only menorah at Beth She'arim that was found on the lintel of a tomb.[16]

15. A lulab carved in sunken relief on the left jamb of the archway between room II and room III of hall A in catacomb 18. It is 46 cm high (Pl. XXV, 3).

16. A lulab carved in high relief on the jamb opposite the one described above. It is 55 cm high (Pl. XXV, 2). For additional details on the lulabim, see p. 77.

We shall now attempt to classify the types of menoroth discovered at Beth She'arim. From a technical point of view, the menoroth of the first group (nos. 1–6) are usually executed on a higher standard than those of the second group, since they were done by professionals. Only the first three menoroth were styled realistically. The rest are schematically executed and vary in their standard of workmanship; most of them have parallels in catacombs 1–4.

The most common type of menorah is the one with rounded branches culminating at the same height, and separated one from the other (nos. 1–3, 5, 8–9, 14). This seems to have been the first standard form of menorah generally in use in the Second Temple period, as evidenced by the shape of the menoroth on coins of Matityahu Antigonus,[17] the tomb of Jason,[18] Titus's Arch,[19] at the Jewish quarter in Jerusalem,[20] and for a long period after the destruction of the Temple[21] as attested by the finds in the synagogues and tombs both in Palestine and in other countries as well.[22]

The second type (nos. 4, 6, 11, and 12) differs from the first in having a horizontal band connecting the tops of the branches along the entire width of the menorah. This type is apparently later than the first type,[23] since no menoroth of this type antedating the destruction of the Second Temple have been found until now; even among the early menoroth appearing after the destruction, it is still rare. The horizontal band is not decorative but functional: it connects the tops of the branches and serves as a base for the oil lamps.[24] It is difficult to establish the date of its first appearance. The examples from Beth She'arim are probably earlier than the middle of the fourth century; chronologically, it is difficult to distinguish them from the other types. One of them, no. 4, classified with type 2, is engraved on a marble tablet together with a Greek epigram which has been attributed to the end of the third century C.E. on paleographical grounds. The lintel of the synagogue in Kfar Naburiyeh (Nabratein), upon which a menorah of this type was also carved,[25] should likewise be attributed to approximately the same date. In the course of time, the distribution of menoroth of this type increased.

The menorah with oblique branches (no. 11 and perhaps also nos. 10 and 12) is a variant of the two types just described. These sloping branches were not accidentally drawn by inexperienced draftsmen but were copied from existing examples. This is evidenced by the menorah on the Holy Ark of the synagogue in Dura-Europos (the beginning of the third century C.E.),[26] depicted in a distinctively realistic style.

A third type of menorah is no. 13, which is characterized by branches graduating downward from the center to the sides. This type was also found in the earlier excavations of Beth She'arim,[27] and is well known from the catacombs in Rome[28] and from other places.

The rendering of the menorah branches by means of links (nos. 1–3 and 11) is an obvious imitation, though schematic and inaccurate, of the "button and flower" pattern which is described in the Bible as embellishing the Temple menorah. Numerous versions of this decorative style are exhibited by many types of menoroth in the known repertoire. The simpler menoroth have undecorated branches.

The base of the menorah is second in importance. Two main kinds of bases are displayed by our menoroth, presumably similar to those used in reality. Generally the menorah is mounted on a tripod (nos. 2, 4, 6, and 11); however, sometimes it is borne on a square base (nos. 1 and 14). Menorah no. 3 cannot have been stable since it lacks a third leg. The absence of bases on menoroth nos. 5, 9, 12, and 13 is very probably just a graphic deletion.

The size of the third component, the shaft, (i.e., the part between the branches and the base), determines the height of the menorah. Menoroth may be classified as short or tall depending on the dimensions of the shaft. The short-shaft type is probably the earlier of the two.[29]

While the menorah is doubtlessly the most important cult utensil depicted in Jewish art, it is frequently flanked by all or part of a group of other ritual articles, namely, shofar, lulab, ethrog, and incense shovel. These assemblages of religious emblems are very common in synagogal and Jewish fine art; they are also frequently encountered on tombstones of the catacombs in Rome as well. On Palestinian tombs, on the other hand, they are relatively rare. At Beth She'arim the numerous menoroth carved on the walls of catacombs 1–4 are not flanked by additional symbols. Therefore, the triple occurrence of this group of objects (alongside menoroth nos. 2, 4, and 5) in our assemblage of menoroth is surprising. However, it should be borne in mind that these menoroth were not actually found on graves but on a lead coffin and on two marble tablets which were presumably brought from the Diaspora together with the deceased. If this is so, it provides further verification of our theory that Palestinian Jews used religious emblems very sparingly on their tombs, whereas Diaspora Jews employed them frequently. From this viewpoint, it is very interesting that two solitary carved lulavim were found on the walls of catacomb 18 (see above, nos. 15–16).[30]

NOTES

1 Y. Meshorer, *Jewish Coins from the Second Temple Period,* Tel Aviv, 1967, Pl. V, 36–36a.

2 L. Y. Raḥmani, "The Tomb of Jason," *IEJ,* XVII (1967), p. 61.

3 N. Avigad, *IEJ,* XX (1970), p. 4, frontispiece.

4 Goodenough, *Symbols,* IV, pp. 71–98 (see additional bibliography there).

5 *Ibid.,* nos. 2–3.

6 *Ibid.,* III, nos. 706–818.

7 *Beth She'arim,* I, fig. 29.

8 Cf. *ibid.,* Pl. XXVII.

9 In general it bears somewhat of a resemblance to the menorah on the Arch of Titus (Goodenough, *Symbols,* IV, no. 1).

10 *Qadmoniot,* vol. 1, no. 4, Pl. 2 (Hebrew).

11 *Bulletin,* III, Pl. VIII, 1; *Eretz-Israel,* VI (1961), Pl. 22, 1 (Hebrew). See: H. Strauss, "The Fate and Form of the Hasmonean menorah," *Eretz-Israel,* VI, p. 125 (Hebrew).

12 This feature is similar in this respect to the menorah from the Second Temple period discovered in the Jewish Quarter of Jerusalem (see above, n. 3).

13 For two other examples of this type see: Goodenough, *Symbols,* III, nos. 444 and 618. The incense shovel is usually depicted as a closed square; see: Goodenough, *Symbols,* III, nos. 293, 334–337, 478, 639, and 651.

14 See: Y. Yadin, *The Finds from the Bar Kochba Period in the Cave of the Letters,* Jerusalem, 1963, p. 58, fig. 14.

15 See: *Beth She'arim,* I, Pl. XXVII.

16 A menorah on the lintel of a tomb was also found at Kfar Tamra in Western Galilee. See: N. Avigad, *Eretz-Israel,* VII, (1964), p. 20, Pl. X, 1 (Hebrew).

17 See above, n. 1.

18 Raḥmani, "The Tomb of Jason," fig. 7.

19 Goodenough, *Symbols*, IV, no. 1.

20 See above, n. 3.

21 A. Negev was the first to try to catalogue the menorah typologically and chronologically. See: "The Chronology of the Seven-Branched Candelabrum." *Eretz-Israel*, VIII (*Sefer Sukenik*, 1963), pp. 193–210 (Hebrew). As a starting point for his study he uses the menoroth dated prior to the destruction of the Second Temple (on coins of Matityahu Antigonus, the Tomb of Jason, and the Arch of Titus) which he calls the "classical" type: "The branches are graduated in such a way that their height diminishes from the central branch outwards." (*ibid.*, p. 193; see also pp. 206, 209). But this observation is mistaken, for in actual fact the candelabrum branches on the coins and on Titus' Arch are not graduated but culminate at the same height; and in Jason's tomb the only reason for the unequal heights is the careless incising: on this menorah some of the branches are short and others tall without conforming to any definite order. See: Raḥmani, "The Tomb of Jason," fig. 7. Further on in his work Negev uses the same term "classical" for all the menoroth which he defines as having "equal branch height." This ambiguous definition caused confusion in the typological classification.

22 For a general survey on menoroth in synagogues see: Goodenough, *Symbols*, III (Illustrations); IV, pp. 71–98; XII, p. 79. For a list of the finds see: Negev, "The Chronology of the Seven-Branched Candelabrum."

23 Negev (*ibid.*, p. 207) was the first to determine the chronological order of the two types of menoroth. He defines the second type as "the menorah with a horizontal bar along the tops of the branches."

24 See the stone menorah from Ḥammath-Tiberias, which has depressions on top (Goodenough, *Symbols*, III, no. 562), and the menorah from Sardis (M. A. Hanfmann, *BASOR*, 174 [1964], fig. 20).

25 These two menoroth are mistakenly classified by Negev as classical ("Chronology," pp. 195 and 197). On the menorah from Nabratein see: N. Avigad, *BRF*, III (1960), Pl. XIII, 1.

26 C. H. Kraeling, *The Excavations at Dura-Europos, Final Report, VIII*, 1: *The Synagogue*, New Haven, 1956, Pl. LI; Goodenough, *Symbols*, III, no. 603.

27 *Beth She'arim*, I, fig. 29, top.

28 Goodenough, *Symbols*, III, nos. 712 and 788–789.

29 Cf. the menoroth from the Second Temple period that were mentioned at the beginning of the chapter.

30 Cf. also: *Beth She'arim*, I, Pl. XXXIV, on the right side.

CHAPTER VII

JEWISH FIGURATIVE ART. A HISTORICAL REVIEW

Our discussion of the decorated sarcophagi from Beth She'arim does not clear us from the need to examine the contribution of these exceptional finds in clarifying the essence of Jewish figurative art. However, such an examination should first be preceded by a brief review of the role of Jewish figurative art in the various periods of the history of the Jewish people.

Any discussion of Jewish art or of the art of the Jews in antiquity is constantly pervaded by the Second of the Ten Commandments: "Thou shalt not make unto thee any graven image, or any likeness of any thing that is in heaven above, or that is in the earth beneath, or that is in the water under the earth: Thou shalt not bow down thyself to them, nor serve them" (Exodus 20:4, 5; Deuteronomy 5:8, 9). Due to this prohibition, nothing definable as "original art" or "national art" could possibly have developed among Jews, as it did among other peoples. However, in a way, art is like the Tree of Knowledge: one cannot resist its temptation. Despite the injunction, figurative art was cultivated to a certain extent also among Jews, not continuously nor out of the keenly inventive drive which produces original artistic creations, but by a process of borrowing and adapting forms and designs from other nations.

The extent to which figurative art was used among Jews always depended upon two factors: *(a)* the degree of influence of the neighboring peoples; and *(b)* the degree of strictness or tolerance with which the rabbis interpreted the Biblical prohibition, i.e., does this injunction pertain to all images as such; or does it refer mainly to the verse "thou shalt not bow down thyself to them, nor serve them." This question was a focal point of conflicting opinions

and vehement arguments for many generations. It seems to me that in order to understand the spirit of the injunction, we must look for evidence dating as closely as possible to the time of its legislation.

The first violation of this prohibition occurred immediately after the giving of the Law. While the children of Israel were still encamped at the foot of Mt. Sinai, when Moses's vigilant eye was momentarily turned away, they immediately began to worship the golden calf, saying: "These be thy gods, O Israel" (Exodus 32:1–4). For this they were severely punished. It is easy to understand this act since the Law had just been revealed to a people who were still under the influence of pagan customs. However, it is difficult to comprehend how Moses could have made the copper serpent under divine command: the very authority which prohibited any graven image permitted the making of a serpent which, as is well known, symbolized healing power for many ancient peoples. Furthermore, the image of the serpent with its magic properties accompanied the Israelites during their long trek through the desert and was ultimately placed for safekeeping in the Temple at Jerusalem.

For our discussion, the two golden cherubim (winged sphinxes) which decorated the cover of the Ark of the Covenant, also by the commandment of God, are of particular significance. The Ark of the Covenant which escorted the Israelites in their wanderings and wars and was finally placed in the Holy of Holies of Solomon's Temple, was the most revered object for the people of Israel. However, the God of Israel is an abstract God — perhaps too abstract for the Israelites wandering in the desert to grasp. On the other hand, a God residing "between the two cherubim which are upon the ark of the testimony" (Exodus 25:22), or "the lord of hosts which dwelleth between the cherubim" (I Samuel 4:4) was more readily conceivable by the people since they were familiar with the great importance attached to cherubim in the traditional mythologies of ancient peoples, including Israel. Therefore, in order to make his presence more tangible, God commanded the cherubim to be made as a symbol of His throne — though at that time it could well have been suspected that the people would forget about the Spirit hovering between the cherubim and would pay attention to the cherubim themselves. Apparently, the cherubim on the Ark of the Covenant should be viewed as an indication of the legislator's true intent, prohibiting the worship of a statue and not the image as such. However, in order to prove this point more concretely, let us continue our review of developments in this field during the First Temple period, and consider particularly the Temple itself.

When Solomon wanted to enhance the reputation of the Temple both among his own people and the neighboring nations, he had no choice but to build it in the popular fashion of that time. However, being inexperienced in such matters, he turned to the King of Tyre for assistance. This accounts for the typically Canaanite-Phoenician style of the Temple, both in architecture and in decoration. Two colossal cherubim (ten cubits high), made of olive wood and overlaid with gold, sheltered the Ark of the Testimony in the Holy of Holies, with their wings. Images of cherubim ornamented the curtain of the Ark, the walls, and the doors of the sanctuary and the Holy of Holies. On the wheeled cart there were carvings of cherubim and lions. In the vision of Ezekiel, the Temple is also described as being decorated with cherubim; there is even a very important allusion as to the form of the cherubim: they have the faces of a man, on a young lion, and of

an eagle. These mythological creatures evidently had various forms, and many suggestions of their supposed shape have been offered. In Canaanite-Phoenician art, the cherubim are depicted as demonic creatures with the body of a lion, the wings of an eagle, and the face of a man (the winged sphinx); or the face of a bird (the griffin); or the face of some other animal. These figures, appearing in stone reliefs and in ivory carvings found in Syria and Palestine, are frequently pictured beside the throne of a king or the seat of a god. It might obviously be argued that, since these cherubim are hybrid creatures which have no likeness "in the heavens above" or "in the world below" or "in the water below the land," they are not subject to the prohibition against graven images, as some commentators have indeed maintained. However, this argument is hardly valid since, in the courtyard of Solomon's temple, there was also the Sea of Bronze, held aloft by twelve bronze oxen; and Solomon's throne itself was decorated with carvings of lions which are, after all, ordinary animals.

Not one of the prophets of Israel or the religious reformers of those days found fault with the "prohibited" figures in the Temple, though at that time paganism was indeed a potential danger for Israel. Only about the copper serpent which Moses made are we told that, in the days of King Hezekiah, the serpent was destroyed because the people of Israel burned incense to it (II Kings 18:4). Hence, the other images, which served no ritual purpose but were purely functional or decorative, were not disqualified for the Temple even during Hezekiah's reform. It is noteworthy that in later generations as well neither the Rabbis nor the subsequent commentators took offense at the figures in the Temple but condoned them on the grounds that the people did not worship them. Only Josephus Flavius, who lived at a period of virtual abstinence from figurative art objected vehemently to the lions of Solomon's throne.

Except for the Temple, there was no place for cultivating Jewish monumental art; indeed, no evidence of such an art has been found in any of the archaeological excavations. In the fine arts, on the other hand, lavish use was made of the Temple motifs with the addition of many others from the repertoire of Canaanite-Phoenician art. On the ivory plaques which adorned the palace of the Kings of Israel in Samaria there are cherubim, serpents, lions, oxen, magic symbols, and mythological figures of Egyptian and other origin. These motifs also served to decorate Israelite stamp seals from the First Temple period. The winged beetle, originally an Egyptian mythological emblem, became a royal symbol of Judah and was impressed on official jars. We know little about the art of painting during that time; however, judging by the painting preserved on a shard from the royal Citadel in Ramat Raḥel[1] which depicted the figure of a bearded king (?) seated on his throne in the finest style of that period, we may assume that this branch of art was also cultivated to a certain extent in Israel. The art of sculpture is evidenced by the numerous clay figurines of women and animals which were found on Israelite sites. It is generally thought that magic properties were attributed to these figurines.

It transpires, therefore, that in the very period when the Ten Commandments were handed down and in the subsequent era, the Second Commandment was not viewed as an absolute prohibition against the making of animate images, but against images which might be used for pagan worship. This proscription was sufficient to turn Israel into a distinctively aniconic nation; but it was not sufficient to totally prevent the use of artistic products for personal pleasure (for which purpose the prohibition was apparently not intended); nor did it impede the artistic expression of mythological traditions prevailing among the people. On the contrary, an object of art like the cherubim served to represent the presence of the God of Israel and to exalt His name among the people. Any depiction which was valid in the Temple was surely legitimate in secular life, though the extent to which the people related to art of course was very restricted, due to the Torah injunction. In any case, the prophets of Israel did not warn against phenomena of this type but against the high places upon which the people worshipped pagan gods. Moreover, the prophets were closer both in time and in spirit to the handing down of the injunction than the sages of later generations. In discussing the synagogal figurative art of the Mishnaic and Talmudic period, we frequently overlook the use of this art in Solomon's Temple.

Our knowledge of conditions after the fall of the First Temple is extremely restricted since the archaeological finds from the Persian period are so meager. It seems that the proscription against using animate images was not rigorously observed during this period. In the province of Yehud, which was apparently partly governed by High Priests, coins were struck with the image of a pagan god seated on a winged wheel, human heads, and birds, as was customary on the coins of the neighboring peoples in that era. This phenomenon very probably reflects the influence of Persian rule. Stamped jar-handles frequently bear figures of animals.

The situation in the Hasmonean and Herodian periods was entirely different. Then, triumphant Hellenism began its assault on Judaism by attempting to force its culture and religion on the Jews. The Jews, in turn, felt the deepest obligation to defend themselves against Hellenism. Naturally, at a time when foreign rulers were bent on introducing statues of gods or of themselves into the Temple and forcing Jews into idolatry, the use of any image whatsoever was stringently prohibited. Thus, during this period, the enforcement of the Torah injunctions was infinitely stricter than at any other time in Jewish history. There are several references to this uncompromising orthodoxy in the literature The most famous is the story about the image of the eagle which was placed on the gate of Herod's Temples and was removed by the Zealots, for which act they paid with their lives. Probably, what mainly aroused the ire of the Jews was the eagle as a symbol of Roman rule and not simply the eagle as an image in itself. Josephus Flavius was similarly motivated when he hurried to Tiberias to destroy the palace of Herod the Tetrarch since, in Josephus's opinion, it was decorated with figures of animals prohibited by the Torah. Obviously, this religious argument also had political overtones; however, the very use of such an argument reflects the spirit of the time.

The archaeological finds from the Second Temple period reveal a very strong Hellenistic influence on the architecture and decorative art of Jewish tombs; nevertheless, this art was absolutely aniconic. Not a single animate motif is to be found on the tomb façades or on the hundreds of decorated ossuaries and sarcophagi unearthed up to the present: only floral and geometric designs were used. It is true that a charcoal sketch of a reclining deer and figures of people in boats was discovered in the corridor of Jason's tomb in Jerusalem, dated to the Hasmonean period.[2] However, these drawings are not an integral part of the design of the tomb but crude sketches by visitors. Also, the meager traces of human figures are most schematic and difficult to distinguish. Similarly, in Herod's palace at remote Masada not a single animate image was found, the magnificent mosaics having been decorated only with floral and geometric designs. Herod may be assumed to have decorated the rest of his palaces in the country in the same style, since even the remains of the elaborate palace in Jericho, attributed to Herod or to another member of his family, does not display different characteristics.

After the fall of Jerusalem the situation changed with regard to the use of figurative art; however, it is not surprising that during the difficult trials of the Bar Kochba war, there were still vestiges of fanaticism on this subject. For example, the human faces on the Roman bronze vessels found in the Cave of the Letters in the Judean Desert were deliberately mutilated. On the other hand, neither the pagan images on one of the vessels (showing a Greek mythological scene), nor a seal used for stamping Bar Kochba's letters (which bore a figure of Heracles struggling with a lion) were destroyed.[3]

At the end of the second, and especially during the third century C.E., a major change took place, and a new page was opened in the history of Jewish art. The disasters of the Bar Kochba war were followed by a period of reorganization within the Jewish community, then concentrated mainly in Galilee. This was a period of political peace, normalized relations with the Roman government, economic prosperity, and spiritual flourishing. The Sanhedrin, the Patriarchy, and the Rabbis formed the spiritual image of the community, and the *halakhah* had absolute control over everyday life. Now, during the heyday of this period, the barriers with which the Jewish nation surrounded itself for protection against foreign artistic influences were suddenly shattered. The Jews appropriated some customs from the peoples who lived in their midst or in whose midst they lived, and steadily they began to cultivate figurative art. They decorated their synagogues and even their tombs with animate motifs, including typically pagan designs.

This phenomenon was first discovered when Galilean synagogue ruins began to be unearthed at the end of the nineteenth and the beginning of the twentieth centuries. To many people this discovery came as a rude shock. The ornamental patterns on these synagogues, built at the end of the second and during the third centuries C.E., included a host of figures carved in stone, for example, human beings, animals (eagles, dolphins), and mythological figures (medusas, sea-goats, winged victories, and others). An even larger variety of figures was displayed in the mosaic floors of the synagogues from the Roman-Byzantine period. From the standpoint of possibilities for artistic expression, mosaic work closely resembles painting; and indeed, Jewish communities and Jewish artists exploited this medium to the utmost. First, we must mention the mosaic drawings with themes from Biblical narratives. The best picture of this type was discovered on the floor of the Beth Alpha synagogue, where the sacrifice of Isaac is depicted in full. In Na'aran near Jericho, there are remains of a depiction of Daniel in the lion's den; and at Gerasa in Transjordan, part of a beautiful portrayal of the story of Noah's Ark is preserved. On the synagogue floor at Yaphia, near Nazareth, the emblems of the twelve tribes seem to have been delineated. The content of these biblical themes seems very appropriate for synagogue decoration; however, the use of the Zodiac with the sun-god in his horse-drawn chariot in the center, surrounded by figures of women symbolizing the four seasons of the year, seems surprising. Yet these particular motifs appear on synagogue floors in Na'aran, Beth Alpha, and Hammat-Tiberias. This is apparently the most pagan theme in the synagogue mosaics. Furthermore, many synagogue floors are decorated with figures of animals, e.g., lions alongside religious symbols (like the menorah or the Ark of the Law), and animals and birds in various decorative combinations.

A most interesting depiction of a biblical figure in pagan dress was recently discovered in Gaza on a mosaic floor dating to the fifth century C.E. King David is portrayed as Orpheus playing the harp, flanked by different animals listening to the sounds. The word *David* is written in Hebrew near the figure.[4] The largest and most important

assemblage of ancient Jewish art was discovered in the third century C.E. synagogue at Dura-Europos on the banks of the Euphrates River, consisting of a series of ten variegated mural paintings whose subjects are derived from biblical narratives. These paintings opened a new chapter in the history of Jewish iconography.

Of particular importance to our subject is the mosaic floor in a private house recently discovered at Beth She'an.[5] Among other objects depicted on this floor there are figures from the Homeric tale of Odysseus and the Sirens and a figure of the Nile-god. The owner of the house, Leontius (probably a Hellenized Jew), went to extremes in choosing a pagan/mythological theme for decorating his home. His Judaism is demonstrated by a menorah inserted into a Greek commemorative inscription which also mentions his brother Jonathan. This was the first time that concrete evidence was found of the style in which an affluent, secular Jew might decorate his house during the Byzantine period.

The discovery of the necropolis of Beth She'arim supplemented our knowledge, formerly based only on material discovered in ancient synagogues, of the extent to which figurative art was propagated among Jews. It transpires that Jews ornamented not only their synagogues but even their tombs with figures of people and animals, including motifs borrowed from pagan art. By now it is evident that the paintings in the Jewish catacombs in Rome, whose profusion of pagan themes aroused such intense dispute at the time of their discovery, were not an isolated phenomenon but an integral product of a general trend deriving from the influence of a foreign environment on the one hand, and the relaxed observance of the Second Commandment on the other. The archaeological discoveries prove beyond doubt that at the end of the period of the Mishnah and the Talmud it was common practice for Palestinian Jews to decorate their synagogues, tombs, and private homes with animate figures — in carving, painting, and mosaics. The themes of these decorations were not only Jewish or universal but even specifically pagan. Furthermore, the inscriptions testify that the contributors and the artists who executed the work were also Jews.

Such were the facts shown by archaeological research. Initially, these findings caused such surprise that the first scholars who dealt with this subject and who still did not have all the information at their disposal made the strange conjecture that the Galilean synagogues were really built by Roman emperors who benevolently donated them to the Jewish community. However, as archaeological data accumulated and began to be reconsidered in the light of conditions prevailing during that period, these newly uncovered facts no longer seemed puzzling since the environment from which they sprang is clearly reflected in Talmudic literature. From the long discussions in the tractates on idolatry (the halakhot on Avodah Zarah) in the Mishnah and Talmud, it transpires that among the people there were serious infringements of the prohibition specified in the Torah "Thou shalt not make unto thee any graven image or any likeness of any thing...," and that the strict self-control of the previous period had been relaxed. The auspicious political and economic circumstances prevailing at the end of the second and subsequent centuries, the tolerant attitude of the Roman authorities who no longer attempted to force idolatry on the Jews, residence in Gentile cities, and economic contacts with the mixed population in Palestine, all intensified the influence of foreign culture on the Jews and mitigated their suspicions about the dangers inherent in this influence. Instead of indiscriminately applying the absolute proscription against figurative art, the Rabbis began to deal with each case individually, i.e., whether a particular representation was the unavoidable product of the times and devoid of religious

meaning or whether it was a potentially dangerous source of pagan worship.

This is not the place to deal with the myriads of complicated definitions of idolatry in the halakhah. We shall also not quote the unequivocal convictions of the orthodox, nor the halakhic debates which deal at one and the same time with prohibitions and allowances of different images from the point of view both of form and execution. There is such a plethora of contradictory halakhot (laws) that they can hardly assist us in understanding the phenomena under discussion here. Instead, we shall merely note a few events referred to in the Talmud that clearly reflect the transformation which had taken place in the rabbinical attitude toward figurative art and its manifestations in the everyday life of that period.

It is related that Rabbi Gamaliel the Second, one of the great Tannaim of the second century C.E., entered a bathhouse in which there was a statue of Aphrodite.[6] His excuse for his conduct was that the building was just a bathhouse and that the statue was only there for ornamentation; since the pagans themselves did not revere the statue, it is surely meaningless. This interesting story is sufficient to indicate the new spirit which began to pervade even among some eminent Rabbis, a more tolerant spirit which could differentiate between important and trivial issues. This approach obviously had a direct influence on the opinions of broad sections of the public.

Rabbi Jonathan (third century C.E.) is said not to have protested when his contemporaries began to paint pictures on walls.[7] In the time of R. Abun (first half of the fourth century C.E.), it is related that he, too, did not object when Jews began to make mosaic drawings.[8] These two facts vividly delineate the true state of affairs at that time and explain the existence of the mural decorations at Dura-Europos and the ornamental mosaic floors in the synagogues. If two such great Rabbis did not object or attempt to prevent these activities, it means that they viewed such practices as legitimate, in keeping with the customs of the time. There is also a rather strange account of Rab and Shmuel bar Shmuel from Nehardea in Babylonia (circa third century C.E.) who went to pray in the Shaf-Yativ synagogue, even though it contained a statue.[9] This is the only reference to a statue inside a synagogue; however, we have no information as to what kind of statue it was. Furthermore, this particular synagogue's importance was renowned: it is even said that the *Shekhinah* (Divine Presence) appeared there twice.

There is also a tale about another Babylonian synagogue where the Tanna Rab once prayed on a fast day.[10] At a certain point in the prayers, when all the congregation knelt on the stone floor, he did not kneel because he maintained that it is written: "You shall not place figured stones in your land to bow down unto them." From this it emerges that the mosaic floor was decorated with figures. The pictures on the floor did not prevent Rab from praying in the synagogue; however, he was careful to observe the commandment "Thou shalt not bow down to them." In this respect, there is a most interesting translation in Targum Yonathan of Leviticus 26:1: "Ye shall make you no idols nor graven image, neither rear you up a standing image, neither shall ye set up any image of stone in your land, to bow down unto it: for I am the Lord your God." Yonathan adds his interpretation to this verse: "However, if there are stoae with engraved pictures, or figures on the floor of your synagogues, do not bow down to them for I am your God." Since the Aramaic translation was intended for popular instruction of the Torah, it obviously reflects the conditions prevailing at the time of Yonathan ben Uziel. This unique piece of evidence reveals the degree of tolerance toward figurative art which prevailed during that period.

The preceding discussion thus demonstrates that among the Rabbis approaches varied as to the meaning of idolatry. The rigorously orthodox looked upon the slightest deviation from the proscription as idolatry. On the other hand, other Rabbis understood that it was almost impossible to abrogate the new reality; they, therefore, took a more tolerant stand in their interpretation of the Second Commandment by emphasizing the second sentence: "Thou shalt not worship them." The same spirit is evinced in the previously cited verse from Leviticus 26:1, where the emphasis is placed mainly on the prohibition of idols. This is the basis for the Rabbis' concessions in the *halakhot* of Avodah Zarah, wherein it is stated that the prohibition is applicable only to an image about which there is proof that it was worshipped or suspicion that it will be worshipped. At that time, there was evidently good reason for supposing that such suspicions were unfounded. Scholars have shown that the Jewry of that period was indeed quite immune to, and unafraid of, idolatry; therefore, the Rabbis could afford to take a more permissive attitude toward a prohibition with which the public would not have complied in any case. This liberality, within limits, of course, reflects a certain pragmatic flexibility and acceptance of the existing circumstances.

The people who pursued figurative art, whether for business or pleasure, abided by the liberal approach. This was expressed not only in their private homes, for which archaeological evidence is still rather limited, but mainly in their synagogues and tombs which were decorated with various images, some even borrowed from the pagan world, without arousing any suspicion of idolatry.

Though the use of figurative art was widely accepted, there still were, nevertheless, large segments of the Jewish population that observed the proscription rigorously and could not compromise with behavior which in their view was unadulterated pagan worship. During times of trouble or edicts against Jews, religious fanatics became predominant. They would then mutilate "prohibited" figures on synagogues and deface them so badly that today the original images are scarcely discernible. Such iconoclasm is evident in many places: all the reliefs of animate figures in Capernaum, Kfar Bar'am, and other places were so effectively damaged that their exact form can no longer be determined. The same fate befell the figures on the mosaic floor of the Na'aran synagogue.

Two major questions are posed by Jewish figurative art: *(a)* Why was such an art used at all? *(b)* Why were pagan themes used?

If the very use of figures for decorative purposes was an infringement of the Torah commandment "Thou shalt make no graven image...," then the use of pagan themes was doubly so. After all, the image of a lion or an eagle is hardly comparable to a mythological figure like a centaur or a Nike: the insult of pagan content is added to the already existing injury of making "a graven image." It was difficult for scholars to understand why Jews used these motifs and why they did not confine themselves to Jewish themes or to decorations with no symbolic value. Their usual excuse was that in the course of time these motifs lost their original pagan/symbolic significance and evolved into purely decorative designs. This opinion is accepted today by most scholars, Jew and Gentile alike (except for E. Goodenough, whose theories will be discussed shortly); the present writer has also expressed the same opinion on various occasions. However, despite the apparent plausibility of this explanation it is actually an oversimplification which does not elucidate many problematical details of this intricate subject.

Let us take the Zodiac signs as an example. On the floors of three synagogues — Na'aran, Beth Alpha, and Ḥammath-Tiberias — this theme occupies a very

important place — near the tablet depicting the Ark of the Law. In the Na'aran mosaic it is also near the picture of Daniel in the lion's den; and in the Beth Alpha synagogue floor it is located between the illustrations of the Ark of the Law and the Sacrifice of Isaac. It is inconceivable that a theme which was meaningless for the congregation would consistently be assigned so central a place, right next to the subjects of deepest religious and symbolic significance. The names of the constellations, written in Hebrew beside the figures, attest that these symbols were indeed deliberately chosen. The very need for a Hebrew translation for the constellation names customarily used by Gentiles means that our forefathers also pursued astrology and consulted the constellations. In fact, scholars have pointed out that the existence of representations of the Zodiac in synagogues indicates that Jews, too, were not invincible to the prevailing belief in the influence of the constellations on world events, a belief which infiltrated into all the cultures and was accepted by all the peoples of the ancient world. Such sentiments were widely held by the common people and even the Rabbis were not immune to their impact. Depictions of the Zodiac were also a favorite subject in Jewish art in the Middle Ages for the ornamentation of prayer books, manuscripts, and calendars. In synagogal decorations, the Zodiac has been used throughout the ages, right up to our days.

In the inner circle of the Zodiac there is a depiction of Helios, the sun-god, on his horse-drawn chariot; in the Beth Alpha mosaic the moon and stars also appear in the background. This would seem to be the most pagan motif in the synagogue decorations since it is a personification of the sun[11] as the center of the universe, together with the symbols of the constellations and the seasons of the year, a typical graphic expression of the conception "stars and planets," which is just a synonym for idol worship. Nevertheless, among Jews this particular depiction became a favorite illustration of the heavenly host and occupied an important position in synagogal decorations throughout the generations, without arousing suspicions of idolatry.

The representation of the sun in the synagogue mosaics was borrowed from the ancient portrayals of Helios in Greek art. However, the same pictorial representation of the sun is expressed in the Midrashic literature. For example, in Bamidbar Rabba 12, there is the following interpretation of verse 3:10 of the Song of Songs "his chariot of purple..., etc." or "This is the sun on high, rising in his chariot and illuminating the world and riding bedecked like a groom, as it is written: which is as a bridegroom coming out of his chamber..." (Psalms 19:5). A similar description is also preserved in the "Sayings of Rabbi Eliezer," chapter 6. An allegorical description of the cosmic forces is not foreign to Jewish thought which portrays the God of Israel in the following manner: "And he rode upon a cherub and did fly; yea, did he fly upon the wings of the wind" (Psalms 18:10). In the Tabernacle and Solomon's Temple, while the cherubs took on the customary form employed in Canaanite-Phoenician art, the God of Israel "seated among the cherubs" remained invisible and intangible. Apparently, for the congregation in the synagogue the figure in the chariot was not a personification of the god Helios, but the sun itself as a component of the cycle of cosmic forces depicted in the Zodiac: the sun and the moon, the constellations symbolizing the twelve months, and the four seasons of the year. Once the Jews were permitted to depict figures at all, they did not refrain from appropriating certain mythological and symbolic figures from pagan art which had also become accepted in the legends and *midrashim*. We have already seen how conscious use was made of these symbols in the Zodiac. The question now remains: did Jews attribute any symbolic significance to the rest of the

pagan motifs, or were these motifs strictly ornamental?

This problem has been exhaustively dealt with recently by the late Professor Erwin R. Goodenough, the eminent scholar of Hellenistic religion and thought who dedicated his giant work of thirteen volumes to the subject of Jewish symbolism in the Hellenistic-Roman Period. All the documentary evidence, both archaeological and literary, is assembled in this monumental undertaking. Goodenough devoted his brilliant mind and keen analytical insight both to the presentation and attempted solution of this problem. In brief, this is the essence of his thesis:

During the Second Temple period, the Jews did not cultivate figurative art due to the predominating influence of the Pharisees. However, after the destruction of the Temple, the Jews appropriated the ornamentation and symbolism of the Hellenistic world in all its forms. This phenomenon can only be explained by postulating that after the political loss of the country the strict control of the religious leadership was weakened, and the defenses of Jewish religion were breached. Many Jews were intrigued by foreign culture, including the arts of painting and sculpture. They even went so far as to use the pagan art of their neighbors in synagogues and tombs, though completely aware of the idolatrous/symbolic character of these forms. Though these symbols were indeed devoid of their original pagan content, they were assigned a new ritual value associated with a mystic, eschatological belief in immortality of the soul and hope for resurrection. This phenomenon is comparable to the development in Christian art, which also employed pagan symbols but invested them with new meaning. The followers of this new mystic movement, which apparently embraced extensive sectors of the people, did not actually become estranged from Judaism; however, their use of pagan symbols was anathema to the Rabbis and, by using these symbols, they excluded themselves from normative Jewry. In Goodenough's opinion, official Judaism never permitted the use of any image at any time, despite the liberal attitude of a few individual Rabbis. He also sees a certain resemblance between this mystic trend and the Reform movement in present-day Jewry, which is adapting the performance of ritual to the spirit of the times and the style of the Gentile environment, and which does not recognize the authority of the orthodox *halachic* religious leadership.

Most scholars did not accept Goodenough's thesis; on the contrary, his conjectures were generally met with outright rejection.[12] A small minority was prepared to accept a few of his assumptions. This is not the place to unfold all the details of the dispute on this extensive subject; recently, it has been summarized in a most lucid and trenchant article by Morton Smith.[13] In Smith's opinion, the universal mystic/ritual paganism on which Goodenough bases his system is simply a product of his imagination, as is his interpretation of pagan symbols. Thus, Goodenough's visualization of a mystic, anti-rabbinical Judaism throughout the Roman Empire, deduced from his interpretation of Jewish symbols, must be totally dismissed.

Nevertheless, two of Goodenough's basic assumptions are worthy of careful consideration: *(a)* all the motifs appearing in synagogal and Jewish sepulchral art have an inherent mystic symbolism; *(b)* the people who used these symbols belonged to a mystic movement of Hellenized Jews. This movement caused a schism within normative Judaism, which did not employ any type of art whatsoever.

One of the main faults of Goodenough's system lies in its sweeping generalizations. Almost all the graphic motifs from Palestine assembled in his books are indiscriminately presented as Jewish motifs, without considering their origin, i.e., whether they are definitely or possibly Jewish; or

definitely non-Jewish. He assigns symbolic significance to all the motifs, geometric, architectural, floral, and animal alike, Moreover, he maintains that these symbols did not have a mere superficial significance, but a deep mystic/eschatological meaning, frequently associated with Dionysian belief in sacramental salvation. All this is aimed at proving his thesis about the existence of a mystic/religious Jewry which had splintered off from official Jewry. In Goodenough's opinion, after the destruction of the Temple a united Jewry comprised of a broad gamut of different trends no longer existed; instead, Jewry was split: orthodox on the one hand, and mystic/Hellenized on the other. Furthermore, this partisan faction was not a small sect, but a large influential congregation which, according to the archaeological finds, must have almost displaced official Judaism.

It is no wonder that such comprehensive evaluations were so decisively, and justifiably, rejected by scholars. However, if we restrict our examination to some of the problems which Goodenough raised, we must admit that a few of his arguments sound reasonable even if we cannot accept his conclusions. For example, when dealing with themes that Jewish art borrowed from pagan art, we have frequently asserted that these themes became devoid of all content and evolved into strictly decorative designs. Goodenough objects to this argument; he maintains that the consistent selectivity of the same borrowed motifs testifies that their choice was deliberate, and that they do, therefore, have symbolic significance. We have already seen that the Zodiacs in the synagogues retained the symbolic values of the constellations. However, this significance is straightforward and well known: the constellations are simply graphic representations of values which were openly accepted by the Judaism of that period, and not mystic/religious symbols of deep significance, as Goodenough contended.

It is in this spirit that mythological

figures like the centaurs (Dura-Europos, Chorazain), the sea-goat (Dura-Europos, Capernaum), the siren (Beth She'an), and others were depicted. Jews were familiar with these figures not only from their neighbors' art, but also from Midrashic literature.[14] The tremendous influence of Midrashic literature on Jewish art is particularly conspicuous in the biblical scenes at Dura-Europos (third century C.E.). The winged victories bearing a wreath (Beth She'arim, Kfar Bar'am, Ramah, and others) very probably lost their original significance even in the pagan art of that period and became accepted among Jews as associations with winged Jewish mythological figures (cherubim, angels[?]). Since the lion and the eagle are deeply rooted in the poetry of the Jewish people, their frequent appearance in Jewish art both as a vague symbol (e.g., of power, kingship, and so on) and as a purely decorative motif should not cause surprise. The different birds and animals, occurring both individually and in groups (Na'aran, Ma'on/Nirim, and others) are usually conventional designs which were copied from pattern pages that were widely distributed in the ancient world.

The most widespread and characteristic floral design employed in Jewish art is the vine. If we want to look for a symbolic significance for the vine, then we may say quite simply that it is one of the "seven kinds" (Deuteronomy 8:8) with which the country was blessed, and there is absolutely no reason for associating it with a mystic Dionysian ritual as Goodenough does. The universality of the vine as a decorative motif is also evidenced by the lead coffins found at Beth She'arim, which were manufactured in advance for people of different religions (see above, the discussion on the lead coffins, pp. 173–182). Each customer could add a symbolic decoration of his own choice: Jews, a menorah; Christians, the chi-rho; and pagans, a pagan mythological figure. Among the reliefs at Chorazain, only the vintage scenes might have been borrowed from Dionysian art; however, even in this case, there is no reason for attributing any significance to them other than plain, straightforward grape harvesting. The wreath motif doubtlessly originates in Hellenistic art, where it symbolized the bestowing of honor and praise both upon the living and the dead. This concept is foreign to Jewish thought; however, the fact remains that it became accepted among Jews during the rigorously orthodox Hasmonean period and that it neither impaired nor offended the principles of Jewish religion. This inference also applies to other motifs which we consider purely decorative, like the rosette. The compass-made rosette is very common in Jewish art; among the ossuary decorations, it is the most frequently encountered design. Whether or not it had magic significance at one time is an open question; in either case, it is not relevant to our problem since the use of certain magic symbols is universal and surely cannot furnish a criterion for the degree of Hellenization among Jews. The only conclusion deducible from archaeological data is that the rosette, in all its variants, evolved into a conventional decorative pattern which was easy to execute by compass and to use wherever it was needed.

In the clarification of the problem of pictorial art among Jews, Beth She'arim occupies a special position since it is the only site except for the catacombs at Rome where this art was also employed on Jewish tombs. If we were dealing only with a single grave at Beth She'arim or with a tomb in other places about the country, we could interpret this figurative art as the product of non-observant Hellenized Jews. We might even be able to view these Jews as mystic dissenters, in Goodenough's vein. However, we are discussing the large, central necropolis of Beth She'arim, which was revered both by Jews in Palestine and in the Diaspora as the burial place of Rabbi Judah Ha-Nassî. Nobody can deny the fact that Beth She'arim was under the control of rabbinical Judaism; nor can one assume that this leadership would have permitted the burial of Jewish dissenters, who did not recognize rabbinical authority and were even suspected of heresy, to be buried within the precincts of the city. Furthermore, it is totally inconceivable that mystical reformed Jews, from far and near, would have sought to be buried precisely in Beth She'arim. Thus, it emerges that all the deceased at Beth She'arim, including those whose way of life had become Hellenized, belonged to official Jewry. Indeed, it is evident that there was no other Jewry during that period.

The same liberal attitude on the part of Judaism toward figurative art was also revealed most convincingly by the discovery of catacomb 20. We were already aware of this permissive spirit, which Goodenough flatly repudiates, from the synagogue remains and the earlier finds at Beth She'arim: in one and the same catacomb, rabbis and their families are interred in hewn graves and simple coffins alongside other individuals of unknown identity who are interred in sarcophagi decorated with human and animal figures. Rabbis designated as "the holy ones" who, during their lifetime, probably refrained from even looking at a coin bearing an image, were buried in undecorated coffins beside Jews interred in elaborate sarcophagi decorated with idolatrous, mythological scenes. It is very likely that the deceased buried in these pagan sarcophagi were greatly influenced by foreign culture; they may have been "progressive," or even Hellenized, Jews. Nevertheless, they must have been staunch, conscientious Jews, otherwise they would not have requested to be brought from afar in order to be buried in the same cemetery as Rabbi Judah Ha-Nassî. The burial of individuals from such different backgrounds, in close proximity in the same catacomb, a phenomenon not due to objective reasons since there was no lack of space in the other catacombs, also attests to a Jewish community life of mutual understanding and tolerance. Historical circumstances dictated this state of affairs; otherwise, the Jewish people might well have split along the lines which Goodenough so mistakenly imagined.

NOTES

1 Y. Aharoni, *Excavations at Ramat Raḥel — Seasons* 1959–1960, Rome, 1962, Pl. 28.

2 L. Y. Raḥmani, "The Tomb of Jason," *IEJ*, XVII (1967), p. 61, figs. 5–6.

3 Y. Yadin, *The Finds from the Bar Kochba Period in the Cave of the Letters*, Jerusalem, 1963, fig. 45, Pl. 17.

4 A. Ovadiah, "The Synagogue at Gaza," *IEJ*, XVIII (1968–69), p. 124.

5 N. Zori, "The House of Kyrios Leontis at Beth Shean" *IEJ*, XVI (1966), pp. 123–134.

6 M. Avodah Zarah, 3, 4.

7 Talmud Jer. Avodah Zarah, 3, 42d.

8 See: Y. N. Epstein, "Additional Fragments of the Jerushalmi," *Tarbiz*, III (1932), p. 121.

9 Bab. Talmud Avodah Zarah, 43b.

10 *Ibid.*

11 On this subject see: M. Dothan, "The Figure of Sol Invictus in the Mosaic of Ḥammath-Tiberias," *All the Land of Naphtali*, Jerusalem, 1968, pp. 130–134.

12 See below, in the bibliography, no. 8.

13 *Ibid.*, no. 15.

14 *Ibid.*, no. 2.

SELECTED BIBLIOGRAPHY FOR CHAPTER VII

1 E. L. Sukenik, *The Synagogue of Dura-Europos and its Frescoes,* Jerusalem, 1947, pp. 164–170 (Hebrew).

2 J. Braslavi, "Symbols and Mythological Figures in the Early Synagogues in Galilee," *All the Land of Naphtali,* Jerusalem, 1968, pp. 106–129 (Hebrew).

3 G. Talpir, "Jerusalem in Jewish Art," *Gazit,* XXV (1967–1968), pp. 173–192 (Hebrew).

4 N. Avigad, "Excavations at Beth She'arim, 1953," *IEJ,* IV (1954), pp. 88–107; Pls. 8–12.

5 *Idem,* "Excavations at Beth She'arim, 1954," *IEJ,* V (1955), pp. 205–239; Pls. 25–33.

6 *Idem,* "Excavations at Beth She'arim, 1955," *IEJ,* VII (1957), pp. 73–92, 239–255; Pls. 17–24.

7 *Idem,* "Excavations at Beth She'arim, 1958," *IEJ,* IX (1959), pp. 205–220; Pls. 21–24.

8 E. E. Urbach, "The Rabbinical Laws of Idolatry in the Second and Third Centuries in the Light of Archaeological and Historical Facts," *IEJ,* IX (1959), pp. 149–165, 229–245.

9 L. Blau, "Early Christian Archaeology from the Jewish Point of View," *Hebrew Union College Annual,* III (1926), pp. 169–203.

10 N. Frey, "La question des images chez les juifs à la lumière des récouvertes," *Biblica,* XV (1934), pp. 265–300.

11 Goodenough, *Symbols,* IV, pp. 3–24.

12 C. H. Kraeling, *The Excavations at Dura-Europos,* VIII, 1: *The Synagogue,* New Haven, 1956, pp. 340–346.

13 E. Goodenough, "The Rabbis and Jewish Art in the Greco-Roman Period," *Hebrew Union College Annual,* XXXII (1961), pp. 269–279.

14 J. Neusner, "Jewish Use of Pagan Symbols after 70 C.E.," *Journal of Religion,* XLIII (1963), pp. 285–294.

15 M. Smith, "Goodenough's 'Jewish Symbols' in Retrospect," *Journal of Biblical Literature,* LXXXVI (1967), pp. 53–68.

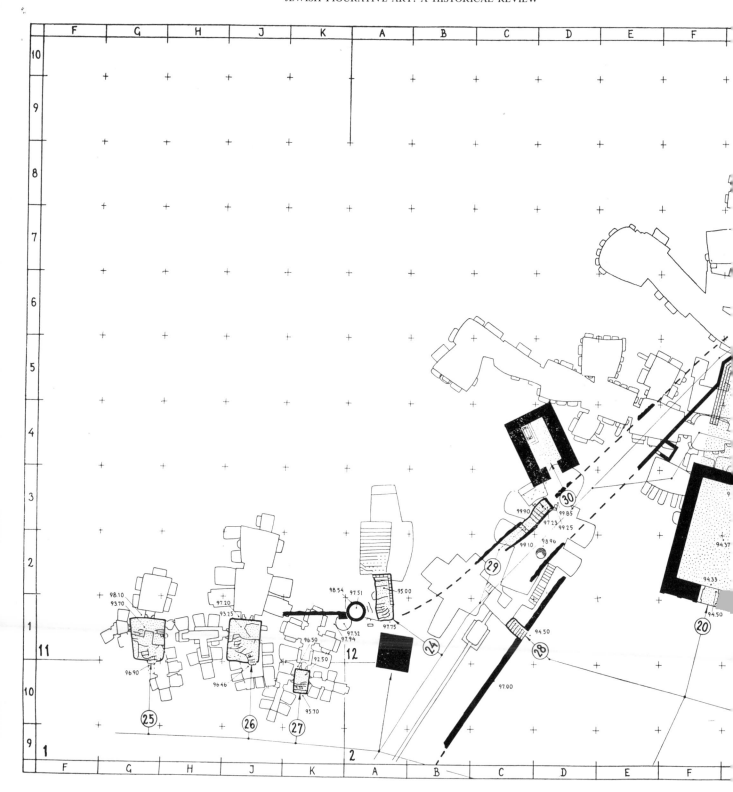

Fig. 131 General plan of catacombs 12–30

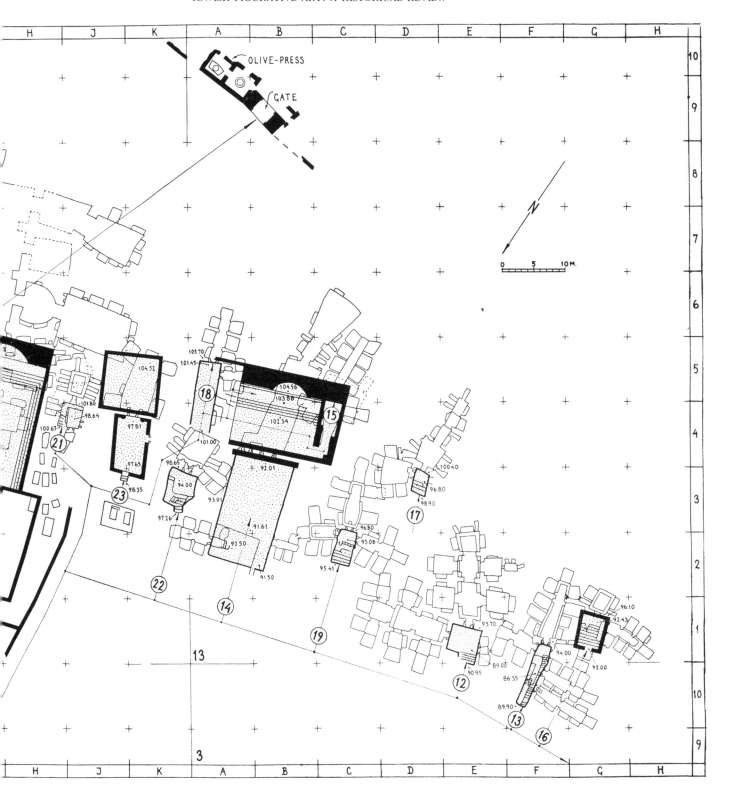

PLATES

The northern slope of the Beth She'arim hill after the excavations and development of the site.
View of catacombs 12–23.

PLATE II

1. *The excavations on the Beth She'arim hill in 1954. View from north.*
In the center, the benches above catacomb 14.

2. *The excavations in catacombs 17, 15, 14, and 18, from right to left.*

PLATE III

1. Looking toward room III.

2. Looking toward room V.

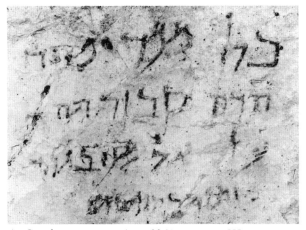

3. Aramaic inscription (no. 1) in room III.

4. Greek inscription (no. 134) in room III.

5. Arcosolium 3 in room III. Above the arcosolium, left, the Greek inscription. Inside the arcosolium, right, the Aramaic inscription; bottom left, the breach leading to catacomb 13.

Catacomb 12, Hall A

PLATE IV

1. The door at the entrance.

2. Room I, looking south.

◀ *3. Room VIII, looking south.*

4. Aramaic inscription (no. 2) in room VIII.

Catacomb 12, Hall A

PLATE V

1. Room I.

2. Relief of menorah in room I. Breach to hall A.

3. Right doorpost of archway to room V.

5. The "Esther from Tyre" inscription.

◀ 4. The "Kalliope from Byblos" inscription.

Catacomb 12, Hall B

PLATE VI

1. *Greek inscriptions at entrance to room IV.*

2. *Arcosolium 2 in room IV.*

3. *The inscription of the "Head of the Council of Elders from Antioch" to the right of the entrance to room IV.*

5. *Entrance door to hall C.*

4. *Arcosolium 2 in room V.*

Catacomb 12, Hall B

PLATE VII

Catacomb 13, the courtyard. Looking north.

PLATE VIII

Catacomb 13, the courtyard. Looking south.

PLATE IX

1. Door of hall D with Greek inscription
(no. 150) above it.

2. Door of hall E.

3. Door of hall J.

4. Door of hall K.

PLATE X

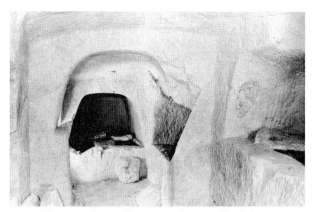

1. *Hall B. To the right, arcosolium with Hebrew inscription.*

3. *Carved menorah in room II of hall K.*

2. *Inscription "Judan ben Levi" (no. 5) hall B.*

4. *Hall I. Looking from room II to room VI, through room IV.*

Catacomb 13

PLATE XI

4. *Marble plaque with Greek inscription (no. 149).*

1. *Greek inscription (no. 162) in hall D.*

2. *Hall D.*

5. *Hall F.*

3. *Greek inscription (no. 163) in hall D.*

6. *Inscription (no. 167) in hall J.*

PLATE XII

1. Entrance to hall.

2. Room I, view of entrance.

3. Greek inscription (no. 168) on lintel of entrance to hall.

8. Greek inscription (no. 169c).

5. Greek inscription (no. 169b).

4. Room II with its inscription.

6. Greek inscription.

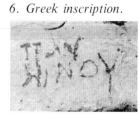

7. Greek inscription (no. 169a).

9. Greek inscription.

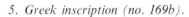

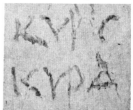

Catacomb 13, Hall G

PLATE XIII

1. Entrance to hall L.

2. The tomb of Aristeas in hall L with two Greek inscriptions above it.

3. The "Aristeas" inscription in hall L (no. 171).

4. "Aristeas the Sidonian" (no. 172) inscription in hall L.

5. Hall J. Looking toward the room with the kokhs.

6. Greek inscription (no. 170) in room II, hall J.

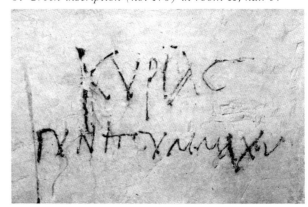

PLATE XIV

Catacomb 14. Arched façade and the benches above.

PLATE XV

1. *The benches above the catacomb.*

2. *The apse and the upper benches.*

PLATE XVI

1. The bench complex, looking east. At bottom, catacomb 15.

2. Two bronze hinges of the main door viewed from above, the side, and below.

Catacomb 15

PLATE XVII

1. The western arch.

3. Pilaster of the eastern arch.

2. Detail of the western arch.

4. Doorway
of Hall B.

Catacomb 14

PLATE XVIII

1. Central door in the arched façade.

3. The main entrance from inside. One half is blocked by stones.

2. The main entrance prior to the removal of the external blockage.

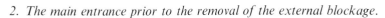

Catacomb 14

PLATE XIX

1. The main room of hall A, looking south.

2. The graves of "Rabbi Shim'on" and "Anina haQatan" in the corner of Room I.

Catacomb 14

PLATE XX

1. Built archway between rooms I and III.

2. The same archway seen from room III.

PLATE XXI

1. The built tomb in room II.

2. The built tomb. View of the inside.

3. Clay sarcophagus in room V.

4. Breach in the courtyard, blocked with stones.

Catacomb 14

PLATE XXII

1. *Hebrew inscription (no. 12) in room III.*

2. *Inscription in unidentified script in room I.*

3. *The "Rabbi Shim'on" inscription (no. 8).*

4. *The "Rabbi Gamaliel" inscription (no. 9).*

5. *The "Anina haQatan" inscription (no. 11).*

6. *The "Rabbi Aniana" inscription (no. 10).*

Catacomb 14

PLATE XXIII

1. *Entrance to hall A.*

2. *Hall A, looking south.*

PLATE XXIV

1. Greek inscription in catacomb 15 (no. 176).

2. Doorway of hall A, catacomb 16.

3. Courtyard of catacomb 17.

4. Coin from catacomb 17.

5. Greek inscription (no. 182) in catacomb 17.

PLATE XXV

1. Main door to hall A and the Greek inscription (no. 184) on the lintel.

2. Relief of lulab on the right doorpost of the archway between rooms II and III.

3. Relief of lulab on the left doorpost of the arch.

PLATE XXVI

1. *Greco-Jewish epigram on marble plaque.*

2. *Detail of the plaque showing menorah and other ritual objects.*

PLATE XXVII

1. The courtyard, looking south.

2. Entrance door to the western hall.

PLATE XXVIII

1. Entrance door to hall A.

2. Concentric circles carved on the walls of room I.

3. Greek inscription (no. 191) in arcosolium 2, room I, hall A.

4. Relief of menorah in room I, hall A.

Catacomb 19

PLATE XXIX

1. Entrance door to hall B.

4. The "Benjamin" inscription (no. 189) in hall B.

◀ *2. Hall B.*

5. The "Daniel" inscription on marble plaque.

3. The "Justus" inscription in hall B (no. 190).

PLATE XXX

1. Benches above the catacomb.

2. Entrance to courtyard.

Catacomb 20

PLATE XXXI

1. The façade after its discovery.

2. The arched façade after its reconstruction.

Catacomb 20

PLATE XXXII

1. *Stone of the restored entablature on the upper part of the façade.*

2. *The restored western arch.*

PLATE XXXIII

1. The western side of the façade after it was uncovered.

3. One of the central door panels.

2. Opening to the courtyard. View from inside.

PLATE XXXIV

1. *Room III. On the right, the sarcophagus of the "Holy Ones."*

2. *Room IV.*

3. *Room V, looking east.*

4. *Room VIII₃. On the left, the "Lions" sarcophagus.*

5. *Rockfall in room XVIII, looking south.*

6. *Room XXVI. On the left, the "Menorah" sarcophagus.*

Catacomb 20 after excavation

PLATE XXXV

1. Room VIII, looking west. To the left the "Circles" sarcophagus.

2. Room XI. To the left the "Eagles" sarcophagus.

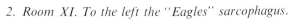

PLATE XXXVI

1. Carved menorah on the wall of room XXIII.

2. A built wall in room XIII.

3. Human figure incised on wall of room XIX.

PLATE XXXVII

1. View from room XIII toward room XIV through the archway.

2. Room XIV.

PLATE XXXVIII

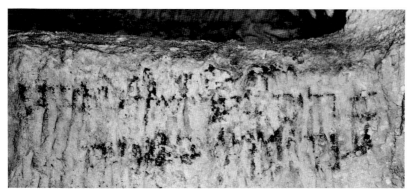

1. The "Miriam" inscription (no. 21).

2. The "Kyrilla" inscription (no. 18).

3. The "Holy Ones" inscription (no. 17).

4. The "Rabbi Hillel" inscription (no. 28).

5. The "Kyra Mega" inscription (no. 24).

PLATE XXXIX

1. *The "daughters" sarcophagus (no. 25).*

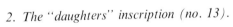

2. *The "daughters" inscription (no. 13).*

PLATE XL

1. The "lions" sarcophagus.

2. The "hunt" sarcophagus.

PLATE XLI

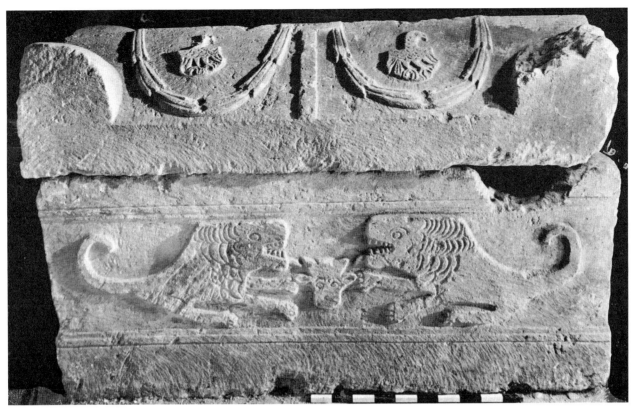

1. The "eagles" sarcophagus, front.

2. The "eagles" sarcophagus, back.

PLATE XLII

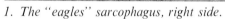 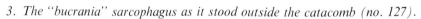

1. *The "eagles" sarcophagus, right side.*   2. *The "eagles" sarcophagus, left side.*

3. *The "bucrania" sarcophagus as it stood outside the catacomb (no. 127).*

PLATE XLIII

1. The "shell" sarcophagus (no. 117).

2. The "shell" sarcophagus, right side.

3. The "shell" sarcophagus, left side.

PLATE XLIII A

1, 2. Details of the "shell" sarcophagus.

PLATE XLIV

1. The "gable" sarcophagus (no. 103).

2. Hebrew inscription (no. 25)
on the "gable" sarcophagus.

3. Continuation of the inscription on the left side.

4. The "gable" sarcophagus, left side.

PLATE XLV

1. The "mask" sarcophagus (no. 84).

 2. The "mask" sarcophagus, right side.

3. The mask.

Catacomb 20

PLATE XLVI

1. The "Nikae" sarcophagus (no. 125).

2. The "menorah" sarcophagus (no. 122), right side.

3. The "menorah" sarcophagus, left side.

Catacomb 20

PLATE XLVII

1. The "acanthus" sarcophagus A (no. 101).

2. Right side.

3. Left side.

Catacomb 20

PLATE XLVII A

1. *Detail of the "acanthus" sarcophagus A.*

2. *The lid of the "gate" sarcophagus; view from above.*

PLATE XLVIII

1. The "acanthus" sarcophagus B (no. 97).

2. Detail of the "acanthus" sarcophagus B.

3. Left side.

PLATE XLIX

1. The "gate" sarcophagus (no. 46).

3. The "circles" sarcophagus (no. 43), right side.

2. The "gate" sarcophagus, right side.

PLATE L

1. The "column" sarcophagus (no. 124).

2. Grooved sarcophagus in the courtyard (no. 126).

3. Sarcophagus no. 27; detail

4. Marble plaque with Greek inscription from courtyard (see p. 83).

5. Fragment of lead sarcophagus.

PLATE LI

1. The "tabula-ansata" sarcophagus (no. 54).

2. Sarcophagus no. 96.

3–4. Sarcophagus no. 119.

PLATE LII

Marble fragments.

Catacomb 20

PLATE LIII

Marble fragments.

PLATE LIV

Marble fragments.

Catacomb 20

PLATE LV

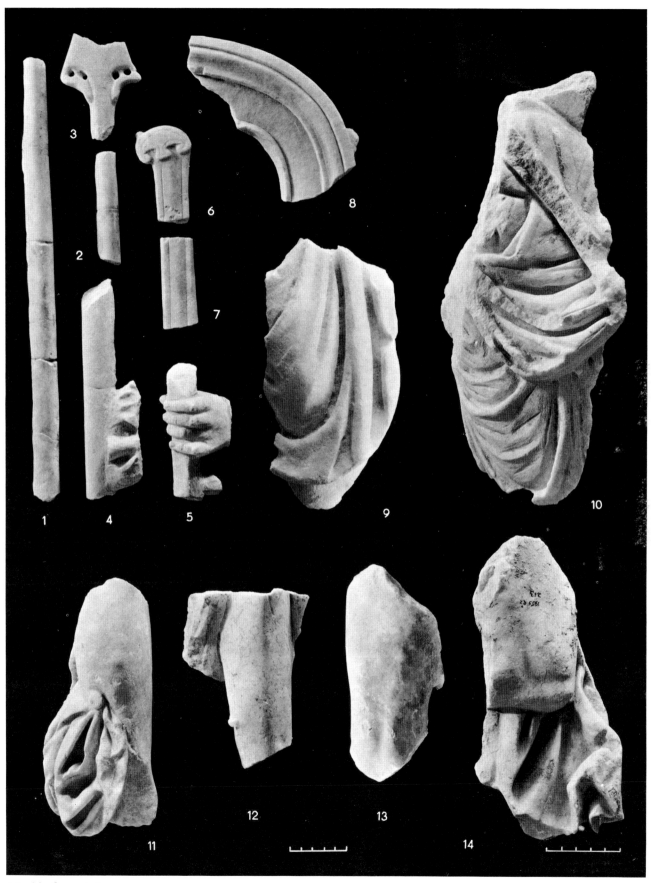

Marble fragments.

PLATE LVI

Marble fragments.

Catacomb 20

PLATE LVII

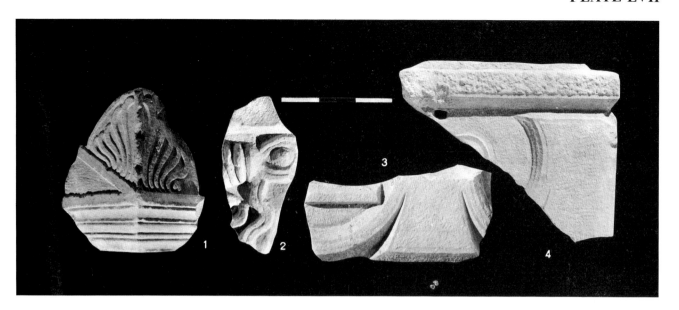

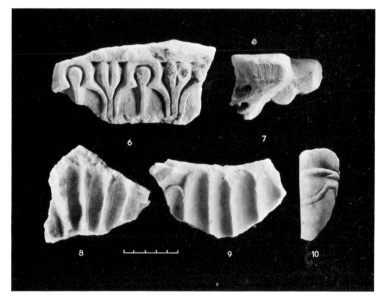

1–3. Marble fragments.

*4. Stone bolts from various
catacombs.*

PLATE LVIII

1. Looking toward the entrance of hall A.

3. The courtyard, looking south.

2. The small niche.

Catacomb 21

PLATE LIX

a. Hall A. Entrance prior to the removal of the blockage.

b. Hall A. Entrance and the blocking stone.

c. Entrance to Hall D.

d. Entrance to Hall G.

1. Catacomb 21

2. The ''Kalliope'' inscription (no. 200) on marble plaque in courtyard of catacomb 21.

3. Stone sarcophagus in catacomb 23.

Catacombs 21 and 23

PLATE LX

1. The main room in catacomb 22; view toward the entrance.

2. Terrace wall to the west of catacomb 20.

PLATE LXI

1. Outer tombs above catacomb 20.

2. Stone covering of tomb 1.

3. Tomb 1 after the removal of the stone covering.

4. Tomb 11.

PLATE LXII

3. *The long side; detail.*

2. *The long side.*

1. *The lid.*

Lead Sarcophagus No. 1

PLATE LXIII

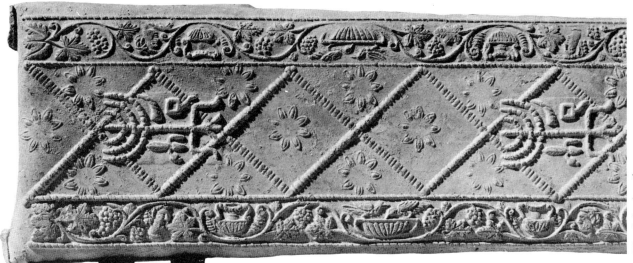

2. The lid; detail.

1. The narrow side.

Lead Sarcophagus No. 1

PLATE LXIV

1. The lid.

2. The long side.

3. The long side; detail.

Lead Sarcophagus No. 2

PLATE LXV

2. *The lid; detail.*

1. *The narrow side.*

Lead Sarcophagus No. 2

PLATE LXVI

4. The lid: detail.

Lead Sarcophagus No. 3

5. The arch on the narrow side.

2. The long side.

3. The narrow side.

1. The lid.

PLATE LXVII

1. The lid.

2. The long side.

3. The lid; detail.

4. The narrow side.

Lead Sarcophagus No. 4

PLATE LXVIII

Glassware

PLATE LXIX

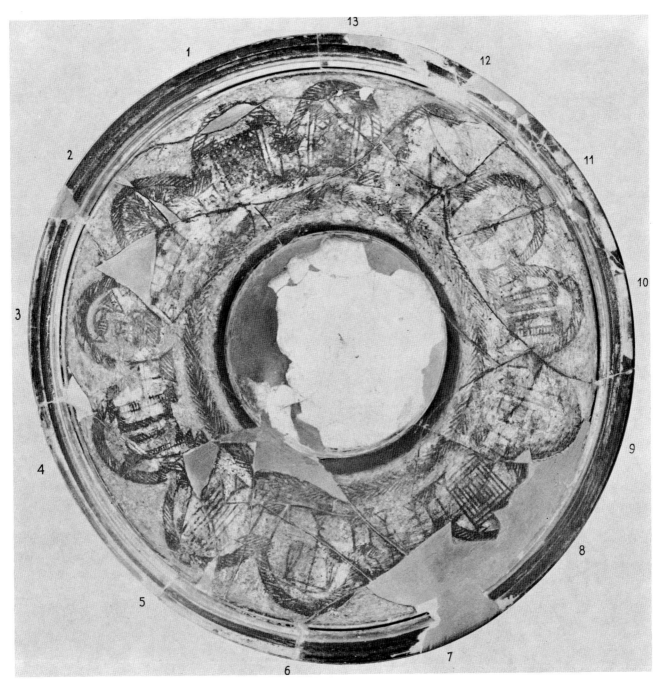

1. View from above.

2. View from the side.

Decorated Glass Plate

PLATE LXX

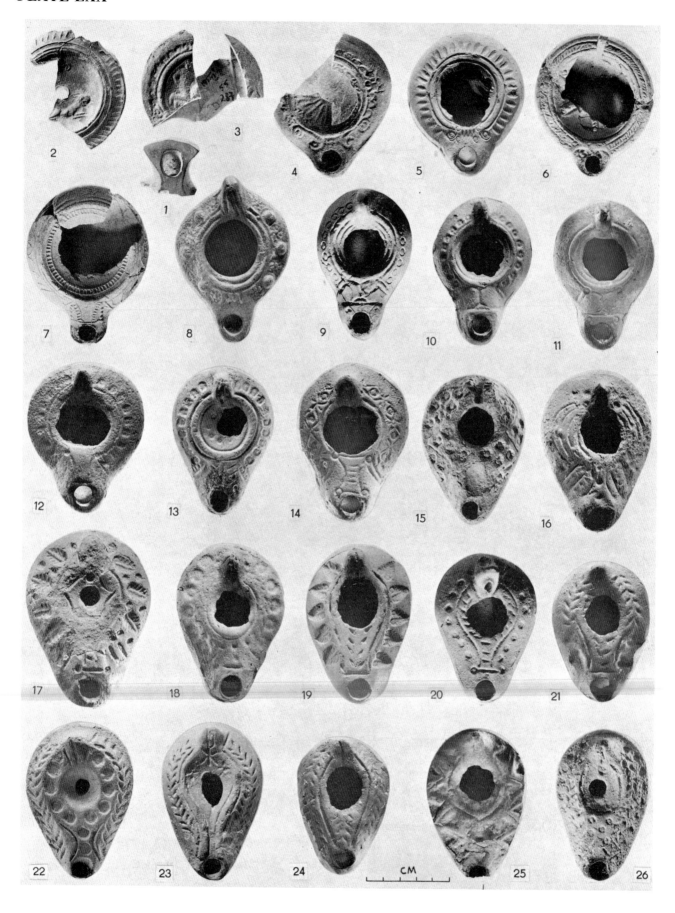

Lamps

PLATE LXXI

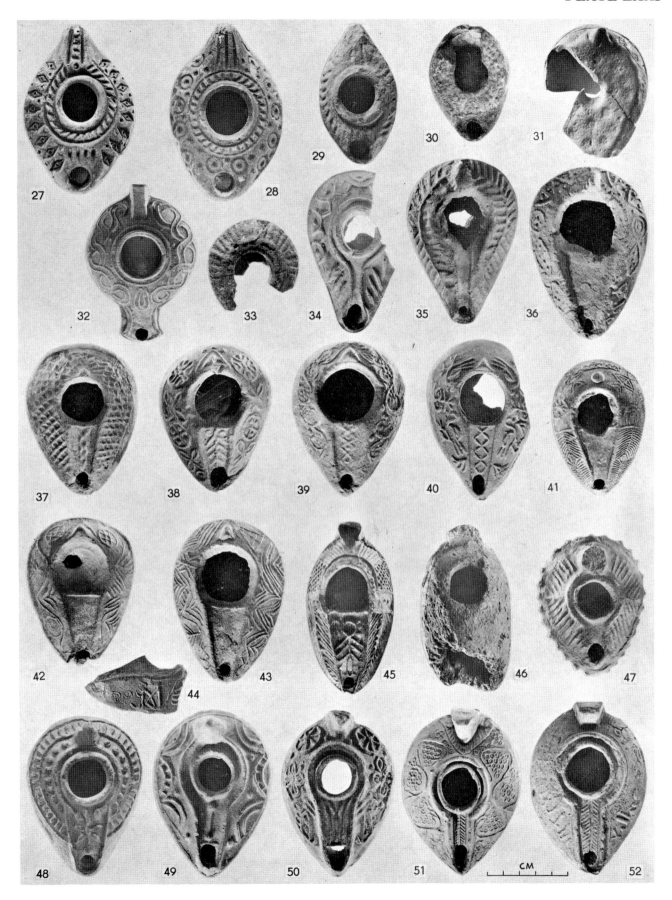

PLATE LXXII

Pottery

PLATE LXXIII

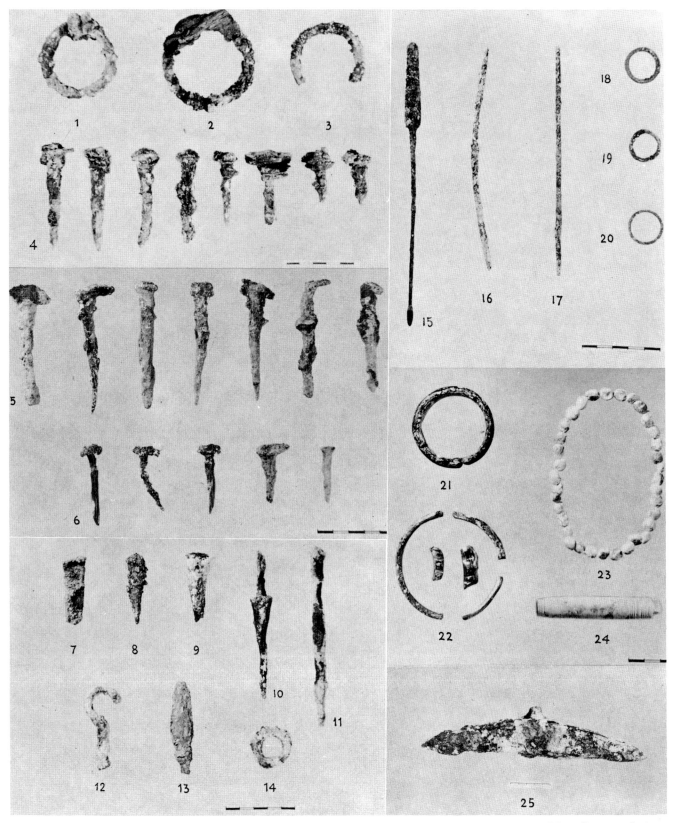

Miscellaneous finds

PLATE LXXIV

1. Greek inscription in catacomb 16.

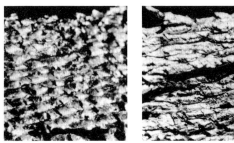

*2. Gold embroidery from lead sarcophagus no. 1.
(ca. 20:1)*

*3. Lead sarcophagus from Ḥederah; relief on
narrow side.*

4. Lead sarcophagus from Ḥederah; decoration on long side.

Appendix A

EXAMINATION OF ROCK SAMPLES FROM THE BETH SHE'ARIM BURIAL CAVES

U. Würzburger

At the request of Prof. N. Avigad an excursion was arranged to the Beth She'arim catacombs, with the aim of examining the rocks from which some of the sarcophagi and the doors of Catacombs 14 and 20 are made.

During the excursion samples of nine sarcophagi were taken from Catacomb 20, and the arches and doorposts in the entrance of this catacomb and Catacomb 14 were examined. The rocks were described and identified by means of comparison with the rocks in the vicinity as well as in the general area. Petrographic and micropalaeontological analyses were carried out, the latter by Dr. Z. Reiss, Head of the Palaeontology Department in the Geological Survey.

RESULTS OF ANALYSES

Catacomb 20 is quarried from white chalk whose age was determined as the upper part of the Middle Eocene. The material is relatively soft and hence easy to work with simple mechanical tools. This chalk appears to be fresh in the walls of the caves, where a layer of *Nari* (caliche) has developed on its surface. The rocks from which the arches at the entrance and the sarcophagi were made can be divided into three main groups.

1. **Coarse-grained limestone**

This rock is similar to the type called *Meleke*. This is a relatively hard stone, which is not found in the vicinity of Beth She'arim. The stone blocks were perhaps brought from the Carmel Range where such rock types can be found. The age of the rock was determined as Cenomanian-Turonian. This type of rock is easy to work but is well preserved. Sarcophagi 44, 55, 56 and 119 and the area in the entrance to Catacomb 20 and to hall A of Catacomb 14 are built of this stone.

2. **Fine-grained crystallized limestone**

This rock is similar to the type known as *Mizzi Ḥilu*. This is a relatively hard limestone which does not occur in the vicinity of Beth She'arim but is found in the Carmel Range and the Shefar'am region.

Sarcophagi 12 and 60 of Catacomb 20, the left doorpost in the entrance to this catacomb, and the door slab lying in the courtyard in front of this entrance are made from this stone.

3. **Hard white chalk**

The age of the chalk is Middle Eocene, the same age as the country rocks. Where it occurs as *Nari* it does not contain fossils, and it is therefore difficult to pinpoint its age accurately. It seems that it is taken from the close vicinity, possibly even from the burial cave itself. Sarcophagi 97 and 101 are made of this type.

The ornamented stones of the arch at the upper part of the entrance to Catacomb 20 and sarcophagus 16 are made of *Nari* which is apparently identical to the chalk. It is possible that some of the sarcophagi which have a weathered appearance were cut from this chalk, and the prevailing humidity in the caves has caused a *Nari*-type condition.

PETROGRAPHY OF SOME BETH SHE'ARIM MARBLES

S. Gross

Three marble samples, each of a different color, from the Beth She'arim excavations were submitted for examination by Prof. N. Avigad of the Archaeology Department of the Hebrew University.

Thin sections were prepared from each sample and their mineralogy and petrography were microscopically studied, although detailed fabric analysis which is often applied to marbles was not made.

The following determinations were made of the three samples:

a. A finely crystalline, white marble with a yellowish tint. Microscopically it consists of a mosaic of calcite grains of a granoblastic texture. The crystals range in size from 0.1 to 0.5 mm. Most crystals are twinned. Elongated scales of sericite (fine-grained white mica-muscovite or paragonite), 0.02 mm in length, were observed in the interstices between the calcite grains. They are of low interference colors and give a biaxial negative interference figure with a small axial angle.

b. A coarse-grained, monomineralic, grey marble consisting of a simple mosaic of interlocking calcite grains ranging from 0.1 to 2.0 mm. Average crystal diameter is about 0.75 mm. In most crystals two sets of polysynthetic twins are observed and in some crystals the twin lamellae are foliated.

c. A white marble which resembles the grey marble in texture and is likewise monomineralic. Calcite crystals range from 0.15 to 0.2 mm. Most of the crystals are about 1 mm in diameter. No foliated twin lamellae were observed.

According to the petrography the three samples represent two types of marble: a polymineralic, fine-grained, calcite-sericite marble and a monomineralic, coarse-grained, calcite marble which occurs in two color variants and which is probably of a slightly higher metamorphic grade.

No outcrops of either marble are known in any of the nearby regions.

THE NAMES AND WORDS IN THE HEBREW AND ARAMAIC INSCRIPTIONS

THE PERSONAL NAMES
(number refer to inscriptions and lines)

אבעל (?) 12
אטיו 15:1
אטיון 15:4; 16:2
אליעזר 26:2
אניאנא 10:2; אנינא 17:2; אנינא 11:1
גמליאל 9; 15:2, 5; 26:1
דומנה 20
הלל 28:1; הליל 16:1

טבלה 7
יהודה 15:5; 27
יהושע 16:1; 24:2; 25:2; יושע 23
שליודן 5:2, 9; 6:2 יודן 22
יוחנן 2:2
יונתן 21:1
לוי 5:2, 3, 10; לווי 6:3; 24:3; 28:1

מגה 24:1
מיאשה 22
מרים 21:1
נחמיה 15:2
קירילא 18
שמעון 2:2; 8:2

THE HEBREW WORDS

אח — אחיה 13
אלו 17:1
ארון — ארונה 24:1; 23; 26:1; ארונן 28:1; הארון 25:1; ארון 22; ארונות 17:1
אשת — אשתו 24:2
את 28:2

בירבי 16:1
בן 5:2, 10; 6:2; 15:2; 16:2; 24:3; 26:2; בנו 15:5; 22; 26:1; 28:1; בניו 17:3; 22
ברכה — לברכה 25:4; 26:4
בת 15:3, 6; בתו 15:1, 4; 21:1; 25:2; בנותיה 21:2
בתולה 15:3

היה — יהי 5:5
הן 15:1

זה 5:1; 6:1; הזה 25:1; 26:1
ז 9; 10:1; 23; 24:1; 28:1; זוא 22; הזו 28:2

זכר 25:3; 26:3
חודשים 15:8
חיצונית — והחיצונית 17:1
כן 15:1
מנוחה — מנוחתה 20:1
מערה — המערה 28:2
משכב — משכבו 5:1; 6:1; 16:2
מונח — מנחות 15:1
מות — שמתה 15:2, 6
עולם — לעולם 5:3; לעום 6:3
על 14
עם 21:2
עמידה — עמידת(ן) 15:8
עשה — שעש(ה) 28:1
עשר — שבע עשרה 26:2
עשרין ושתים 15:3
פנימית — הפנימית 17:1

צדיק — צדיקין 25:4; 26:3
קדוש — הקדושים 17:3
קטן — הקטן 11:2
קירה — שלקירא 24:1; שלקירה 19; 20:1
רבי 8:1; 16:1; שלרבי 9; 10; 15:1, 4, 5; 17:2; 21:1; 22:1; 23; 24:2; 25:2; 26:2; 28:1
ש־ שמתה; שעשה
שבע עשרה 26:2
שוי 5:6
שלום — בשלום 5:4, 8; see also "שלום"
של־ שליודן, שלקירה, שלרבי, שלשלושת
שלום 14; 19:3; 24:3; בשלום 16:3; see also: "שולם"
שלושת — שלשלושת 22
שנים 15:7; שנה 15:4; 26:3
ששה — ושסה 15:8
שתים — שתי 21:2; ושתים 15:3
תשע 15:6

THE ARAMAIC WORDS

עַל 1:3; עֲלוֹי 2:4

דִיפְתַח – פְּתַח 1:1; 2:4; 3

קְבוּרָה – קְבוּרְתָה 1:2

קְבִיר – דקְבִיר 2:1

שְׁבוּעָה – וּבִשְׁבוּעָה 2:3

הֱוָה – יְהִי 2:4

כֹּל – דְכֹל 1:1; 3; 2:3

מוֹת – מֵאִית 2:5; יְמוּת 1:4; שָׁמְתָה 15:16

מִן 1:3; 3

סוֹף – בְּסוֹף 1:4; 2:5

בַּר 2:2

בִּישׁ 1:4; 2:6

גּוֹ – דְּבְגוֹה 1:3

ד־ – דְבְגוֹה, דִיפְתַח, דְקְבִיר

דָה – הָדָה 1:2

דִין – בְּהָדִין 2:1

THE NAMES IN THE GREEK INSCRIPTIONS

THE PERSONAL NAMES
(numbers refer to pages)

Ἀδδώ 82
Ἀγρίππας 102
Ἀιδέσιος 27
Ἄλυπις 51
Ἄνθος 27
Ἀννιανός 37   53
Ἀριστέας 40
Ἀστήρ (אסתר) 27   68
Βαριοσαῖ 68
Βαριωσῆ 31
Βενιαμίν (בנימין) 81
Γαμαλιήλ 54
Δανιήλ (דניאל) 82
Διοδώρα 73
Δομνικά 103
Ελάσονος 31
Ειούδας (יהודה) 71
Ειούσστα 41
Ἐλπιδία 24
Ἐπιτύχιος 73

Εὐσέβιος 36
Ζηνοβία 77
Ἡσυχις 27
Θεοδοσία 118
Θεοδώρα 31
Ἰάσων — ν. Ελάσονος
Ἰεσοῦς (ישוע) 26
Ἰούδας — ν. Ειούδας
Ἰούλιος 81
Ἰοῦστα — ν. Είούσστα
Ἰοῦστος 81
Ἰωσήφ (יוסף) 71
Καλιόπη 27   118
Καρτερία 77
Κυρία 39
Κυρίς 38
Κυρίλλα 27
Λαζάρ (לעזר) 68
Μάγνος 27
Μακρόβιος 81

Μαρῖνος 41
Μικκή 37
Παυλῖνος 38
Πρειμόσα 76
Προκόπιος 118
Προσδοκίς 37
Σαβέρις 81
Σαβῖνος 37   81
Σακέρδως 76
Σάρα (שרה) 31   118
Σατορνεῖλος 31   36
Σιρικία 31   37
Σιρικίς 80
Σύμμαχος 39
Σωκράτης 81
Ὑπερέχις 80
Φαυόνις 31
Χωήν (כהן) 30

THE ETHNICA

Αντιοχέως 27
Βηρίτιος 30   Βηρίτων 36
Βιβλίας, Βίβλον 26

Ἰαμουρίτης 26
Ἰουδέα 31
Σιδωνίου 40

Τυρία 27   Τυρέου 82
Φαινήσιος 71

INDEX

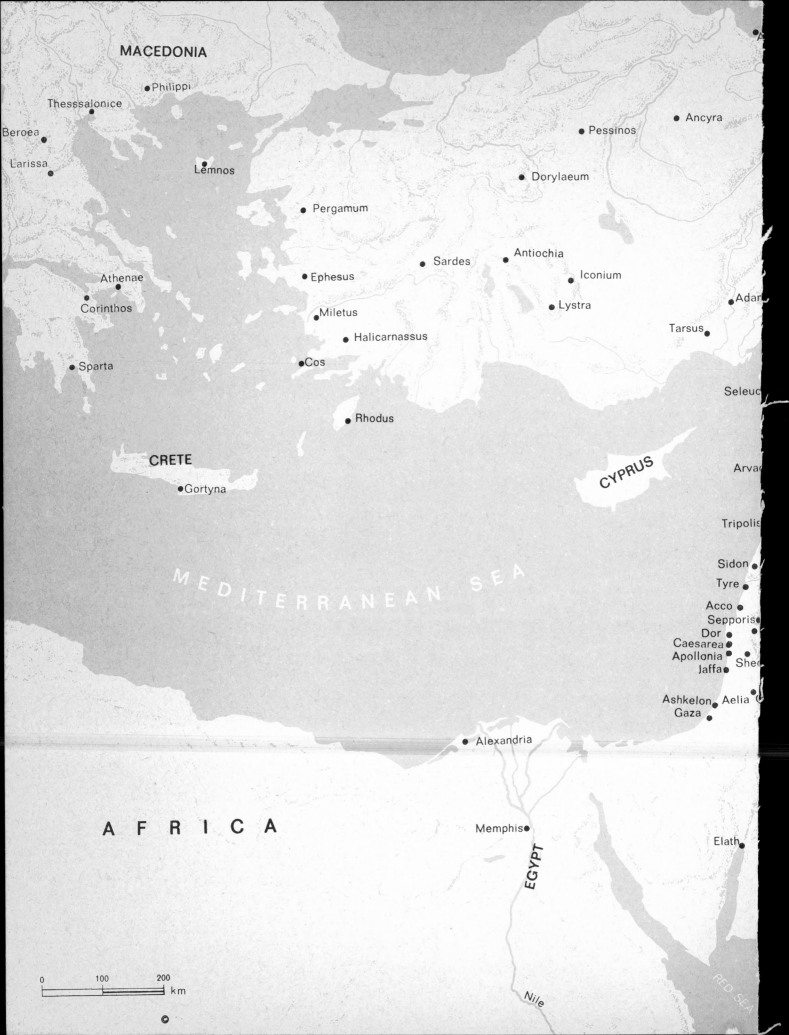

MACEDONIA

Philippi

Thesssalonice

Beroea

Larissa

Lemnos

Pergamum

Ancyra

Pessinos

Dorylaeum

Sardes

Antiochia

Ephesus

Iconium

Miletus

Lystra

Adar

Halicarnassus

Tarsus

Athenae

Corinthos

Cos

Sparta

Rhodus

Seleuc

CRETE

CYPRUS

Arva

Gortyna

Tripolis

MEDITERRANEAN SEA

Sidon

Tyre

Acco

Sepporis

Dor

Caesarea

Apollonia

Shec

Jaffa

Ashkelon

Aelia

Gaza

Alexandria

AFRICA

Memphis

Elath

EGYPT

0   100   200
km

Nile

RED SEA

©